Practitioner Series

Springer

London
Berlin
Heidelberg
New York
Barcelona
Hong Kong
Milan
Paris
Singapore
Tokyo

Other titles in this series:

The Project Management Paradigm
K. Burnett
3-540-76238-8

The Politics of Usability
L. Trenner and J. Bawa
3-540-76181-0

Electronic Commerce and Business
Communications
M. Chesher and R. Kaura
3-540-19930-6

Key Java
J. Hunt and A. McManus
3-540-76259-0

Distributed Applications
Engineering
I. Wijegunaratne and G. Fernandez
3-540-76210-8

Finance for IT Decision Makers
M. Blackstaff
3-540-76232-9

The Renaissance of Legacy Systems
I. Warren
1-85233-060-0

Middleware
D. Serain (Translator: I. Craig)
1-85233-011-2

Java for Practitioners
J. Hunt
1-85233-093-7

Conceptual Modeling for User
Interface Development
D. Benyon, T. Green and D. Bental
1-85233-009-0

Computer-Based Diagnostic
Systems
C. Price
3-540-76198-5

The Unified Process for Practitioners
J. Hunt
1-85233-275-1

Managing Electronic Services
Å. Grönlund
1-85233-281-6

Real-Time and Multi-Agent Systems
A. Attoui (Translator: S. Ingram)
1-85233-252-2

Tony Sammes and Brian Jenkinson

Forensic Computing
A Practitioner's Guide

Springer

A.J. Sammes, BSc, MPhil, PhD, FBCS, CEng
Head, Department of Informatics and Simulation, Royal Military College of Science, Cranfield University, Shrivenham, Swindon, Wiltshire SN6 8LA, UK

B.L. Jenkinson, BA, BSc (hon), MBCS
Forensic Computer Consultant. Detective Inspector (retired), former head of Cambridgeshire Constabulary Fraud Squad, Chairman of the Forensic Computer Group Training Committee and member of the ACPO Computer Crime Group.

ISSN 1439-9245
ISBN 1-85233-299-9 Springer-Verlag London Berlin Heidelberg

British Library Cataloguing in Publication Data
Sammes, A. J.
    Forensic Computing : a practitioner's guide. -
    (Practitioner series)
    1.Forensic science - Data processing 2.Microcomputers
    I.Title II.Jenkinson, B.
    363.2'5'0285416

ISBN 1852332999

Library of Congress Cataloging-in-Publication Data
Sammes, A. J.
    Forensic computing : a practitioner's guide / A.J. Sammes and B. Jenkinson.
        p. cm. -- (Practitioner series)
    Includes bibliographical references and index.
    ISBN 1-85233 -299-9
        1. Forensic engineering--Data processing. I. Jenkinson, B., 1950- II. Title. III. Series.

    TA219 .S36 2000
    363.25--dc21   00-037163

© Springer-Verlag London Limited 2000
Printed in Great Britain
2nd printing 2001
3rd printing 2002
4th printing 2003

Typesetting: Ian Kingston Editorial Services, Nottingham UK
Printed and bound by the Athenæum Press Ltd., Gateshead, Tyne & Wear
34/3830-543 Printed on acid-free paper SPIN 10942420

Dedication

To Joan and Val

Acknowledgements

The authors would like to thank all the members and former members of the FCG Training Committee and all those law enforcement officers who have so generously given of their time for their kind support and the valuable contributions that they have made to this work. In particular our grateful thanks go to Steve Buddell (Inland Revenue), Tony Dearsley (Customs & Excise), Geoff Fellows (Northamptonshire Police), Paul Griffiths (Greater Manchester Police), Mike Hainey (Serious Fraud Office), Dave Honeyball (Thames Valley Police), Peter Lintern (Avon & Somerset Police), John McConnell (Greater Manchester Police), Keith McDonald (Customs & Excise), Geoff Morrison (Wiltshire Constabulary), Laurie Norton (Customs & Excise), Kathryn Owen (Serious Fraud Office) and Stewart Weston-Lewis (Inland Revenue). Our thanks also go to all the students of the seven Forensic Computing Foundation Courses that have so far run for their helpful comments and to the members of the DoIS staff who have provided such valuable support to us. Finally, a word of thanks for our publisher, our editor and our families who have all tolerated our intolerance as we have gone through the ups and downs of writing this book.

Series Editor's Foreword

With the benefits of computing come the inevitable human misuses. This unique book, written by two authors with extensive practical experience, provides the reader with a sufficient depth of technical understanding to search for, find and confidently present any form of digital document as admissible evidence in a court of law. So the book has two classes of readership: a forensic computing analyst, and someone wanting to know the intrinsic technicalities of computers.

Chapters 2–5 provide the technical content, culminating with Disk Geometry in Chapter 5, the "real technical meat of the book". Chapter 6 considers the issue of process as put forward by the Association of Chief Police Officers (ACPO) in their *Good Practice Guide for Computer Based Evidence*. Chapter 7 looks at personal organizers, which tend not to have hard disks and therefore make the analysis memory based. The final chapter is a lookahead chapter, a springboard I would guess for future editions of this valuable book.

The material in this book has been tried and tested on students in Tony Sammes' department at the Royal Military College of Science at Shrivenham. Having been an external examiner there, I know how rigorous the material has to be. But more importantly, the experience distilled in this book has been gleaned and tested on numerous real cases by the authors. There can be no better evidence of its value.

Ray Paul

Contents

Appendices

1. Forensic Computing

Introduction

Throughout this book you will find that we have consistently referred to the term "Forensic Computing" for what is often elsewhere called "Computer Forensics". In the UK, however, this latter name has been adopted by a commercial company operating in the forensic computing field and we felt that it was not appropriate for us to use a name that carried with it commercial connotations. Hence our use of "Forensic Computing". Having said that, however, we will need on occasion to refer to "Computer Forensics" particularly when quoting from overseas journals and papers which use the term and our use in such circumstances should then be taken as synonymous with that of "Forensic Computing" and not as a reference to the commercial company.

In point of fact, we will start with a definition of Computer Forensics that has been given by Special Agent Mark Pollitt of the Federal Bureau of Investigation as: "*Computer forensics is the application of science and engineering to the legal problem of digital evidence. It is a synthesis of science and law*" (Pollitt, undated). In his paper he contrasts the problems of presenting a digital document in evidence with those of a paper document, and states: "*Rarely is determining that the* (paper) *document physically exists or where it came from, a problem. With digital evidence, this is often a problem. What does this binary string represent? Where did it come from? While these questions, to the computer literate, may seem obvious at first glance, they are neither obvious nor understandable to the layman. These problems then require a substantial foundation being laid prior to their admission into evidence at trial*". These are questions for which we try to provide the requisite technical knowledge in Chapters 2, 3, 4 and 5.

In a second paper (Pollitt, 1995), Special Agent Mark Pollitt suggests that in the field of computer forensics: "*Virtually all professional examiners will agree on some overriding principles*" and then gives as examples the following three: "*...that evidence should not be altered, examination results should be accurate, and that examination results are verifiable and repeatable*". He then goes on to say: "*These principles are universal and are not subject to change with every new operating system, hardware or software. While it may be necessary to occasionally modify a principle, it should be a rare event.*" In Chapters 6 and 7 we will see that these overriding principles are in complete accord with the practices that we recommend and with those that have been put forward in the Good Practice Guide for Computer Based Evidence (ACPO, 1999) of the UK Association of Chief Police Officers (ACPO).

In short, it is the essence of this book to try to provide a sufficient depth of technical understanding that will enable forensic computing analysts to search for, find and confidently present any form of digital document[1] as admissible evidence in a court of law.

▪ ▪

Origin of the Book

The idea for this book sprang originally from a course that had been developed to support the forensic computing law enforcement community. The UK Joint Agency Forensic Computer Group[2] had tasked its Training Sub-Committee with designing and establishing education and training courses for what was seen to be a rapidly developing and urgently needed discipline. The first requirement was for a foundation course that would establish high standards for the forensic computing discipline and would provide a basis for approved certification. The Training Sub-Committee, in collaboration with academic staff from Cranfield University, designed the foundation course such that it would give successful candidates exemption from an existing module in Forensic Computing that was available within the Cranfield University Forensic Engineering and Science MSc course programme. The Forensic Computing Foundation (FCF) course was thus established from the outset at postgraduate level and it continues to be formally examined and accredited by the university.

The FCF course, of two weeks duration, is jointly managed and delivered by staff from both the forensic computing law enforcement community and the university. It covers the fundamentals of evidence recovery from mainly PC based computers and the successful presentation of that evidence before a court of law. The course does not seek to produce computer experts. Rather it sets out to develop forensic computing analysts who have a proven capability for recovering evidential data from computers while preserving the integrity of the original and who are fully competent in presenting that evidence in an understandable form before a court of law.

At the time of writing, five cohorts have successfully completed the FCF course and the taught material of the course has been continually revised and updated in the light of much useful feedback and experience. It is this material that forms much of the substance of this book.

The structure of the book differs a little from the way in which the material is presented on the course itself and this is to make the sequencing more pertinent to the reader. Nevertheless, it is intended that the book will also serve well as a basic text book for the FCF course.

---

1 Document here refers to a document in the widest sense. It includes all forms of digital representations: photographic images, pictures, sound and video clips, as well as spreadsheets, computer programs, text as well as fragments of all of these.

2 The Joint Agency Forensic Computer Group is a made up of representatives of ACPO, the Inland Revenue, HM Customs and Excise, the Forensic Science Service and the Serious Fraud Office.

Structure of the Book

Picking up on one of the key questions raised by Special Agent Mark Pollitt in the earlier quotes ("...*What does this binary string represent?*") we start our investigation in Chapter 2 by considering what information is and just what binary strings might represent. We look at number systems in some detail, starting with decimal and then moving to binary, ranging through little endian and big endian formats, fixed point integers and fractions, floating point numbers, and BCD and hexadecimal representations. We then look at characters, records and files, file types and file signatures (or magic numbers) and hexadecimal listings. A number of file formats are then considered, with particular reference to some of the better known word processing, graphic and archive file formats. To complement this chapter, the ASCII, Windows ANSI and IBM Extended ASCII character sets are listed in Appendix 1, and the magic number signatures of many of the standard file formats are listed in Appendix 2. In addition, the order code for the Intel 8086 processor is listed in hexadecimal order in Appendix 7. These appendices provide a useful reference source for the analysis of binary sequences that are in hexadecimal format.

In Chapter 3, we look at fundamental computer principles: at how the von Neumann machine works and at the stored program concept. The basic structure of memory, processor and the interconnecting buses is discussed and a worked example for a simplified processor is stepped through. The ideas of code sequences, of programming and of breaking sequence are exemplified, following which a black box model of the PC is put forward.

Chapter 4 continues on from Chapter 3 and aims to achieve two goals: to put a physical hardware realization onto the abstract ideas of Chapter 3 and to give a better understanding of just what is "inside the box" and how it all should be connected up. We need to do this looking inside and being able to identify all the pieces so that we can be sure that a target system is safe to operate, that it is not being used as a storage box for other items of evidential value, and that all its components are connected up and working correctly. We again start with the black box model and relate this to the motherboard and to the various system buses. Next we look at the early Intel processors and at the design of the PC. This leads on to the development of the Intel processors up to that of the Pentium III and then a brief look at some other compatible processors. Discussion is then centred round memory chips and this is followed by a brief mention of disk drives, which receive a very much more detailed treatment in a chapter of their own. Finally, a number of other peripheral devices and expansion cards are discussed. Diagrams and photographs throughout this chapter aim to assist in the recognition of the various parts and their relative placement.

Chapter 5 (Disk Geometry) provides the real technical meat of the book. This is the largest chapter by far and the most detailed. In order to understand the second question posed by Special Agent Mark Pollitt in the above quotes: "*Where did it* (this binary string) *come from?*" we need to know a little about magnetic recording and rather a lot about disk drives. The chapter opens with an introduction to five main issues: the physical construction of disk drives; how addressable elements of memory are constructed within them; the problems that have arisen as a result of rapid development of the hard drive and the need for backward compatibility; the ways in which file systems are formed using the addressable elements of the disk; and where and how information might be hidden on the disk. Discussion initially centres on the physical construction of disks and on CHS addressing. Encoding methods are next considered together with formatting. This leads on to hard disk interfaces and the problems that have been caused by incompatibility between them. The 528 Mbyte barrier is described and the workaround of CHS translation is explained. LBA is discussed and a number of BIOS-related problems are outlined. A summary of the interface and translation options is then given. This is followed by a detailed explanation of the POST/boot sequence to the point at which the bootstrap loader is invoked. A full discussion of the master boot record and of partitioning then follows and a detailed analysis of extended partitions is presented. Since our explanations do not always fully conform with those of some other authorities, we expand on these issues in Appendix 6 where we explain our reasoning and give results from some specific trials that we have carried out. FATs, directories and DOS file systems are next described together with long filenames and additional time and date fields. We then give a summary of the known places where information might be hidden and discuss the recovery of information that may have been deleted. We conclude the chapter with a short section on RAID devices.

A detailed technical understanding of where and how digital information can be stored is clearly of paramount importance both from an investigative point of view in finding the information in the first place and from an evidential point of view in being able to explain in technically accurate but jury-friendly terms how and why it was found where it was. However, that admitted, perhaps the most important part of all is *process*. Without proper and approved process, the best of such information may not even be admissible as evidence in a court of law. In Chapter 6 (The Treatment of PCs), we consider the issues of process. We start this by looking first at the principles of computer based evidence as put forward in the ACPO Good Practice Guide (ACPO, 1999). Then we consider the practicalities of mounting a search and seizure operation and the issues that can occur on-site when seizing computers from a suspect's premises. Guidelines are given here for each of the major activities, including the shutdown, seizure and transportation of the equipment. Receipt of the equipment into the analyst's laboratory and the process of examination and the production of evidence are next considered. A detailed example of a specific disk is then given, and guidance on interpreting the host of figures that result is provided. Finally, the issues of imaging and copying are discussed.

In the treatment of PCs, as we see in Chapter 6, our essential concern is not to change the evidence on the hard disk and to produce an image which represents its state exactly as it was when it was seized. In Chapter 7 we look at the treatment of organizers and we note that for the most part there is no hard disk and the concern here has to be to change the evidence in the main memory as little as possible. This results in the first major difference between the treatment of PCs and the treatment of organizers. To access the organizer it will almost certainly have to be switched on and this effectively means that the first of the ACPO principles, not to change the evidence in any way, cannot be complied with. The second major difference is that the PC-compatible is now so standardized that a standard approach can be taken to its analysis. This is not the case with organizers, where few standards are apparent and each organizer typically has to be approached differently. The chapter begins by outlining the technical principles associated with electronic organizers and identifying their major characteristics. We then go on to consider the application of the ACPO Good Practice Guide principles and to recommend some guidelines for the seizure of organizers. Finally, we discuss the technical examination of organizers and we look particularly at how admissible evidence might be obtained from the protected areas.

The final chapter attempts to "look ahead" but only just a little bit. The technology is advancing at such an unprecedented rate that most forward predictions beyond a few months are likely to be wildly wrong. Some of the issues that are apparent at the time of writing are discussed here. Problems with larger and larger disks, whether or not to image, the difficulties raised by networks and the increasing use of encryption form the major topics of this chapter.

References

ACPO (1999) *Good Practice Guide for Computer Based Evidence V2.00*, The Association of Chief Police Officers (ACPO) Computer Crime Group.

Pollitt, Mark M. (undated) *Computer Forensics: An Approach to Evidence in Cyberspace*, Federal Bureau of Investigation, Baltimore, MD.

Pollitt, Mark M. (1995) Principles, practices, and procedures: an approach to standards in computer forensics, *Second International Conference on Computer Evidence*, Baltimore, MD, 10–15 April 1995. Federal Bureau of Investigation, Baltimore, MD.

2. *Understanding Information*

Introduction

In this chapter we will be looking in detail at the following topics:

- What is information?
- Memory and addressing
- Decimal and binary integers
- Little endian and big endian formats
- Signed numbers, fractions and floating point numbers
- BCD and hexadecimal numbers
- Characters and computer program codes
- Records, files, file types and file signatures
- The use of hexadecimal listings
- Word processing and graphic file formats
- Archive and other file formats

We note that the fundamental concern of all our forensic computing activity is for the accurate extraction of information from computer-based systems, such that it may be presented as admissible evidence in court. Given that, we should perhaps first consider just what it is that we understand by this term *information* and then we might look at how it is that computer systems are able to hold and process what we have defined as information in such a wide variety of different forms.

However, deciding just what it is that we really mean by the term *information* is not easy. As Liebenau and Backhouse (1990) explain in their book *Understanding Information*: "*Numerous definitions have been proposed for the term 'information', and most of them serve well the narrow interests of those defining it.*" They then proceed to consider a number of definitions, drawn from various sources, before concluding: "*These definitions are all problematic*" and "*...information cannot exist independently of the receiving person who gives it meaning and somehow acts upon it. That action usually includes analysis or at least interpretation, and the differences between data and information must be preserved, at least in so far as information is data arranged in a meaningful way for some perceived purpose*".

This last view suits our needs very well: "*...information is data arranged in a meaningful way for some perceived purpose*". Let us take it that a computer system holds *data* as suggested here and that any *information* that we (the receiving persons) may extract from this data is as a result of our analysis or interpretation of it in some meaningful way for some perceived purpose. This presupposes that we have to hand a set of interpretative rules, which were intended for this purpose, and which we apply to the data in order to extract the information. It is our application of these rules to the data that results in the intended information being revealed to us.

This view also helps us to understand how it is that computer systems are able to hold information in its multitude of different forms. Although the way in which the data is represented in a computer system is almost always that of a *binary* pattern, the forms that the information may take are effectively without limit simply because there are so many different sets of interpretative rules that we can apply.

Binary Systems and Memory

That computer manufacturers normally choose to represent data in a two-state (or *binary*) form is an engineering convenience of the current technology. Two-state systems are easier to engineer and two-state logic simplifies some activities. Provided that we do not impose limits on the sets of interpretative rules that we permit, a binary system is quite capable of representing almost any kind of information. We should perhaps now look a little more closely at how data is held in such binary systems.

In such a system, each data element is implemented using some physical device that can be in one of two stable states: in a memory chip, for example, a transistor switch may be on or off; in a communications line, a pulse may be present or absent at a particular place and at a particular time; on a magnetic disk, a magnetic domain may be magnetized to one polarity or to the other; and, on a compact disc, a pit may be present or not at a particular place. These are all examples of two-state or binary devices.

When we use such two-state devices to store data we normally consider a large number of them in some form of conceptual structure: perhaps we might visualize a very long line of several million transistor switches in a big box, for example. We might then call this a *memory*. We use a notation borrowed from mathematics to symbolize each element of the memory, that is, each two-state device. This notation uses the symbol "1" to represent a two-state device that is in the "on" state and the symbol "0" to represent a two-state device that is in the "off" state. We can now draw a diagram that symbolizes our memory (or at least, a small part of it) as an ordered sequence of 1s and 0s, as shown in Fig. 2.1.

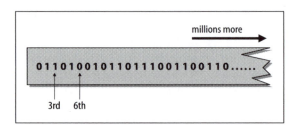

Fig. 2.1 Memory.

Each 1 and each 0 is a symbol for one particular two-state device in the structure and the value of 1 or 0 signifies the current state of that device. So, for example, the third device from the left in the sequence is "on" (signified by a "1") and the sixth device from the left is "off" (signified by a "0").

Although we can clearly observe the data as an ordered sequence of 1s and 0s, we are not able from this alone to determine the information that it may represent. To do that, we have to know the appropriate set of interpretative rules which we can then apply to some given part of the data sequence in order to extract the intended information.

Before we move on to consider various different sets of interpretative rules, however, we should first look at some fundamental definitions and concepts that are associated with computer memory. Each of the two symbols "1" and "0", when representing a two-state device, is usually referred to as a *binary digit* or *bit*, the acronym being constructed from the initial letter of "binary" and the last two letters of "digit". We may thus observe that the ordered sequence in Fig. 2.1 has 24 bits displayed, although there are millions more that are to the right of the diagram.

Addressing

We carefully specified on at least two occasions that this is an *ordered* sequence, implying that position is important, and this, in general, is clearly the case. It is often an ordered set of symbols that is required to convey information: an ordered set of characters conveys specific text; an ordered set of digits conveys specific numbers; an ordered set of instructions conveys a specific process. We therefore need a means by which we can identify position in this ordered sequence of millions of bits and thus access any part of that sequence, anywhere within it, at will. Conceptually, the simplest method would be for every bit in the sequence to be associated with its unique numeric position; for example, the third from the left, the sixth from the left, and so on, as we did above. In practical computer systems, however, the overheads of uniquely identifying every bit in the memory are not justified, so a compromise is made. A unique identifying number, known as the *address*, is associated with a group of eight bits in sequence. The group of eight bits is called a *byte* and the bytes are ordered from address 0 numerically upwards (shown from left to right in Fig. 2.2) to the highest address in the memory. In a modern desktop personal computer, it would not be unusual for this highest address in memory to be of the order of 64 million.

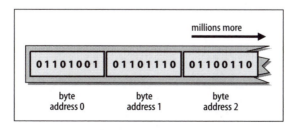

Fig. 2.2 Byte addressing.

Table 2.1 Units of memory.

● Nibble	= half a byte	= 4 bits
● Byte	= 1 byte	= 8 bits
● Word	= 2 bytes	= 16 bits
● Double word	= 4 bytes	= 32 bits
● Kilobyte	= 1024 bytes	= 2^{10} bytes
● Megabyte	= 1 048 576 bytes	= 2^{20} bytes
● Gigabyte	= 1 073 741 824 bytes	= 2^{30} bytes
● Terabyte	= 1 099 511 627 776 bytes	= 2^{40} bytes

Our ordered sequence fragment can now be represented as the three bytes shown in Fig. 2.2.

Today the byte is used as the basic measure of memory size, although other terms are still often met: a *nibble* is half a byte = 4 bits; a *word* is 2 bytes = 16 bits; a *double word* is 4 bytes = 32 bits. As computer memory and disk sizes have become very much larger, so the byte has become a comparatively small unit, and various powers of two are now used to qualify it: a kilobyte is 2^{10} = 1024 bytes; a megabyte is 2^{20} = 1 048 576 bytes; a gigabyte is 2^{30} = 1 073 741 824 bytes; and a terabyte is 2^{40} = 1 099 511 627 776 bytes. Traditionally, computing scientists have always based their memory units on powers of 2 rather than on powers of 10, though this is a matter of some contention within the standards community[1]. In Williams (1996), the practical implications of some of these units are compared: a kilobyte is likened to a very short story, a megabyte to a small novel, 5 megabytes to the complete works of Shakespeare and a gigabyte to a truck filled with paper. Some of these units are shown for reference in Table 2.1.

We can now move on to another very important idea. We can associate a particular set of interpretative rules with a particular sequence of byte addresses in the memory. This then tells us how the patterns of 1s and 0s at those addresses are to be interpreted in order to extract the information that the data held there is intended to represent[2]. It is important to note that these associations of rule sets with addresses are completely flexible; in general, in a computer system any associations can be made with any sequence of bytes, and these can be changed at any time.

There are, however, some standard interpretative rule sets which all computer systems share, and we will start by considering the best known of these: the interpretation of a binary data pattern as a decimal number.

---

1   The issue is whether the prefixes kilo, mega, giga etc. should be raised to powers of two as traditionally implemented by the computing fraternity or to powers of ten as decreed by the General Conference of Weights and Measures for SI units. If they were to be changed to powers of ten, kilo would become 10^3 = 1000 and mega would become 10^6 = 1 000 000 (see Williams, 1996).

2   The association of a set of interpretative rules with a sequence of memory addresses is known as *typing*. In a *strongly typed* system, the computer programs will not only contain rules about the interpretation that is to be applied to data at given memory addresses, but will also contain rules that limit the ways in which that data may be manipulated to those appropriate to the interpretation.

Number Systems

Before we look at the interpretative rules for binary data patterns we should remind ourselves of the rules for decimal data patterns. In the representation of numbers generally, we use a notation that is positional. That is, the position of the digit in the pattern is significant and is used to determine the multiplying factor that is to be applied to that digit when calculating the number. In the decimal system, each digit in the pattern can range in value from 0 to 9 and the multiplying factor is always some power of 10 (hence the *decimal* system).

The particular power of 10 depends on the actual position of the digit relative to the decimal point. The powers of 10 start from 0 immediately to the left of the decimal point, and increase by one for each position we move to the left and decrease by one for each position we move to the right. When writing down whole numbers, we tend not to write down the decimal point itself but assume it to be on the extreme right of the positive powers of ten digit sequence. Hence, we often write down "5729" rather than "5729.0". All of this, which is so cumbersome to explain, is second nature to us because we have learned the interpretative rules from childhood and can apply them without thinking. As an example of a whole number, we read the sequence "5729" as five thousand, seven hundred and twenty-nine. Analyzing this according to the interpretative rules we see that it is made up of:

$$5 \times 10^3 + 7 \times 10^2 + 2 \times 10^1 + 9 \times 10^0$$

or, in terms of the expanded multiplying factors, as shown in Fig. 2.3:

$$5 \times 1000 + 7 \times 100 + 2 \times 10 + 9 \times 1$$

As we described above, the powers of 10 which form the multiplying factors, increase by one for every move of digit position to the left and decrease by one for every move of digit position to the right. The use of this style of interpretative rule set is not limited to decimal numbers. We can use the concept for any number system that we wish (see Table 2.2). The number of different digit symbols we wish to use (known as the *base*) determines the multiplying factor; apart from that, the same rules of interpretation apply. In the case of the decimal system (base 10) we can see 10 digit symbols (0 to 9) and a multiplying factor of 10. We can have an *octal* system (base 8) which has eight digit symbols (0 to 7) and a multiplying factor of eight; a *ternary* system (base 3) that has three digit symbols (0 to 2) and a multiplying factor of three; or, even, a *binary* system (base 2) that has two digit symbols (0 and 1) and a multiplying factor of two. We will later be looking at the *hexadecimal* system (base

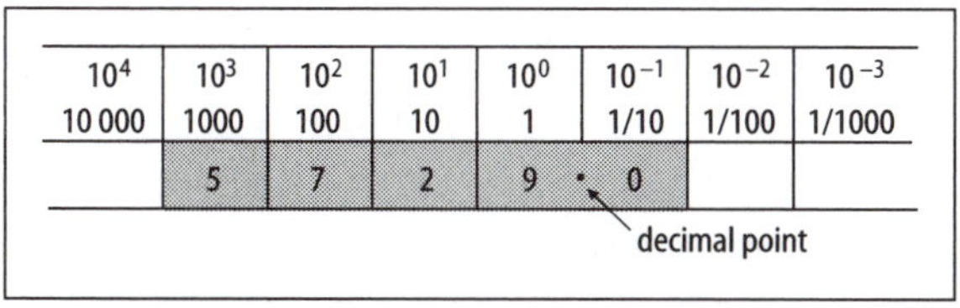

10^4	10^3	10^2	10^1	10^0	10^{-1}	10^{-2}	10^{-3}
10 000	1000	100	10	1	1/10	1/100	1/1000
	5	7	2	9 .	0		

decimal point

Fig. 2.3 Rules for decimal numbers.

Table 2.2 Other number systems.

Binary	Base 2	0 and 1
Ternary	Base 3	0, 1 and 2
Octal	Base 8	0 to 7
Decimal	Base 10	0 to 9
Hexadecimal	Base 16	0 to 9 and a to f

16), which has 16 digit symbols (the numeric symbols 0 to 9 and the letter symbols a to f) and a multiplying factor of 16.

Binary Numbers

Returning now to the binary system, we note that each digit in the pattern can range in value from 0 to 1 and that the multiplying factor is always some power of two (hence the term "binary"). The particular power of two depends on the actual position of the digit relative to the *binary point* (compare this with the decimal point referred to above).

The powers of two start from 0 immediately to the left of the binary point, and increase by one for each position we move to the left and decrease by one for each position we move to the right. Again, for whole numbers, we tend not to show the binary point itself but assume it to be on the extreme right of the positive powers of two digit sequence (see Fig. 2.4). Now using the same form of interpretative rules as for the decimal system, we can see that the binary data shown in this figure (this is the same binary data that is given at byte address 0 in Fig. 2.2) can be interpreted thus:

$$0 \times 2^7 + 1 \times 2^6 + 1 \times 2^5 + 0 \times 2^4 + 1 \times 2^3 + 0 \times 2^2 + 0 \times 2^1 + 1 \times 2^0$$

which is equivalent, in terms of the expanded multiplying factors, to:

$$0 \times 128 + 1 \times 64 + 1 \times 32 + 0 \times 16 + 1 \times 8 + 0 \times 4 + 0 \times 2 + 1 \times 1$$

and this adds up to 105. It is left for the reader to confirm that the data in the other two bytes in Fig. 2.2 can be interpreted using this rule set, as the decimal numbers: 110 and 102.

Taking the byte as the basic unit of memory, it is useful to determine the maximum and minimum decimal numbers that can be held using this interpretation. The pattern 00000000 clearly gives 0 and the pattern 11111111 gives:

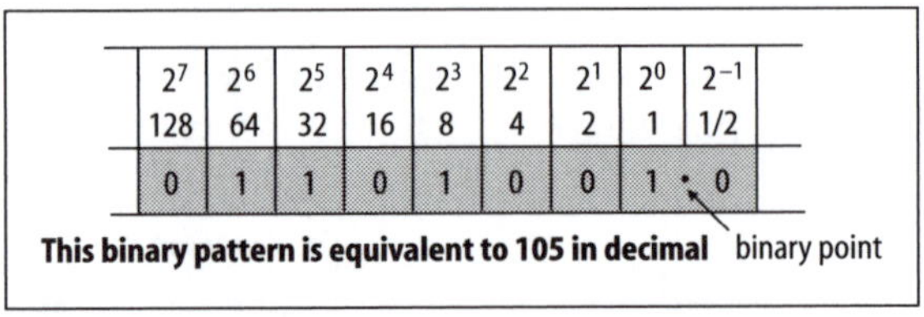

2^7	2^6	2^5	2^4	2^3	2^2	2^1	2^0	2^{-1}
128	64	32	16	8	4	2	1	1/2
0	1	1	0	1	0	0	1	0

This binary pattern is equivalent to 105 in decimal   binary point

Fig. 2.4 Rules for binary numbers.

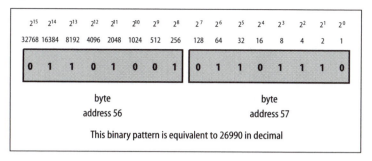

Fig. 2.5 A number in a word.

$$1 \times 2^7 + 1 \times 2^6 + 1 \times 2^5 + 1 \times 2^4 + 1 \times 2^3 + 1 \times 2^2 + 1 \times 2^1 + 1 \times 2^0$$

which is equivalent to:

$$1 \times 128 + 1 \times 64 + 1 \times 32 + 1 \times 16 + 1 \times 8 + 1 \times 4 + 1 \times 2 + 1 \times 1$$

and this is equal to 255. The range of whole numbers that can be represented in a single byte (eight bits) is therefore 0 to 255. This is often found to be inadequate for even the simplest of arithmetic processing tasks, and two bytes (a word) taken together are more frequently used to represent whole numbers. However, this poses a potential problem for the analyst, as we shall see. We can clearly implement a number in a word by using two bytes in succession as shown in Fig. 2.5.

The question now arises of how we should interpret the pair taken together. The most obvious way is to consider the two bytes as a continuous sequence of binary digits as they appear in Fig. 2.5. The binary point is assumed to be to the right of the byte at address 57. As before, we have increasing powers of two as we move to the left through the byte and, at the byte boundary with byte address 56, we simply carry on. So, the leftmost bit of byte address 57 is 2^7 and the rightmost bit of byte address 56 continues on as 2^8. Using the rules that we established above, we then have the following interpretation for byte address 57:

$$0 \times 128 + 1 \times 64 + 1 \times 32 + 0 \times 16 + 1 \times 8 + 1 \times 4 + 1 \times 2 + 0 \times 1$$

together with this for byte address 56:

$$0 \times 32768 + 1 \times 16384 + 1 \times 8192 + 0 \times 4096$$
$$+ 1 \times 2048 + 0 \times 1024 + 0 \times 512 + 1 \times 256$$

The decimal number interpretation of the two bytes taken together in this way is the total of all the individual digit values and is equal to 26990.

The range of numbers for the two bytes taken together can now readily be established as 00000000 00000000 to 11111111 11111111. The first pattern clearly gives 0 and the pattern 11111111 11111111 gives 65535. The range is therefore 0 to 65535. This is left to the reader to confirm. It is also apparent that we could use a similar argument to take more than two bytes together as a single number; in fact, four bytes (a double word) are often used where greater precision is required.

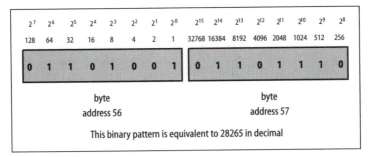

Fig. 2.6   Little endian format.

Little Endian and Big Endian Formats

The approach adopted here of taking the two bytes as a continuous sequence of binary digits may seem eminently sensible. However, there is an opposing argument that claims that the two bytes should be taken together the other way round. The lower powers of two, it is claimed, should be in the lower valued byte address and the higher powers of two should be in the higher valued byte address. This approach is shown in Fig. 2.6 and is known as *little endian format*, as opposed to the first scheme that we considered, which is known as *big endian format*[3].

Here we see that the digit multipliers in byte address 56 range from 2^0 to 2^7 and those in byte address 57 range from 2^8 to 2^{15}. Using this little endian format with the same binary values in the two bytes, we see that from byte address 56 we have:

$$0 \times 128 + 1 \times 64 + 1 \times 32 + 0 \times 16 + 1 \times 8 + 0 \times 4 + 0 \times 2 + 1 \times 1$$

and from byte address 57 we have:

$$0 \times 32768 + 1 \times 16384 + 1 \times 8192 + 0 \times 4096$$
$$+ 1 \times 2048 + 1 \times 1024 + 1 \times 512 + 0 \times 256$$

The decimal number interpretation of the same two bytes taken together in this little endian format is 28265, compared with the 26990 which we obtained using the big endian format.

The problem for the forensic computing analyst is clear. There is nothing to indicate, within a pair of bytes that are to be interpreted as a single decimal number, whether they should be analyzed using little endian or big endian format. It is very important that this factor be correctly determined by the analyst, perhaps from the context in which the number is used or perhaps from a knowledge of the software that is used to read or write the binary data. It is known, for example, that Intel uses little endian format when reading or writing two byte and four byte numbers in its

---

3   The notion of big endian and little endian comes from a story in *Gulliver's Travels* by Jonathan Swift. In this story the "big endians" were those who broke their breakfast egg from the big end and the "little endians" were those who broke theirs from the little end. The big endians were outlawed by the emperor and many were put to death for their heresy!

Table 2.3 Little endian and big endian.

● Little endian	Times 1 then times 256
● Big endian	Times 256 then times 1

80x86 processor range and that Motorola uses big endian format for the same purpose in its 68000 family[4].

Application software, on the other hand, may choose to represent numbers in either little endian or big endian format, as well as many other formats. The simplest way of calculating little endian or big endian pair values is by taking the value of the left-hand byte and adding to it 256 times the value of the right-hand byte for little endian format, or, by taking the value of the left-hand byte, multiplying it by 256 and adding to it the value of the right hand byte for big endian format. These rules are summarized in Table 2.3.

Signed Numbers

So far we have only considered the representation of positive whole numbers. Negative numbers are also required and these can be represented by taking out of use one of the digit positions and re-employing it as a *sign bit*. The digit position that is chosen is the leftmost bit in the sequence; in the case of a single byte, this is the 2^7 digit position. If this particular bit is set to 1, by definition, the number is negative; if it is set to 0 by definition the number is positive as indicated in Fig. 2.7.

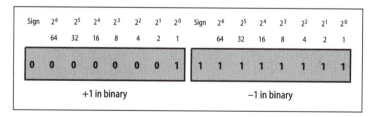

Fig. 2.7 Two signed numbers.

In this diagram we have shown two bytes, which, unlike previous diagrams, are not to be considered as a single number. Instead, for this example, each byte is to be interpreted as a separate signed number. The left-hand byte represents +1 and the right-hand byte represents −1. The data pattern in the right-hand byte may not appear as expected for a representation of −1 and this may need some explanation. In order to ensure that the mathematics of positive and negative numbers works systematically we have to have a representation where the binary number +1 when added to the binary number −1 gives us the binary number 0. In a single byte, the binary number +1 is represented as expected, and as shown in Fig. 2.7, by:

---

4   As reported on page 46 of Messmer (1997).

Sign 2^6 2^5 2^4 2^3 2^2 2^1 2^0

0   0   0   0   0   0   0   1   +1 in binary

It is positive because the sign bit is 0 and it is of value 1 because only the 2^0 column is set . Now we have agreed that negative numbers by definition will have the sign bit set, so the most obvious pattern for –1 might simply be:

Sign 2^6 2^5 2^4 2^3 2^2 2^1 2^0

1   0   0   0   0   0   0   1   a suggestion for −1 in binary

This would be negative because the sign bit is set to 1, and it would be of value 1 because only the 2^0 column is set. However, if we add the +1 and suggested –1 patterns together using the rules[5] of binary addition, the result is:

Sign	2^6	2^5	2^4	2^3	2^2	2^1	2^0	
0	0	0	0	0	0	0	1	+1 in binary
1	0	0	0	0	0	0	1	a suggestion for −1 in binary
1	0	0	0	0	0	1	0	

which, according to our same rules is –2; a negative number because the sign bit is set to 1 and of value 2 because the 2^1 column is set.

In order to overcome this problem, negative numbers are held in what is known as *two's complement* form. To make a negative binary number in two's complement form, we first write down the positive binary number, and then change all the 0 digits for 1s and all the 1 digits for 0s, and then finally we add 1 in binary to the result. So, the steps in making –1 in binary are:

Sign	2^6	2^5	2^4	2^3	2^2	2^1	2^0	
0	0	0	0	0	0	0	1	write down +1 in binary
1	1	1	1	1	1	1	0	change all the 1s to 0s and vice versa
0	0	0	0	0	0	0	1	add 1 in binary to result
1	1	1	1	1	1	1	1	to give −1 in binary

This is, in fact, just what we have shown in Fig. 2.7 as –1. We can now see that +1 in binary added to –1 in binary does indeed give 0 in binary

Sign	2^6	2^5	2^4	2^3	2^2	2^1	2^0	
0	0	0	0	0	0	0	1	+1 in binary
1	1	1	1	1	1	1	1	−1 in binary
0	0	0	0	0	0	0	0	gives a sum of zero

though this result of 00000000 may need a little explanation[6].

---

5   In binary addition: 0 + 0 = 0; 0 + 1 = 1; 1 + 0 = 1; and 1 + 1 = 0 carry 1 to the next digit on the left.

Table 2.4 Integers.

● Smallest unsigned integer in one or two bytes	0
● Largest unsigned integer in one byte	255
● Largest unsigned integer in two bytes	65535
● Smallest signed integer in one byte	−128
● Largest signed integer in one byte	+127
● Smallest signed integer in two bytes	−32768
● Largest signed integer in two bytes	+32767

The range of *signed numbers* that can be represented in a single byte (the range we considered previously was that of *unsigned numbers*) can now be seen to be from:

$$\text{Sign} \quad 2^6 \ 2^5 \ 2^4 \ 2^3 \ 2^2 \ 2^1 \ 2^0$$

$$0 \quad 1 \quad 1 \quad 1 \quad 1 \quad 1 \quad 1 \quad 1 \quad +127\text{, the largest positive integer, to}$$

$$1 \quad 0 \quad 0 \quad 0 \quad 0 \quad 0 \quad 0 \quad 0 \quad -128\text{, the largest negative integer}$$

that is, +127 (sign bit is zero) to −128 (sign bit is 1) and the range of signed numbers for two bytes can just as readily be calculated as +32767 to −32768. A summary of this is shown in Table 2.4.

Fractions and Mixed Numbers

So far we have only looked at the representation of whole numbers or *integers* and the form of representation that we have been considering is generally known as *fixed point*. Although we will only touch on this here, fixed point representation can be used for fractions and mixed numbers as well simply by considering the binary point to be at some position other than at the extreme right-hand side of the digit sequence. So, for example, in Fig. 2.8 the binary point is considered to be between the two bytes that are to be taken together as a single number.

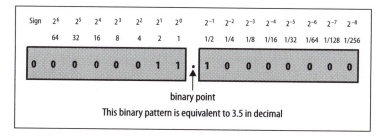

Fig. 2.8 Mixed numbers.

---

6   Note that there is an *overflow*; that is, the result is too big for the eight bits available. The leading bit therefore "falls off" the end. This condition will be detected by most arithmetic units and in the case of signed binary arithmetic would be classed as an acceptable condition.

As a result the rightmost digit of the left-hand byte has a multiplying factor of 2^0 (which is 1) and the leftmost digit of the right-hand byte has a multiplying factor of 2^{-1} (which is ½). With all that has gone before we can readily see that the left-hand byte may be interpreted as:

$$0 \times \text{Sign} + 0 \times 64 + 0 \times 32 + 0 \times 16 + 0 \times 8 + 0 \times 4 + 1 \times 2 + 1 \times 1$$

and the right-hand byte may be interpreted as:

$$1 \times 1/2 + 0 \times 1/4 + 0 \times 1/8 + 0 \times 1/16 + 0 \times 1/32 + 0 \times 1/64 + 0 \times 1/128 + 0 \times 1/256$$

In decimal, the right-hand byte becomes:

$$1 \times 0.5 + 0 \times 0.25 + 0 \times 0.125 + 0 \times 0.0625 + 0 \times 0.03125$$
$$+ 0 \times 0.015625 + 0 \times 0.0078125 + 0 \times 0.00390625$$

and adding all the digits from this pair of bytes, we see that this represents the number +3½ or +3.5.

As an exercise, attempt the interpretation of the two bytes in Fig. 2.5 as a mixed decimal number with the binary point assumed to be between byte address 56 and byte address 57. The result, you will find, is +105.4296875. A simpler way of calculating the mixed number value than adding up all the fractional parts is to take the whole number value and *scale* it. In decimal arithmetic, dividing the number by 10 is equivalent to shifting the decimal point one position left. Similarly, in binary arithmetic, dividing the number by two is equivalent to shifting the binary point one position left. Using big endian interpretation, the whole number value for Fig. 2.3 was found to be 26990. If we wish the binary point to be between the two bytes, this is equivalent to shifting the binary point 8 positions to the left (the width of a byte) which is also equivalent to dividing the number by $2^8 = 256$. The number 26990 divided by 256 does indeed result in +105.4296875.

Floating Point

All the forms of number representation that we have so far considered belong to the family of *fixed point* numbers. Another common form of number representation is that of *floating point*. In this format, several bytes are used to represent a number. The basis for this representation is the so called *scientific notation*. In this notation, numbers are represented (on paper) in a form such as $+2.5 \times 10^{+2}$ which is equivalent of course to 250. The signed mixed number (+2.5), which is restricted by definition to be between 1 and 10 is known as the *mantissa* and the signed power of 10 (+2) is known as the *exponent*. In order to represent a number in this format, the mantissa has to be adjusted until there is just one digit before the decimal point and the remaining digits are after it. To maintain the overall value of the number, the exponent then has to be increased or decreased accordingly. It is this adjustment of the position of the decimal point that results in the term "floating point" as opposed to our earlier considerations of fixed point format.

In representing floating point numbers in a binary system, one sequence of bits is used for the exponent and another sequence of bits is used for the mantissa. The base to which the exponent is raised is 2 in the binary system as opposed to 10 in the decimal system. Both the mantissa and the exponent may have positive or negative values, so the problem of representing negative numbers in binary patterns arises in both cases. In the case of the mantissa, by definition, a sign bit and two's complement approach is taken, as we have seen before (see the section on Signed Numbers above). For the exponent, again by definition, it is more usual to utilize a so-called *bias*. In this form of representation, a fixed value (the bias) is added to the exponent value on constructing the data and subtracted when analyzing the data. By this means, the exponent data is always kept positive. For example, with a bias of 127 and an exponent value of 42, the constructed value placed in the exponent field would be 127 + 42 = 169. On analyzing the exponent field of 169, the bias would be subtracted giving 169 – 127 = 42, resulting, of course, in the original exponent value. For a negative exponent value of, say, –5, the constructed value would be 127 + –5 = 122 and the analyzed value would be 122 – 127 = –5. In both cases, the values stored in the exponent field are positive.

Complications arise because there are several different formats. Most systems comply with the IEEE formats which define three floating point types: short real (1 bit for the sign of the mantissa, 8 bits for the exponent, and 23 bits for the mantissa itself), long real (1 bit for the sign of the mantissa, 11 bits for the exponent, and 52 bits for the mantissa itself) and temporary real (1 bit for the sign of the mantissa, 15 bits for the exponent, and 64 bits for the mantissa itself)[7]. In addition, Microsoft have traditionally used their own (different) floating point formats in their BASIC programming interpreters. Shown in Fig. 2.9 is an example that uses the format for the IEEE short real representation.

The sign bit refers to the mantissa and therefore, in this case, indicates a positive number. The exponent is not signed but has a 127 bias as explained above. This means that the value of the exponent is the binary value of the data in the exponent field with the value of 127 subtracted from it. The binary value of the data in the exponent field is clearly: $1 \times 2^7 + 1 \times 2^0 = 128 + 1 = 129$. The value of the exponent is therefore $129 - 127 = 2$. The binary value of the mantissa field is clearly $1 \times 2^{-1} = 0.5$. However, with this format, by definition and as indicated in the diagram, the value of the mantissa always has an implied $2^0 = 1$ added to it (note that it starts at 2^{-1} in the

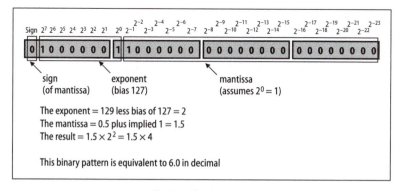

Fig. 2.9 Floating point.

<hr>

7   For further details see pages 165–170 of Messmer (1997).

Table 2.5 IEEE floating point formats.

● Short real	4 bytes	1 sign, 8 exponent, 23 mantissa
● Long real	8 bytes	1 sign, 11 exponent, 52 mantissa
● Temporary real	10 bytes	1 sign, 15 exponent, 64 mantissa

diagram). As a result, the actual value of the mantissa is $0.5 + 1 = 1.5$. The overall decimal value of the number is thus: $1.5 \times 2^2 = 1.5 \times 4 = 6.0$.

Most modern computer systems have a mathematical coprocessor which implements floating point arithmetic in the IEEE formats (see Table 2.5) and uses these floating point representations for storing and manipulating so-called *real* numbers.

Binary Coded Decimal

Another number format which is often used is that of *binary coded decimal,* or BCD. In this interpretation, the binary value of each byte in a sequence of bytes represents directly a single decimal digit. So the decimal number 105 would be represented in BCD by the three bytes shown in Fig. 2.10. The problem with this approach is that it is very wasteful of storage. Each byte is capable of holding 256 different values (0 to 255) and this form of BCD only uses 10 different values (the digits 0 to 9). A more efficient use is known as *packed BCD,* where each decimal digit is held in a nibble (4 bits) instead of a byte. A byte in this representation can therefore hold two decimal digits, as shown in Fig. 2.11.

All that has been done here is that the value 00000001 from the first byte of Fig. 2.10 has been reduced to a nibble of value 0001 and placed in the first nibble of the first byte of Fig. 2.11. The value 00000000 from the second byte of Fig. 2.10 has been reduced to a nibble of value 0000 and placed in the second nibble of the first byte of Fig. 2.11. The value 00000101 of the third byte of Fig. 2.10 has been reduced to a nibble of value 0101 and placed in the first nibble of the second byte of Fig. 2.11. All that has been lost in each case are leading zeros which do not contribute to the value of the digit. What was in three bytes has now been *packed* into the three nibbles, leaving room for another three digits to be represented (I have arbitrarily chosen "7",

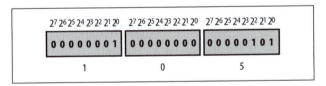

Fig. 2.10 Binary coded decimal.

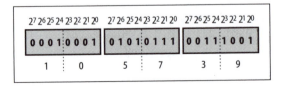

Fig. 2.11 Packed binary coded decimal.

"3" and "9" in the figure). Figure 2.11 therefore represents the decimal number 105739 held in three successive bytes in packed BCD form.

Hexadecimal

Before leaving number systems, we should briefly return to the hexadecimal number system. This, you will recall, utilizes base 16 and therefore has 16 digit symbols (the numeric symbols 0 to 9 and the letter symbols a to f) and a multiplying factor of 16.

Its real value to the analyst is in providing a much more compact form for listing and interpreting long binary sequences and one that can be very readily translated to and from binary. If we examine the binary equivalent of each of the 16 hexadecimal digits shown in Table 2.6 we note that we need exactly four binary digits to represent one hexadecimal digit (this should not surprise us, since 16 is of course 2^4). What it does mean, however, is that each four-bit half byte (that is, each nibble), can be represented by exactly one hexadecimal digit. A full byte can therefore be exactly represented by two hexadecimal digits. By memorizing the values in Table 2.6, translation between hexadecimal and binary can be carried out by simple inspection.

For example, consider the binary data in the two bytes at addresses 56 and 57 of Fig. 2.5. We can now see that this data can equally well be represented by the hexadecimal values 69 and 6E as is shown in Fig. 2.12. We simply look up the values from Table 2.6. What we have achieved using hexadecimal is a reduction in size of the binary sequence from 4 to 1 (four binary digits are represented by one hexadecimal digit) without losing awareness of the binary pattern.

The letters in hexadecimal numbers may be written in upper or lower case, and hexadecimal numbers may be identified with an upper or lower case "H" following them, thus: 69H and 6EH. Alternatively, 0x may be put in front of the number, thus:

Table 2.6 Hexadecimal code table.

Hex	Binary	Hex	Binary	Hex	Binary	Hex	Binary
0	0000	4	0100	8	1000	C	1100
1	0001	5	0101	9	1001	D	1101
2	0010	6	0110	A	1010	E	1110
3	0011	7	0111	B	1011	F	1111

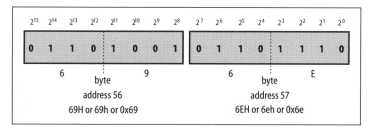

Fig. 2.12 Hexadecimal representation.

0x69 and 0x6e. Throughout the book, we use a variety of forms for representing hexadecimal numbers, in line with the screenshots from different software packages.

Characters

After numbers, the next most obvious sets of interpretative rules are those for characters. By "character" we mean a single symbol that is to be printed on a printer or displayed on a visual display unit and which includes within the set of all characters, the letters of the alphabet, both upper and lower case, and the digits 0 to 9. In most binary representations, a single character is represented by the data pattern in a single byte. Since a byte can hold 256 different patterns (recall that the range of numbers in a byte is 0 to 255), then up to 256 different characters can be defined.

Any character we wish could be associated with any of the 256 binary patterns. So, for example, we could define quite arbitrarily that the character "A" be represented by "00001000" and the character "B" be represented by "00001001" and so forth. In practice, the association between a particular character and particular binary pattern has to be standardized so that, for example, printers and display units will operate compatibly between different systems. The most common set of associations is the American Standard Code for Information Interchange, or *ASCII* as it is universally known. The ASCII code only actually defines characters for the first 128 binary values (0 to 127) and of these the first 32 are used as non-printing *control characters* originally intended for controlling data communications equipment and computer printers and displays. IBM introduced for its personal computer (PC) an *extended ASCII* code which is also in common use, as is the *Windows ANSI* code, which is used in Microsoft Windows. In addition to the original ASCII meanings, these codes each assign (typically different) particular character symbols to all those binary values in the range 128 to 255. These two sets of extended ASCII characters are given in Appendix 1.

Figure 2.13 shows the three bytes we started with at Fig. 2.2, interpreted now as three ASCII characters in sequence. The result is the three letters "inf". Clearly, given the page layout and punctuation characters that are available in ASCII, this approach can be used for representing arbitrarily long text documents. A sequence of characters such as this is often known as a *string*. In many systems, the end of a text string is marked by a binary all-zeros byte (ASCII code 0), and this is often referred to as an *ASCIIZ string*.

Although ASCII code is certainly the most widely used representation for characters, one other 8 bit code is still sometimes met with, particularly on IBM

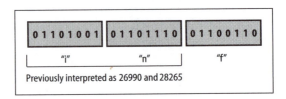

Fig. 2.13 ASCII characters.

mainframes. This is known as extended binary-coded decimal interchange code, or *EBCDIC*. In addition, many personal information managers and electronic organizers use their own particular modified versions of ASCII, which are often not published. An analyst will need to know these when looking at internal memory.

More recently, a two-byte code, known as *Unicode*, has been coming to prominence. On the Web site at `http://www.unicode.org/` can be found the following description: *The Unicode Worldwide Character Standard is a character coding system designed to support the interchange, processing, and display of the written texts of the diverse languages of the modern world. In addition, it supports classical and historical texts of many written languages.* We will consider this code again briefly when we discuss long filenames in Microsoft Windows 9x.

Computer Programs

There is one more standard form of interpretative rule set which we need to mention before leaving this section. That is the interpretation of binary byte sequences as a program of instructions to the computer. Because of the complexity of this topic, however, detailed discussion is best left until we have considered the way in which a computer operates. Suffice to say here that the binary patterns in a sequence of bytes may be interpreted by the processor as an ordered sequence of operations that it must perform. There are therefore sets of interpretative rules that the processor follows to interpret the bit patterns as instructions to itself. We will consider this further in a later chapter.

Records and Files

We have now looked at a number of different interpretations for the eight bit binary patterns that can be held in one, two, three or four bytes[8] (see the summary in Table 2.7).

The interpretations for one, two, three and four bytes that we have looked at are by no means exhaustive even for the very limited set of interpretative rules that we have considered. Clearly, for example, we could have a mixed number or a fraction in a single byte and we could have a fixed point whole number in four bytes. As we have also seen, we can have a sequence of bytes of arbitrary length to represent a string of characters of arbitrary length.

The byte is often (though not always) used as the fundamental unit for making more useful structures such as *records* and *files*. A record is a sequence of bytes, which, typically will have different sets of interpretative rules associated with different parts of the byte sequence. Say, for example, we require to hold a military

---

8 The forensic computing analyst needs to be aware that sequences of four bytes (double words) for fixed point numbers can also be in big endian or little endian format. Thus, the double word number (in hexadecimal) 0x89ABCDEF would be stored in four bytes in little endian format as: EF CD AB 89.

Table 2.7 Some possible interpretations.

● One byte	One fixed point unsigned whole number (0 to 255)
	One fixed point signed whole number (+127 to −128)
	One ASCII character
● Two bytes	One fixed point unsigned whole number (0 to 65535)
	One fixed point signed whole number (+32767 to −32768)
	One fixed point mixed number or fraction
	Four hexadecimal digits
● Three bytes	Three BCD digits
	Six packed BCD digits
	Three ASCII characters
● Four bytes	One IEEE "short real" floating point number

vehicle registration number in a record. Such registration numbers are made up of a two-digit decimal number followed by two letters followed again by another two digit decimal number, thus: 41 XY 73. We could define a military vehicle registration record in four bytes as follows. The first two-digit decimal number is held as packed BCD in the first byte, then there are two ASCII character bytes and finally the second two-digit decimal number is again held as packed BCD in the fourth byte, as shown in Fig. 2.14.

Our definition above defines the interpretative rules for both the construction and the interpretation of our military vehicle registration record. In order to make "sense" of these four bytes, the analyst must know, or be able to deduce, the interpretative rules for this particular record. Clearly, there is no limit to the different types of record that are possible nor to the complexity of any given record structure. If the wrong[9] interpretation is not to be made, it is essential that the analyst is able to prove that the interpretative set of rules applied to the four bytes are those intended by the originator for that record structure.

A sequence of records may be called a *file*. The records in the file may all be of the same type, or they may be of a variety of types; they may be very complex or they may be as simple as a single byte each. Again, there is no limit on the different types of file possible. A file is the basic element that is normally stored in a *file system*. In most file systems the file is given a name and often a type description. So, for example, in the MS-DOS[10] file system, a file is given a file name of up to eight characters and a file

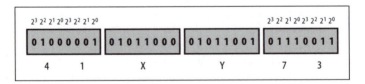

Fig. 2.14 Military vehicle registration record.

---

9 By "wrong" here we mean "not that intended" by the originator of the record.

10 Microsoft Disk Operating System.

type of up to three characters. When written down, it is normal practice to show the filename separated from the file type by a period thus: TEST.TXT signifies a file of file name "TEST" and file type "TXT".

File Types and Signatures

File types may be used to signify the types of record that are held in the file. This is useful to the analyst as a starting point for deducing the appropriate set of interpretative rules for the file. Some software packages use the file type to confirm initially that a suitable file is being processed, but this is never a sufficient test and further checks are invariably made of the actual data. There is no guarantee that any particular system will conform to the file typing practice and, indeed, a conscious attempt to deceive subsequent analysis may have been made by deliberately misusing a particular known file type. Some files may have a sequence of bytes at the beginning of the file that specifically indicate the type of file. This is known as the *file signature*. Although this too can be deliberately changed to hinder recognition by the analyst, it is less likely to be done, since the associated application software would then be unable to recognize the file until the signature had been restored.

Use of Hexadecimal Listings

One of the simplest and most common forms of file is that of the *plain text file*. In this, all the records are single bytes and each byte represents one ASCII character. Such files are sometimes called *ASCII files* and they are often signified by a file type of "TXT". Even with something as simple as this there are variations: the end of each line of text in the file may be indicated by the two byte values 0dH followed by 0aH, which represent the characters "carriage return" and "line feed" respectively, or, it may be indicated by the single byte 0aH, or, it may be indicated by the single byte 0dH. All three approaches are in common use, but few application software packages recognize all three. Figure 2.15 shows an example of an ASCII text file (TEST.TXT) in the form of a so-called *hexadecimal listing*. This form of listing is very useful to the

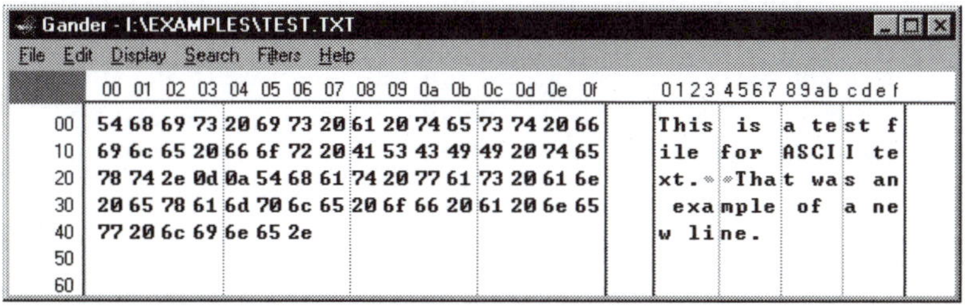

Fig. 2.15 Hexadecimal listing of TEST.TXT.

analyst and it is displayed here by means of a shareware program called Gander for Windows[11].

The listing of Fig. 2.15 shows the actual byte values in the file: in hexadecimal number form in the left-hand panel and in ASCII character form in the right-hand panel. If we examine the left-hand panel, we can see that the address of each byte is given, also in hexadecimal number form, by the sum of the row and column numbers. So, for example, the third byte in the sequence (of value 69H) is at address row 00H + column 02H = 02H (remember addresses start from 0); the sixteenth byte (of value 66H) is at address row 00H + column 0fH = 0fH; and the thirty-sixth byte (of value 0dH) is at address row 20H + column 03H = 23H. It is at addresses 23H and 24H that we see an example of the carriage return (0dH) line feed (0aH) sequence that we referred to above. In the right-hand panel of the listing, we see the ASCII character interpretation for each byte, but only where that interpretation results in a visible character. So, for example, the effects of the ASCII characters associated with addresses 23H and 24H (carriage return 0dH and line feed 0aH respectively) are not implemented (we would get a new line of text in the display, if they were) but instead a blob is put in their place, and this is repeated for all non-visible characters. The ASCII text file, when printed out, displays the visible text shown in Fig. 2.16.

> This is a test file for ASCII text.
> That was an example of a new line.

Fig. 2.16 Printout of TEST.TXT.

Word Processing Formats

In practice, there is not much to gain from using a hexadecimal listing with a plain text ASCII file. The real benefits come when the file is not made up solely of ASCII characters. Most word processors use a modified form of ASCII for the text and embed their own word processing codes into the file. These codes signify, for example, the page layout, the type of printer and all those other elements that determine the appearance of the document, such as bold, italic, underline and the font types and point sizes etc. They normally also include a file signature.

WordPerfect

Figure 2.17 shows a hexadecimal listing of some of the byte patterns that result when this same text is processed using Corel® WordPerfect® version 8. The listing has been limited to two small parts: the first part is from addresses 00H to 3fH and the second part is from addresses 730H to 7aaH. The detail between addresses 3fH and 730H has been deliberately omitted in this example for the purposes of clarity.

---

11 Gander for Windows (1991), Dave Lord, shareware. Available from http://www.gsw.com/welcome/2112.htm.

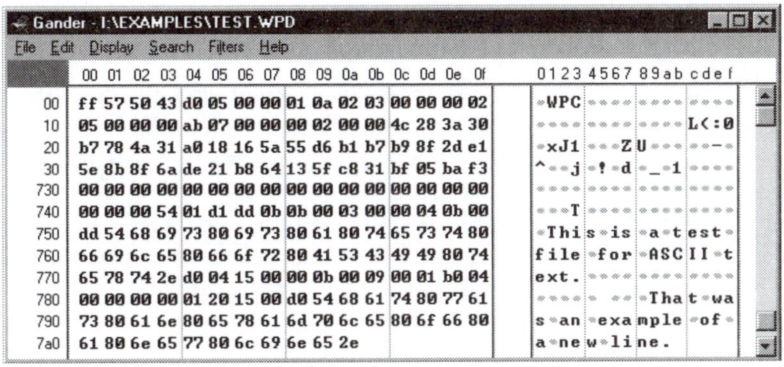

Fig. 2.17 Hexadecimal listing of WordPerfect file.

The first point to note is the significant increase in size of the word processor file over that of the original ASCII file. The word processor file is 7abH bytes long (equal to 1963 bytes) and the ASCII file is 47H bytes long (equal to 71 bytes). The second point to note is the presence of a file signature in the first few bytes of the file. Here we see in the first four bytes of this file the hexadecimal codes: ff 57 50 43[12] and this is the known signature[13] for a Corel® WordPerfect® word processor file. The third point we may note is that the ASCII text, which starts at 751H with the byte value 54H for the character "T", has been modified. The space character in ASCII is 20H (for an example, see byte address 04H in Fig. 2.15), but here the space character has been replaced with 80H (see, for example, byte address 755H in Fig. 2.17). In addition, there is nothing recognizable as a carriage return or line feed character, 0dH and 0aH respectively, between the two lines of ASCII text, in the area of addresses 774H to 789H.

The Software Development Kit[14] provided with Corel® WordPerfect® Suite 8 includes full details of all these file format codes. Using this information, we are able to interpret the entire file should we so wish. This we will not do, but a few simple examples will make the point. The four-byte sequence 01 0a 02 03 at addresses 08H to 0bH defines that the document was written by a WordPerfect program, that it is a WordPerfect document and that it is WordPerfect version 8. The two-byte sequence ab 07 at addresses 14H and 15H is in fact the file size in little endian fixed point whole number format. That is, it is the number 07abH, equal to 1963 bytes, as we noted above. Finally, the sequence of bytes that starts d0 04H at addresses 774H and 775H and ends 00 d0H at addresses 787H and 788H is called an "end-of-line group" and represents the end of line characters between the two lines of text.

---

12 The WordPerfect signature is often written as −1, "WPC".

13 Many file signatures are listed in books such as *The File Formats Handbook* (Born, 1997) and *Encyclopedia of Graphics File Formats* (Murray and vanRyper, 1996). See Appendix 2 for some examples.

14 See WordPerfect Document File Format, Corel WordPerfect Suite 8 Software Development Kit in an installed WordPerfect 8 system at Corel/SDKs/Suite8/ DOCS/A_FRNTFF.htm.

Microsoft Word for Windows

Of course, all word processors are typically different, and In Fig. 2.18 we see a hexadecimal listing of some of the byte patterns that result when the same ASCII text is processed using Microsoft Word for Windows 95 version 7. The listing this time has been limited to three small parts: the first part is from addresses 00H to 1fH, the second part is from addresses 4f0H to 54fH, and the third from addresses 2be0 to 2bff. Here we note that the Microsoft Word for Windows file is very much larger, 2c00H bytes (equal to 11 264 bytes) compared with the WordPerfect file of 1963 bytes and the ASCII file of 71 bytes. We also note that the signature for a Microsoft Word for Windows file appears[15] to extend from addresses 00H to 07H and consists of the eight hexadecimal codes: d0 cf 11 e0 a1 b1 1a e1[16]. At address 507H we note that the space character is held with its ASCII value of 20H and that at address 523H the end of line is indicated by an ASCII carriage return character with a byte value of 0dH.

Table 2.8 compares the file size of the ASCII text with the equivalent WordPerfect 8 and Microsoft Word for Windows word processor file sizes.

The detailed formats for the Microsoft Word for Windows files were not found in the public domain at the time of writing. Concerns were also being expressed, of particular interest to the forensic computing analyst, about the so-called "trash blocks" in Microsoft Word for Windows files. These are where memory blocks that have been used by other applications are reused within the Word for Windows file without being modified. The effect of this is that sensitive information from another

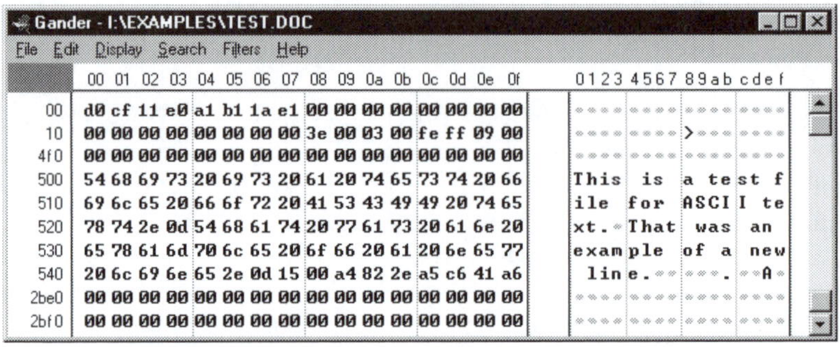

Fig. 2.18 Hexadecimal listing of MS Word for Windows file.

Table 2.8 Typical file sizes.

● ASCII text file	71 bytes
● WordPerfect 8	1963 bytes
● Word for Windows 7	11264 bytes

15 Born (1997) notes in *The File Formats Handbook* that "*...the complete structure of the Winword format is confidential and may not be published here.*"

16 This signature is identified by Schwartz (1997) in his LAOLA file system as signifying a "wrapper" file for a variety of Microsoft applications, including Word 97, Excel 97 and PowerPoint 97.

application could become inadvertently saved within the Word for Windows file. While such information would not be accessible through the Word for Windows program, it would be accessible to an analyst using, for example, a hexadecimal listing program such as Gander. Examination of such blocks could provide useful additional information about other applications that have been run on the target machine. There is also the possibility that such information could be passed inadvertently from one system to another when Word for Windows documents are enclosed in email messages. Of course, it would also be possible for sensitive information to be hidden deliberately within a Word for Windows file and sent openly as an email enclosure.

Rich Text Format

In the previous two word processor examples we have been seeing a mixture of binary control codes and ASCII text. For the last example in this section, we note in Fig. 2.19 the same information encoded in *Rich Text Format* (RTF), which was designed to use only the displayable ASCII characters[17]. In this example the listing has been limited to two parts: from addresses 00H to 4fH and from addresses d0H to 13aH. The file signature is evident at the beginning of the file as "{\rtf1\ansi" and the text clearly starts at address e5H. In addition, it is apparent that the formatting information is also held in text form; thus we see ASCII character details about font and colour as well. Many applications support RTF, so it can be used as a useful exchange medium between different products.

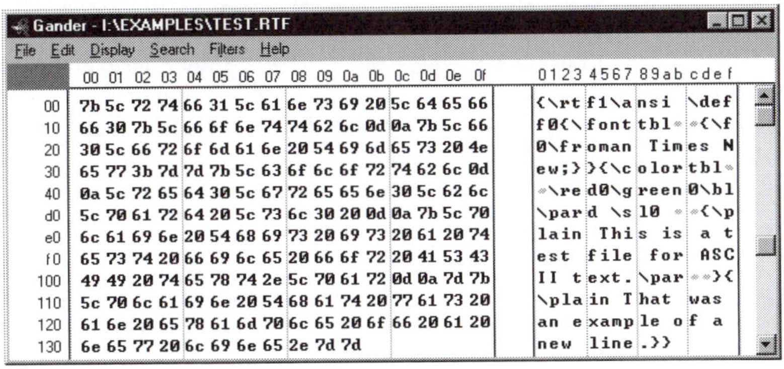

```
Gander - I:\EXAMPLES\TEST.RTF                                          _ □ ×
File  Edit  Display  Search  Filters  Help

        00 01 02 03 04 05 06 07 08 09 0a 0b 0c 0d 0e 0f    0123 4567 89ab cdef
  00   7b 5c 72 74 66 31 5c 61 6e 73 69 20 5c 64 65 66   {\rt f1\a nsi  \def
  10   66 30 7b 5c 66 6f 6e 74 74 62 6c 0d 0a 7b 5c 66   f0{\ font tbl· ·{\f
  20   30 5c 66 72 6f 6d 61 6e 20 54 69 6d 65 73 20 4e   0\fr oman Tim es N
  30   65 77 3b 7d 7d 7b 5c 63 6f 6c 6f 72 74 62 6c 0d   ew;} }{\c olor tbl·
  40   0a 5c 72 65 64 30 5c 67 72 65 65 6e 30 5c 62 6c   ·\re d0\g reen 0\bl
  d0   5c 70 61 72 64 20 5c 73 6c 30 20 0d 0a 7b 5c 70   \par d \s l0 · ·{\p
  e0   6c 61 69 6e 20 54 68 69 73 20 69 73 20 61 20 74   lain This  is  a t
  f0   65 73 74 20 66 69 6c 65 20 66 6f 72 20 41 53 43   est  file  for  ASC
 100   49 49 20 74 65 78 74 2e 5c 70 61 72 0d 0a 7d 7b   II t ext. \par ··}{
 110   5c 70 6c 61 69 6e 20 54 68 61 74 20 77 61 73 20   \pla in T hat  was
 120   61 6e 20 65 78 61 6d 70 6c 65 20 6f 66 20 61 20   an e xamp le o f a
 130   6e 65 77 20 6c 69 6e 65 2e 7d 7d                   new  line .}}
```

Fig. 2.19 Hexadecimal listing of RTF file.

Magic Numbers

It is not just modern word processing packages that use file signatures to identify their application files. The idea has been around since the very early days of

---

17 This format was designed by Microsoft as a method of encoding formatted text and graphics for ease of transfer between different applications. It is used by the clipboard in Windows. (From Born (1997).)

computing, and in the *Unix* community in particular the first few bytes of a binary file are often used to indicate type. This is generally referred to as its *magic number* and is defined as: "*Special data located at the beginning of a binary data file to indicate its type to a utility. Under Unix, the system and various applications programs (especially the linker) distinguish between types of executable file by looking for a magic number. Once upon a time, these magic numbers were PDP-11 branch instructions that skipped over header data to the start of executable code*"[18]. There are now thousands of such magic numbers, many not documented, many proprietary and many simply picked at random. Attempts[19] are being made to document and standardize magic numbers as well as specifying basic rules for their future selection. A preliminary draft document[20] is now in existence which states: "*...it is very desirable that files should generally present themselves as self-describing objects from which an application launcher or navigation tool can readily deduce both their uses and at least some of the semantics of their contents*". Clearly, this work is of much interest to the forensic computing analyst, since it could make the recognition and interpretation of well-behaved files a routine activity[21]. We consider in a later section the problem of badly behaved files and deliberate attempts to hide information.

Graphic Formats

It is in the digital representation of graphic images that we find perhaps the greatest range of different file formats. Just to give a flavour for some of these graphic formats, we will use the digital image of a Zeon Tech digital diary, shown in Fig. 2.20, as our example. A high-resolution digital image was first taken with a digital camera and then processed using a graphics software package (Paint Shop Pro) to give a series of lower resolution 256 grey-scale images in a number of different graphic formats.

The first of these that we will consider is that of the Graphics Interchange Format, or GIF, developed by Compuserve in 1987 to permit the passing of graphic images by email.

Graphic Interchange Format

GIF enables several pictures to be stored in the one file and it uses a loss-free compression algorithm[22] to reduce the file size. The specification published in 1987

---

18 Quoted from URL http://sunsite.nstu.nsk.su/jargon/m/magicnumber.html.

19 See URL http://sagan.earthspace.net/~esr/magic-numbers/ for the Magic Numbers Group Home Page.

20 Rfc-draft, v1.2 1996/11/20 available at URL http://sagan.earthspace.net/~esr/magic-numbers/rfc-draft/.

21 In Unix, there is a special program, file(1), which attempts to identify the type of any given file from its magic number.

22 Lempel–Ziv–Welch (LZW) compression. See Blackstock (undated) for an outline of the process.

Fig. 2.20 Zeon Tech digital diary.

	00	01	02	03	04	05	06	07	08	09	0a	0b	0c	0d	0e	0f	0123 4567 89ab cdef
00	47	49	46	38	39	61	40	01	d6	00	f7	00	00	00	00	00	GIF89a@
10	01	01	01	02	02	02	03	03	03	04	04	04	05	05	05	06	
20	06	06	07	07	07	08	08	08	09	09	09	0a	0a	0a	0b	0b	
30	0b	0c	0c	0c	0d	0d	0d	0e	0e	0e	0f	0f	0f	10	10	10	
40	11	11	11	12	12	12	13	13	13	14	14	14	15	15	15	16	
300	fb	fc	fc	fc	fd	fd	fd	fe	fe	fe	ff	ff	ff	2c	00	00	,
310	00	00	40	01	d6	00	00	08	fe	00	37	5d	9a	b4	68	12	@ 7] h
320	24	44	87	12	0d	0a	f4	e7	0f	9f	3e	0c	f9	fc	f1	03	$D >
330	b1	a1	c3	3c	7b	0a	11	02	f4	a7	0f	20	3f	7c	f6	f4	< { ?!
340	e9	18	88	e2	48	89	7e	28	e6	c1	43	47	4f	a2	4d	99	H ~< CG O M

Fig. 2.21 Hexadecimal listing of GIF file.

is referred to as "GIF87a" and an extended version published in 1989 is known as "GIF89a". In the case of our example, the resulting GIF file is 64 kilobytes in size and two small segments of the file, examined using the Gander hexadecimal viewer, are shown in Fig. 2.21.

The file signature (or magic number) can readily be seen in the first few bytes as 47 49 46 38 39 61 or "GIF89a". This is followed immediately by the *logical screen descriptor block*, starting at address 06H, which specifies the width of the logical screen in pixels as 40 01 (in little endian this becomes 0140H = 320 decimal) and the height of the logical screen in pixels as d6 00 (again, in little endian, this is 00d6H = 214 decimal). It also shows at address 0aH that there is a *global colour table* and that the colour resolution is 8 bits for each primary colour in the colour table[23]. The

---

23 For these and similar details see page 684 *et seq.* of Born (1997).

global colour table starts at address 0dH with 00 00 00 and consists of 256 triples, each triple representing the red, green, blue (RGB) intensity values of one of the 256 possible colours in the colour palette. In this case, the colours in the palette are all grey-scale colours. We can tell this because the intensities of each of the R, G and B values for each colour triple are identical, thus resulting in a palette of grey/black tones.

Two small segments of the file have been shown. The second segment, starting with address 300H, shows the last entry of the colour table at address 30aH with RGB values ff ff ff. The next value, at address 30dH, is 2c, and this signals the start of a GIF picture (there may be more than one). This is the first byte of the *image descriptor block* which defines at address 30eH the left coordinate of the picture in pixels (0000), at address 310H the top coordinate of the picture in pixels (0000), at address 312H the width of the picture in pixels (again little endian, thus 0140H = 320 decimal) and at address 314H the height of the picture in pixels (also little endian, 00d6H = 214 decimal). Immediately following this is a single flags byte and then, starting from address 317H is the first *raster data block*. This will typically be followed by a number of *raster data sub-blocks*.

In constructing the GIF file, the original picture has been analyzed, starting in the top left-hand corner, and working, pixel by pixel, from left to right and from top to bottom. Each pixel of the picture has been coded as a colour byte, the value of which is the relative entry in the colour table of value 0 to 255. This stream of pixel bytes has then been encoded using LZW compression and the resulting output stream has been used to form the raster data block and sub-blocks, the first bytes of which are the block lengths. Each data block therefore contains LZW compressed data, which we will not attempt to analyze here. The first of the data blocks commences with a *code size* byte which is used in the decompression process. In our example, this byte is at address 317H (of value 08H) and the first raster data block starts at address 318H and has a length of feH. The compressed data for this block starts at address 319H.

LZW Legal Problems

Although GIF became one of the most widely used formats for graphic files, legal difficulties have arisen in recent years. Abraham Lempel and Jakob Ziv (1977) developed the first of the LZ compression algorithms (LZ77) which are found in archiving programs such as *zoo*, *lha* and *pkzip*. In 1984, Terry Welch, while working for Sperry Corporation, produced a modified version known as the LZW algorithm. It is this algorithm which is used today in the GIF and TIFF graphic file formats. In 1985, Sperry Corporation was granted a patent for the LZW algorithm and the ownership of this was transferred to Unisys when the new company was formed. In 1994, Compuserve and Unisys came to an agreement whereby the use of the LZW algorithm would be licensed for application in the GIF file format. This created many problems with the user community, who had understood from Compuserve that the GIF format was freely available for unrestricted use. Now, since 1995, licences have been required from Unisys for all software that reads or writes the GIF format (Unisys, 1995).

Portable Network Graphic

The recent reaction to this problem has been to move away from GIF and towards a new format called Portable Network Graphic (PNG) format[24]. This uses a LZ77 variant of the compression algorithm which is not part of the Unisys patent. The unofficial expansion of the acronym PNG is "PNG's Not GIF".

The PNG work has been well received by the graphics community and many graphics packages now support it. Murray and vanRyper (1996) state: "*We are happy to report that the PNG specification is one of the most complete, well-thought-out, and well-written file format specifications yet examined by the authors of this book.*"

Our second graphics example of the picture in Fig. 2.20 shows, in Fig. 2.22, one small segment of a PNG file, again examined using the Gander hexadecimal viewer. This file is 44 kilobytes in length. The file signature is the first eight bytes and is always 89 50 4e 47 0d 0a 1a 0a. This is not a random choice of values since the bytes are used to assist in detecting various kinds of errors. The value 89, for example, is used to detect whether the file has passed through a 7 bit data transmission channel, in which case the 89 would become 09. The characters "PNG" give an immediately recognizable text signature. The byte pair 0d 0a is used to determine whether or not the file has been manipulated by software that alters carriage return and newline sequences, and the byte 1a prevents the listing of the file on MS-DOS operating systems since this byte value is the MS-DOS end of file marker, Control-Z.

Immediately after the signature is the Header *chunk*. The length of the data in the chunk is given by the double word starting at address 08H and of value 00 00 00 0d. Note that this format uses big endian storage, and thus the value is equivalent to decimal 13. Next follows the signature for the chunk, the characters "IHDR" at address 0cH and then the 13 data bytes of the chunk starting at address 10H. These take the form of a double word for the width of the image in pixels 00 00 01 40 (big endian format results in 320 decimal) followed by a double word for the height of the image in pixels 00 00 00 d6 (big endian format results in 214 decimal). Finally, the last five bytes 08 00 00 00 00, starting from address 18H, indicate an 8 bit per pixel grey-

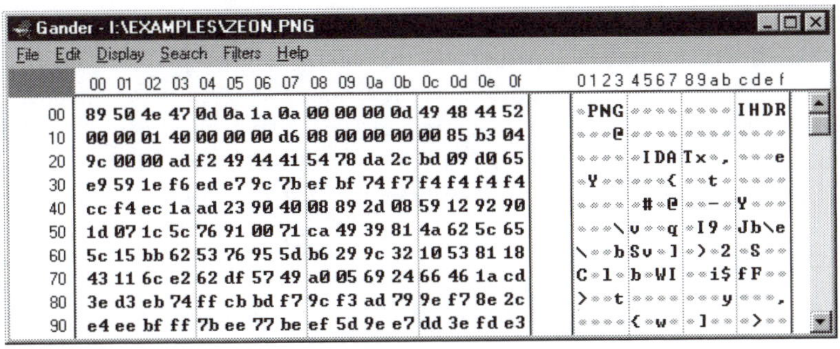

Fig. 2.22 Hexadecimal listing of PNG file.

---

24 See article by Atzberger and Zolli (1997).

scale colour depth[25]. These are exactly the same results as we obtained from interpreting the equivalent GIF file.

The chunk ends at 1dH with a double word cyclic redundancy check and the next chunk starts at address 21H with a chunk data length of 00 00 ad f2 which is equivalent to 44530 in decimal. The signature for this chunk, the Image Data chunk, is the characters "IDAT" and the 44530 bytes of compressed data start at address 29H. The image data is laid out as a bitmap which has been scanned from left to right and from top to bottom and it is compressed using a variation of the *deflate*[26] compression method developed by Phil Katz, the author of the *pkzip* archiving program. Again, we will not attempt to decode the compressed data of this example.

JPEG Compression

Both the graphic formats so far considered use lossless[27] compression methods and, at best, in practice, will achieve only an approximate halving of the file size. The final example we will look at is a graphic format that utilizes lossy compression methods and one that can achieve much higher compression ratios. The Joint Photographic Experts Group (JPEG) is a standards committee that was formed in 1987 from two separate bodies, a CCITT (International Telegraph and Telephone Consultative Committee) sub-group and an ISO (International Organization for Standardization) sub-group. Both sub-groups had been researching compression methods for the transmission of graphic images and the combining of the two groups permitted the establishment of a single standard.

JPEG, unlike the previous formats, is not based on a single compression method[28]. Rather, it is a toolkit of methods that may be altered to fit the needs of the user. Different compression methods may be used to trade quality of image against file size. As mentioned above, JPEG also differs in that it primarily uses lossy methods of compression. These work by discarding information that normally goes unnoticed by the human eye. As a result, there need be no perceptible degradation in quality despite achieving compression ratios of the order of 20:1.

The JPEG ISO standard (ISO, undated) describes the compression methods for images, but it does not define a common file interchange format which will enable JPEG bitstreams to be exchanged between a variety of platforms and applications. The JPEG File Interchange Format (JFIF) has been designed just for this. In the 1992 specification (Hamilton, 1992), the author states: "*...the only purpose of this simplified format is to allow the exchange of JPEG compressed images*". Image files with file types such as JPG, JIF, JPEG or JFIF are most likely therefore to be in JFIF format and our final example of the picture in Fig. 2.20 is in just this format.

---

25 For these and similar details see pages 700 *et seq.* of Murray and vanRyper (1996).

26 See the file *Application.zip* available from URL: http://www.pkware.com/.

27 In a lossless system, the original bit pattern can be restored in its entirety from the compressed version.

28 See pages 191 *et seq.* of Murray and vanRyper (1996) for a discussion of JPEG compression.

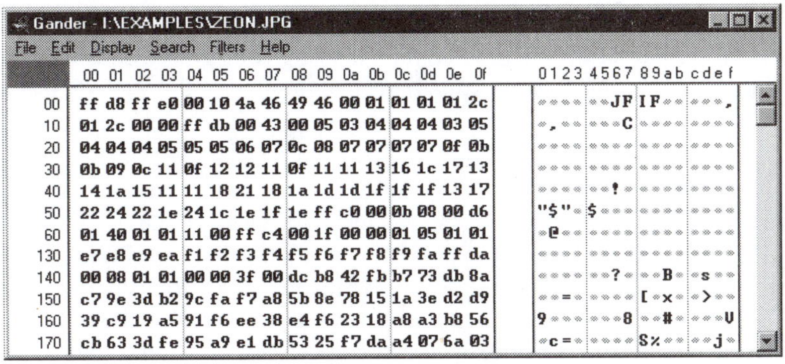

Fig. 2.23 Hexadecimal listing of JPG file.

JPEG File Interchange Format (JFIF)

Figure 2.23 shows two small segments of the JPG file, again examined using the Gander hexadecimal viewer. This file is only 17 Kilobytes in length as a result of the lossy compression. The quality of the image, however, is little different from that of the GIF and PNG versions. The file signature is effectively the first four bytes ff d8 ff e0 although these are part of two separate blocks. The *start of image marker* block, ff d8, is required by the JPEG standard to signal a JPEG file and the ff e0 indicates an *application marker* block which together with the characters "JFIF" starting at address 06H identify this as a JFIF file.

Also of interest is the sequence that starts at address 59H of value ff c0. This is a *start of frame marker* block which at address 5dH has the bits per pixel value of 08. At address 5eH is a two-byte word giving the height of the image in pixels, 00 d6 (big endian format results in 214 decimal), and at address 60H is a two-byte word giving the width of the image in pixels 01 40 (big endian format results in 320 decimal). Once again, these are exactly the same results as we obtained from interpreting the equivalent GIF and PNG files.

In the second segment of the file, starting with address 13eH, we see the *start of scan marker*, ff da, and this is then followed at 148H by the compressed image data, also scanned from left to right and from top to bottom. It is at this point, once again, that we will leave the analysis[29].

There are many other graphic file formats: BMP, FLI, FLC, MAC, ICO, IMG, PAL, PIC, PCX and TIF, to name but a few. Some file signatures are listed in Appendix 2, but reference books such *as The File Formats Handbook* (Born, 1997) and *Encyclopedia of Graphics File Formats* (Murray and vanRyper, 1996) are essential for detailed analysis.

Archive formats

The file archive program *pkzip* has already been mentioned in the context of the LZ compression algorithms, as have similar products such as *zoo* and *lha*. Archivers

---

29 For more details see pages 895 *et seq.* of Born (1997).

such as these carry out two separate functions: they compress one or more files using lossless compression and they archive the resulting compressed files into a single archive file, which, in the case of *pkzip*, is given a file type ZIP.

Pkzip

To demonstrate an archive format, the two word processing files TEST.DOC and TEST.WPD were archived using *pkzip* to form the file TEST.ZIP. Figure 2.24 shows two small segments of the resulting file, using the Gander hexadecimal viewer. The ZIP file is 2597 bytes long compared with the 11 264 bytes of TEST.DOC and the 1963 bytes of TEST.WPD. The file signature can be seen in the first four bytes as 50 4b 03 04 and this is most readily recognized as starting with the characters "PK". This signature is part of the *local file header* and is repeated for every file in the archive. Immediately after the signature are a series of bytes detailing the *pkzip* version number, general-purpose flags, the compression method used, the last modified date and time of the file, a cyclic redundancy check, the compressed and uncompressed file sizes and the filename in characters[30]. The name of the first file in the archive starts at address 1eH and is seen to be "TEST.DOC". The compressed file size is the four bytes 7c 05 00 00 starting at 12H, which in little endian double word format becomes 0000057c equal to 1404 in decimal.

The original file size is the four bytes 00 2c 00 00 starting at 16H, which in little endian double word format becomes 00002c00 equal to 11 264 in decimal (entirely as we expect). It is interesting to note the very significant reduction in file size that is possible with compressing this kind of word processing file. Immediately following the filename at address 26H is the start of the compressed data of the word processing file. Each of the files in the archive follows a similar pattern: a local file header followed by the compressed file data. At the end of the sequence of files, a *central directory record* is established. In the second segment of the ZIP file, starting with address 9d9H, we see the signature 50 4b 01 02 of the second (and last)[31] *file*

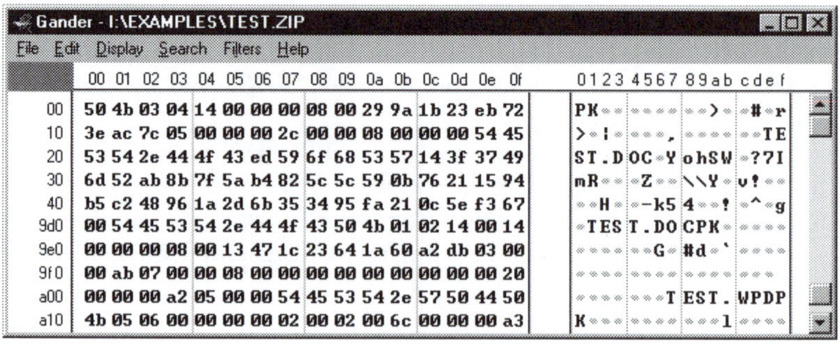

Fig. 2.24 Hexadecimal listing of ZIP file.

---

30 For these, and details of the compression algorithms, see PKWARE (undated).

31 The start of the first file header of the central directory structure occurs at an address not shown in Fig. 2.24.

header in this central directory record. Each header contains very similar information to that held in the local file header, including, as can be seen at address a07H, the filename in character form. The central directory record (and the ZIP file) is terminated by an *end of central directory record*, starting at address a0fH with signature 50 4b 05 06.

From the viewpoint of the forensic computing analyst, it is useful to note that even if the ZIP file has been password-protected, the filenames and other details are still available, both in the local file headers and in the central directory record.

Other Applications

The final format considered in this chapter is the record structure found in the memory of some Sharp organizers. The structure, shown at Fig. 2.25, takes the form of a record signature, made up of the three bytes 20 07 00, which is preceded by two counts, each of which are two bytes in length held in little endian format. Immediately after the signature are the character bytes of the record itself. The first two byte count specifies the length of the record, including the count bytes, and the second two byte count specifies the length of the preceding record.

In the first entry of the example shown in Fig. 2.25, the first count is 15 00, which, in little endian format gives 0015H equal to 21 in decimal and, taking into account the seven bytes of the two counts and the signature, gives a text character record size of 14 bytes. The second count of this record indicates that the *previous* record is 1c 00 (or 001cH little endian) which is equal to 28 (in decimal) bytes long. The second entry shows the first count as 1a 00 (or 001aH in little endian) which is equal to 26 (in decimal) and, once again, taking into account the seven bytes, gives a text character record size of 19 bytes. The second count of this record is, of course, the same as the first count of the previous record.

Finally, Fig. 2.26 shows a hexadecimal listing of part of the memory of a Sharp organizer which uses this format for its record structure. Starting from address 529H can be seen the two counts of values, 15 00 and 1c 00, followed by the signature at address 52dH of 20 07 00. Following this are the 14 text character bytes of the record. In this format 00H is used to represent a newline. The next record then starts at 53eH with the counts of values 1a 00 and 15 00

Of interest to the forensic computing analyst is the fact that the signature in this format is changed for secret records to A0 07 00, although the text characters remain

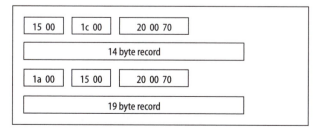

Fig. 2.25 Structure of a Sharp organizer record.

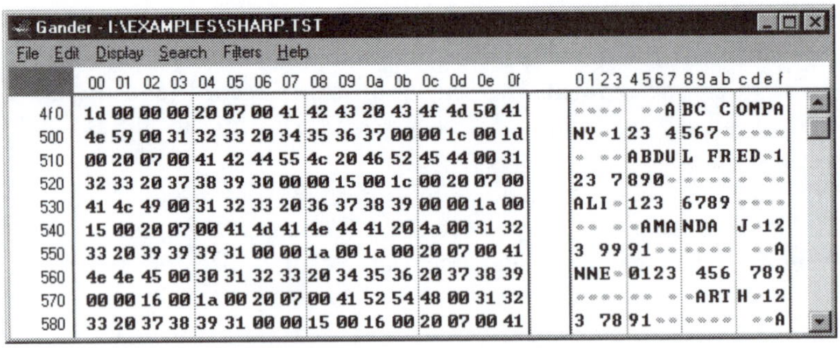

```
Gander - I:\EXAMPLES\SHARP.TST                                    _ □ ✕
File  Edit  Display  Search  Filters  Help

        00 01 02 03 04 05 06 07 08 09 0a 0b 0c 0d 0e 0f   0123 4567 89ab cdef
 4f0 | 1d 00 00 00 20 07 00 41 42 43 20 43 4f 4d 50 41 | ····  ·ABC COMPA
 500 | 4e 59 00 31 32 33 20 34 35 36 37 00 00 1c 00 1d | NY·123 4567····
 510 | 00 20 07 00 41 42 44 55 4c 20 46 52 45 44 00 31 | ·  ··ABDUL FRED·1
 520 | 32 33 20 37 38 39 30 00 00 15 00 1c 00 20 07 00 | 23 7890······ ··
 530 | 41 4c 49 00 31 32 33 20 36 37 38 39 00 00 1a 00 | ALI·123 6789····
 540 | 15 00 20 07 00 41 4d 41 4e 44 41 20 4a 00 31 32 | ·· ··AMANDA J·12
 550 | 33 20 39 39 39 31 00 00 1a 00 1a 00 20 07 00 41 | 3 9991······ ··A
 560 | 4e 4e 45 00 30 31 32 33 20 34 35 36 20 37 38 39 | NNE·0123 456  789
 570 | 00 00 16 00 1a 00 20 07 00 41 52 54 48 00 31 32 | ····· ·  ·ARTH·12
 580 | 33 20 37 38 39 31 00 00 15 00 16 00 20 07 00 41 | 3 7891······ ··A
```

Fig. 2.26 Hexadecimal listing of part of a Sharp organizer memory dump.

unchanged. Direct access to the memory and a knowledge of the record structure permits the analyst to extract password-protected records from this model of organizer.

Quick View Plus

This chapter would not be complete without reference to the file utility Quick View Plus[32]. This program uses the file signature in a file to identify the file format and then display it in accordance with the rules of that format. The help file of the most recent version (5.1.1) at the time of writing states: "*Quick View Plus gives you easy access to files created in over 200 programs, regardless of whether you have those programs on your computer. With Quick View Plus you can work effortlessly with files or parts of files created in the format of text, spreadsheets, databases, presentations, and graphics.*"

A utility such as this, together with a hexadecimal viewer (also included in Quick View Plus), is an essential tool for the forensic computing analyst. It should be noted, however, that some members of the forensic computing community take the view that computer output that is to be presented in evidence should always be produced using the application software that was used to create it. Quick View Plus and other tools are thus seen to be useful to assist in identification, but evidence needs to be produced, wherever possible, using the original software.

Exercises

2.1   Interpret each of the pairs of binary byte patterns that follow as:

(1) a little endian unsigned decimal integer

(2) a big endian unsigned decimal integer

(3) two signed decimal integers

---

32 This is a commercial product produced by Inso Corporation, Ltd, The Old Telephone Exchange, 12 Compton Road, Wimbledon SW19 7QD, UK (URL: http://www.inso.com/).

(4) a big endian unsigned mixed decimal number with the binary point between the two bytes

(5) a packed binary coded decimal number

(6) a hexadecimal number

(7) two ASCII characters

Where a value is not relevant such as a non-printing ASCII character or a BCD digit outside of the range 0 to 9, write a "?" symbol.

(a) 01010111 01110110

(b) 10000000 01111111

(c) 01000110 01011001

(d) 00000101 10001000

(e) 00110111 10011001

(f) 01110010 00111111

(g) 10010001 01000010

(h) 01010101 01100001

2.2 Write down the binary patterns in two bytes for the following:

(a) 7f 43 hexadecimal little endian

(b) 18ab hexadecimal big endian

(c) "Az" ASCII characters

(d) 1904 packed BCD

(e) 18956 unsigned decimal big endian

(f) 51423 unsigned decimal little endian

(g) −4 and −60 two signed decimal numbers

(h) 103.75 unsigned mixed decimal big endian with the binary point between the two bytes

2.3 Write down the binary patterns in four bytes for the following short real floating point numbers:

(a) +12.0

(b) +16.0

(c) +127.0

(d) −127.0

2.4 Write down the short real floating point numbers represented by the following four byte sequences:

(a) 41 c6 00 00H

(b) c1 c6 00 00H

(c) 44 f8 40 00H

(d) c5 9d 08 00H

2.5 Examine the partial hexadecimal listing in Fig. 2.27 and answer the following questions about the file to which it relates:

(a) Can you confirm that this is a graphics file?

(b) What are the dimensions of the image?

(c) Is the image colour or grey-scale?

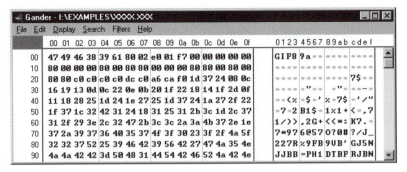

Fig. 2.27

References

Atzberger, P. and Zolli, A. (1996) *Portable Network Graphics, Trincoll Journal.* URL: http://www.trincoll.edu/~tj/tj10.31.96/articles/tech.html.

Blackstock, S. (undated) *LZW and GIF explained.* URL: http://excel.riga.lv/encyclopedia/gif.html.

Born, G. (1997) *The File Formats Handbook.* International Thompson Publishing, London.

Hamilton, E. (1992) *JPEG File Interchange Format Version 1.02,* C-Cube Microsystems, 1778 McCarthy Blvd, Milpitas, CA 95035, USA.

ISO (undated) ISO DIS 10918-1.

Liebenau, J. and Backhouse J. (1990) *Understanding Information – An Introduction.* Macmillan Press, Basingstoke and London, pp. 1–3.

Messmer, H.-P. (1997) *The Indispensable PC Hardware Book.* Addison-Wesley, Reading.

Murray, J. D. and vanRyper, W. (1996) *Encyclopedia of Graphics File Formats.* O'Reilly & Associates, San Francisco.

PKWARE Inc. (undated) *Application Notes for PKZIP.* URL: ftp://ftp.pkware.com/appnote.zip.

Schwartz, M. (1997) *Elser Word convertress.* URL: http://wwwbs.cs.tu-berlin.de/~schwartz/pmh/elser/elser.html.

Schwartz, M. (1997) *LAOLA file system.* URL: http://wwwbs.cs.tu-berlin.de/~schwartz/pmh/guide.html.

Unisys (1995) *License Information on GIF and Other LZW-based Technologies,* Press Release 1/10/95. URL: http://corp2.unisys.com/LeadStory/lzwfaq.html.

Williams, R. (1996) *Data Powers of Ten.* URL: http://www.cacr.caltech.edu/~roy/dataquan/.

Ziv, J. and Lempel, A. (1977) A universal algorithm for sequential data compression, *IEEE Transactions on Information Theory,* 23(3), 337–343.

3. *IT Systems Concepts*

Introduction

In this chapter we will be examining the following topics:

- The memory and the processor
- Address and data buses
- The stored program concept
- Format of instructions
- The processor mechanism
- A worked example of processor execution
- Stepping through the worked example
- Program and data and rules and objects
- Software and programming
- Breaking sequence
- A black box model of the PC

In the previous chapter we saw how we can use binary patterns, physically implemented as the two-state devices of a computer memory, to represent information in a wide variety of forms. We have looked, in some detail, at the representation of numbers, of text, and of graphics and briefly, at some other complex file structures, and we may well have formed the view that perhaps we can represent any real-world object by means of binary patterns in a computer memory. For all practical purposes, this is indeed the case. We may recall that the reason for this unbounded diversity of what can be represented stems from the limitless sets of rules that we may use to interpret and manipulate the binary patterns. In all that we have talked about so far, however, we as individuals have been applying the relevant rules of interpretation and manipulation to the patterns of binary data we have been observing and by so doing we have each had the intended information revealed to us.

In this chapter, we examine the idea that rules of interpretation and manipulation, instead of just being in our heads for us to apply, might also be held in computer memory as a sequence of binary patterns. As such they could then be interpreted by the computer as an ordered set of instructions which cause it to carry out a series of actions. If, in carrying out these actions, the computer were to manipulate and interpret other binary patterns of data in its memory, we might see this as little different in principle from our own interpretation of such patterns. We might then view the computer, when executing instructions, as a device that is capable of extracting information from data.

The part of the computer that carries out the function of executing instructions is called the *processor*, and the relationship between this and the memory is what we now need to examine in more detail. We will do this by means of a worked example, showing, step by step, the principles involved and how data in the memory is interpreted and manipulated by the processor. In order not to confuse the reader with unnecessary detail at this stage, some simplifying assumptions will be made, but these do not alter the principles that will be described.

Two Black Boxes

We start with a very simple diagram (Fig. 3.1) showing a processor and a memory as two black boxes connected together by two arrowed lines. The black boxes are shown as separate because they are most likely to be implemented using two different electronic chips: a processor chip and a memory chip (or set of chips). They are connected together by flexible cables (or tracks on a printed circuit board) which are made up of several wires in parallel. Such multiple connections are called *buses*.

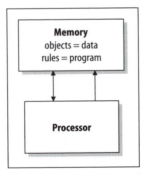

Fig. 3.1 Processor and memory.

Buses

One bus (the *address bus*) has a single arrow on it indicating a one-way transfer of data and the second bus (the *data bus*) has two arrows indicating a two-way transfer of data. If we consider the requirement to pass binary patterns between the processor and the memory we might consider an appropriate unit as being the byte. Recalling that a byte consists of eight binary bits, a suitable form of connection that would permit all eight bits of a byte to be transferred in one go would be eight parallel lines; a separate line for each bit. This is precisely the form that a bus takes: a set of parallel lines that permits the transfer of several bits of data all at once. Buses come in many sizes, and the eight-bit data bus suggested by this example is now very dated.

However, it will serve our purposes well enough here and we will consider bus sizes again in a later chapter.

The Stored Program Concept

Within the memory box we have indicated binary patterns that represent both *objects* and *rules*. The objects are typified by the real world objects that we were considering in Chapter 2: numbers, text, pictures, record structures etc. It is perhaps unfortunate that in this context such objects are also sometimes referred to as "data", an association that should not be confused with our earlier use of the word. The rules are ordered sequences of instructions that are to be interpreted by the processor and which will cause it to carry out a series of specific actions. Such sequences of rules are called *programs* and the idea that the computer holds in its memory instructions to itself, in this way, is sometimes referred to as the *stored program concept*.

So we have the situation where the first of the two black boxes in the diagram, the memory, contains not only the binary patterns that represent the real-world objects (the data) but also the binary patterns that represent the rules (the program). The rules specify what is to be done to, as well as the interpretations that are to be placed upon, the binary patterns that are the data and it is these program rule patterns that are to be interpreted by the second of the two black boxes shown in the diagram: the processor.

Instructions

Now let us consider the form that one such instruction or rule might take. Applying our simplifying assumptions, we will define a rule, for our example processor, as consisting of the patterns in two consecutive bytes in memory, as shown in Fig. 3.2. For our simplified processor, we will decree that the pattern in the first byte of the pair (and we will take them as being big endian) is to represent a *doing* code to the processor. This is an imperative: *do this thing*; the details of what particular thing is to be done being determined by the pattern in the doing byte. In Fig. 3.2 this pattern is 00000101, and we have arbitrarily determined that this should represent the action *subtract*. We will further decree that the pattern in the second byte is to represent the object on which the doing code action is to be carried out. We have called this the *using* code. In Fig. 3.2 this pattern is 11000101, which in decimal is 197. Frequently, the value of this second byte will refer to a place where an object to be manipulated resides in memory; that is, it will be a memory byte address.

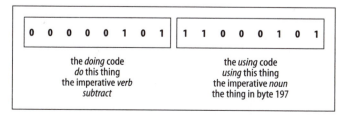

Fig. 3.2 An instruction.

Table 3.1 Example doing codes.

Action	Doing code
Load a byte	00000001
Store a byte	00000010
Add a byte	00000100
Subtract a byte	00000101

The two-byte pattern may therefore be interpreted as an instruction, or rule, as "subtract the thing in byte 197". In a practical processor, we would have a variety of different doing codes available, known collectively as the *order code* for the processor, and these would relate specific patterns in the doing byte to specific actions available in the hardware of the processor. Typical examples might include: add a byte, subtract a byte, multiply a byte, divide a byte, input a byte, output a byte, move a byte, compare a byte and so forth.

There may be similar actions which relate to two or more bytes taken together. The range and functionality of these doing codes are defined by the hardware of the processor[1]. For our example processor, however, we will only consider four such doing codes: *load a byte*, *store a byte*, *add a byte* and *subtract a byte* and we will decree that load a byte is to be 00000001, store a byte is to be 00000010, add a byte is to be 00000100, and subtract a byte is to be 00000101, as shown in Table 3.1.

The Processor

The basic mechanism for our example processor is very simple. The idea of the stored program concept, as implemented in a modern computer, was first expounded by John von Neumann[2] in 1945. This idea decrees that instructions are held sequentially in the memory and that the processor executes each one, in turn, from the lowest address in memory to the highest address in memory, unless otherwise instructed.

To achieve this the processor maintains a record of where it has got to so far in executing instructions. It does this using a so-called *counter register* or *sequence control register*. This is a small element of memory that is internal to the processor which normally holds the address in the main memory of the next instruction that the processor is about to execute. The processor will go through a series of steps to execute an instruction. In the *fetch* step, it will first of all use its counter register to send a message to the main memory requesting that it be sent a *copy* of the next instruction to be executed. It will do this using the address bus. The memory will then respond by sending back a copy of the binary patterns that it holds at the

1 Two approaches have been adopted by processor chip manufacturers: designs with large numbers of complex instructions, known as Complex Instruction Set Computers (CISC), and designs with a minimal set of high-speed instructions known as Reduced Instruction Set Computers (RISC).

2 See von Neumann, John (1945), *First Draft of a Report on the EDVAC*, 30 June 1945, Contract No W-670-ORD-492, Moore School of Electrical Engineering, University of Pennsylvania, Philadelphia.

address it has been given. It will do this using the data bus. The processor will then take from the data bus the binary patterns that represent the instruction and place them in its *instruction registers* in readiness for decoding. Once the transfer is complete, the processor will then enter the *interpret* step, where it will interpret or *decode* the patterns as an imperative instruction. Part of the pattern will be used to select the action that the processor should perform and part will be used to determine the object to which this action should be applied. On completion of its preparations to perform the instruction, the processor will then enter the *update* step. In this step, the processor prepares its program counter so that it is ready for the next instruction in sequence. It does this by calculating the length in bytes of the current instruction and adding that value to its program counter. Given that the system is obeying the rules of sequential instructions, the program counter will thus be pointing to the start of the next instruction in the sequence. Finally, the processor enters the *execute* step where it causes the action defined in the interpret step to be applied to the object defined in the interpret step. To do this, it may well use an additional register as a scratchpad for interim results, sometimes known as an *accumulator* or *general purpose register*. After that, the processor repeats the cycle starting with the fetch step once again.

The Worked Example

Figure 3.3 shows a more detailed view of the two black boxes that we considered earlier, now rotated through 90° and expanded so that we can see something of what they contain. Here we are able to see into a small portion of the main memory on the left-hand side and observe exactly what patterns are in the bytes with addresses 3, 4 and 5 and 31 through to 36.

All that we require for the processor, on the right-hand side, is a small element of internal memory for the registers and a four-step cyclic control mechanism which we can usefully compare with the four-stroke internal combustion engine. Where we have "suck", "squeeze", "bang" and "blow" for the four strokes of the internal combustion engine we have "fetch", "interpret", "update" and "execute" for the four

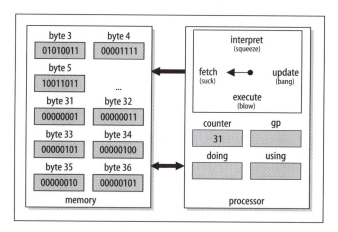

Fig. 3.3 Looking inside.

steps of the processor cycle. One rather important difference between the two models, however is their rotational speed. In the case of a typical processor, the Intel Pentium Pro for example, the speed of operation is of the order of 100 million revolutions per second, and since each revolution causes one instruction to be carried out, this is equivalent to 100 MIPs[3]. The processor is shown connected to the main memory by the two buses, the address bus at the top and the data bus at the bottom. There is a third bus, not shown on the diagram for the sake of clarity, known as the *control bus* and this is concerned with control activities such as the direction of data flow on the data bus and the general timing of events throughout the system.

As was described above, the counter register in the processor holds the address of where in main memory the next instruction that the processor is to execute can be found (in this example, address 31) and the *doing* and *using* registers are our versions of the instruction registers used by the processor to interpret the current instruction. The *gp* register is the general-purpose scratchpad register that was also referred to earlier. We have used throughout registers that are only one byte in size so as to keep the example simple. Again, this does not affect the principles, but practical processors are likely to have two, four or even eight byte registers.

The in-built control mechanism of our example processor causes it to cycle clockwise through the four steps: fetch, interpret, update and execute, over and over again, repeating this same cycle continuously all the while that the processor is switched on. We have earlier likened this to the four strokes of the internal combustion engine: suck, squeeze, bang and blow, and these are shown on the diagram.

The rate at which the processor cycle is executed is controlled by a system *clock* and, as mentioned above, this may be running at many millions of cycles per second[4].

Executing the Worked Example

Using our example machine, we can now step through the processor cycle for ourselves and determine exactly what happens at each stage and how each pattern in memory is interpreted by the system. We start with the beginning of the fetch step, as shown in Fig. 3.4. Here the value of the counter register, shown as decimal 31 in the diagram, is placed on the address bus by the processor and sent across to the memory in binary by means of the eight parallel connections referred to earlier[5]. The memory is by this means requested to transfer a copy of what is in bytes 31 and 32, that is, the patterns of the next instruction, to the processor[6].

In Fig. 3.5 we see copies of the two bytes being passed across the data bus in binary, one after the other, back to the processor. As these copies are received so the

---

3 Millions of Instructions Per Second or, as the cynics would tell you, a Meaningless Indicator of Performance.

4 One point that arises from this speed of operation. Should you happen to note that your PC is starting to behave suspiciously and you try to stop the current operation as quickly as you can, you are, almost certainly, many millions of instructions too late in the most rapid action that you could possibly take!

5 In practice the address bus will be larger than 8 bits; more likely between 16 and 32 bits.

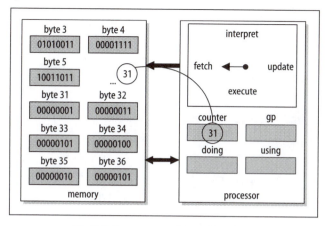

Fig. 3.4 Processor puts 31 on address bus.

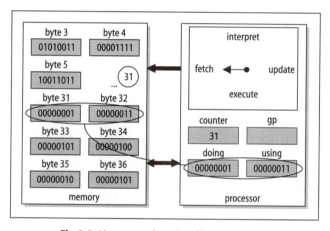

Fig. 3.5 Memory sends copies of bytes 31 and 32.

processor places them in its doing and using registers respectively. On completion, it then moves on to the interpret step, as shown in Fig. 3.6. The "handshaking" process we have seen here is typical of the way in which the various parts of the computer system interact with one another. Requests are sent across the address bus and results are returned across the data bus with control being exercised by signals on the control bus, which for clarity we have not shown on our diagrams. In Fig. 3.6, we see that the patterns in the doing and using registers have been interpreted as the instruction "load byte 3". We can interpret the doing code 00000001 from Table 3.1 as "load a byte" and the using code 00000011 as the address of byte 3. In practice, the processor would at this step have adjusted its internal circuitry such as to be ready to carry out the action "load byte 3" when it reaches the execute step.

6 An assumption is made here that the memory somehow "knows" that instructions are two bytes long. In practice the processor would request the appropriate number of bytes for the particular instruction. This simplification does not affect the principles of the example.

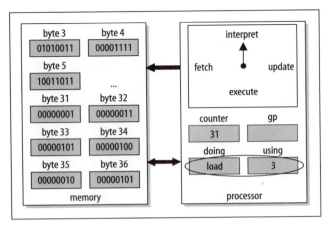

Fig. 3.6 Interpret as load byte 3.

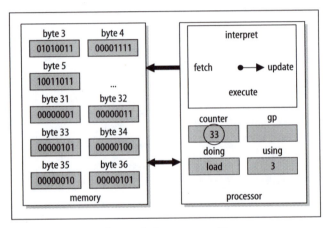

Fig. 3.7 Update counter to 33.

In Figure 3.7, we see the effect of the update step. Here 2 has been added to the counter register so that it now holds the address of the next instruction in the sequence, 33. In the execute step, the instruction "load byte 3" is carried out by the processor. First of all a copy of the using register, shown as decimal 3 in Fig. 3.8, is placed on the address bus by the processor and sent across to the memory in binary[7].

This requests the memory to transfer a copy of byte 3 to the processor over the data bus. We see this happening in Fig. 3.9. When the processor receives the copy of byte 3, it places the value, 01010011, into its general purpose (gp) register as shown in the diagram. This completes the execution of one instruction. The processor then moves on to the next step, which is the fetch step for the next instruction, as shown in Fig. 3.10.

---

7   For clarity of the example, we have shown the values of the counter register and the using
    register together with the transfer of all addresses across the address bus as *decimal*
    numbers on all the diagrams. In practice, of course, they are in binary like everything else.

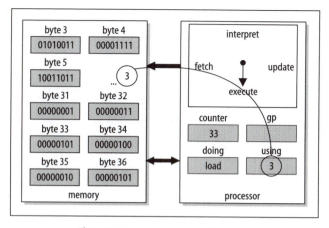

Fig. 3.8 Processor puts 3 on address bus.

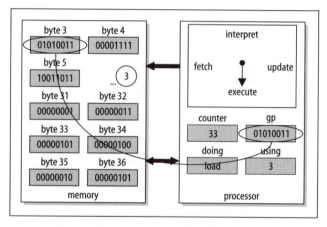

Fig. 3.9 Memory sends copy of byte 3 to processor.

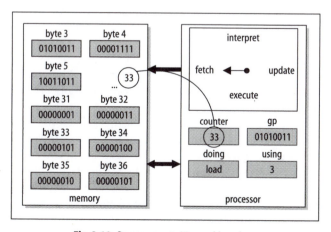

Fig. 3.10 Processor puts 33 on address bus.

Here we see the start of a similar cycle of events as before. The processor places the value of the counter register, shown as decimal 33 in the diagram, onto the address bus, thus requesting the memory to transfer a copy of what is in bytes 33 and 34, the patterns of the next instruction, to the processor. The memory responds, in a similar manner to that shown before, by transferring copies of bytes 33 and 34 across the data bus. In this case, 00000101 is sent first followed by 00000100, and these are written by the processor into its doing and using registers respectively. This situation is then as shown at Fig. 3.11.

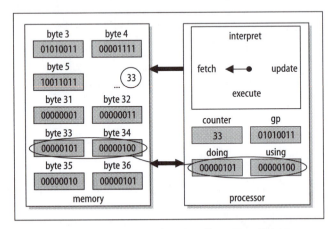

Fig. 3.11 Memory sends copies of bytes 33 and 34.

From all that has gone before, it is not difficult to work out what will happen at the interpret step (not shown as a separate diagram). The processor decodes the doing register as "subtract a byte" (see Table 3.1) and the using register as "byte 4". The instruction set up internally by the processor is therefore "subtract byte 4". For the update step (also not shown as a separate diagram), the processor simply adds 2 to the counter register which then becomes 35, to take account of the fact that this is a von Neumann sequential machine and that each instruction is two bytes in length. Given all of that, the start of the execute step is then as shown in Fig. 3.12. As before, a copy of the using register, shown as decimal 4 in figure 3.13, is placed on the address bus by the processor and sent across to the memory in binary.

This requests the memory to transfer a copy of byte 4 to the processor over the data bus, and we see this happening in Fig. 3.13. This time, however, something rather different happens. The doing action here is not "load a byte" but "subtract a byte", so rather than loading the value coming across the data bus straight into the gp register, as occurred before, the processor this time *subtracts* the value from that already held in the gp register, putting the result back into the gp register. We see, therefore, the action, in binary, of 01010011 subtract 00001111 equals 01000100.

This completes the execution of the second instruction and the processor moves on to the next step, which is the fetch step for the third instruction. Once again, the processor puts the counter register value, decimal 35, onto the address bus (not shown as a separate diagram) and the memory sends copies of the two bytes at addresses 35 and 36 across the data bus to the processor. As before, these are placed in the doing and using registers, and this outcome can be seen in Fig. 3.14.

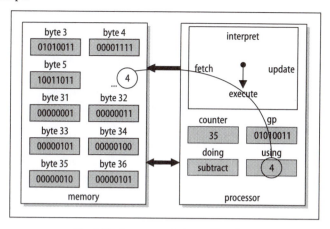

Fig. 3.12 Processor puts 4 on address bus.

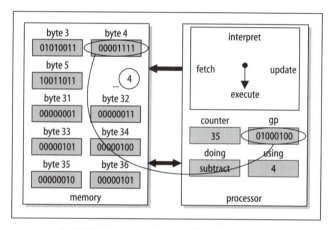

Fig. 3.13 Memory sends copy of byte 4 to processor.

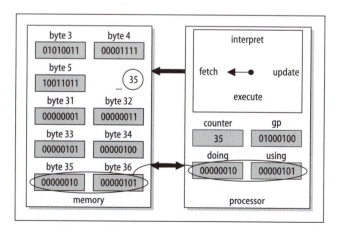

Fig. 3.14 Memory sends copies of bytes 35 and 36.

It now becomes very easy to work out that, for the interpret step, the processor decodes the doing register as "store a byte" (see Table 3.1) and the using register as "byte 5". The instruction is therefore set up by the processor as "store byte 5" (not shown as a separate diagram). For the update step, the processor again adds 2 to the counter register which now becomes 37 (again, not shown as a separate diagram). The result of all of this, is that at the start of the execute step we have the situation that is shown in Fig. 3.15.

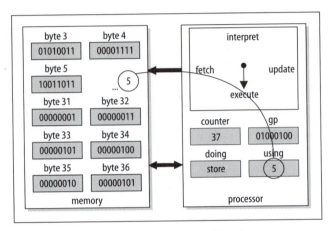

Fig. 3.15 Processor puts 5 on address bus.

As before, a copy of the using register, shown as decimal 5 in Fig. 3.15, is placed on the address bus by the processor and sent across to the memory in binary. This time, however, the request to the memory is rather different. Because the action in the doing register is "store a byte", the processor requests the memory not in this case to send it a byte but rather to be prepared to receive a byte. The memory must be prepared to store at the address given on the address bus (in this case decimal 5), the value which is about to come across the data bus. The processor achieves this outcome by setting a special *write enable* signal on that third bus referred to earlier, the control bus, which tells the memory that this is a write action rather than a read action.

In Fig. 3.16 we see this happening. The pattern 01000100 from the gp register is sent by the processor across the data bus and stored by the memory in the address specified on the address bus, that is in byte address 5, completely overwriting what was originally there. This then completes the execution of the third instruction and the processor now moves on to the next step, which is the fetch step for the fourth instruction. However, that is as far as we are going to take this example, and we will leave the processor at Fig. 3.17, calling for copies of the bytes at addresses 37 and 38; addresses that happen not to be shown on our diagrams.

Having seen three instructions executed, we should now have a sound understanding of the processes involved, and this in turn should give us a good insight into the workings of all digital computers that are based on the von Neumann architecture. This includes, for example, the personal computer or PC architecture. In a practical system, of course, this entire process of executing three instructions would

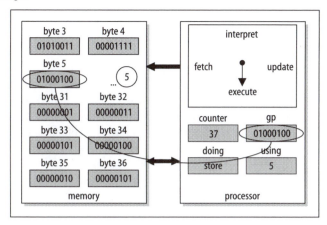

Fig. 3.16 Processor sends gp value over data bus.

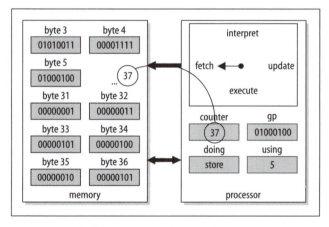

Fig. 3.17 Processor puts 37 on address bus.

have taken no more than a few hundred-millionths of a second. The processor would not stop as we have done after the third instruction, but it would continue to interpret and execute binary patterns as instructions, taking them in sequence from bytes 37 and 38 onwards, until it was switched off.

Program, Data, Rules and Objects

Now is a very good time for us to observe just how the various binary patterns in the main memory have been interpreted. Interpreted, it is important to recognize, not by us, but by the computer system itself. Referring again to Fig. 3.17, we see that the binary patterns in the pairs of bytes 31 and 32, 33 and 34, and 35 and 36 have clearly been interpreted by the processor as instructions or rules, and this interpretation has been driven by the changing value in the processor's counter register. It is the current value in the counter register, by definition, that determines which patterns in memory are to be interpreted as the next instruction.

The patterns in bytes 3, 4 and 5, however, have not been interpreted directly by the processor as instructions. Instead, they have been manipulated as a result of the actions that resulted from the processor executing the three instructions in bytes 31 to 36 and this manipulation has imposed a particular interpretation upon them. Analyzing the manipulation, we see that the pattern in byte 3 has been loaded into the processor's gp register, the pattern in byte 4 has been subtracted from it using the rules of binary arithmetic, and the resulting pattern has been placed in byte 5. The patterns in bytes 3, 4 and 5 have therefore been interpreted, by the execution of the three instructions in bytes 31 to 36, as binary whole numbers or integers; in other words, as data, as real-world objects.

Hence we have a situation in which the execution by the processor of one set of patterns in memory as a *program* of instructions or *rules* has given meaning to another set of patterns in memory as *data* or real-world *objects*. Patterns in memory can therefore represent whatever objects we choose them to represent; the specific meaning of the patterns is determined only by the set of rules that we cause to be applied. It rests upon us, however, to ensure that the set of rules that we use to interpret and manipulate such patterns is consistent with the set of rules that were used to establish the patterns in the first place. If we don't do this, the *wrong*[8] meaning may be obtained.

This is particularly important to the forensic computing analyst, who must be sure that the *correct*[9] interpretations are being placed on observed patterns. This is one reason for recommending that the original software be used in analysis: to minimize the likelihood of incorrect interpretations being made.

As far as the processor is concerned, it would have been equally acceptable for the counter register to have been set initially to 3, in which case the patterns in the byte pairs 3 and 4 onwards would have been interpreted as rules. It could then be said that the processor was extracting the wrong meaning from the patterns; it would be executing patterns as rules that were perhaps intended by the original programmer to be interpreted as numbers. This is not an uncommon problem. The processor slavishly, and at very high speed, executes as rules whatever patterns it is directed to by its counter register, regardless of what the intentions of the programmer might have been. The stored program computer is completely general-purpose, and in most systems any part of the memory can be used for any purpose: for program or for data, for rules or for objects. It is solely the responsibility of the programmer to ensure that such use is always consistent with the intended interpretations. In most modern machines, however, the programmer will be assisted in this activity by some form of hardware controls.

---

8   By "wrong" here we mean "not that intended by the designer or originator".

9   Similarly, by "correct" we mean "consistent with the interpretation used to establish the patterns".

Software Development

Given our understanding of the von Neumann mechanism and the concepts of representation and meaning, it is not difficult to believe that we ought to be able to make a digital computer process representations of anything that we wish, simply by designing the appropriate sets of rules and objects (or programs and data). However, it is not always as simple as it may sound. Practical difficulties lie in designing and implementing effective programs; in understanding and formulating complete and consistent sets of rules; and in representing objects completely, or at least adequately. These are the problems of *software development*. We will now look at one aspect of software development, that of programming, and how it is that the instruction patterns actually get into the machine.

Programming

If we return to our original example program, held in bytes 31 to 36 of the memory (see Fig. 3.18) it is instructive to ask ourselves how those patterns came to be there?

One possible answer would be for each bit of those six bytes to be implemented as a physical on–off switch on some control panel accessible to the user. Programming could then simply be achieved by setting up the switches appropriately: *off off off off off off off on* (byte 31); *off off off off off off on on* (byte 32); and so forth. This is truly "programming in binary", and some very early computers were programmed just like this. However, it is such an error-prone and tiresome task that had no alternative approach been developed, it is doubtful whether the modern digital computer would ever have come about.

A much better approach to programming is to utilize the digital computer itself to assist the process. There is no reason why we should not devise a computer program that is designed to manipulate representations of rules or instructions; in other words, to manipulate programs. If we arrange for an external representation of the instructions to be convenient to us as users then we can get the computer running

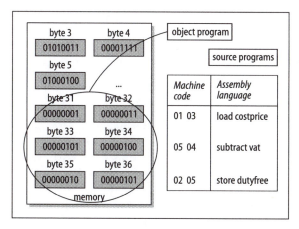

Fig. 3.18 Object and source programs.

this *translator* program to convert the representation that is convenient to us to the much less convenient binary form and place the resulting binary patterns in the appropriate places in memory for us.

Perhaps the simplest form of external representation that we might use is the hexadecimal equivalent of the binary values. We could then lay the three instructions out on a piece of paper or type them it in at a terminal in the following format:

```
01  03
05  04
02  05
```

We have here arranged for the doing code to be separated from the using code by a space and for each separate instruction to start on a new line. We would also need to specify to the translator program where in memory the sequence was to be placed (in our example, from byte 31 onwards). All that we have done is to use an external abstraction that is a little more readable to us than the internal binary patterns. We have in fact defined a very simple *programming language*, and in this format the program statements would be known as *machine code*.

There is no reason, however, why we should limit ourselves to a numeric language representation. We know that 00000001 means "load a byte", 00000101 means "subtract a byte" and 00000010 means "store a byte", so we could use the words "load", "subtract" and "store" to represent the equivalent doing codes. In addition, we could replace the byte addresses 3, 4 and 5 with suitably chosen names to give us a much more readable format thus:

```
load        costprice
subtract    vat
store       dutyfree
```

It matters not to us which actual addresses in memory are used for the data, provided that their use is consistent, so we can name them costprice, vat and dutyfree and permit the translator to decide exactly where in memory they are put. One of the benefits of this is that the purpose of the rules can then become much clearer if the names are sensibly chosen. In this format the program statements would be known as *assembly language* and the translating program would be called an *assembler*.

It is possible to go further and develop a much more complex programming language together with its translating program, then more usually called a *compiler*, that permits statements such as:

```
dutyfree := costprice - vat;
```

These may then be *compiled* into the internal binary representation that the machine requires. Such statements are typical of so-called *High Order Languages* (HOLs); that is, languages that have been specifically designed to assist programming at a high level of abstraction. Some examples of these are ALGOL, COBOL, FORTRAN, Pascal, C, C++ and Ada. It should be noted that what the programmer writes down in the programming language is often called the *source code* and what is actually executed by the computer may be called the *object code*.

Practical Programming Systems

In a practical programming system, such as an *integrated development environment*[10] (IDE), there will be more complications than this, of which the forensic computing analyst needs also to be aware.

Source code files will often have a file type that indicates the programming language in which they are written: PAS for Pascal, C for C, and CPP for C++ for example. Such files will invariably be in ASCII text format. Many systems also use ASCII text files of type H for configuration and header information. In practice, most compilers do not compile source code directly to the object code of the computer but rather generate an intermediate or *semi-compiled* file format that permits the linking of library and other files to this semi-compiled file before the generation of the final executable program. Such semi-compiled files often have the file type OBJ. Files of type OBJ may also be grouped into library files of type LIB using *library manager* software. The final executable program, of file type COM or EXE, is normally produced by the *linker*. This takes the semi-compiled OBJ file and links to it all necessary library files and any other specified OBJ files to produce the final executable form that we called above the object code.

If, during analysis, a programming system is come upon, all of these types of files are likely to be found. In addition there may be DSK, PRJ and TC files which are used by the programming environment to control the desktop, the project and the programming environment configurations respectively[11].

Breaking Sequence

In all that has been described so far, the processor has no option but to execute one instruction after the other in sequence through the memory. This occurs because the counter register is automatically incremented by two within the processor control cycle, and the counter register always points to the next instruction that the processor is to execute. In practice, however, this is not very useful by itself. Many processes are highly repetitive and we would often like to be able to repeat a sequence of instructions many times. This can be achieved if we provide instructions with doing actions that change the value of the counter register. This can be made even more useful if we make the carrying out of these doing actions conditional on some other register value.

So, we might invent a new instruction for the processor with doing code 00001000, say, which has the following doing action: "*if the gp register is not equal to zero then subtract the value of the using code from the counter register*".

How might this work? Before we look at an example, it would be as well to establish a method that avoids us having to draw quite so many diagrams as we used for the previous example.

---

10 See, for example, Borland (1994) *Borland C++ User's Guide, Version 4.5*, Borland International, Inc., Scotts Valley, CA 95067-0001.

11 For details of these and other file signatures see Appendix 2.

Table 3.2 Finger check of the worked example.

Counter register	Doing		Using code	gp	Address		
	Code	Action			03	04	05
31	01	load	03	53	53	0f	9b
33	05	subtract	04	44	53	0f	9b
35	02	store	05	44	53	0f	44
37							

Finger Checks

When programming at very low level or when attempting to deal with a particularly elusive bug, programmers will sometimes use what used to be known as *finger checks*. As shown in Table 3.2 for the worked example of Fig. 3.4, the current values of the processor registers and of any relevant memory addresses are placed in the columns of a table and each row of the table is used to represent the execution of a single instruction. In this way, the effects of the execution of each instruction by the processor can be examined in detail without the need for all the diagrams that we used above.

In this instance, Table 3.2 encapsulates the effects of the execution of the three instructions from our worked example. The counter register starts at 31 referring to the instruction "load 03" and the execution of this results in the gp register being set to 53H[12]. Meanwhile, the counter register has been stepped to 33.

The next instruction, at 33, is "subtract 04" and the result of this execution is that 0fH is subtracted from 53H in the gp register, giving 44H. Again, the counter register has been stepped, now to 35, so the instruction "store 05" is executed. This results in the value in the gp register, 44H, being put into memory address 5. The counter register is now at 37, where we leave the example.

A Revised Example

Let us now consider a revised example, shown in Fig. 3.19, which incorporates our new break sequence instruction, 00001000. We need to give this new instruction a name, and in most programming languages it will be called something like: *jump*, *branch*, or *goto*, and the conditional versions would be called *jump if* etc. We will call ours "jump back if gp not zero" to describe its action, and then use an acronym such as "jbnz". This is typical of the kinds of names that are given by processor manufacturers to their assembly language codes.

Now we will use our finger check technique to step through the actions of the example in Fig. 3.19, the relevant table for which is shown in Table 3.3. The counter register starts at 31 referring to the instruction "load 07" and the execution of this results in the gp register being set to 03H. Meanwhile, the counter register has been

---

12 Note that we have used here hexadecimal format (hence the "H") rather then the binary format that appears in the worked example.

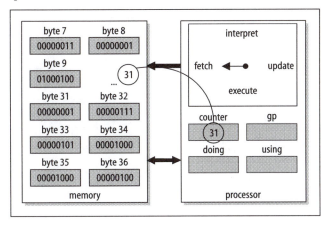

Fig. 3.19 Example with break sequence instruction.

Table 3.3 Finger check of the new example.

Counter register	Doing		Using code	gp	Address		
	Code	Action			07	08	09
31	01	load	07	03	03	01	44
33	05	subtract	08	02	03	01	44
35	08	jbnz	04	02	03	01	44
37 – 4 = 33	05	subtract	08	01	03	01	44
35	08	jbnz	04	01	03	01	44
37 – 4 = 33	05	subtract	08	00	03	01	44
35	08	jbnz	04	00	03	01	44
37							

stepped to 33. The next instruction, at 33, is "subtract 08", and the result of this execution is that 01H is subtracted from 03H in the gp register, giving 02H. Again, the counter register has been stepped, now to 35, whence our new instruction "jbnz 04" comes into effect.

By this time, the counter register has been stepped to 37[13] when the action *"if the gp register is not equal to zero then subtract the value of the using code from the counter register"* is carried out. The gp register is 02H, which is not zero, so the counter register is changed to 37 – 4 = 33, which has the effect of executing the *"jump back if gp not zero"* doing code. The instruction at 33, "subtract 08", is therefore repeated and the result of this execution is that 01H is subtracted, this time from 02H in the gp register, giving 01H. Again, the counter register has been stepped to 35, and our new instruction "jbnz 04" comes into effect once more. This time the gp register

---

13 Recall that the update step takes place before the execute step, so the counter register is set to the *next* instruction *before* the current instruction is executed.

is 01H, which is still not zero, so the counter register is changed once more to 37 – 4 = 33.

So the process repeats again. The instruction at 33, "subtract 08", is executed once more and the result of this execution is that 01H is subtracted, this time from 01H in the gp register giving 00H. Again, at 35, our new instruction "jbnz 04" comes into effect, but this time the gp register is 00H, which is indeed zero. So, on this occasion, the value of the using code is *not* subtracted from the counter register, which therefore remains at 37. From here on the processor continues to execute instructions in sequence through the memory *until instructed otherwise by some other jump type instruction*.

Some analysis of this construct is useful. The two instructions at 33 and 35 were executed in sequence three times: precisely the number of times that is specified by the value in byte 7. The gp register was used as the counter, was set initially to the value of byte 7, and was then reduced by one each time the *loop* of instructions was executed until it reached zero. This is a typical construct for controlling a loop. What has been demonstrated with this example is a *counter-controlled loop*.

If what has been covered to this point is clear, then a very reasonable under-standing of the principles by which all von Neumann architecture computers operate and are programmed should have been gained. In a later chapter we will examine the specific architecture and workings of the PC, but this should not now hold any surprises in store for us. To complete this chapter, we should now develop our two black boxes of processor and memory into a complete system.

An Information Processing System

Expanding on our two black boxes of Fig. 3.1, we now include an input device, an output device and a backing store to obtain the black box model of a complete infor-mation processing system, as shown in Fig. 3.20. This is a typical black box model of a PC.

A typical input device would be a *keyboard* and a typical output device would be a *visual display unit* (VDU). Many other kinds of input and output devices can of

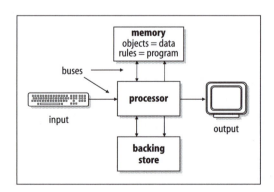

Fig. 3.20 Black box model of an information processing system.

course be connected, ranging, for example, from *printers* and *sound cards*, to *modems* and *mice*. All have access to the processor and memory via the address, data and control buses.

Because the main memory is volatile and loses all information at power-down, it is essential that we are able to load previously developed programs and data from some external source into main memory and save our programs and data that we wish to use again onto a more permanent medium. A device which provides this facility is called a *backing store*, and this is the lower black box in our diagram.

In principle, at least, a backing store is very simple. When it is required to save a program or a piece of data, the binary patterns in memory representing the relevant information are transferred, for example, to a magnetic disk, where they are used to record equivalent magnetic patterns on the surface of the disk. When it is required to restore the program or piece of data, the relevant part of the magnetic disk is played back and the resulting binary patterns are used to reset the memory addresses to their original values. In this way, any information may be saved and reloaded from disk.

Several forms of magnetic disk have become available in recent years, including various sizes of *floppy disk*, various sizes of *hard disk* and several versions of *Zip disk*. Magnetic disk is not the only medium for backing store. Magnetic tape was first used, with rows of large reel-to-reel systems once typifying the layperson's image of a computer centre. Today, magnetic tape is still used, though more usually in the form of *cartridge tapes*.

Non-magnetic systems are also widely used, the most common of these being CD-ROM devices, where the binary patterns are implemented as pits in the surface of the disc and are read back by laser light. Originally these were classed as *worm*[14] systems that could not be written to, but nowadays so called *rewritable CD-ROM* devices have become very common. At the time of writing, DVD (which originally stood for Digital Video Disc but is now more usually called Digital Versatile Disc) was becoming the major substitute for CD-ROM drives on higher end systems. DVD operates in a similar manner to CD-ROM using lasers to read pits on the surface of the disk and it is of the same physical dimensions. The major differences, however, are that it uses a higher frequency laser, has a smaller track pitch and pit size and can be double-layered and double-sided. In comparison with a CD-ROM, which has a capacity of 650 Mbyte, the single-sided, single-layered DVD has a capacity of 4.7 Gbyte and a double-sided, double-layered DVD can hold up to 17 Gbyte.

Exercises

3.1   Using Table 3.1 and a finger check table as required, determine the actions that will occur when the instructions shown in Fig. 3.21, from address 31 onwards, are executed.

---

14 Write Once Read Many times.

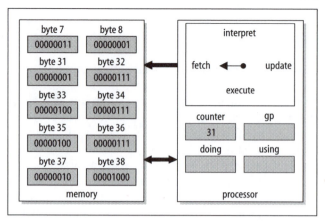

Fig. 3.21

3.2   Examine the diagram in Fig. 3.22. This is a more extensive piece of program code and data than we have used before. For this reason, a diagram such as Fig. 3.21 has not been used, but rather the program code and data segments have been written down in a tabular form, much as early programmers used programming sheets. Assuming that the counter register starts at 31, and using the doing codes that we have defined, determine the final value of memory address 09. What process has been established by this code?

program			data	
Memory address	Doing code	Using code	Memory address	Value
31	01	05	05	04
33	02	06	06	00
35	01	07	07	01
37	04	08	08	01
39	02	09	09	00
3b	01	08	0a	01
3d	02	07		
3f	01	09		
41	02	08		
43	01	06		
45	05	0a		
47	02	06		
49	08	16		

Fig. 3.22

3.3   List a sequence of instructions, using only "jbnz" and those listed in Table 3.1, that will result in the value in memory address 05 being multiplied by the value in memory address 06 and the byte result left in memory address 07. Assume that memory address 05 contains the value 3 and that memory address 06 contains the value 7. Confirm, after execution of the program, that memory address 07 contains 21. Because this is quite difficult, three hints are given as follows. (1) Note that multiplication can be implemented by successive addition. (2) You will need to use some additional memory bytes for temporary storage. (3) The program is at least 11 instructions long.

4. *PC Hardware and Inside the Box*

■ ■

Introduction

In the previous two chapters we have looked first at how information can be represented and then at how the principles of a von Neumann machine may be used to construct an information processing system. In this chapter we will take the black box model of Chapter 3 and develop from that the actual hardware of a modern PC. As we do that, we will look inside the box so that we can identify all the pieces. This is an important part of an analyst's task. A detailed internal examination of a PC is invariably going to be required, since we will wish to know firstly that it is safe to operate, and then to see whether it is being used as a storage box for other items of possible evidential value, and finally whether all its components are connected up correctly. An ability to recognize what should be there and how the bits should be connected together is therefore of some considerable importance. This is summarized as follows:

- Revision of the black box
- The motherboard and all the buses
- Packaging of chips
- The 8088 and the design of the PC
- System resources
- The Intel processors
- Static RAM, dynamic RAM and ROM
- Connection of backing store devices
- Connection of peripherals
- Expansion cards

■ ■

The Black Box Model

Just to remind us, the black box model of Chapter 3 is shown again as Fig. 4.1. We can use this to identify the elements of a real PC that we will need to look at. The first

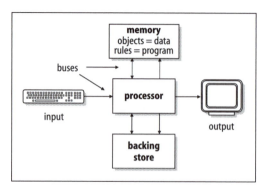

Fig. 4.1 Black box model of an information processing system.

element we are going to consider, rather surprisingly perhaps, is the mechanism by which the major elements are connected up.

We have shown in the diagram the interconnections between the major elements, and we referred to these in Chapter 3 as the address and data buses. Recalling that they are simply sets of electrical connections, it will be no surprise to note that they tend to be implemented as parallel tracks on a printed circuit board (PCB). This brings us then to the most important component of all, the *motherboard*. This normally hosts the processor and the memory chips, and as a result the buses between them are usually just parallel tracks on the motherboard. Also on the motherboard is the *chipset* that carries out all the housekeeping needed to keep control of the information transfers between the processor, the memory and all the peripheral devices. In addition, the motherboard hosts the real-time clock and the *Basic Input Output System* (BIOS) *Read-Only Memory* (ROM). One particularly clever idea in the original design of the PC was to arrange for the various buses to be accessible in a standard form so that *expansion cards* could be fitted into *expansion slots* on the motherboard and thus gain access to all the buses. The motherboard normally has a number of these expansion slot connectors either directly fitted onto the motherboard itself, or fitted onto a separate *riser board* or *daughterboard* that often connects at right angles to the motherboard.

The next item we need to look at is the processor. This technology has advanced at an unprecedented rate, in terms of both performance and price, over the past 15 years, and a little bit of the history of the PC needs to be covered because of the way that various legacy issues still affect us today. Then we must look at the memory, and this too has advanced rapidly in both performance and price, resulting in much greater capacities becoming the norm. We need also to look at the backing store, of which the floppy disk and the hard disk are the most common examples. Although we will examine these in much greater detail in Chapter 5, we need here to note the various other kinds of backing store that we might come across, and be able to recognize them and understand how they are connected into the system.

For the external peripherals of the system, such as the display, the mouse, the keyboard, the printer and the scanner, we will do no more than mention how they are connected. Finally, we need to look at some of the possible expansion cards, such as the video card, the network card and the sound card, at least in enough detail to be able to recognize them.

The Buses and the Motherboard

We start our exploration with the buses. As we have seen earlier, the buses are no more than a set of parallel electrical connections; one connection for each bit of information. Hence, an 8 bit bus can transfer one byte of information at a time. From this, it becomes apparent that although the speed at which the processor operates is a very important factor in the overall performance of the system, it is the data transfer rates across the system buses which effectively act as bottlenecks and limit the performance of the whole. For this reason, there has been much development of buses throughout the life of the PC to try to overcome these various performance bottlenecks as the major elements of the system have all become so much faster.

Three Buses

A simplistic view of the PC considers the major elements to be interconnected by means of three main buses: the *address bus*, the *data bus* and the *control bus*. In Fig. 4.2 we have taken as an example the interconnections of these three buses between the processor unit and the memory unit.

Here, the address bus provides the means by which, for example, the processor can signal the memory with the address of a byte to which it wants access. We saw this in action in Chapter 3. More generally, the address bus is used by any autonomous[1] device to specify the address of some other device (or the address of part of some other device, such as a memory byte) with which it wishes to communicate. The data

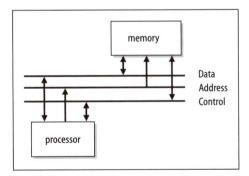

Fig. 4.2 Three buses.

---

1   Autonomous devices are devices that can operate without every action being controlled by the main processor. The writing of a memory block to a hard disk drive, for instance, would be initiated by the processor, but the disk controller might then carry out the detailed transfer of each byte of memory autonomously, referring back to the processor with an interrupt only when the transfer was complete. This is sometimes also referred to as Direct Memory Access (DMA).

bus, in the above diagram, provides the means by which the data bits are passed, in parallel, between the memory and the processor after the address of the required byte has been specified by the address bus. Again, we saw this in action in Chapter 3. The control bus carries, as you might expect, a number of control lines concerned with the housekeeping that is necessary to make this all work. Examples of such control lines include signals to indicate that the data bus is being used to *read* a byte from memory, the data bus is being used to *write* a byte into memory, the address bus is currently active, the processor is using the system buses, and so forth. In addition, a number of clock timing signals are also distributed by means of the control bus.

The three bus model derives from the early processors, with their sets of data, address and control pins, which were used to construct the first PCs. The buses are implemented in such a way as to provide a standard interface to other devices. In this way, expansion cards containing new devices can easily be slotted into spare sockets on the motherboard and connected directly to the three buses.

Size of Buses

Clearly the size of the data bus, that is, the number of bits that can be transferred in parallel, is going to be a major factor in determining overall system performance. The wider the bus, the more data that can be passed in parallel on each machine cycle and hence the faster the overall system should be able to run. The data bus width is often used to categorize processors. Very early processors are known as *8 bit*, because they have only eight pins for access to their external data bus. In the mid-1970s came the first of the *16 bit* processors and today's Intel Pentium processors are *64 bit* which means that they can transfer 8 *bytes* at a time over their external data bus. One point worth noting, in passing, is that modern processors are likely to have much larger internal data buses than the external data buses that are evident to the rest of the system. In the case of the Intel Pentium II, the internal data bus, on the chip itself, is 300 bits wide.

The width of the address bus, on the other hand, determines the maximum number of different devices or memory bytes that can be individually addressed. In practice, it imposes a limit on the size of the memory that is directly accessible to the processor, and thus dictates the memory capacity of the system.

Packaging of Chips

Obviously then, for high performance and high capacity, we want the data and address buses to be as large as possible. One limitation that is imposed on the size of these buses is the need to connect each separate contact point on the tiny processor chip to a corresponding pin on some supporting container package and then to be able to plug that package into a suitable socket on the printed circuit board.

One standard packaging arrangement that has been around since the early days of the PC is for the *Dual In Line* (DIL) chip, as shown in Fig. 4.3 (from the Microsoft ClipArt Gallery 2.0), and this is often known as a *Dual In line Package* (DIP). For the processor at the heart of the original IBM PC, the Intel 8088, the DIL package has 40 pins, with 20 down each side. The data bus is 8 bits wide and the address bus is 20 bits wide, but 20 pins on the package are also used for control signals and power supply.

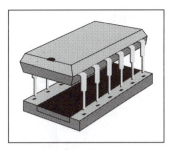

Fig. 4.3 A typical DIL chip.

In order to fit all of this onto a 40 pin package, many of the pins have to be used for more than one purpose at different times in the processor cycle. With the Intel 8088, the address pins 0 to 7 also double up as the 8 data bus pins, and the address pins 16 to 19 carry status information as well. This technique is known as *multiplexing* and obviously adds additional complication to the motherboard in separating out the various signals. DIL packages with more than 40 legs were found to be very unwieldy and difficult to plug into their sockets, although the Texas Instruments TMS9900 had 64 pins in a DIL package[2]. In later processor systems, as the number of pin connections required increased, the DIL packaging was found to be too limiting and was replaced by a square-shaped package with several rows of pins on each side known as a *pin grid array.*

With this packaging, now often referred to as the *form factor* of the chip, we see the more frequent use of *Zero Insertion Force* (ZIF) sockets which allow the relatively easy replacement and upgrading of pin grid array processor chips. A ZIF socket allows a chip to be inserted into a socket without using any significant force. When the chip is properly seated in the socket, a spring-loaded locking plate is moved into place by means of a small lever, which can be seen to the left of Fig. 4.4, and this grips all the pins securely, making good electrical contact with them. In Fig. 4.4 the lever is shown in the down, locked, position on a Socket 7 ZIF socket. The form factors of processor chips for the PC introduced by Intel over the past few years have been a variety of pin grid array systems known as *Socket 1* through to *Socket 8*, as shown in Table 4.1[3].

More recently still, Intel has introduced what it calls a *Single Edge Contact* (SEC) cartridge for the newer Pentium II processors. This form factor is called *Slot 1* and is a 242 contact daughter card slot. Since the Xeon version of the Pentium II, Intel have increased the number of contacts on the SEC cartridge to 330, and this has become known as *Slot 2*. There is much current industry concern about all these changes, and there is a move by other processor manufacturers to try to standardize on a form of Socket 7.

A more radical approach to the packaging problem is to place the die (or silicon chip) directly onto the printed circuit board and bond the die connections straight onto lands set up for that purpose on the PCB. The die is then covered with a blob of

---

2   See *Master Handbook of Microprocessor Chips* (Adams, 1981).

3   See *Upgrading and Repairing PCs* (Mueller, 1998).

Fig. 4.4 A ZIF Socket 7 fitted to a motherboard.

Table 4.1 Socket numbers.

Socket	No. of pins	Layout	Processor types
Socket 1	169	17 × 17	486SX, SX2, DX, DX2, DX2 and DX4 Overdrive
Socket 2	238	19 × 19	486SX, SX2, DX, DX2, DX2 and DX4 Overdrive 486 Pentium Overdrive
Socket 3	237	19 × 19	486SX, SX2, DX, DX2, DX4 486 Pentium Overdrive
Socket 4	273	21 × 21	Pentium 60, 66 and Pentium 60, 66 Overdrive
Socket 5	320	37 × 37	Pentium 75–133, Pentium 75 + Overdrive
Socket 6	235	19 × 19	486DX4, 486 Pentium Overdrive
Socket 7	321	37 × 37	Pentium 75–200, Pentium 75 + Overdrive
Socket 8	387		Pentium Pro

resin for protection. This technique is known as Chip on Board (COB) or Direct Chip Attach (DCA) and is being seen used increasingly often at the time of writing in the production of electronic organizers.

Bus Routes

In order to reduce the data transfer bottlenecks, a modern PC has a number of different buses, which may be called the *processor bus*, the *I/O* (input–output) *bus* and the *memory bus*. In Fig. 4.5 we see the processor bus connecting both to the bus

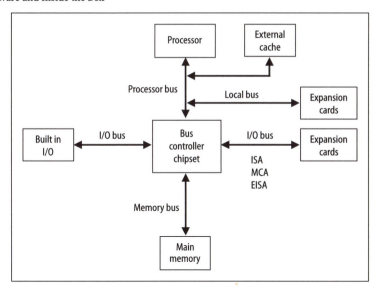

Fig. 4.5 Bus routes.

controller chipset and the external cache memory (ignoring for the moment the connection to the local bus). This processor bus is a high-speed bus which in the Pentium has 64 data lines, 32 address lines and various control lines, and it operates at the external clock rate. For a 66 MHz motherboard clock speed, this means that the maximum transfer rate, or *bandwidth*, of the processor data bus is $66 \times 64 = 4224$ Mbit per second.

The memory bus is used to transfer information from the processor to the main *dynamic random access memory* (DRAM) of the system. It is often controlled by special memory controller chips in the bus controller chipset because the DRAM operates at a significantly slower speed than the processor. The main memory data bus will be the same size as the processor data bus and this is what defines a *bank* of memory. When adding more DRAM to a system, it has to be added, for example, 32 bits at a time if the processor has a 32 bit data bus. For 30 pin, 8 bit SIMMs (see later section on memory), four modules will be required to be added at a time. For 72 pin, 32 bit SIMMs, only one module is required to be added at a time.

The I/O bus is the main bus of the system. It connects the processor, through the chipset, to all the internal I/O devices, such as the primary and secondary *IDE* (*Integrated Drive Electronics*) controllers, the floppy disk controller, the serial and parallel ports, the video controller and, possibly, an integrated mouse port. It also connects the processor, through the chipset, to the expansion slots. Newer chipsets incorporate what is called *bus mastering*, a technique whereby a separate bus controller processor takes control of the bus and executes instructions independently of the main processor.

I/O bus architectures have evolved since the first PC, albeit rather slowly. The requirement has always been quite clear. In order to capitalize on the rapid improvements that have taken place in chip and peripheral technologies, there is a need to increase significantly the amount of data that can be transferred at one time and the speed at which it can be done. The reason for a relatively slow rate of change in this area has been the need to maintain backward compatibility with existing systems, particularly with respect to expansion cards.

The original IBM PC bus architecture used an 8 bit data bus which ran at 4.77 MHz and became known as the *Industry Standard Architecture* (ISA). With the introduction of the PC-AT, the ISA data bus was increased to 16 bits, and this ran first at 6 MHz and then at 8 MHz. However, because of the need to support both 8 bit and 16 bit expansion cards, the industry eventually standardized on 8.33 MHz as the maximum transfer rate for both sizes of bus, and developed an expansion slot connector which would accept both kinds of card. We still see ISA connector slots on most motherboards today.

When 32 bit processors became available, manufacturers started to look at extensions to the ISA bus which would permit 32 data lines. Rather than extend the ISA bus again, IBM developed a proprietary 32 bit bus to replace ISA called *Micro Channel Architecture* (MCA). Because of royalty issues, MCA did not achieve wide industry acceptance and a competing 32 bit data bus architecture was established called *Extended Industry Standard Architecture* (EISA), which can handle 32 bits of data at 8.33 MHz.

All three of these bus architectures (ISA, MCA and EISA) run at relatively low speeds, and as graphical user interfaces (GUIs) became much more prevalent, this speed restriction proved to be an unacceptable bottleneck, particularly for the graphics display. One solution to this was to move some of the expansion card slots from the traditional I/O bus and connect them directly to the processor bus. This became known as a *local bus*, and an example of this is shown in Fig. 4.5. The most popular local bus design was known as the *Video Electronics Standards Association* (VESA) *Local Bus* or just *VL-Bus*, and this provided much improved performance to both the graphics and hard disk controllers.

Several weaknesses were seen to be inherent in the VL-Bus design. In 1992 a group led by Intel produced a completely new specification for a replacement bus architecture. This is known as *Peripheral Component Interconnect* (PCI). Where VL-Bus links directly into the very delicate processor bus, PCI inserts a bridge between the processor bus and the PCI local bus. This bridge also contains the memory controller that connects to the main DRAM chips. The PCI bus operates at 33 MHz and at the full data bus width of the processor. New expansion sockets that connect directly to the PCI bus have been designed and these can be found on most modern motherboards. The design also incorporates an interface to the traditional I/O bus, whether it be ISA, EISA or MCA, so backward compatibility is maintained. Clearly, an expansion card that can take advantage of the PCI bus and slots into a PCI socket is going to perform much better than the traditional ISA card.

Two further advances are worthy of mention before leaving this section. *FireWire* is a relatively new bus technology with very high transfer rates which has been designed largely for audio and video multimedia devices. The official specification is IEEE-1394[4], and it supports up to 63 devices daisy chained to a single adapter card.

---

4 See *More About IEEE 1394 and FireWire* (Apple Computer Inc., 1999).

The second advance is that of *Universal Serial Bus* (USB)[5] and this allows for up to 127 peripheral devices to be daisy-chained from a single adapter card.

A Typical Motherboard

Figure 4.6 shows a typical motherboard, an Elonex MS-5156[6]. On the diagram we can see clearly the three ISA expansion slots, which have two sections, permitting both 8 bit and 16 bit expansion cards to be fitted. The very different PCI expansion slots, of which there are four, are also clearly marked, as is the ZIF Socket 7 for the processor. The two IDE connectors for the ribbon cables to the hard disks, the two power connectors and the two serial port connectors are also evident. The motherboard chipset, which is the Intel 82439TX, can be seen in the centre of the diagram and the lithium battery which provides backup for the real-time clock and the CMOS memory is to the left of the ZIF Socket 7. On the far left of the diagram is the BIOS ROM chip, which is in a DIL socket and can thus readily be upgraded if necessary. The main memory is fitted into the *SIMMs* (*Single In-line Memory Modules*) and *DIMMs* (*Dual In-line Memory Modules*) slots. This motherboard supports a maximum of 256 Mbyte of memory using up to four 72 pin SIMMs or up to two 168 pin DIMMs. As for most motherboards, there are various rules about what mix of memory modules are permitted in the memory banks.

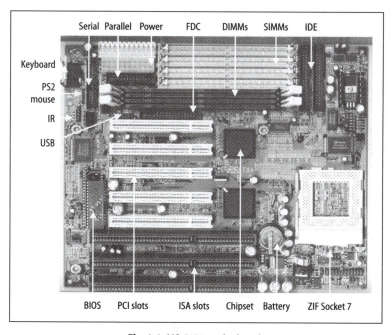

Fig. 4.6 MS-5156 motherboard.

---

5 See *Universal Serial Bus Specification* (USB, 1998).

6 See *MS-5156 User's Manual* (Elonex plc, 1997).

Intel Processors and the Design of the PC

The original IBM PC architecture, dating from 1981, was based on the Intel 8088 processor chip. This architecture became known as the *PC/XT*, with XT referring to *Extra Technology*. The Intel 8088 is a later version of the Intel 8086, a processor chip that was first produced in 1976. Microcomputer systems of this time were all 8 bit and the 8086, which was one of the first chips to have an external data bus of 16 bits, did not gain widespread support, mainly because both the chip and the 16 bit mother-board designed to support it were, at the time, very expensive. In 1978, Intel intro-duced the 8088, which is almost identical[7] to the 8086, but has an 8 bit external data bus rather than the 16 bits of the 8088. Both these processors have a 16 bit internal data bus and fourteen 16 bit registers. They are packaged as 40 pin DIL chips and have an address bus size of 20 bits, enabling them to address up to 2^{20} bytes; that is, up to 1 048 576 bytes or 1 Mbyte. With the XT architecture designed round the 8088 chip it was able to use the then industry-standard 8 bit chip sets and printed circuit boards that were in common use and relatively cheap. Bus connections in the original XT architecture were very simple. Everything was connected to everything else using the same data bus width of 8 bits and the same data bus speed of 4.77 MHz. This was the beginning of the 8 bit ISA bus that we discussed above.

The PC Memory Map

The layout of the PC memory map (see Fig. 4.7) and part of the basic design of the PC is a consequence of the characteristics of the Intel 8088 and 8086 processors. The memory map is, of course, limited to 1 Mbyte, which is the address space of this processor family (20 bits). The first 1024 bytes of this address space are reserved by

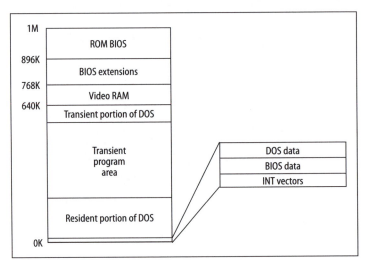

Fig. 4.7 The PC-XT system memory map.

---

7   See *The 8086 Family User's Manual* (Intel, 1979).

the processor for its *interrupt vectors*, each of which is a four byte pointer to an interrupt handling routine elsewhere in the address space. To ensure a flexible and upgradable system, the interrupt vectors should be held in RAM so that they can be modified. In addition, when the processor is first switched on, and before any volatile memory has yet been loaded with programs, it expects to start executing code from an address that is 15 bytes from the top of the address space. This indicates that this area will have to be ROM.

The memory map that results is thus not surprising. The entire address space of 1 Mbyte cannot all be RAM. The compromise made was to arrange for the lower 640 kbyte to be available as the main RAM memory[8] and the upper part of the address space to be taken up with the ROM BIOS, with the video RAM and to give room for future expansion with BIOS extensions. The reason for the 640 kbyte figure is said to be that the original designers looked at the then current microprocessor systems[9], with their user areas of 64 kbyte of RAM, and felt that 10 times this figure was a sensible compromise for the new PC. In practice, of course, the *transient program area* in which the user's application programs run does not get the whole of the 640 kbyte. Some is taken up by the interrupt vectors and by BIOS data, and some by the *disk operating system* (DOS), as shown in Fig. 4.7.

Design of the PC

The basic philosophy behind the design is very sound. The ROM BIOS, produced by the manufacturer, provides the programs for dealing in detail with all the vagaries of the different kinds and variations of the specific hardware. The operating system and the application programs can interact with the standard interface of the BIOS, and, provided that this standard is kept constant, both the operating system and the application programs are transportable to any other PC that observes this standard.

The standard BIOS interface utilizes yet another feature of this processor family, that of the *software interrupt*. This works in a very similar manner to the hardware interrupt. On detection of a particular interrupt number, the processor saves the current state of the system, causes the interrupt vector associated with that number to be loaded and then transfers control to the address to which it points. In the case of a hardware interrupt, this will be code to deal with some intervention request from the hardware. In the case of a software interrupt, which calls on the BIOS, this will have been issued as an INT instruction code by some calling program, and will cause an appropriate part of the BIOS ROM code to be executed. In both cases, when the interrupt is complete, the original state of the system, saved at the time of the interrupt, is restored.

One of the major benefits of this approach is the ability to change the interrupt vectors, because they are held in RAM. Let us consider, for example, that we are using the original BIOS to control our graphics display, and this, therefore, has a set of programs which control the actual display controller chip which is on our

---

8 Because of the relatively high cost of memory, many early systems did not have the whole of the 640 kbyte populated with memory chips.

9 One of the most popular chips of the time was the Zilog Z80 using the CP/M operating system.

motherboard. When one of our applications uses the display, it will issue a standard BIOS software interrupt which will have been set up to transfer control to these original BIOS graphics programs. Now consider the case in which we purchase a superb, high-performance modern graphics controller expansion card and fit that into one of the expansion slots on our PC. On the graphics expansion card will be new BIOS routines for dealing with this specific graphics controller. What is arranged for us by the system is that the graphics controller interrupt vectors are changed from pointing to the original BIOS addresses to now point to the appropriate addresses in the BIOS extensions area of the memory space where our new graphics card BIOS has been installed. We will see precisely how the interrupt vectors are changed when we look at the bootstrap sequence in Chapter 5. It is enough for now to recognize that the same application, issuing the same software interrupt as before, now automatically gets access to the new high-performance graphics controller system.

PC System Resources

Hardware interrupts are transmitted along *interrupt request channels* (IRQs) which are used by various hardware devices to signal to the motherboard that a request needs to be dealt with. Such a request may arise, for example, because input data is now available from the hardware and needs processing, or because output data has now been dealt with by the hardware and it is ready for the next tranche. There are a limited number of IRQs available and each has its own specific address in the interrupt vector table which points to the appropriate software driver to handle the hardware that is assigned to that IRQ. Many IRQs are pre-assigned by the system to internal devices, and allocation of IRQs to expansion cards must be carried out with great care, since the system is not able to distinguish between two hardware devices which have been set to use the same IRQ channel. Often, an expansion card will have *DIP (dual inline package)* switches which enable a number of different IRQ channels to be selected for a given configuration in an attempt to avoid IRQ conflicts.

Autonomous data transfer, which is the sending of data between a hardware device and the main memory without involving the main processor, is provided by *direct memory access* (DMA) channels and these too are a limited resource. Again, some of the channels are pre-assigned by the system and others are available for use by expansion cards and may also be set by DIP switches on the card. Conflicts can arise if two different hardware devices are trying to use the same DMA channel at the same time, though it is possible for different hardware devices to share channels providing that they are not using them simultaneously.

The third system resource is the *I/O port address*. The Intel 8088 processor, in addition to being able to address 1 Mbyte of memory, can also address, quite separately, up to 65535 I/O ports. Many hardware device functions are associated with an I/O port address. Issuing, for example, an IN instruction to a particular port address may obtain from the hardware associated with that address the current contents of its status register. Normally a particular hardware device will be allocated a range of port addresses.

The final system resource, and perhaps the one in greatest demand, is that of main memory address space in the upper part of the memory map. This is required for the use of BIOS extensions in particular.

When a new expansion card is fitted, therefore, consideration has to be given to what of these limited system resources it is going to require. It may have to be allocated an IRQ, a DMA channel, a set of port addresses and, possibly, some address space in the main memory range. The concept of *Plug and Play* has now been introduced to try to automate this process of assigning the limited system resources.

The Intel 80286 and the AT Architecture

In 1981 a new processor chip was introduced by Intel, the 80286[10] (often just called the 286). This offers an external data bus of 16 bits and a wider address bus of 24 bits. The 24 bits of the address bus potentially give access to 2^{24} bytes of memory, that is, to 16 Mbyte, and memory above the 1 Mbyte region then became known as *extended memory*. The 80286 chip is fully compatible with the 8086 and 8088 chips and it adds a new mode of operation called *protected* mode, which enables access to the extended memory. The original mode of operation became known as *real* mode.

IBM developed the *AT* (*Advanced Technology*) architecture, based on this new chip, because it was fully compatible with the 8088 and all software that ran on the earlier systems should be able to run on the AT. The new chip was much faster than the 8088, and the original AT, which first ran at 6 MHz, was some five times faster than the 8088 running at 4.77 MHz. In practice, the AT systems using the 80286 were seen, from a user viewpoint, to be little more than very fast XTs, though there were some other important changes in the architecture. For example, the combined 8 bit and 16 bit ISA expansion slots were introduced to take advantage of the new 16 bit data bus without losing the legacy 8 bit systems. The IRQ and DMA channel allocations used by the system were changed and an increased range of both IRQ and DMA channels was made available. However, because the operating system and much of the available software was unable to use the new protected mode of the chip, useful advantage could not be taken of the additional memory access that the system could provide.

The 80386 Chip

When Intel introduced the 80386 (often just called the 386) in 1985, it rightly promised a vast improvement in the performance of PCs. The chip can operate at clock speeds from 16 MHz up to 33 MHz. With its 24 bit address bus, it provides an address space of 4 Gbyte and with a 32 bit internal and a 32 bit external data bus it can transfer 4 bytes at a time. It is fully compatible with the 8086, 8088 and the 80286 processors and it adds yet a further mode to the protected and real modes of its predecessor, that of *virtual 8086* mode, which is sometimes called *virtual real* mode.

---

10 Before this Intel had produced the 80186 and 80188 chips. These are very similar to their 8086 and 8088 predecessors but incorporate onto the same chip several other of the 8086 family of components. This provides for a reduced chip count over the original 8086 family.

This new mode allows a control program to create what are in effect a series of "virtual" 8086 systems on the one PC, each of which is operating in a protected mode which prevents it from interfering with the others.

Many variations of the 386 chip exist. The original 80386 became known as the 386DX when Intel introduced a cheaper version of the chip known as the 386SX. While retaining the internal 32 bit data bus, the external data bus on the 386SX was reduced to 16 bits. This move took advantage of the large number of 16 bit ISA cards which by now were in common use, and the 386SX-based system rapidly became a popular entry level system. A *coprocessor*, used to perform floating point arithmetic in hardware and thus improve the performance of scientific and engineering calculations, was produced for the 80386, and this was designated the 80387.

The 80486 Chip

The 80486, which is normally called the 486, is essentially an 80386 with an enhanced 80387 coprocessor built onto the chip. It also incorporates enhanced memory management, 8 kbyte of internal *cache* memory and a more efficient design. A 486 will run for the same clock speed about twice as fast as the equivalent 386, and the chip is fully compatible with the 8086, 8088, 80286 and 80386 processors. Initial chips ran at a clock rate of 25 MHz, but later ones were available in 33 Mhz and 50 MHz versions. The 486 effectively created a revolution. Before its introduction, *graphical user interfaces* (GUIs), such as Windows, had not achieved widespread popularity, largely because of performance limitations, often characterized by the dreaded appearance of the hourglass icon. The 486 changed that, providing a performance that made GUIs acceptable.

Many variations of the 486 chip also exist. The original 80486 chip became known as the 486DX when the cheaper 486SX was introduced. This is essentially a 486DX without the onboard maths coprocessor. The early 486SXs were simply 486DXs with the maths coprocessor element disabled, although later the chip became established as a design in its own right. Intel also produced the 487SX as a separate maths coprocessor for those who wished subsequently to upgrade their 486SX systems. Motherboards of upgradable systems were fitted with an extra socket into which this 487SX could be fitted. In practice, the 487SX is a 25 MHz 486DX, and when it is installed in its socket, it completely disables the original 486SX via a new signal from one of its pins, and takes over all processor functions from the 486SX.

The big advance, based on this same idea, was the introduction of the *OverDrive* processor. This was before the widespread use of ZIF sockets and the prising out of one processor chip and replacing it with another was not a recommended practice. Instead, the idea of fitting a new processor chip into a separate upgrade socket, which automatically disabled the existing processor, was a very sensible strategy. The 486DX2 overdrive processor uses the same pinout as the 487SX and therefore can be fitted into the same upgrade socket. The 486DX2 achieves clock speed doubling by running at twice the speed of the motherboard clock. For a 33 MHz clock this means that the 486DX2 runs internally at 66 MHz. Similarly, the 486DX4 triples the clock speed.

None of these chips is being marketed today, although forensic computing analysts are still likely to come across systems using them. The separate OverDrive socket idea has also now been dropped in favour of the ZIF socket. The original OverDrive socket is now called Socket 1; see Table 4.1. The current upgrade strategy is to remove the processor chip from its ZIF socket and replace it with the upgrade rather than to add a second chip which disables the first.

The Pentium, Pentium Pro, Pentium II and Pentium III

In 1993, Intel shipped the first of what it designated the Pentium processor. As part of a natural progression, it might well have been called the 80586, but, since a number cannot be trademarked, Intel chose this time to give the chip a name in order to try to protect itself against possible future clones. The original chip was about twice as fast as the 80486 for the same clock rate. It can effectively be thought of as two 80486 processors with separate 8 kbyte code and 8 kbyte data caches connected internally by a 256 bit data bus. The chip has an external data bus of 64 bits and an address bus of 32 bits, and is fully software compatible with the 386 and 486 processors. Like the 486DX, the Pentium incorporates an internal maths coprocessor, which is much improved over its predecessors. As mentioned above, the Pentium processor is designed to connect to the rest of the system through the PCI bus which runs at 33 MHz and can be 32 or 64 bits wide.

The first generation systems ran at 60 MHz and 66 MHz clock speeds. Second generation systems run at 75, 90, 100, 120, 133, 150, 166 and 200 MHz from basic motherboard speeds of 50, 60 and 66 MHz. This range is achieved by on-chip clock multiplication, which is activated by two pins on the chip labelled BF1 and BF2. The four combinations possible with these two pins give clock multipliers of 1.5, 2, 2.5 and 3, resulting in the variety of Pentium speeds already quoted. Most motherboards have jumper pins which allow these settings to be changed. Selecting a setting that is above that recommended for the processor is known as *overclocking*. The third generation of Pentium processors incorporate *MMX* (*multimedia extension*) technology and have additional instructions and data types that have been designed for high-performance multimedia and communications applications. These run at 166, 200 and 233 MHz.

The Pentium Pro was introduced in 1995 with clock speeds of 150, 166 and 200 MHz. It became commercially available in early 1996 but was rapidly replaced by the Pentium II, which at the time of writing (August 1999) are available with clock speeds from 233 MHz to 450 MHz. At this same time, the Pentium III is now being offered with clock rates from 550 MHz up to 1 GHz.

Compatible Processors

A number of compatible processors are produced by manufacturers other than Intel, most notable AMD (Advanced Micro Designs) and Cyrix. Their chips are fully compatible in terms of emulating the processor instructions and some are also pin-compatible. For those that are not pin-compatible, specialist motherboards are provided. Typical of the AMD chips are the K5 (75–166 MHz), K6 (166–233 MHz) and Athlon (up to 1 GHz), ranges with performances comparable to the equivalent

Fig. 4.8 The AMD K6 200 MHz processor – top and bottom views.

Pentiums. Cyrix similarly produce the M1 (120–233 MHz) and M2 (180–255 MHz) ranges. Figure 4.8 shows the top and bottom views of an AMD K6 200 MHz processor.

A Few Words about Memory

Memory chips are made up of an array of transistor-type cells, each of which can be in one of two states: either on or off, representing 1 or 0. *Random access memory* (RAM) is characterized by being *volatile* (that is, it loses its information when power is removed) and by being capable of easy modification (that is, it accepts both read and write operations).

SRAM and DRAM

Static RAM (SRAM) uses between 4 and 6 transistor memory elements for each switch cell[11] to form a logical unit known as a bistable flip-flop. The flip-flop may be in one of two stable states and, once set in a particular state, and provided the power remains applied, it will continue in that state until a new state is set. *Dynamic RAM* (DRAM), on the other hand, uses a single transistor-based capacitor[12] for each switch cell and the small charge on the capacitor is used to determine its state. As a result of leakage current, however, the charge on each capacitor dissipates quite quickly and thus has to be refreshed at regular intervals, of the order of a few tens of microseconds or so. It is this characteristic that gives it the name *dynamic* RAM. Because of the need for this regular refresh, additional circuitry is required, internal addressing is much more complicated and the speed of access is reduced. However,

---

11 IBM uses 6 transistor memory elements for an SRAM cell. See *Understanding Static RAM Operation* (IBM, 1997).

12 In IBM DRAM this is known as a *trench capacitor*. See *Understanding DRAM Operation* (IBM, 1996a).

DRAM is much cheaper to manufacture than SRAM, since DRAM requires only one memory element to every six for SRAM.

These characteristics determine the way in which we use the two kinds of RAM in the PC. Since DRAM is relatively cheap, it is used for the whole of the main RAM memory, perhaps as much as 256 Mbyte. However, since its performance is slow compared with SRAM and it would significantly delay the modern processor, a *cache memory* is often provided on the motherboard which is populated with the higher speed, but more expensive, SRAM chips. Such a cache may be of the order of 512 kbyte and its purpose is to provide a high-speed buffer between the processor and the slower main memory.

Memory chips are packaged in many ways. Older chips still use the DIL standard package that we have referred to before, and we may still find some SRAM in sockets on the motherboard in this form. More likely today, however, SRAM will be in *PLCC* (*Plastic Leaded Chip Carrier*) or *TQFP* (*Thin Quad Flat Plastic*) packages that are surface mounted onto the motherboard. For the DRAM we may find 30 pin (less likely now) or 72 pin SIMMs (single in-line memory modules; see Fig. 4.9) and 168 pin DIMMs (dual in-line memory modules) in sockets on the motherboard. You may recall that our example motherboard of Fig. 4.6 has four 72 pin SIMM sockets and two 168 pin DIMM sockets. Typical memory module sizes range from 256 kbyte to 128 Mbyte, and, as we have discussed, various rules as to the mix of modules permitted are associated with each motherboard.

Fig. 4.9 A 72 pin SIMM.

Advances in the performance of DRAMs have come over the last five years or so from making changes to the basic DRAM architecture of the chip. The internal layout of a DRAM chip can be likened to that of a spreadsheet with all of its cells in a series of columns and rows. Access to any particular cell may then be made by selecting a specific column and row address. Because of the refresh cycles that have to take place, selecting both the column and the row address takes time. One improvement in the design of the DRAM is to arrange for the rows to have a relatively large number of columns and then to ensure that successive data items are held in the same row. This has the benefit of saving the time needed to select the row address when accessing successive data items, since it already remains selected. Each row can be considered to be a page, and chips using this mode of operation are often called *Fast Page Mode* (FPM) DRAMs. A further extension to this idea is implemented in *Extended Data Out* (EDO) DRAMs[13]. Normally, the cell data is only available while the row and

---

13 See *Understanding EDO (Hyper Page Mode)* (IBM, undated).

column addresses remain selected. We have seen that, with FPM, the row address remains selected between accesses, but clearly the column address cannot if we want to select another element. With EDO, the DRAM holds the data valid on its output pins, even after the column selection has become invalid for the current element and we are starting to access the next element. This speeds up the rate of access and gives an extended period of time over which the processor can access the data. Clearly the motherboard must be "EDO aware" for this to work. EDO is also sometimes called *Hyper Page Mode*.

A more recent advance is seen in *Synchronous DRAM* (SDRAM)[14]. Where FPM and EDO DRAMs are driven asynchronously, with each access being initiated by control signals from the processor, SDRAM is operated synchronously with all its accesses controlled by the same external clock as that used by the processor. This, together with a burst capability, permits much faster consecutive read and write operations compared with FPM and EDO. In addition, SDRAM may have two internal banks, so that while one bank is being accessed, the other is being prepared.

Video RAMs (VRAMs) and *Synchronous Graphics RAMs* (SGRAMs)[15] are DRAMs that have been designed to make them particularly suitable for graphics applications. VRAMs are based on the standard asynchronous DRAM architecture but have the addition of a high-speed serial port and a serial access memory (SAM) which is designed to hold part of a page of data from the DRAM array. They also have the standard DRAM interface which permits data to be read from or written to the VRAM while serial data is continuously being written to the video interface. This is sometimes referred to as *dual port*. SGRAM is a video RAM that is very similar in operation to that of SDRAM.

ROM

Read-Only Memory (ROM) is characterized by being non-volatile and read-only. The information stored may be built into the chip during manufacture or it may be subsequently placed there by *programming* the chip. Chips capable of being programmed after manufacture are known as *Programmable ROMs* (PROMs). The simplest form is programmed by permanently fusing selected links in the memory chip so that it retains the required binary pattern. This is a one-time process and such chips cannot be reused.

Reusable read-only memory chips are called *Erasable PROMs* (EPROMs) or *Electrically Erasable PROMs* (EEPROMs). EPROMs together with *Flash Memory* are looked at in more detail in Chapter 7 when we consider the significance of the memory type in the treatment of organizers. An example of an EPROM is the BIOS chip seen on the motherboard of Fig. 4.6.

---

14 See *Synchronous DRAMs: the DRAM of the future* (IBM, 1996b).

15 See *Understanding VRAM and SGRAM operation* (IBM, 1996c).

Backing Store Devices

A variety of devices can be used for backing store, of which the most familiar are probably the standard 3.5 inch *floppy disk* drive and the *hard disk* drive. We devote the main chapter of the book, Chapter 5, to the topic of magnetic disk drives, since it is of such fundamental importance to the forensic computing analyst. Other backing store devices of some importance include the newer 120 Mbyte floppy disk drives, *CD-ROM (Compact Disk Read-Only Memory)* drives (and possibly CD-R writers), *DVD (Digital Versatile Disk)* drives, Iomega Zip drives, and a wide assortment of magnetic tape units. Most of these devices come in two flavours: internal fitting, where they are connected to an IDE slot or to a SCSI card, and external fitting, where they are often connected via the parallel printer port. We still may even see the old 5.25 inch floppy disk drive on some elderly systems.

Hard Disk Drive Units

Figure 4.10 is a picture of a typical hard disk drive. It is a Seagate Medalist 8641, Model ST38641A, and the CHS parameters are given on the label as Cylinders 16,383, Heads 16 and Sectors 63. The disk has an 8.4 Gbyte capacity. On the left-hand side of the figure, in the top corner, can be seen fitted a typical standard power supply connector which is recognizable by its four coloured leads: a red, two blacks and a

Fig. 4.10 A Seagate Medalist 8641 hard disk drive.

yellow. The connector is shaped so that it will only fit in the socket one way round. To the right of the power connector can be seen fitted the IDE ribbon cable connector. The ribbon cable is 2 inches wide and contains 40 parallel lines. One line is invariably coloured red and this is line 1 of the cable. Current ribbon cable sockets and connectors tend not to be shaped or to have guards which prevent incorrect connection, and it is thus very important to match the red line of the cable with pin number one at both ends of the cable. Incorrect connection will certainly ensure that the disk drive does not work and may damage it. The other end of the ribbon cable, of course, connects to one of the two IDE slots that we saw in Fig. 4.6 on the motherboard. Many current motherboards have two slots which permit up to four IDE devices, such as hard drives, CD-ROM and 120 Mbyte floppy disks, to be connected to the system. One slot is the IDE primary and the other is the IDE secondary. From each slot, the ribbon cable can connect up to two devices, a master and a slave. Which is master and which is slave is determined not by position on the cable but by jumper settings on the unit.

We also show, in Fig. 4.11, the details of the sockets found on the Seagate Medalist drive of Fig. 4.10. On the left-hand side of the figure can be seen the 40 pin socket for the IDE ribbon cable. Pin number 1, the red line, is on the right-hand side of this socket.

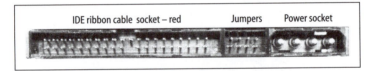

Fig. 4.11 Disk drive sockets and jumpers.

On the right-hand side of the figure can be seen the power socket and the shaping that ensures that its connector can only be fitted one way round. In between the two sockets can be seen four pairs of jumper pins. A jumper is set by sliding a small black connector over both the top and bottom pins of a pair which then makes an electrical connection between the two. Reference to the disk manufacturer's documentation should provide details of what all the various jumper settings do. In the case of this disk, no jumpers fitted, as shown in the figure, sets the disk up as a slave. Other settings switch it into master mode or limit the drive capacity to 2.1 Gbyte (for the reasons why this might be a good idea, see Chapter 5). A check of these jumper settings is of much importance to the forensic computing analyst to ensure that the disk has been set up correctly.

Floppy Disk Drive Units

These are connected via a similar 1.75 inch wide ribbon cable to the Floppy Disk Controller (FDC) slot on the motherboard. This can be seen marked FDC in Fig. 4.6. This ribbon cable again has one line coloured red to identify pin 1, and it has a total of 34 lines. It is easily recognizable in the system because the ribbon cable is split and has 8 lines that have one full twist in them just before it connects to one of the two floppy disk units that it supports. Power connectors are identical to those for hard drive units in the case of 5.25 inch floppy drives and similar but rather smaller for 3.5 inch floppy drives.

External Peripherals

Most of the external peripherals connect to the buses of the motherboard by means of appropriate sockets, connectors and cables. The keyboard has its own PS/2 socket on the motherboard, and this is shown in Fig. 4.6. In some systems, the PS/2 socket on the motherboard will not be accessible from outside the casing and a short connecting cable will be fitted from the PS/2 socket on the motherboard to an external PS/2 socket on the casing of the main unit.

The mouse also has a socket on the motherboard for a PS/2 cable connection, though not itself a PS/2 socket. This too will require a cable to the casing of the main unit as described for the keyboard connection. Similarly, short ribbon cables will be needed to connect the two serial port sockets and the parallel port socket, seen in Fig. 4.8, to the appropriate serial and parallel port sockets on the main casing. The serial ports may be used for devices such as the mouse, a modem, a digital camera and perhaps PC links to organizers, mobile phones and other electronic equipment. The parallel port may be used for devices such as printers, plotters, and scanners, and perhaps for interconnecting with other PCs. This particular motherboard also has a connector for the new USB standard and an infrared connector for wire-less communication.

The only major peripheral not so far dealt with, is the display. For this motherboard, the display will have its own expansion card, slotted into one of the expansion slots, and a socket on the card will provide the video connection to the display. Some older motherboards will have on-board display controllers and then there will be a video socket for this purpose on the board.

Expansion Cards

A very brief look at some typical expansion cards now follows. The first of these is shown in Fig. 4.12 and is an AWE Sound Blaster card. A number of points are noteworthy with respect to this card.

First of all it can be seen that this is a 16 bit ISA card by the split connectors at the bottom of the figure. Also just visible on the right-hand side of the figure is the metal plate which forms part of the outer casing, and a number of sockets through which various sound connections can be made. This particular model, in common with many sound cards manufactured before IDE CD-ROM drives became available, has three different CD-ROM interface sockets on the left-hand side of the figure. These enable a CD-ROM drive to be fitted which interfaces through the Sound Blaster card.

This next card, in Fig. 4.13, is a graphics card, and this time the connection at the bottom of the figure is by means of a PCI connector. The slot in this PCI connector is just a key.

Fig. 4.12 AWE32 Sound Blaster card.

Fig. 4.13 Graphics card.

The final picture (Fig. 4.14) is of a simple network card. Again, this has a PCI connection, shown at the bottom of the diagram, and we can just see a network cable plugged into a 10BaseT socket on the left-hand side of the card.

Although there are very many different kinds of expansion card, these three examples should give a reasonable view of what to expect inside the box. Often, the purpose of an expansion card becomes evident from the connections that are made to it. Equally often, there is useful information screen-printed on to the printed circuit board which will help identify the manufacturer of the card and its type.

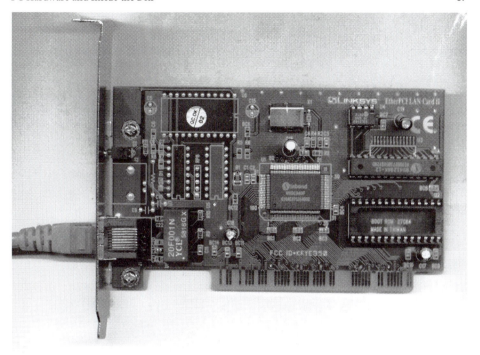

Fig. 4.14 Simple network card.

References

Adams, C. K. (1981) *Master Handbook of Microprocessor Chips*, Tab Books Inc., New York.

Apple Computer Inc. (1999) *More About IEEE 1394 and FireWire*. URL: http://developer.apple.com/hardware/FireWire/More_about_Firewire.htm.

Elonex Plc (1997) *MS-5156 User's Manual, Rev 1.21*.

Freer, J. (1987) *Systems Design with Advanced Microprocessors*, Pitman, London.

IBM (1996a) *Understanding DRAM operation*, IBM Applications Note, 12/96, International Business Machines Corp. URL: http://www.chips.ibm.com/.

IBM (1996b) Synchronous DRAMs: the DRAM of the future, *IBM MicroNews*, First Quarter, 4–6.

IBM (1996c) *Understanding VRAM and SGRAM operation*, IBM Applications Note, 12/96, International Business Machines Corp. URL: http://www.chips.ibm.com/.

IBM (1997) *Understanding Static RAM operation*, IBM Applications Note, 03/97, International Business Machines Corp. URL: http://www.chips.ibm.com/.

IBM (undated) *Understanding EDO (Hyper Page Mode)*, IBM Applications Note, International Business Machines Corp. URL: http://www.chips.ibm.com/.

Intel (1979) *The 8086 Family User's Manual*, Intel Corporation.

Khambata, A. J. (1982) *Microprocessors/Microcomputers Architecture, Software, and Systems*, John Wiley & Sons, New York.

Mueller, S. (1998) *Upgrading and Repairing PCs*, 8th edn, Macmillan Computer Publishing, New York.

USB (1998) *Universal Serial Bus Specification, Revision 1.1*, 23 September. Compaq Computer Corporation, Intel Corporation, Microsoft Corporation, NEC Corporation. URL: http://www.us.org/developers/data/usb11.pdf.

5. *Disk Geometry*

Introduction

In Chapter 5 we look in detail at the geometry of floppy and hard disk drives to find out exactly how information is stored and how it might be hidden. The topics we are going to consider are:

- The development of the hard disk
- Physical construction - heads, tracks and cylinders
- Formation of addressable elements
- Encoding methods and formats for floppy disks
- Encoding methods and formats for hard disks
- The formatting process
- Hard disk interfaces
- IDE/ATA problems and workarounds
- The boot sequence and POST
- The master boot record and partitions
- Directories and file systems
- Hiding information

A Little Bit of History

One of the most important devices from a forensic computing viewpoint is the hard disk drive, which today may contain many gigabytes of information. It is of more than passing historical interest to note, however, that the very early IBM Personal Computers, released in 1981, were not provided with any kind of hard disk drive; indeed there was no program code[1] in their BIOS that could recognize a hard drive nor any provision in the early versions of their operating systems for hard disk support. PC-DOS versions 1.0 and 1.1 and MS-DOS versions 1.0 and 1.25 had no support at all.

---

1 From *Technicians' Guide to PC Hard Disk Subsystems* (Majors, 1995).

It was not until MS-DOS version 2.0, released in March 1983, that hard disk support was provided in the operating system code[2]. In addition, the lack of any subdirectory facilities in the file structure of these operating systems meant that there was a very low upper limit[3] on the number of files that could be stored on a disk. MS-DOS 1.0 and its file system was based on the 16 bit operating system 86-DOS, and this, in turn, had been designed by Seattle Computer Products to be upwards compatible with C/PM-80, the Digital Research 8 bit operating system, which was then the current standard for the Intel 8080 and Zilog Z-80 microprocessors. In the CP/M file systems, the directory area on the disk is of fixed size and typically can contain only some 64 entries. This does not necessarily represent even 64 files, since multiple directory entries may be needed for a single file[4]. However, since these file structures were designed solely for floppy disk support, and these, at the time, had a capacity of only 160 kilobytes per disk, this did not pose a real problem.

Five Main Issues

From a forensic computing viewpoint, there are five main issues that we need to consider with respect to disk drive units. These are: the physical construction of the unit itself; the way in which addressable elements of memory are formed within the unit; the variety of interfacing issues and problems that have arisen as a result of rapid development; the implementation of file systems using the addressable elements of memory; and the ways in which information might be hidden on the disk. In this chapter, we will consider each of these five issues in turn.

Physical Construction of the Unit

We will start with floppy disk units, not only because these were the sole forms of backing store available on the early PCs, but also because they are the simplest in structure and in concept.

We see in Fig. 5.1 a simple conceptual model of a floppy disk drive unit. A magnetic disk or *platter*, contained in a protective envelope or hard plastic case, is inserted into the drive and automatically locked onto a spindle. It is then rotated at a constant speed by means of a spindle motor. The disk itself is a circular piece of very flexible plastic (hence the term *floppy* disk), coated on both sides with a magnetic material. A *head assembly*, consisting of two magnetic read/write heads, one in contact with the upper surface of the disk and one in contact with the lower surface of the disk, may be moved in discrete steps across the disk by means of a stepper motor.

---

2   From *Advanced MSDOS Programming* (Duncan, 1988).

3   From *Advanced MSDOS Programming* (Duncan, 1988).

4   From *The Amstrad CP/M Plus*, Clarke and Powys-Lybbe (1986).

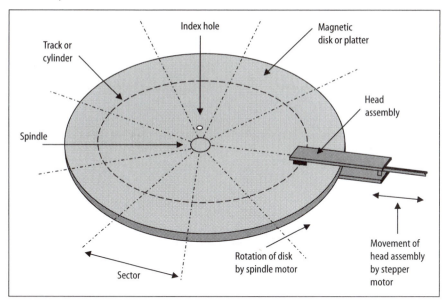

Fig. 5.1 Physical construction.

Because the magnetic read/write heads are in contact with the two surfaces of the disk, physical wear occurs and the rotational speed has to be limited to ensure a reasonable life for the disk and drive unit. For the standard 3.5 inch, 1.44 Mbyte floppy, the rotational speed is limited to 360 revolutions per minute.

Tracks and Cylinders

Given that the head assembly is held at some particular position in its series of steps across the surface of the disk, the area of magnetic material that is passing under the upper head as a result of the rotation of the disk is seen to be a very narrow circular strip.

This is shown as a dashed oval in Fig. 5.1. The strip is called a *track*, and, since there is one track swept out by the upper head and a second track swept out by the lower head, the two tracks taken together are referred to as a *cylinder*. The number[5] of possible cylinders for a given drive is clearly determined by the number of discrete steps available to the stepper motor. This concept of a cylinder is more explicitly illustrated in Fig. 5.2, where three disk platters and six tracks are shown[6].

Clearly, information may be magnetically recorded onto a given track by moving the head assembly to the appropriate step position, switching to one of the two heads electronically, and writing electromagnetically to the disk surface for the period of

---

5   For the standard 3.5 inch 1.44 Mbyte floppy, the number of possible steps and hence the number of cylinders is 80.

6   We will use the terms *track* and *cylinder* from now onwards, usually without distinguishing between them, to mean a particular positioning of the head assembly.

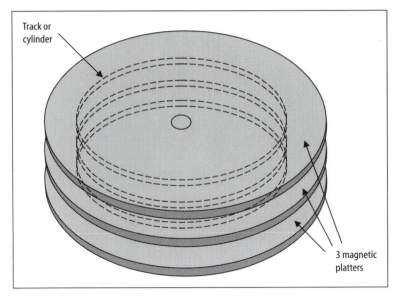

Fig. 5.2 A cylinder.

one rotation. Similarly, the information may be "played back" by moving the head assembly to the appropriate step position, switching to the appropriate head, and reading electromagnetically from the disk surface for a period of one rotation. One problem that becomes evident from this simple approach is the determination of where a track, which is circular, begins and ends. This is where the index hole (see Fig. 5.1) comes in for older floppy disks; it helps to mark the beginning and end of a track. For the standard 3.5 inch 1.44 Mbyte floppy, a metal slot on the floppy disk is mated with a pin on the drive spindle which registers the disk in relationship to the spindle motor. Given this registration, timing pulses can be used to help determine the start and end of tracks.

Formation of Addressable Elements

In practice, the track is found to be too large a unit for storing information, so it is divided into a number of equal sized *sectors*. Shown in Fig. 5.1 are 9 *sectors per track* (*spt*) which is typical for the older 5.25 inch floppy disks. The later ones use 15 sectors per track, while the standard 3.5 inch 1.44 Mbyte floppy has 18 sectors per track.

The position of each sector can be determined by timing pulses that are generated in conjunction with the index hole and the rotation of the spindle motor. In this way, any information unit on the disk can be uniquely identified and accessed. First the head assembly must be moved to the correct cylinder position, then the appropriate head must be switched in electronically to access the correct track, and then the read process must start when the timing pulses indicate that the correct sector is passing under the head.

CHS Addressing

This has led to the common use of so-called *CHS addressing*: C for the cylinder number (starting from 0), H for the head number (starting from 0) and S for the sector number (starting from 1). The formation of addressable elements of disk memory is achieved by means of this *physical CHS address*, which uniquely identifies every sector on the disk[7].

Encoding Methods and Formats for Floppy Disks

The *format* of the information recorded on the track and on each sector within the track is also very important in helping to identify sector addresses. A track consists of a serial sequence of bits which are all interpreted as 8 bit bytes. One might reasonably assume that these bit patterns are simply recorded directly onto the magnetic platter as a sequence of small magnetized areas, with a "0" being represented by, say, a "north–south" magnetized area and a "1" by a "south–north" magnetized area.

In practice, this is not done, because the magnetic heads operate by detecting *changes* in magnetization, so a long run of 1s or 0s using our simple-minded approach would not generate any signals. Instead, an *encoding* method is used which ensures that there are plenty of changes in the magnetization, whatever the bit pattern of our track data happens to be.

To clarify the distinction between the encoding method and the format we should note that the *encoding method* determines how a *bit* is actually encoded on the magnetic surface of the disk and the *format* determines what sequences of *bytes* are used to represent the various data structures that are required. These data structures include, for example, the CHS address for each sector, the sector data blocks and any error detecting or correcting codes.

FM and MFM Encoding

Two encoding methods exist for floppy disks: Frequency Modulation (FM) and Modified Frequency Modulation (MFM). Figure 5.3 shows the FM and MFM encoding methods compared for the same data pattern. This is a byte of value 41h representing the character "A". The byte is shown, for example purposes, with leading and trailing 0s to make it up to the 10 bit sequence: 0010000010. The information is written as a continuous bit stream onto the magnetic surface.

In the case of FM, information is stored in a *bit cell* and this consists of a *clock bit* and a place for a *data bit*. Electromagnetic theory tells us that only a flux change can create a signal so every bit needs to be implemented by some kind of flux change, usually a reversal of magnetization. Each set clock or data bit is therefore established by a reversal of magnetization. Typical of FM is a clock bit present for every bit cell and a data bit present only where there is a 1 in the data stream and absent where

---

7   The outermost cylinder on the disk is normally cylinder 0 and the topmost head is normally head 0.

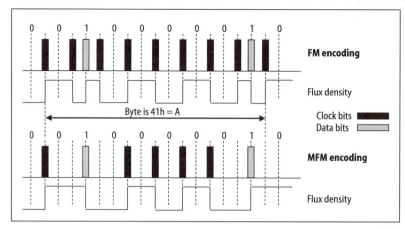

Fig. 5.3 FM and MFM encoding.

there is a 0 in the data stream. In the FM encoding section of Fig. 5.3 we can see, as magnetic flux density reversals, the clock bits for each bit cell and the two set data bits for the byte 41h (0100 0001).

It was very soon recognized that, for FM encoding, many of the clock bits are, in fact, redundant. Their presence is only required to identify the start of a bit cell and thus help to maintain synchronization of the controller with the data stream. However, this is only a problem where the data stream consists of a series of 0s together and a reversal does not occur for some time. Provided reversals occur frequently enough, synchronization can be maintained.

In the MFM encoding method, two simple rules were established that determined when a clock bit needed to be written in order to maintain synchronization and when it could be ignored. The rules are shown in Table 5.1. What these rules are doing is to set a clock bit whenever a run of two 0 data bits occurs. This can be clearly seen from the MFM encoding section of Fig. 5.3, which shows the same byte, 41h, encoded using the rules.

Table 5.1 Rules for MFM encoding.

- A data bit is always written if it is equal to 1.
- A clock bit is only written if the preceding bit cell as well as the current bit cell does not have a data bit set.

By comparing the flux reversals in the two sections it is not difficult to see that MFM will permit, on average, twice the information density over that of FM for the same recording density. As a result, FM encoding is almost never used today.

Floppy Disk Low-level Format

A slightly different low-level format is specified for the two encoding methods, but both of these formats require, for each track on the disk, a *start of track* sequence of

Table 5.2 5.25 inch floppy disk format MFM encoding.

GAP 4A	80 bytes 4eh	Start of track
SYNC	12 bytes 00h	
IAM	4 bytes c2h c2h c2h fch	
GAP 1	50 bytes 4eh	
SYNC	12 bytes 00h	Start of sector 1
IDAM	4 bytes a1h a1h a1h feh	
ID	4 bytes cylinder head sector sector-size *1024 cylinders, 256 heads, 63 sectors*	
CRC	2 byte CRC value	
GAP 2	22 bytes 4eh	
SYNC	12 bytes 00h	
DAM	4 bytes a1h a1h a1h fbh (or f8h)	
Data	512 bytes data	
CRC	2 byte CRC value	
GAP 3	80 bytes 4eh	End of sector 1
...		Sectors 2 to 15
GAP 4B	?? bytes 4eh	End of track

bytes, a *sector format* sequence which includes the CHS address and the data block for each of the sectors, and an *end of track* sequence of bytes.

As mentioned earlier, bytes are recorded sequentially along the track, with each byte itself being recorded as eight serial bits. Table 5.2[8] shows the sequence of bytes that are required for a 5.25 inch floppy disk track in IBM format using the MFM (Modified Frequency Modulation) encoding method that we discussed in the previous section.

Referring to Table 5.2, we note that a track always starts with a so-called GAP 4A sequence which consists of 80 bytes each of value 4eh. This is the hex value that is used for all gaps in this format. Although a floppy disk controller can recognize the beginning of the track by means of the index hole on the floppy, as we mentioned above, the physical size of this hole is far too large and its physical position is far too imprecise to determine precisely where the track begins[9]. The 80 byte 4eh pattern warns the disk controller that the track is about to start and gives the electronics time to synchronize with the 12 byte sequence of 00h which follows. This is known as the *synchronization* (SYNC) block.

The four bytes of the *Index Address Mark* (IAM) tell the controller that the sectors of the track are about to follow and immediately after this there is another gap of 50

---

8 See *The Indispensable PC Hardware Book* (Messmer, 1997) p. 791.

9 Data bits on a 15 sector per track floppy are only about 2 micrometres apart, whereas the index hole is about 1 mm in diameter.

bytes of 4eh, GAP 1. It is this Index Address Mark that signals the true start of the track[10].

After the start of track sequence, the sectors proper begin. Each of the sectors, and in this format there are 15 of them, has 10 sections, of which only those for sector 1 are shown in the diagram. After another synchronization (SYNC) sequence of 12 bytes of 00h, the *ID Address Mark* (IDAM) follows, which indicates the start of the *ID* or identification field for the sector concerned. This is where the CHS address is held. The ID field is made up of four bytes, of which three are used for *cylinder, head* and *sector* addressing and the fourth is used to indicate the *sector size* for floppy disks and as a *flag* byte for hard disks, the details of which we will look at later. Figure 5.4 shows the layout of the first three of the four ID bytes which provide the CHS address for the sector. Ten bits are used for the cylinder[11] address, with the *leading* two bits of that address being taken from the high end of the sector byte (the third byte). This gives a maximum cylinder address of 1023, and since the cylinder count starts from 0, we may address up to 1024 cylinders. Eight bits are used for the head address (the whole of the second byte), giving a maximum value of 255, and since the head count starts from 0 we may address up to 256 heads. Only six bits are used for the sector address (the remainder of the third byte) giving a maximum value of 63, and, since the sector count conventionally always starts from 1, we may address up to 63 sectors.

Because of the importance of these ID marks, a two-byte *Cyclic Redundancy Check* (CRC)[12] is calculated and stored at format time for the IDAM and ID fields. Another gap then follows of 22 bytes of 4eh, GAP2, which is deliberately put there to give the controller time to check this CRC, and then there is another synchronization (SYNC)

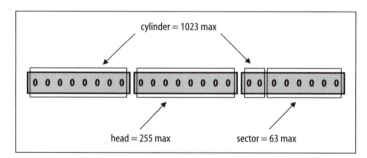

Fig. 5.4 CHS of ID field.

---

10 Floppy disks used to fail rather more frequently than today and the error message would often be "Missing address mark".

11 Recall that *cylinder* numbers are the same as *track* numbers; they represent the position of the head assembly.

12 A cyclic redundancy check is a form of checksum that can be used to detect certain kinds of error. For a good detailed explanation see pages 796–800 of *The Indispensable PC Hardware Book* (Messmer, 1997).

sequence of 12 bytes of 00h. This is followed by the *Data Address Mark* (DAM), which signals the start of the actual 512 bytes of data[13].

After this data block comes another two-byte CRC, calculated for the whole of the data area, and the sector is finally terminated by another gap, GAP3, of 80 bytes of 4eh. This gap is designed to be long enough to allow for any variations in recording speed and thus avoid the inadvertent overwriting of the following sector. This first sector is then followed by the other 14 sectors, using exactly the same format, and then the *End of Track* is written as GAP 4B, a variable number of 4eh bytes forming a flexible buffer which finally links up with GAP 4A. With all of this laid down during formatting, we can easily see why a formatted disk has less usable data space than an unformatted disk. We can also see how a disk controller can confirm that it has accessed the correct CHS address from the sector ID field.

The 8.4 Gbyte Barrier

Having now discussed track and sector formatting in some detail, it might be useful at this point to consider what implications, if any, these data structures might have on hard disk capacity. Although there is not going to be any problem for current floppy disks with their very limited capacity, it is important to understand that we have, at the level of the disk format itself, imposed limits on the range of CHS addresses that are possible. This is because we have used a fixed size for the bit space that has been allocated to each of the three parameters, namely: 1024 cylinders (10 bits), 256 heads (8 bits) and 63 sectors (6 bits).

The maximum number of sectors it is thus possible to address is $1024 \times 256 \times 63$, and given that the normal sector data size is 512 bytes, we can calculate the theoretical maximum size of a formatted disk as $1024 \times 256 \times 63 \times 512$ bytes = 8 455 716 864 = 8.4 Gbyte[14]. Here is one of the factors that can result in the so-called *8.4 Gbyte barrier*. This ID field structure is the structure of the original low-level format design for floppy disks which was carried over with little modification into the ST412/506 low-level format design when hard disks first became available. We will be looking at this in detail in the next section in order to understand many of the hard disk design concepts. Hard disk manufacturers have tended subsequently in their low-level formatting design to utilize these four ID bytes in rather different ways in order to help overcome this barrier, as we shall note later. However, since the low-level format structure is completely hidden from the outside world by the disk controller in modern hard disks, some manufacturers[15] have radically revised the data structures which they use to low-level format their hard disks, and the 8.4 Gigabyte barrier no longer applies because of this factor.

---

13 Data sizes other than 512 bytes are possible and these would be indicated appropriately by the setting in the fourth byte of the ID. However, 512 bytes is the size most usually adopted.

14 Note that this figure is calculated using SI units in powers of ten for kilo, mega and giga. If we were to use the traditional computing community powers of two we would then get a result of 7.8 Gbyte.

15 IBM has designed a new low-level format which does not use ID bytes at all. It is called the No-ID™ sector format (IBM, 1995).

Construction of Hard Disk Systems

One of the big differences between floppy disks and hard disks is that the heads do not (normally) touch the surface of a hard disk except when at rest. The hard disk is, as the name suggests, made up of a number of rigid hard *platters* and the *head–disk assembly* is enclosed in a dust-free environment.

All the heads are fixed to the same *actuator* and fly free, just above the surface of the disk, held up by aerodynamic pressure (Fig. 5.5). At the time of writing, a common size of disk platter, usually referred to as the *form factor*, is 3.5 inches though 2.5 inches is often used for notebook computers. The number of heads is likely to be between two and six and the rotational speeds are typically from 3600 to 7200 revolutions per minute[16]. Servo control circuits are used to position the head assembly and to reduce any rotational variations in speed to approximately plus-or-minus 0.1%. A nice analogy for the standard of engineering required is quoted here from Seagate (1995a): *"Today's new generation of disc drives achieve the engineering equivalent of a Boeing 747 flying at Mach 4 just two meters above the ground, counting each blade of grass as it flies over."*

As in the case of floppy disks, except for high-performance systems and RAID (see later section), only one head is active at any one time for reading or writing data. Having said that, in modern hard disk systems, one of the disk surfaces[17] may be

Fig. 5.5 Western Digital Caviar (with kind permission of Western Digital Corporation).

16 The Cheetah from Seagate has a rotational speed of 10,033 r.p.m. (Seagate, 1997a).

17 Usually the topmost.

used for holding pre-formatted control information, and thus its associated head is also in use at the same time as the data head for servo control purposes. Tracks on this surface are called *servo tracks* or *index tracks* and the head itself is known as the *servo head* or the *index head*. Disks that use this technique often appear to have an odd number of heads, since one has been reserved for servo use. Other systems may instead embed the servo information into the data tracks as *servo sectors* (IBM, 1995). The head assembly, instead of being positioned by a stepper motor actuator[18] is controlled by a linear motor system which is often referred to as a *voice coil actuator*. In this system, the head reads the preset data on the servo tracks and uses this with a feedback loop to position the voice coil actuator and the head assembly very accurately to any particular cylinder position. It is this approach that has led to a rapid expansion in the capacity of hard disks by radically increasing the number of cylinders[19]. This development was apparently not foreseen by the early designers who, if the low-level format ID data structure sizes are any indication, expected instead the number of heads to increase to 256. We recall from our discussion above of the 8.4 Gbyte barrier that the ID field in a sector only has scope to specify up to 1024 cylinders. This is yet another limitation to which we will return shortly.

When the drive is switched off, the heads rest on the surface. Most modern disks "park" their heads automatically onto an unused track as they power down, though earlier disks had a special PARK program designed for this purpose. It is certainly unwise practice to use any version of this program with a modern self-parking disk!

Typical distances for heads flying free are 0.2 to 0.5 micrometers above the surface, or some 12 millionths of an inch. By comparison, a fingerprint and a smoke particle are some five to ten times thicker at 3 micrometres and a hair is some thirty times thicker at 10 micrometres. Contamination can therefore be a serious potential problem.

Hard disks have an internal air filter which is used for filtering the air already in the case. To avoid the head disk assembly exploding as a result of low external air pressure, such as might occur in an aircraft cabin at high altitude, the case has a ventilation slit which is also protected by an air filter.

Encoding Methods and Formats for Hard Disks

A very similar approach to encoding and low-level formatting has been adopted for hard disks. Indeed, the approaches can be seen to have developed directly from their floppy disk controller antecedents. Three encoding methods may be met with: *Modified Frequency Modulation* (MFM) encoding, *Run Length Limited* (RLL) encoding and *Advanced Run Length Limited* (ARLL) encoding. Again slightly different low-level formats are used for the different encoding methods and also between hard disk manufacturers.

---

18 An out-of-date mechanical head positioning system that was used with early hard disks drives and is still used for floppy disk drives.

19 The Cheetah from Seagate has 6526 cylinders (Seagate, 1997a).

RLL Encoding

We will first look briefly at RLL encoding and compare it with MFM. It is an area that tends to be shrouded in mystery, quite unjustifiably so as it turns out.

We saw earlier how MFM can provide, on average, a 2 to 1 improvement over FM by writing a clock bit only if two 0 data bits occur in succession. However, if we were to have all 512 data bytes in a sector filled with 0s we would still have 4096 clock bits using MFM. With RLL, there are no clock bits, but this means that with long sequences of 0 data bits we would have no 1 bits set at all in the recorded stream and the controller would quickly lose synchronization.

What *Run Length Limited* means is that although there are no clock bits in the recorded stream, we limit the run length of any sequence that can occur without a 1 bit to something that is short enough for the controller to maintain synchronization. With one of the most widely used RLL methods[20], there are, by definition, at least two and at most seven 0 bits between any two 1 bits in the recorded stream. This is achieved by re-encoding the original data bit pattern in terms of a well-defined set of (what I have called here) *data chunks*. These data chunks together with their appropriate RLL 2,7 codes are shown in Table 5.3. You will note if you look at the resultant code fragments that you can never have sequences that have fewer than two or more than seven 0s, no matter what sequences of RLL 2,7 code you use. If, as shown in the example, we wanted to encode a sequence of nine 0s we would use the 000 chunk three times, thus generating 000100 000100 000100. We note two things from this: first that the largest run length that has been generated is five and the smallest run length is two, fulfilling the required conditions, and that there has been a significance increase in size with 9 bits becoming 18. On average, we find that RLL 2,7 doubles the number of bits needed for any given data sequence.

If we now consider Fig. 5.6 we see the same example that we used before in Fig. 5.3 to compare FM with MFM; that is, the data bits 0010000010, representing the character "A" of byte value 41h with a leading and trailing 0. The data bits have been re-encoded into RLL 2,7 form using the three chunks 0010, 000 and 010 resulting in the RLL 2,7 recorded bit stream of 00100100 000100 100100. The MFM flux density encoding for this recorded bit stream is shown in the upper half of the diagram. In

Table 5.3 Code for RLL 2,7.

Data chunk	RLL 2,7 code
000	000100
10	0100
010	100100
0010	00100100
11	1000
011	001000
0011	00001000

---

20 Known as RLL 2,7.

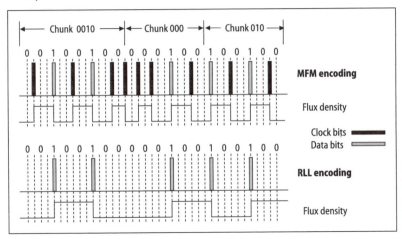

Fig. 5.6 RLL encoding.

the lower half of the diagram, the same bit stream is shown, but here with all the clock bits removed, thus giving us RLL encoding.

From this we can clearly see the advantage when we look at the two flux densities. For RLL we have no clock bits at all, and hence there is a significant saving, of the order of 3 to 1. However, because we have increased the recorded bit pattern size by re-encoding it into RLL 2,7 code, there is also a loss of the order of 2 to 1. Combining these two, we find a net gain on average, using RLL 2,7 over MFM, of about 1.5 to 1. One problem with the RLL method is that if the system does lose synchronization, a burst error of up to five bits can result. This requires much more sophisticated error detection and correction, so RLL controllers tend to use *error correcting codes* (ECC) in their formats rather than the simpler CRC codes we saw in the MFM format. Other RLL methods exist which may be referred to as *Advanced RLL* or *ARLL*. Examples include RLL 1,7 and RLL 3,9. In both these cases the encoding overhead is even higher and the larger number of 0 bits permitted between two 1 bits makes greater demands on system synchronization. The payoff, however, is that data density improvements of up to 90% over that of MFM can be realized.

Hard Disk Low-Level Format

As in the case of the floppy disk low-level format, the original hard disk low-level format requires, for each track on the disk, a start of track sequence of bytes, a sector format sequence which includes the CHS address and the data block for each of the sectors, and an end of track sequence of bytes. As before, bytes are recorded sequentially along the track with each byte itself being recorded as eight serial bits. It should be noted that for hard disks, the actual format is very controller dependent, and this usually means that the format performed by one controller cannot be utilized by another.

Table 5.4[21] shows the hard disk format for an ST412/506 controller using RLL encoding. As can be seen, the fields and sectors are very similar to those for the 5.25 in floppy disk format using MFM encoding that we saw in Table 5.2.

Table 5.4 ST412/506 hard disk format RLL encoding.

SYNC	11 bytes 00h	Start of track
IAM	2 bytes a1h fch	
GAP 1	12 bytes ffh	
SYNC	10 bytes 00h	Start of sector 1
IDAM	2 bytes 5eh a1h	
ID	4 bytes cylinder head sector flags *1024 cylinders, 256 heads, 63 sectors*	
ECC	4 byte ECC value	
GAP 2	5 bytes 00h	
SYNC	11 bytes 00h	
DAM	2 bytes 5eh a1h	
Data	512 bytes data	
ECC	4 byte ECC value	
GAP 3	3 bytes 00h and 17 bytes ffh	End of sector 1
...		Sectors 2 to 26
GAP 4B	approx. 93 bytes 00h	End of track

The first point to note is that all the gaps are very much smaller (GAP 1 is 12 bytes instead of 50, GAP 2 is 5 bytes instead of 22, and GAP 3 is 20 bytes instead of 80). This reduction in gap size is made possible because the rotation of the disk is much more stable, partly because of the lack of any friction between the surface of the disk and the heads and partly because of the servo feedback loop that we referred to earlier. We might also note the 4 byte error-correcting code (ECC) fields in place of the 2 byte cyclic redundancy checks (CRCs) that we saw with MFM encoding.

When discussing RLL encoding above, we identified the need for more extensive error correction in order to deal with the burst errors that can be a feature of this form of encoding. Some formats use 6 bytes for the ECC fields, permitting the controller electronics to detect and correct an even greater range of errors. The ID[22] fields again use four bytes and the first three bytes specify cylinder, head and sector numbers, exactly as for the MFM encoded format (see Fig. 5.4). The implication is, of course, that the 8.4 Gbyte barrier will still apply to hard disks that are formatted in this way.

The fourth byte is not used to specify sector size, as is the case with the floppy disk MFM encoded format, but instead it is used as a *sector flag* which enables the controller to perform *bad sector mapping*. The details of this sector flag are shown in Fig. 5.7.

---

21 See page 859 of *The Indispensable PC Hardware Book* (Messmer 1997).

22 The ID field is shown here (and in Table 5.2) as 63 sectors because the sector count starts from 1.

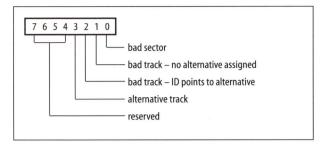

Fig. 5.7 Sector flag details.

Bad Sector Mapping

The need for bad sector mapping and the sector flag arises because of micro-defects that are found to exist on the magnetic surface of the disk at the time of manufacture. Seagate (1995) states that there should be less than 1 defect per formatted megabyte and that the disk should be defect-free for the first two cylinders. The defects are of two types: hard, which usually relates to a surface problem, and soft, which is normally some kind of magnetic anomaly. Although hard defects can be relatively easily discovered with low-level formatting software, soft defects can only be found after much testing with very sophisticated test equipment. The manufacturer will normally perform such tests over a period of several hours and from these tests will determine a *manufacturer's defect list* of all the bad sectors. Such lists are often marked on the casing of the drive as a *defect label*, and might be detailed as the three columns shown in Table 5.5.

Each bad sector is specified by its cylinder and head number, which define the track, and the *bytes from index* (BFI)[23] value. This specifies the number of bytes from the start of track index mark to where the bad area exists. This index mark, which is usually generated by a Hall sensor embedded in the spindle motor or encoded onto the servo tracks, is considered the absolute point of reference for the BFI value.

During the low-level formatting process, the controller will perform bad sector mapping to remove the effects of these defects. This is achieved by a number of strategies.

Table 5.5 Defect label.

Cyl	Hd	BFI
72	0	5314
73	0	5315
74	0	5316
161	2	1816

---

23 Sometimes also called the *byte count after index* (BCAI).

If the controller identifies a defect that only affects a single sector of the track it will attempt to shift the sector formatting slightly so that the defect occurs in one of the sector or track gaps, where it will have no effect. This is known as *sector slipping*. If this is not possible, the controller will mark the sector concerned as *bad* by setting bit 0 of the sector flag to 1 (see Fig. 5.7). The controller will not now permit any accesses to this sector. Some controllers may be able to format an additional spare sector on the track to replace this bad sector, thus ensuring that there is no loss of formatted disk capacity.

Where there is more than one sector in a track defective, the controller can apply one of two strategies. It can mark the entire track as bad by setting bit 1 of the sector flag to 1 in all the sectors of the track. The controller will not now permit any access to any of the sectors in this track. The effect of this is to reduce the formatted disk capacity and create a "hole" in the disk address space where the bad track resides.

A better strategy is to mark the complete track as bad by setting bit 2 of the sector flag to 1 in all the sectors of that track and assigning an alternative track starting from the highest numbered cylinder. The CHS address values of the ID fields in all these bad sectors are now set to point to their replacement counterparts in the alternative track. So, when a seek to a sector in a bad track is made, the controller simply looks up the alternative sector address in the ID field of the sector in the bad track and then seeks to that alternative sector instead. Any track that has been assigned in this way as an alternative track has bit 3 of the sector flag set to 1 in all of its sectors. This strategy still results in a loss of formatted disk capacity, in that the alternative track is no longer available for use in its own address position. However, it does have the benefit of ensuring that there is now no "hole" in the disk address space, since the addresses of the bad track all appear to work correctly using the alternative track resources. It is useful to note that there are 4 reserved bits in the sector flag shown in Fig. 5.7. We will return to these when we examine the ATA interface and LBA addressing in a later section.

A Possible Place to Hide

The reader might at this stage be wondering why it should be necessary to examine the hard disk geometry down to this level of detail. The reason is that sectors that have been marked as bad by the controller in this way could well be a very good place in which to hide information. Consider the situation where a particular track is used for storing some incriminating information and then deliberately marked as bad using, for example, the controller command code REASSIGN ALTERNATIVE TRACK. This would not cause a new format to be laid down, so no information would be overwritten, but would simply cause the controller to adjust its bad sector mapping such that all references to this track now point to the specified alternative track. Someone with a reasonable technical competence and a knowledge of the specific controller commands should certainly be able to do this[24]. It would then not

---

24 Note that this argument applies specifically to ST412/506 controllers, which have now
   largely been replaced by IDE disks (see later section). However, it may be possible to
   obtain a similar effect with IDE disks using vendor-specific commands, if these are known.
   On floppy disks, use of the WRITE DELETED SECTOR command will permit the hiding of
   information that can only be read back using the READ DELETED SECTOR command.

be possible for someone else to access this incriminating information, or even necessarily be aware of its existence, without reassigning the track. Although this scenario is not a particularly likely one, forensic computing analysts need to be aware of the possibilities. The best indicator here of something amiss is that there would appear to be one formatted track too few for the known physical disk geometry.

Cylinder Number –1

The first physical cylinder on the disk is often reserved by controllers that carry out bad sector mapping for their own use. When this is the case, the physical cylinder may be assigned the artificial cylinder number "–1". As such, it is accessible only to the controller using specific internal commands, since it does not appear in the normal data address space of the disk. It is on this cylinder that the defect list may be stored, often in two parts: the original manufacturer's defect list as described above and as illustrated in Table 5.5, and a so-called *grown defect list* which is determined by the controller during formatting and added to by the subsequent use of vendor-specific bad sector mapping commands.

The main difference between the two lists is that the sophisticated testing carried out by the manufacturer is able to identify both hard and soft defects and is able to measure the exact byte positions of such defects using the bytes from index (BFI) count. It is these counts that are held in the manufacturer's defect list, as we have seen.

However, the disk controller is not able to identify soft defects and does not normally measure BFIs, so the grown defect list differs in these two respects. In addition, detailed information about the physical disk geometry may be written to cylinder –1 by the manufacturer. This is of particular importance for auto-configuring controllers which can determine their own physical disk geometry by simply reading the first physical sector on the disk.

Table 5.6 shows the way in which the manufacturer's defect list, the grown defect list and the disk geometry information may be written onto cylinder –1. Given 17 sectors per track, we note that the information is restricted to the first two heads (because these are present on all hard disks) and that more than one copy of the lists are held.

Table 5.6 Controller cylinder –1.

Sector	Head 0	Head 1
1	Disk geometry copy 1	Disk geometry copy 3
2	Disk geometry copy 2	Disk geometry copy 4
3–8	Reserved	Reserved
9–10	Manufacturer's defect list copy 1	Reserved
11–12	Manufacturer's defect list copy 2	Reserved
13–14	Grown defect list copy 1	Reserved
15–16	Grown defect list copy 2	Reserved
17	Reserved	Reserved

Table 5.7 Disk geometry information.

Byte	Contents
0–1	Signature 0dabeh of geometric information
2–3	Number of cylinders
4	Number of heads
5	Number of sectors per track
6–7	Reserved
8	Interleave factor
9	BIOS flag byte
10	Number of cylinders for alternative tracks
11	Reserved
12–13	Start cylinder of write precompensation
14–20	Manufacturer's name (ASCII)
21–39	Product name
40–511	Reserved

The structure of the disk geometry information that is held in sectors 1 and 2 of tracks 0 and 1 of cylinder –1 is shown in Table 5.7. Note that these details refer to the older ST412/506 controllers[25]. With the more modern Integrated Drive Electronics (IDE) drives (see later section on interfacing) an IDENTIFY DEVICE command can be issued to the controller to obtain 512 bytes of detailed device information, with the interpretation to be placed on each byte now defined in the ATA-2 ANSI standard (ANSI, 1996).

This information can be used for autoconfiguration by the BIOS. It may also be used in conjunction with specialist software made available by some disk manufacturers[26] to provide a detailed printout of an IDE hard disk as shown in Fig. 5.8.

There are a number of points that arise from Fig. 5.8 that we will be returning to later: the different cylinder, head and sector numbers in the three columns, and the meanings of the terms LBA, DMA and PIO, for example. Before we do that, however, there are still some points related to Table 5.7 that need to be discussed, and the first of these is the *interleave factor*.

The Interleave Factor

This is all to do with the problem of reading two successive sectors and not having enough time to transfer the buffer from the first across the interface into the computer before the second comes under the read head. This may be because we are using error-correcting codes and we have to wait until the whole sector is available in the buffer before it can be checked, or it may be because the interface itself is too slow.

---

25 See page 866 of *The Indispensable PC Hardware Book* (Messmer, 1997).

26 See, for instance, the program FIND-ATA.EXE from Seagate (1994), which was used to produce Fig. 5.8.

```
                                Find-ATA v1.0

        Drive: ST32140A                          Port: Primary (01F0h)
        Serial #:            JB192001  CMOS Type: 1   Unit: 0 - Master

                  Hardware      DOS          Current        Max ECC: 22 bytes
    Cylinders: 4095            1023          4095
        Heads: 16             64            16
      Sectors: 63             63            63
     Capacity: 2,113,413,120  2,111,864,832 2,113,413,120


                         Available   Information
    R/W Multiple Mode:       Yes     32 sectors Max  Current: 32 sectors/block
            LBA Mode:        Yes     4127760
            DMA Mode:        Yes     Single: 0  (0111)  Multi: 1  (0111) 180 nsec
    Advanced PIO Mode:       Yes     (0011)     +,-IORDY: 120 nsec, 180 nsec

    Default PIO Mode: 2, 240 nsec, up to 8.33 MB/Sec

    Buffer: 128 KBytes Type: A dual ported multi-sectored buffer capable of
            simultaneous transfers with a read caching capability.

            Copyright 1994 Seagate Technology, Inc. All rights reserved
```

Fig. 5.8 Disk information from Find-ATA program.

The problem is overcome by interleaving. Instead of having sector 2 physically follow sector 1 on the track, it is placed, for example, physically one sector further on. In this way there is time for the buffer to be emptied between transfers, since we now read every other sector but still receive the sectors in numerical sequence.

Figure 5.9 shows three cases: interleave factor 1:1, which means there is no interleaving; interleave factor 2:1 which is the example we described above with one sector in between; and interleave factor 3:1 where there are two sectors in between. With many older disk controllers it is possible to specify the interleave factor required when performing a low-level format. Software is available to test the effect of different interleave factors on such drives and help determine an optimum value.

In fact, interleaving tends no longer to be an issue with modern hard disk systems. Computer speeds are now very much faster and most disk drives these days have cache memories (Fig. 5.8 shows a 128 kbyte buffer) that hold an entire track at a time, thus obviating the need for any form of interleaving.

```
Interleave factor 1:1
1   2   3   4   5   6   7   8   9   10  11  12  13  14  15  16  17

Interleave factor 2:1
1   10  2   11  3   12  4   13  5   14  6   15  7   16  8   17  9

Interleave factor 3:1
1   7   13  2   8   14  3   9   15  4   10  16  5   11  17  6   12
```

Fig. 5.9 Interleave factors.

Write Precompensation

Also referred to in Table 5.7 is the *start cylinder of write precompensation*. This too applies only to older hard disk systems. These systems use the same number of sectors per track (spt), 17 for the earliest systems, for every cylinder on the disk. Since tracks are concentric circles, that means that as we move in closer to the spindle the physical track length gets less, and hence the packing density of the bits increases[27]. This makes magnetic interactions between some bit patterns more likely, so to limit this effect write precompensation arranges for particular bits in particular bit patterns to be written to the disk a little earlier or later than normal. The outermost cylinder number from which this timing adjustment is to be applied is referred to as the *start cylinder of write precompensation*.

Capacity and performance of hard disk systems have improved radically since those early systems, and one means by which these improvements have been made is to utilize better the so-called *areal density* of the disk: that is, the number of bits that can be packed into each unit of area on the disk. If we are to make the most of the allowable areal density across the whole surface of the disk, it would be a good idea to have different numbers of sectors per track for different groups of cylinders on the disk. Then, as we move outwards from the centre of the disk, and the track length increases, so outer cylinders could have more sectors per track than inner cylinders for the same bit density. Using this technique, of course, write precompensation becomes unnecessary.

Zoned Bit Recording

Having more than one set of sectors per track on the disk is known as *zoned bit recording* (ZBR)[28]. With this approach, tracks are grouped into zones and each zone on the disk has a different number of sectors per track. As we move from the innermost zone outwards, so the sectors per track figure increases such that the bit packing density within all the tracks is now more even.

Figure 5.10 shows the 15 zones of a 3.8 Gbyte Quantum Fireball™ hard disk (Quantum, 1996), with sectors per track ranging from 122 to 232, and with each zone consisting of 454 tracks[29]. We may wish to note the very large number of tracks[30] (15 × 454 = 6810) on this disk and the much larger numbers for sectors per track compared with the 17 of early disks. Not shown on this diagram are the different data transfer rates for the various zones. Since the angular velocity of the disk is constant and there are substantially more sectors on the outer tracks than there are on the

---

27 Clearly, if we are to get the same number of bits (because there are the same number of sectors per track) into a smaller track length, then they have to be closer together.

28 Also known as *multiple zone recording (MZR)* and *zoned constant angular velocity* recording (ZCAV).

29 It is not a requirement that zones be of equal numbers of tracks. This disk just happens to be built this way.

30 Just a reminder that tracks in this context is synonymous with cylinders.

Zone	14	13	12	11	10	9	8	7	6	5	4	3	2	1	0
Spt	122	135	142	153	162	170	180	185	195	205	214	225	225	229	232
Tracks	454	454	454	454	454	454	454	454	454	454	454	454	454	454	454

Fig. 5.10 Zoned bit recording.

inner ones, then the data transfer rates for the outer tracks must be higher than those for the inner ones. An interesting side effect of this feature is that benchmark tests run on the disk when new and after being in use for some time might suggest that the disk is getting slower. In fact, all that is happening is that the benchmark tests are being run on unused tracks that are now closer to the centre than when the disk was new. This is because sectors are assigned by the file system from the outermost cylinder inwards. What the benchmark is telling us is what we already knew: the data transfer rates of the inner zones are slower than those of the outer zones.

This ZBR approach, however, now poses us a problem. Our use of CHS addressing has assumed a known constant sectors per track value for the whole of the disk. If that assumption is invalid, then we would have to know all the zone information for a disk so that we can avoid giving it CHS addresses that exceed the sectors per track value for any given cylinder. This significantly complicates the disk interface.

A much better solution is for the controller to *pretend* that there is no zoning and to provide to the outside world an artificial sectors per track value[31] that is constant for the whole disk. When the controller receives, from the outside world, a CHS address that uses this artificial sectors per track value, it simply *translates* it into its own internal zoned address. In this way, we need have no knowledge of the zoning within the disk system in order to address it. We need also have no knowledge of any of the low-level formatting data structures or encoding methods used by the manufacturer, since the controller hides all of this from us.

This form of *internal translation*, however, should not be confused with the CHS address translation that we are going to be discussing shortly in connection with the various legacy interface problems.

Head and Cylinder Skewing

The last issue that we need to consider in this section is *skewing*. If we consider a drive that has two physical heads, then the sequence for accessing consecutive sectors, assuming there are 17 to the track (this is an old system), will be as follows: cylinder 0, head 0, sectors 1 to 17; then cylinder 0, head 1, sectors 1 to 17; then cylinder 1 head 0, sectors 1 to 17 and so forth.

Clearly, in the interests of performance, the head assembly is left at a particular cylinder position until each head has been accessed before moving it to the next cylinder position. The time taken to switch a head electronically is much shorter than the time taken to move the head assembly one cylinder position. Nevertheless, even the head switching time can be significant when compared with the speed at

---

31 This is often the value 63.

No skewing

Cylinder 0:

| Head 0: | 1 | 2 | 3 | 4 | 5 | 6 | 7 | 8 | 9 | 10 | 11 | 12 | 13 | 14 | 15 | 16 | 17 |
| Head 1: | 1 | 2 | 3 | 4 | 5 | 6 | 7 | 8 | 9 | 10 | 11 | 12 | 13 | 14 | 15 | 16 | 17 |

Cylinder 1:

| Head 0: | 1 | 2 | 3 | 4 | 5 | 6 | 7 | 8 | 9 | 10 | 11 | 12 | 13 | 14 | 15 | 16 | 17 |

Head skew = 2   Cylinder skew = 8

Cylinder 0:

| Head 0: | 1 | 2 | 3 | 4 | 5 | 6 | 7 | 8 | 9 | 10 | 11 | 12 | 13 | 14 | 15 | 16 | 17 |
| Head 1: | 16 | 17 | 1 | 2 | 3 | 4 | 5 | 6 | 7 | 8 | 9 | 10 | 11 | 12 | 13 | 14 | 15 |

Cylinder 1:

| Head 0: | 8 | 9 | 10 | 11 | 12 | 13 | 14 | 15 | 16 | 17 | 1 | 2 | 3 | 4 | 5 | 6 | 7 |

Fig. 5.11 Head and cylinder skewing.

which sectors are passing under the heads. If the head switching time is greater than the time it takes for the gap between sector 17 and sector 1 to pass under the heads and the sectors are physically lined up such that sector 1, head 0 is immediately above sector 1 head 1, as shown in the upper part of Fig. 5.11, then we are going to miss reading sector 1 head 1 immediately after we have read sector 17 head 0. This means that we will have to wait an entire revolution of the disk before we can access it again. *Head skewing* recognizes this problem and arranges for sector 1 head 1 to be physically located further round the track; in the case shown in the lower half of Fig. 5.11 it is physically under head 0 sector 3, giving a head skew of 2.

A similar problem arises with the time it takes to move the head assembly from cylinder 0 to cylinder 1. In this case the time is much longer, but the principle is exactly the same. Here we apply what is known as *cylinder skew*, and shown in Fig. 5.11 is a cylinder skew of 8 such that sector 1 of head 0 cylinder 1 is physically located under sector 9 head 1 cylinder 0. Hence, after we have read sector 17 head 1 cylinder 0, we have the time it takes for 8 sectors to pass before we must start to read sector 1 head 0 cylinder 1; sufficient time to move the head assembly one track position.

The Formatting Process

Another major difference between hard disks and floppy disks is to be found in the formatting process. For floppy disks we identify two stages of formatting: low-level and high-level (see Table 5.8), and for hard disks there are three stages: low-level, partitioning and high-level (see Table 5.9).

Table 5.8 Formatting floppy disks.

● *Low-level formatting*, which is carried out to establish the tracks and sectors with all the address marks, IDs and gaps we have discussed above.

● *High-level formatting*, during which the file system for the particular operating system is established.

Table 5.9 Formatting hard disks.

- *Low-level formatting*, which is carried out to establish the tracks and sectors with all the address marks, IDs and gaps we have discussed above.

- *Partitioning*, which enables more than one logical volume to be associated with a disk.

- *High-level formatting*, during which the file system for the particular operating system is established on a volume.

Floppy Disk Formatting

The two stages for floppy disks are both carried out by the standard DOS program FORMAT. This first of all performs the low-level format function itself by writing on to the floppy disk, a track at a time, all the gaps, address marks, sectors and CRCs that we have described above, together with all the sector data areas filled with a series of f6h bytes. After writing each track, it then reads back all the sectors of that track, recalculating and checking the data area CRCs and making a note of any sectors that are *bad*[32].

The FORMAT program next performs a high-level format by setting up the MS-DOS file system on the disk (of which more in a later section). This involves writing the *boot sector*, the two *file allocation tables* (FATs) and the *root directory*. The FORMAT program then marks the FATs appropriately with any bad sectors that it identified during the low-level formatting process. We will see how this is done in more detail in a later section. Note for now that this is not the same process as the bad sector mapping that we saw carried out by the controller of the hard disk. In this case it is a part of the file system structure (the file allocation table laid down by the high-level format) that is being marked as opposed to the sector flag bytes written by the low-level format that we saw before (see Fig. 5.7).

If, when initiating the FORMAT program, the /S option had been selected, the program then copies onto the floppy disk the system files IO.SYS, MSDOS.SYS and COMMAND.COM, making the disk *bootable*. Finally, the FORMAT program prompts for a *volume label* which is to be set on to the floppy disk, and then the process terminates.

Hard Disk Formatting

What is often a source of confusion concerning the FORMAT program is that it can carry out, without intervention, both a low-level format and a high-level format on floppy disks, yet it is not able to perform a low-level format on any hard disks. It is, however, invariably used for establishing the MS-DOS file system on a hard disk; that is, performing the high-level format.

In the case of hard disks, the low-level format is usually done by the manufacturer and the general advice is never to attempt to carry out a low-level format of a hard disk unless you are an expert. There are some good reasons for wanting to do a low-level format on certain types of hard disk and some very good reasons for not doing

---

32 Bad sectors in this context are those where the CRC calculated from the sector data just read does not agree with the CRC that was written to that sector during the format.

it on other kinds of hard disk. Among the very good reasons for not doing it on some early IDE disks is the risk of losing the factory-written manufacturer's defect list (which includes the soft defect listings that are virtually impossible for a user to determine) and the loss of any optimized interleave and skewing values. On later disks, internal address translation may be implemented. When the disk is in this mode[33], and disks that use zoned bit recording are always in translation mode, a low-level format is harmless to the defect mapping files and the skewing values. If, however, the disk is in physical mode, the defect mapping files and skewing values may again be lost. All the low-level format does when the disk is in translation mode is to "scrub" the data in all the sectors; it does not rewrite the formatting structure. It should be noted, however, that it is completely destructive to all data on the disk. This is sometimes referred to as *intermediate* or *mid-level formatting*[34]. Among the good reasons for perhaps wanting to do this are the contraction of a virus, the increasing incidence of bad sectors, or the complete removal of an operating system.

Since the DOS FORMAT program cannot be used to low-level format a hard disk the manufacturer may provide special programs[35] specifically for this purpose. Alternatively, there may be formatting utilities built into the BIOS of the PC or the BIOS of the hard disk itself which can be accessed using the DOS DEBUG[36] command. Again, none of these utilities should be invoked unless the analyst has a very high level of expertise in hard disk systems.

Given a hard disk with an appropriate low-level format, the next step is to *partition* it, even if only one partition is to be used. Partitioning is the process of dividing the hard disk up into a number of logical pieces, each piece being a partition. This process allows for a logical volume to be associated with each partition and for different operating systems to be associated with different volumes. The standard program that is often used to carry out partitioning is FDISK, though manufac-turers sometimes provide their own utilities[37] and specialist software, such as Partition Magic (PowerQuest, 1996), can make this rather arcane task much easier. We will examine the details of partitions, the *master boot record* and the whole boot process itself in a later section.

The final activity required is a high-level format of each partition. In this respect, a partition may simply be thought of as a very large floppy disk. As for the floppy disk, a high-level format is carried out to establish the file system for the particular operating system that is to be used with this partition. Again, as for the floppy disk, FORMAT is often used for this process and this will involve writing the boot sector, the two file allocation tables (FATs) and the root directory. At this stage in the floppy

---

33 Some drives can be switched between physical mode and translation mode (non-physical geometry).

34 See Seagate (1997).

35 SGATFMT4.EXE is one such program, provided by Seagate for use on its ATA (IDE) hard drives. See Seagate (1995).

36 This DEBUG command takes the form -G=C800:5, where G is for GO and C800 is the upper memory address of the disk BIOS.

37 See *NFDisc v1.20, Partition Record display and maintenance* (Seagate, 1995).

disk format, the FORMAT program would mark the FATs with any bad sectors that it identified during the low-level formatting process. However, in the case of modern hard disks, bad sector mapping has already been carried out by the controller internally, so the disk appears to be perfect to the FORMAT program and there will be no bad sectors to report and to mark in the FATs.

If the /S option has been selected, FORMAT then copies onto the hard disk the system files IO.SYS, MSDOS.SYS and COMMAND.COM, making the hard disk partition bootable under certain conditions (see later). Finally, the FORMAT program prompts for a volume label which is to be set on to the hard disk partition, and then the process terminates.

Hard Disk Interfaces

We have now seen in quite some detail how data is stored on a hard disk and how it is addressed. We now need to consider how data gets transferred between the PC and the hard disk. In other words, we need to look at the various software and hardware interfaces.

The BIOS and Interrupt Vectors

We start with a reminder of how the memory of the PC is laid out (see Fig. 5.12). We will come back to this again when we look at the bootstrap sequence. For now, we need to recall that the design of the PC incorporates the concept of a basic

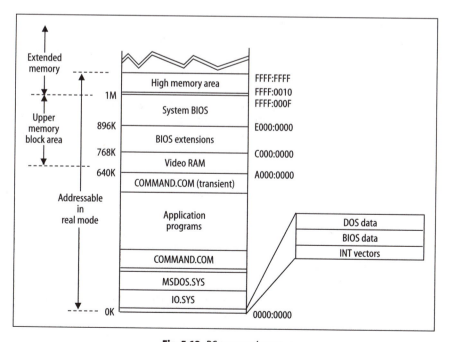

Fig. 5.12 PC memory layout.

input–output system (the BIOS), which is permanent program code held in read-only memory (ROM) in the upper memory block area. This provides us with a standardized low-level interface to the specific hardware of the computer.

The particular functions of the BIOS are accessed by means of interrupt call instruction codes (INTs), and different interrupt numbers access different parts of the BIOS software that controls different parts of the hardware. For example: INT 10h deals with the video system, INT 13h deals with the disk system, INT 14h deals with the serial communications ports and INT 16h deals with the keyboard. In addition, different function numbers within an interrupt carry out different actions. For example, INT 13h function 2 reads a disk sector, INT 13h function 3 writes a disk sector and INT 13h function 5 formats a track. In this way, application software that interacts with the BIOS can be independent of the specific hardware of the particular machine but instead can deal with generic hardware functions that are standardized. This makes any software that uses this BIOS interface portable across PC systems. There is considerable flexibility in the PC design for exactly where the BIOS program code that implements any particular interrupt is located, since all interrupt calls are redirected through an *interrupt vector table* that is held in random access memory (RAM) at address 0000:0400 and below. This table has a 4 byte pointer[38] for each interrupt and is built afresh each time the PC carries out its boot-up sequence. It is therefore possible to cause any interrupt to go to any place in memory simply by changing the 4 bytes of the relevant interrupt vector. This enables us to place interrupt program code anywhere in the memory and, perhaps, change an interrupt from going to the standard BIOS code and to go instead where some revised set of functions have been placed. We will come back to this point again.

Whereas there is considerable flexibility in the way in which the INT routines are implemented, and thus in the functionality that they can exhibit, there can be little flexibility in the form of the interfaces that they present to the software that uses them. This is always the problem with any kind of standard; if it is to be useful it must remain constant, or, at the very least, be backward-compatible with all previous versions if legacy systems are to continue to work.

It is this problem of standards and of legacy systems that, throughout its relatively short history, has so bedeviled the hard disk story and has caused to be imposed a variety of performance and capacity limitations for which often less than elegant solutions have had to be devised. In order to make sense of this we do need to be aware of a little of this history.

The ST412/506 Interface

In the very beginning there were no hard disk drives for PCs and, as a result, no inbuilt BIOS support for them. Hard disks had been available to mainframe and minicomputer systems for many years prior to this time, so it was not long before this technology was targeted at the new Personal Computer.

It initially came in the form of a separate cabinet which contained the hard disk drive itself, the disk controller electronics, and an internal power supply. In addition,

---

38 These are *far pointers*, see later.

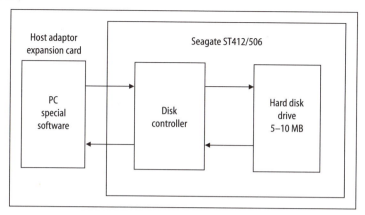

Fig. 5.13 ST412/506 hard disk drives.

an 8 bit *host adaptor expansion card* would be fitted inside the PC in a spare expansion slot and this would be connected by cables to the disk controller in the cabinet. The controller in turn was connected to the hard disk drive (see Fig. 5.13).

Hard disks such as these became known as *Winchester Drives*. The term seems to have been taken from an old IBM drive of the 1960s which had 30 Mbyte of fixed storage and an option for a further 30 Mbyte of removable storage. This drive was informally known as the "30-30" and from this, the term "Winchester", the calibre of the famous Remington rifle, came to signify any fixed disk for a PC.

There were no INT 13h BIOS functions for the PC at this time, so special-purpose software had to be provided. The host adaptor in the expansion slot would be addressed by this special software through which would be sent appropriate commands to the disk controller.

The disk controller would then transfer the required data to and from the hard disk itself. A typical such system of the time was the Seagate ST-506, introduced in 1980, which had a formatted capacity of just 5 Mbyte. Figure 5.14 shows part of its specification[39]. It may be noted that it used MFM encoding, had a stepper type

```
UNFORMATTED CAPACITY (MB) _____6.38
FORMATTED CAPACITY (17 SECTORS) (MB) _____5.0
ACTUATOR TYPE _____STEPPER
TRACKS _____612
CYLINDERS _____153
HEADS _____4
DISCS _____2
MEDIA TYPE _____OXIDE
RECORDING METHOD _____MFM
TRANSFER RATE (mbits/sec) _____5.0
INTERFACE _____ST506
```

Fig. 5.14 Part of the ST-506 specification (with kind permission of Seagate Technology).

39 See *Specifications for ST-506* (Seagate, 1991a).

actuator, 153 cylinders, 4 heads and 17 sectors per track. This gave it a capacity of 153 × 4 × 17 × 512 = 5 326 848 bytes. The ST-506 design incorporated a very well-defined interface between the disk drive and the controller. Introduced about a year later, its successor, the Seagate ST-412[40], had a 10 Mbyte capacity and a slightly modified interface which added a "buffered seeks" facility. It was these two, now obsolete, systems that contributed their interface specifications and their combined names to what became the *de facto* standard for connecting hard disk drives to controllers in the early 1980s: the *ST412/506 Interface*.

In the ST412/506 design, up to two disk drives could be connected to the controller by a single 34 line control cable and separate 20 line data cables for each drive. None of the intelligence was in the drives, which responded to very simple control signals from the controller, such as switch the head assembly to move in a particular direction, step the head assembly one step, select a particular head and so forth. The control program for all of these actions was held in the controller itself, which was also responsible for interpreting all commands from the PC, encoding and decoding read and write serial data to and from the drive, transferring 8 bit bytes to and from the PC, generating and identifying address marks and other formatting information, and similar housekeeping activities. At the PC interface the commands to the controller, sent by the special software referred to above, were the forerunners of the INT 13h BIOS functions, such as read a sector, write a sector, format a track and seek to a specific cylinder.

In 1983, when the *IBM XT* (*eXtended Technology*) became available, with its built-in 10 Mbyte fixed disk, some of these ideas were seen to have evolved further. First of all, the disk controller[41] had been removed from the disk drive box and built right onto a bus interface expansion card, thus doing away with the host adaptor expansion card. Further, program code had been provided on a ROM chip on the controller card itself which supplemented the standard BIOS functions and obviated the need for the special software to be installed. The design utilized interrupt request line 5 (IRQ 5), input–output port addresses 320h to 32fh and *direct memory access* channel 3 (DMA 3). From an earlier section we may recall that the IRQ channel permits a hardware interrupt to be raised by the connected device (in this case the hard disk controller). Such an interrupt will cause the processor to suspend temporarily its current activity and execute code designed to service the device raising the interrupt. In addition, we may recall that the port addresses are the outlets through which commands and data are sent to and received from the hardware device, and the DMA channel permits the hardware device to send and receive data autonomously from the PC's memory without involving the processor.

In 1984, the introduction of the *IBM AT* (*Advanced Technology*) saw a complete overhaul of the hard disk system. The PC command interface to the controller was now incorporated into the ROM BIOS on the motherboard of the PC as the now standard INT 13h functions, thus removing the need for a separate ROM BIOS chip on the controller card. Disk drive parameters as well as other motherboard

---

40 See *Specifications for ST-412* (Seagate, 1991b).

41 These were often called WD1003 controllers after a Western Digital design of that name (Western Digital, undated).

configuration details were held in a low-power *Complementary Metal Oxide Silicon* (*CMOS*) RAM chip that was backed up by a small battery. Some 14 different disk types were initially recognized, ranging from 10 to 112 Mbyte capacity. Any drive with physical parameters which did not match one of the 14 had to be incorporated either by means of a ROM extension on the controller card or by using special device driver software loaded at boot time. The AT design for hard disks utilized interrupt request line 14 (IRQ 14) and input–output port addresses 1f0h to 1f8h, but did not use a direct memory access channel at all. This was because the DMA controller and the buses to which it was connected were found to be too slow for efficient disk data transfers, so *programmed input–output* (*PIO*) was used instead. In this approach, the processor carries out all the transfer activity itself by means of IN and OUT instructions and no autonomous transfers take place.

This is broadly the hard disk system structure that we have today. The number of supported disk types has expanded rapidly, and most current BIOSes provide a user-definable type which allows parameters to be set to match any drive. Many BIOSes now have an auto-configuration mode which enables the drive to be interrogated by the BIOS and to provide its own parameter information at boot time.

Background to the Legacy Problem

The legacy problem of the PC disk system lies in the INT 13h BIOS functions that provide the standard command interface between any software that requires disk facilities and the disk controller. This includes the structure of a CHS address that has to be passed from the BIOS to the controller. This structure[42] exactly mimics that of the CHS address held in the ID field of the hard disk sector format (see Fig. 5.4) and therefore permits a maximum CHS address of 1024 cylinders, 256 heads and 63 sectors. This interface has had to remain constant[43] since 1984 despite some quite radical changes in the physical interfaces between the PC and the controller and the controller and the disk drive. The bus architecture linking the PC to the controller, and the interface between the controller and the hard drive, have both been changed a number of times in the last 15 years in order to take advantage of advances in technology and to improve performance and cost effectiveness. We will look first, very briefly, at the changes in bus architectures.

Bus Architectures

The original bus architecture of the AT, although not formally specified by IBM, eventually evolved into what is now known as the *Industry Standard Architecture* (*ISA*). This has the ability to transfer data at a maximum speed of 8.33 Mbyte/s and has a data bus width of 16 bits. With the introduction of the 386 and 486 processors,

---

42 The cylinder value is part held in the CH register, the head value is in the DL register, and the sector value is held in the last six bits of the CL register, with the leading two bits of the CL register making up the 10 bits for the cylinder value, in close accord with Fig. 5.4.

43 Apart from some relatively recent extensions; see *BIOS Enhanced Disk Drive Specification* (Phoenix, 1995).

which have a 32 bit data bus, an extension to the ISA architecture was made and this is called the *Extended Industry Standard Architecture* (EISA). This can transfer data at up to 33 Mbyte/s and has a 32 bit data bus. Meanwhile, IBM had continued development of the PC and produced the PS/2, which utilized a new bus architecture that it called *Micro Channel Architecture* (MCA). This too has a 32 bit data bus and can transfer data at up to 20 Mbyte/s or 40 Mbyte/s for short periods.

As the technology continued to develop, so even these buses were found wanting, particularly in the area of graphics and disk activity. The *Video Electronics Standards Association* (VESA) developed a Local Bus which became known as *VESA Local Bus* (or just *VLB*) to address this performance problem. It too has a 32 bit data bus but can transfer data at 133 Mbyte/s or 160 Mbyte/s, depending on version.

Finally (so far that is), Intel has developed a new bus architecture that it has designated *Peripheral Component Interconnect* (PCI). The 32 bit standard bus can transfer data at 133 Mbyte/s and this can be expanded to 64 bits with a data rate of 266 Mbyte/s. Most modern Pentium systems use this bus architecture today.

If the bus architectures have changed significantly in the past 15 years, then the disk controller to disk interfaces have changed even more significantly. The typical hard disk capacities have increased from 10 Mbyte to 22 Gbyte and the typical transfer rates have increased from 5 Mbit/s to 220 Mbit/s[44] in the same period. In addition, the form factor has reduced from 5.25 inches to 3.5 inches and the unit cost has become significantly cheaper. We will look at some of these hard disk interface developments next.

The Enhanced Small Device Interface (ESDI)

The ST412/506 interface was soon found to be wanting. Problems arose over data integrity and speed because the raw encoded data was having to travel over lengthy cables between the read/write heads of the drive and the electronics of the controller. In addition, the controller had to be optimized by the user for the drive attached to it by setting interleave factors and so forth.

A first attempt at improving this situation was achieved by moving some of the controller electronics from the controller card on to the hard drive itself. Figure 5.15 shows a number of options for the distribution of controller functions between a separate controller card and the drive itself. The leftmost column of the table shows the ST412/506 situation with all the controller functions on the controller card. The next column to the right shows the data separator electronics and the ST412/506 interface on the drive itself. This has the considerable advantage of getting rid of the lengthy raw data cables and thus improving both performance and error rates.

It was this approach that was adopted in the *Enhanced Small Device Interface* (ESDI) design. Although it was an improvement, it became obsolete very quickly because a much cheaper and more effective solution was seen to be to move *all* of the controller electronics except for a vestigial interface adaptor onto the drive board itself. This became known as *Integrated* (or *Intelligent*) *Drive Electronics* (IDE).

---

44 See *IBM Deskstar 25GP and Deskstar 22GXP Hard Disk Drives* (IBM, 1998).

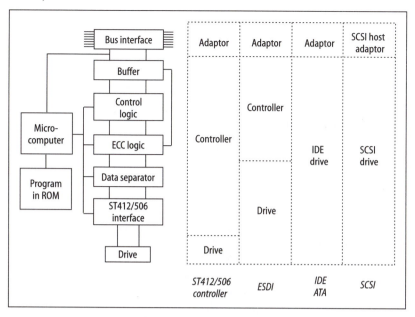

Fig. 5.15 Controllers and drives.

Integrated Drive Electronics (IDE) and AT Attachment (ATA)

The name "Integrated Drive Electronics" or "IDE" was used to signify this placement of all the controller electronics onto the drive itself, as shown in the third column of Fig. 5.15. It is a misleading use of the name (although it is still in very common use today) because other systems, such as the *Small Computer Systems Interface* (SCSI)[45], also integrate the controller electronics onto the drive, as we have indicated in the fourth column of Fig. 5.15.

A much better term is *"AT Attachment"* or *"ATA"*, which defines the standard interface between the hard disk IDE system and the AT-style PC to which it is connected. The specification for this interface eventually became defined as an ANSI standard. This was done by the industry in an attempt to eliminate some of the incompatibility problems that surrounded early IDE/ATA drives. These were particularly evident when attempting to install a master and slave on the same IDE/ATA channel using drives from different manufacturers. Very often the disks would not work together.

The original ATA standard specifies:

---

45 SCSI, pronounced "scuzzy", is not just a hard disk interface. It is a flexible and powerful standard (ANSI X3T9.2) for connecting peripheral devices to computers. Up to eight intelligent devices may be connected to the SCSI bus, one of which is the SCSI host adaptor which connects to the PC. SCSI drives are met much less frequently in PC systems than are IDE/ATA drives and most of the problems that are identified in the next section for the IDE/ATA interface do not apply to the SCSI interface. We therefore do not consider it further here.

- that there is to be a single channel shared by up to two hard disks configured as master and slave;
- that programmed input–output (PIO) modes 0, 1 and 2 are to be supported which are defined as 3.3, 5.2 and 8.3 Mbyte/s transfer rates respectively; and
- that direct memory access (DMA) modes 0, 1 and 2 for single words, defined as 2.1, 4.2 and 8.3 Mbyte/s respectively, and mode 0 for multiwords defined as 4.2 Mbyte/s, are also to be supported.

As we discussed earlier, the basic DMA facilities provided by the standard PC-AT over ISA buses did not make DMA an attractive transfer mechanism for performance reasons, and PIO tended to be used by most disk controllers instead. However, modern IDE/ATA hard disks may have their own DMA controllers and therefore do not need to use the slow DMA controller that is built into the PC-AT. This system is often called *bus mastering* and requires the use of a PCI bus to support it.

The ATA standard also defines a comprehensive command set and protocol which operates between the INT 13h BIOS functions and the ATA/IDE drive. Among the myriad of definitions is the following which we will refer back to in a later section: *A CHS address is made up of three fields: the sector address, the head number and the cylinder number. Sectors are numbered from 1 to the maximum value allowed by the current CHS translation mode but cannot exceed 255. Heads are numbered from 0 to the maximum value allowed by the current CHS translation mode but cannot exceed 15. Cylinders are numbered from 0 to the maximum value allowed by the current CHS translation mode but cannot exceed 65,535*[46].

Although this original standard proved well suited for the early IDE/ATA disks, the rapid improvements in disk technology soon saw the need for faster transfer rates and enhanced features. An *ATA-2* specification, backward-compatible with the original standard, was drawn up which became a second ANSI standard[47]. This adds the following features:

- faster PIO modes, 3 and 4, which are defined as 11.1 and 16.6 Mbyte/s respectively
- faster multiword DMA modes, 1 and 2, which are defined as 13.3 and 16.6 Mbyte/s respectively
- a new block transfer mode
- logical block addressing (LBA), which we will be looking at later
- an improved Identify Drive command which permits BIOS software to obtain more accurate details about the drive

An *ATA-3* unofficial standard has also been drawn up, though this is not much referred to by the disk manufacturers, who have invented a number of marketing names (see below) for their drives to signify additional or enhanced features over the ATA-2 standard. ATA-3 is a minor revision of the ATA-2 standard, with which it is backward-compatible, and it defines means for improving the reliability of the

---

46 See *Information technology – AT Attachment Interface with Extensions (ATA-2)* (Finch, 1999).

47 See *ANSI X3.279-1996 – AT Attachment Interface with Extensions (ATA-2)* (ANSI, 1996).

higher speed transfer modes and introduces the new feature of *Self-Monitoring and Reporting Technology* (SMART).

Ultra-ATA is another unofficial standard that refers to the use of a higher speed DMA transfer mode (multiword DMA mode 3, sometimes called DMA-33) running at 33.3 Mbyte/s. This requires a modified BIOS that supports the Ultra ATA protocol. Ultra-ATA may also be called *Ultra-DMA* or *ATA-33*.

Finally, at least as far as these standards are concerned, the *ATA Packet Interface* (ATAPI) was defined as an ANSI standard to permit CD-ROM and tape drives to be plugged into the standard IDE interface and to be configured as master or slave in just the same way as a hard disk. However, because the ATAPI protocol is not identical to the ATA-2 command set used for the hard disks, a special ATAPI driver has to be installed to communicate with these devices.

As mentioned above, a number of marketing names have been used by some of the disk manufacturers to refer to additional or enhanced features. These are not standards as such, but it is important to be aware of them because the terms are in common use. *Fast ATA* and *Fast ATA-2*[48] are used by Seagate and Quantum to refer to what is essentially ATA-2. Fast ATA complies with ATA-2 except for PIO mode 4 and multiword DMA mode 2, and Fast ATA-2 appears to be no more than just ATA-2. *Enhanced IDE* or *EIDE*[49] is used by Western Digital to refer to systems that in addition to complying with ATA-2, include support for ATAPI and dual IDE/ATA host adaptors, permitting up to four IDE/ATA/ATAPI devices to be used.

Having now looked a little at both the INT 13h BIOS interface and the plethora of standards that make up the IDE/ATA hard disk interface (see Table 5.10) we will now consider in the next section what the problems might be in bringing the two together.

Table 5.10 A plethora of standards.

Bus architectures
Industry Standard Architecture (ISA)
Extended Industry Standard Architecture (EISA)
Micro Channel Architecture (MCA)
Video Electronics Standards Association (VESA) Local Bus (VLB)
Peripheral Component Interconnect (PCI)

Drive interfaces
Seagate Technologies ST412/506
Enhanced Small Drive Interface (ESDI)
Integrated Drive Electronics (IDE) and AT Attachment (ATA)
Small Computer System Interface (SCSI)
ATA, ATA-2, ATA-3
Ultra-ATA, Ultra-DMA, ATA-33, DMA-33
ATA Packet Interface (ATAPI)
Fast ATA and Fast ATA-2, Enhanced IDE (EIDE)

---

48 See *Seagate Fast ATA/Fast ATA-2 Fact Sheet* (Seagate, 1997).

49 See *Enhanced IDE Interface* (Western Digital, 1997).

IDE/ATA Problems and Workarounds

The first serious problem arises from the CHS addressing structure that is used by the INT 13h BIOS interface and the way in which this differs from the CHS addressing structure that is used by IDE/ATA devices. The problem is sometimes known as the *528 Mbyte Barrier*.

The 528 Mbyte Barrier

The details can perhaps best be understood by reference to Table 5.11. Here we see in three columns the CHS addressing structure for the INT 13h BIOS, the IDE/ATA interface and the combined effect of the two connected together labelled "Limitation".

The CHS values for the INT 13h BIOS column are easily recognizable from what has been discussed before: 10 bits for the cylinders resulting in a maximum of 1024 (counting from 0), 8 bits for the heads resulting in a maximum of 256 (counting from 0) and 6 bits for the sectors resulting in a maximum of 63 (because sector counting starts from 1). This gives a total possible disk size in bytes, assuming 512 bytes per sector, of $1024 \times 256 \times 63 \times 512 = 8\ 455\ 716\ 864$. In SI units (powers of ten) this is 8.45 Gbyte and in powers of two units we have to divide by $1024 \times 1024 \times 1024$ to get 7.87 Gbyte[50]. The CHS values for the IDE/ATA column can be determined by reference back to the quote from the ATA interface specification. There we may recall that the quote states that cylinders are permitted to be of value 0 to $65\ 535 = 65\ 536$ (16 bits), heads are permitted to be of value 0 to $15 = 16$ (4 bits), and sectors are permitted to be of value 1 to $255 = 255$ (8 bits). This gives a total possible disk size in bytes of $65\ 536 \times 16 \times 255 \times 512 = 136\ 902\ 082\ 560$. In SI units this is 136.9 Gbyte and in powers of two units it is 127.5 Gbyte.

Table 5.11 Connecting the interfaces.

	INT 13h BIOS	IDE/ATA	Limitation
Cylinders	1024 (10)	65 536 (16)	1024
Heads	256 (8)	16 (4)	16
Sectors per track	63 (6)	255 (8)	63
Bytes per sector	512	512	512
Size in bytes	8 455 716 864	136 902 082 560	528 482 304
SI units	8.45 Gbyte	136.9 Gbyte	528 Mbyte
^2 units	7.87 Gbyte	127.5 Gbyte	504 Mbyte

---

50 We have calculated both sets of units here because either may be quoted in the literature, often without any reference to derivation. We have also seen this value expressed as $8\ 455\ 716\ 864/1024 \times 1024 = 8064$ Mbyte = 8 Gbyte.

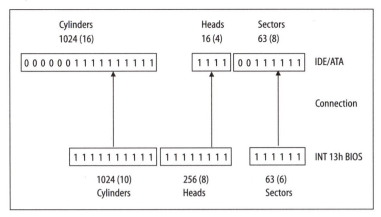

Fig. 5.16 528 Mbyte limitation.

When we connect the two interfaces together we get the worst of both worlds, as we can see in Fig. 5.16. Assuming the highest possible address at the INT 13h BIOS interface which we want to send across to the disk drive, we would have 10 ones for the cylinders, 8 ones for the heads and 6 ones for the sectors. Given that all these bit patterns could cross the interface to the registers at the IDE/ATA drive, the result there would be: 10 ones into the 16 bit cylinders register, 4 ones into the 4 bit heads register (losing the leading 4 ones because the IDE/ATA heads register is too small) and 6 ones into the 8 bit sectors register.

This accounts for what we see in the "Limitation" column of Table 5.11. What has been transferred is 10 bits for the cylinders resulting in a maximum of 1024 (counting from 0), 4 bits for the heads resulting in a maximum of 16 (counting from 0), and 6 bits for the sectors resulting in a maximum of 63 (counting from 1). This gives a total possible disk size in bytes of $1024 \times 16 \times 63 \times 512 = 528\,482\,304$. In SI units this is 528 Mbyte and in powers of two units it is 504 Mbyte. The two interfaces between them limit the maximum possible disk size to 528 Mbyte. It should also be noted, since we will return to this later, that the maximum number of cylinders is limited to 1024 by the same argument.

One might be tempted to wonder why the designers of the IDE/ATA specification had not thought of these problems. Almost certainly they had. It may have been because disks greater than half a Gbyte were not widely available at the time of writing the specification but more likely it is in recognition that development is taking the hard disk into rapidly increasing number of cylinders at the expense of heads and it is the INT 13h BIOS structure that needs to be changed.

Whatever the reasons, the PC user of IDE/ATA disks was limited to 528 Mbyte of hard disk until a workaround could be established.

CHS Translation

A possible solution to this problem can be spotted easily from Fig. 5.16. We could trade some of those leading 4 head bits at the INT 13h BIOS interface, which get lost when we get to the IDE/ATA interface, for some of those leading 6 cylinder bits at the IDE/ATA interface that are missing at the INT 13h BIOS interface. There are, of course, many ways in which this trade could be carried out. The approach chosen by the PC industry is to take the cylinders value at the IDE/ATA interface and, if it is greater than 1023, to divide it by a power of two which makes it less than 1024, before passing the result to the cylinders register at the INT 13h BIOS interface. At the same time, the heads value at the IDE/ATA interface is multiplied by the same power of two before the result is passed to the heads register at the INT 13h BIOS interface. Clearly, when moving from the INT 13h BIOS interface to the IDE/ATA interface, a complementary process is carried out. Because they are powers of two, this algorithm can be implemented by shifting bits the appropriate number of places left or right. For this reason it is often referred to as the *bit shifting method*.

As an example of its use, we can see in Fig. 5.17 the maximum CHS values for a 540 Mbyte hard drive which, at the IDE/ATA interface require a maximum of 1057 cylinders, 16 heads and 63 sectors per track. We note that, at 540 Mbyte, the drive breaches the 528 Mbyte barrier. Using the simple translation algorithm referred to above, the cylinders value at the INT 13h BIOS interface is calculated as $1057/2 = 528$ (rounding down) and the heads value at the INT 13h BIOS interface is calculated as $16 \times 2 = 32$. These CHS values (528, 32, 63) are now well within the range of the INT 13h BIOS registers and the disk appears to the BIOS, and, of course, to all software that uses it, to be of a quite different but entirely acceptable geometry.

It should be noted that we may lose some capacity by this translation process. The original disk geometry of 1057 cylinders, 16 heads and 63 sectors results in a total capacity of $1057 \times 16 \times 63 \times 512 = 545\ 513\ 472$ bytes. The INT 13h BIOS translated geometry results in a total capacity of $528 \times 32 \times 63 \times 512 = 544\ 997\ 376$ bytes, a loss of about 0.1%.

As a further example, we are now in a good position to interpret much of the data that was given by the Find-ATA program for the ST32140A hard disk (see Fig. 5.8). In the "Hardware" column we see that the number of cylinders is 4095, the number of heads is 16 and the number of sectors is 63. The disk capacity is shown as 2 113 413 120. These are clearly the values for the IDE/ATA interface and we can

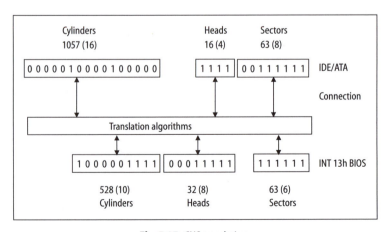

Fig. 5.17 CHS translation.

confirm that $4095 \times 16 \times 63 \times 512$ is indeed 2 113 413 120. In the "DOS" column we are, in fact, seeing the translated values at the INT 13h BIOS interface. The cylinders value is calculated as $4095/4 = 1023$ (rounding down) and the heads value is calculated as $16 \times 4 = 64$, both as shown in the figure. The capacity can then be calculated as $1023 \times 64 \times 63 \times 512 = 2$ 111 864 832, also as shown in the figure. In addition, we should now be familiar with the terms DMA and PIO, which we discussed earlier. The final term, LBA, we will consider very shortly. In some technical papers the term *Logical CHS* or *L-CHS* is being used to refer to the CHS addresses at the INT 13h BIOS interface and the term *Physical CHS* or *P-CHS* is used to refer to the CHS addresses at the IDE/ATA interface.

CHS Translation Options

The translation algorithm that operates between the two interfaces has to reside as some form of software in the PC. There are a number of options for this. A modern BIOS will already have the translation algorithm software built into its INT 13h functions and will automatically be capable of what is sometimes known as *Extended CHS* (ECHS) *Translation* or simply *Large Mode*. Such BIOSes are often referred to as *enhanced*[51] or *translating BIOS*es and the translation algorithm as the *ECHS translation method*. If we have an earlier BIOS, however, which does not incorporate such translation facilities, there are three possibilities for using disks larger than 528 Mbyte.

The first involves using special software drivers that do the translation for us. They are sometimes referred to as *Dynamic Drive Overlays* or *DDOs*. They are typified by EZ-Drive from Microhouse (Western Digital, 1999), and Disk Manager from Ontrack (IBM, 1999), and many hard disk manufacturers provide software of this nature with their disk products in order to deal with the non-translating BIOS problem. Both work in similar ways. During the first setting up of the disk, the DDO establishes itself in some spare disk space just after the partition table and at boot time gets loaded into memory as the CHS translating software. We will look at this process in more detail later. Suffice to say, at this stage, having been loaded in, the CHS translating software also adjusts the INT 13h vector in memory to point to where it now resides so that all INT 13h calls thereafter are automatically handled first by the translation routines. In passing we should note the earlier comment that, without translation, the maximum number of cylinders accessible by the INT 13h BIOS is 1024. This has an important effect when we have a non-translating BIOS and are using a DDO. Prior to the DDO being activated, all INT 13h BIOS calls are subject to the non-translating BIOS limitations. In particular, this means that a boot sector, if it has to be accessed before the DDO is established[52], cannot reside on the disk beyond what is called the *1024 cylinder limit*. A further important point is that DDOs are

---

51 Do not confuse this with the *BIOS Enhanced Disk Drive Specification* (Phoenix, 1995), which introduces entirely new INT 13h functions.

52 This depends upon the stage at which the DDO is loaded and the INT 13h vector gets changed. If this occurs during the analysis of the partition table, then boot sectors beyond the 1024 cylinder limit will be accessible. If it occurs during the sector boot sequence, they will not.

normally established by the hard disk boot sequence. When booting from floppy disk to DOS, with a non-translating BIOS, the hard disk may not be accessible at all because the DDO has not been loaded. Most DDOs provide a workaround process for this problem which may involve either pressing a particular key during the boot sequence or preparing a floppy disk with the DDO installed on it.

The second approach to the problem is to use a disk drive unit which has its own version of the INT 13h translating BIOS routines built into its ROM. During the boot process, the INT 13h vector is adjusted to point to the translating BIOS of the hard disk ROM rather than the standard internal INT 13h BIOS routines. The 1024 cylinder limit always applies here because the INT 13h vector does not get changed until after the boot sector has been accessed, but the floppy boot to DOS problem should not arise in this case.

The third approach to the problem is to change the system BIOS. This can be done either by obtaining an updated chip and replacing the current BIOS with it or, with the more modern flash BIOS systems, downloading a modification patch from the supplier and changing the flash memory.

If we refer back to Table 5.11, we may note that the total number of bits required by the ATA specification is 16 for cylinders + 4 for heads + 8 for sectors/track, giving a total of 28. In the low-level formatting discussion, we saw that three bytes (Fig. 5.4) were used for the CHS of the sector ID field which only gives us 24 bits. However, we also saw (Fig. 5.7) that 4 bits of the sector flag in the sector ID field were "reserved" and using these as well we can obtain 28 bits for CHS addressing.

An approach used by one manufacturer[53] is shown in Fig. 5.18. Here the first two bytes are used to hold the cylinders number (0 to 65 535), the last three bits of the third byte to hold the heads number (0 to 7) and the fourth byte to hold the sectors number (1 to 255).

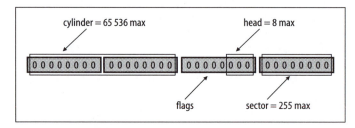

Fig. 5.18 A different use of sector ID bytes.

Logical Block Addressing (LBA)

Logical Block Addressing (LBA) is an alternative form of addressing to that of CHS and it has been included in the ATA-2 specification. In LBA, the 28 bits of the sector ID field are used as a single number, starting from 0 to identify each sector in sequence from the first to the last. The maximum number of sectors is, of course, 2^{28}

---

53 See *SGATFMT4.EXE v4.0, Seagate Format drive utility* (Seagate, 1995a).

= 268 435 456 and this, for 512 byte sectors, results in a maximum size of 137 438 953 472 bytes or 128 Gbyte.

It is important to recognize that LBA is not a solution to the 528 Mbyte problem. All software which uses the INT 13h BIOS interface will be addressing the disk system using CHS addresses. Even though the IDE/ATA interface of the hard disk may be in LBA mode, all LBA addresses will have to be translated to and from the INT 13h BIOS CHS addresses that the software uses. In other words, a translating BIOS is always required and it is the translating BIOS that provides the solution to the 528 Mbyte problem.

The LBA translation algorithm, known as the *LBA assisted method*, is a little different from the bit shifting method we discussed earlier. It is perhaps best understood by looking at Table 5.12. To convert an LBA address to a CHS address, the total capacity (cap) of the drive in bytes is first calculated. Depending upon this capacity a particular line item in Table 5.12 is selected and the cylinders, heads and sectors values calculated according to the appropriate entries. One particular point should be noted from this figure: the heads value and the relevant cylinders divisor for the 4032 to 8032.5 Mbyte capacity is 255 rather than 256. This is because of an operating system problem that we will be looking at shortly.

If we now reconsider the example of Fig. 5.8, we can calculate the highest LBA as 4095 cylinders × 16 heads × 63 sectors = 4 127 760 sectors, and this gives a total capacity of 4 127 760 × 512 = 2 113 413 120 bytes. This is equivalent to 2 113 413 120/ 1024 × 1024 = 2015.5 Mbyte[54]. The appropriate line item in Table 5.12 is therefore the 1008 to 2016 Mbyte line, so the cylinders become 2 113 413 120/(63 × 64 × 512) = 1023.75. Rounding down, this gives us 1023. The INT 13h BIOS translated address for the highest LBA address of 4 127 760 is therefore cylinders 1023, heads 64 and sectors 63. This is exactly the same as that obtained using the bit shifting method above for the highest CHS address at the INT 13h BIOS (DOS) interface. Note that this will not always be the case. The two translation methods produce the same CHS values in many cases, but not in all. The LBA assisted method *always* uses 63 sectors per track. The bit shifting method uses whatever sectors per track the drive reports from the IDE/ATA interface. If this is not 63, the two algorithms will produce completely different results[55]. It can therefore be very destructive of data to change translation

Table 5.12 LBA assisted method.

Capacity	Sectors	Heads	Cylinders
1 < cap < 504 Mbyte	63	16	cap/(63 × 16 × 512)
504 < cap < 1008 Mbyte	63	32	cap/(63 × 32 × 512)
1008 < cap < 2016 Mbyte	63	64	cap/(63 × 64 × 512)
2016 < cap < 4032 Mbyte	63	128	cap/(63 × 128 × 512)
4032 < cap < 8032.5 Mbyte	63	255	cap/(63 × 255 × 512)

54 Note that Table 5.12 is in powers of two units.

55 As an example, the Western Digital WDAC2420, which is a 425 Mbyte disk, specifies 56 sectors per track (Western Digital, 1997b).

modes between ECHS (Large) and LBA on a working drive. The actual sectors accessed could be different between the two modes for the same CHS addresses used by the software.

2 Gbyte Problem

Some implementations of translating BIOSes have difficulty with a cylinders value at the IDE/ATA interface that is greater than 4095. For a drive that has 4096 cylinders, 16 heads and 63 sectors, this results in a capacity of $4096 \times 16 \times 63 \times 512 = 2\ 113\ 929\ 216$ bytes = 2016 Mbyte, hence this is known as the *2 Gbyte problem*. Three problem scenarios have been noted[56]: the BIOS can only see a maximum of 2015.5 Mbyte and truncates the remaining space; the BIOS loses all cylinder bits above 12 and may lose 2016 Mbyte of space or more; the BIOS completely locks up at boot time. A comprehensive solution to this problem is again to use a dynamic drive overlay (DDO). However, if the BIOS locks up at boot time, it will be necessary to configure the drive (incorrectly) as 1023 cylinders, 16 heads and 63 sectors in CMOS Setup. In this way the BIOS does not see the problem and does not lock up. The DDO, when activated, fetches the true CHS parameters from the drive itself and carries out the appropriate translation. One difficulty that may have to be overcome is getting into CMOS Setup. The option to enter Setup comes after the BIOS has detected all the hard drives, and as the lock up will occur when the drive is detected, Setup is not accessible. The way round this problem is to disconnect the offending drive from its cable, then boot and enter Setup to put in the artificial safe parameters. When the drive is reconnected it should then be possible to boot and to establish the DDO.

4 Gbyte Problem

We also need to note that a problem arises with disks that have a cylinders value at the IDE/ATA interface that is greater than 8191. For a drive that has 8192 cylinders, 16 heads and 63 sectors, this results in a capacity of $8192 \times 16 \times 63 \times 512 = 4\ 227\ 858\ 432$ bytes = 4032 Mbyte, hence this is known as the *4 Gbyte problem*. In accordance with the bit shifting method, this requires IDE/ATA interface cylinders to be divided by 16 in order for the translated cylinders value to be in the INT 13h BIOS interface range. However, this then results in a translated heads value of $16 \times 16 = 256$ and it is this translated heads value which causes the problem. The problem, in this case, is not due to a bug in the translating BIOS, but rather it seems that both MS-DOS up to version 6.22 and Windows 95 are unable to deal with translated head values of 256. It may be that this is due to allocating only 8 bits for the heads register and a value of 256 causes a wraparound of the heads register to 0. Although this is an operating system problem, BIOS manufacturers decided to deal with it by modifications to the translating BIOS[57]. These need to be applied both to the bit shifting or ECHS translation method and to the assisted LBA method.

---

56 See *Large Disk Integration* (Western Digital, 1998a).

57 See *Issues with Hard Drives Over 4 GB* (Micro Firmware, 1998).

The *revised ECHS translation method* makes the following adjustment. If, at the IDE/ATA interface, the number of cylinders is greater than 8191 and the number of heads is 16, then the cylinders value is multiplied by 16/15 and the heads value is set to 15 before the standard bit shifting algorithm is applied.

As an example, the Maxtor CrystalMax 1080, model number 84320A8[58] shows 8400 cylinders, 16 heads and 63 sectors per track as the geometry at the IDE/ATA interface. This gives us $8400 \times 16 \times 63 \times 512 = 4\,335\,206\,400$ bytes capacity. Using the standard bit shifting or ECHS translation method this results in 8400/16 = 525 cylinders and $16 \times 16 = 256$ heads, causing the problem that we referred to above. The revised ECHS translation, however, first gives us $8400 \times 16/15 = 8960$ cylinders and 15 heads, and then this in turn is translated to 8960/16 = 560 cylinders and $15 \times 16 = 240$ heads. The resulting capacity is the same as before (this is not always the case), that is: $560 \times 240 \times 63 \times 512 = 4\,335\,206\,400$ bytes.

In the case of the LBA assisted method, the necessary adjustment has already been built into Table 5.12. We noted in passing at the time that for the 4032 to 8032.5 Mbyte capacity the heads value and the relevant cylinders divisor are both 255 rather than the expected 256. This is, in fact, an implementation of the *revised assisted LBA method*.

We can now calculate the translated CHS addresses using the revised LBA mode in the following manner. We note that the total byte capacity is $8400 \times 16 \times 63 \times 512 = 4\,335\,206\,400$ bytes and divided by 1024×1024 this gives us 4134.375 Mbyte. We therefore must use the 4032 to 8032.5 Mbyte entry in the table giving us a cylinders value of $4\,335\,206\,400/(63 \times 255 \times 512) = 527$ when rounded down. The heads figure is 255 and the sectors figure is 63, giving us a total capacity of $527 \times 255 \times 63 \times 512 = 4\,334\,722\,560$. Note that this is not the same value as that obtained using the revised ECHS method. Once again, the two translations are not compatible with one another.

Other BIOS-Related Problems

It has been found[59] that some BIOSes do not properly handle a cylinders value that is in excess of 6322. For a drive that has 6322 cylinders, 16 heads and 63 sectors, this results in a capacity of $6322 \times 16 \times 63 \times 512 = 3\,262\,758\,912$ bytes = 3262 Mbyte (powers of ten), hence this is sometimes known as the *3.27 Gbyte problem*. It generally shows up when the cylinders value in CMOS Setup has been set larger than 6322. As for the 2 Gbyte problem, the computer locks up at boot time and the solution options are very similar. Either set the CMOS Setup values to 1023 cylinders, 16 heads and 63 sectors and use a DDO or obtain an upgrade for the BIOS.

Another problem reported[60] is that of the 240 head limitation. Many BIOSes are only able to report a maximum of 240 heads in the INT 13h function 8 call[61]. This

---

58 See *Maxtor's CrystalMax 1080 Model Number 84320A8* (Maxtor, 1996).

59 See *FAQ Disk Manager Basics, BIOS Limitations* (Seagate, 1998).

60 See *8.4 Gbyte Capacity Barrier* (Western Digital, 1998b).

61 This call is the "Get Drive Parameters" function call which the BIOS uses to build the disk parameter tables.

results in a maximum recognized capacity of 1024 cylinders × 240 heads × 63 sectors × 512 bytes = 7 927 234 560 bytes = 7927 Mbyte (powers of ten) and this is sometimes called the *7.9 Gbyte problem*.

Overcoming the 8 Gbyte Barrier

At the time of writing, disks larger than 8 Gbyte are becoming commonplace on higher end PCs. Referring back to Table 5.11, we can readily see that it is the cylinders, heads and sectors per track maximum sizes of the standard INT 13h BIOS that impose this 8.4 Gbyte limit upon us.

This first has an impact when the drive is being detected and an INT 13h BIOS Function 8, "Get Drive Parameters", is invoked. This will execute code that causes an "Identify Device" command to be issued to the IDE ATA interface. Without going into too much detail, the drive will respond with cylinder, head and sector information in words 1, 3 and 6 of the data structure it returns. Each of these words can contain up to the value 65 535, so this is not restricting us. However, the INT 13h BIOS registers can only hold, and hence identify, maximum values for cylinders up to 1024, heads up to 256 and sectors up to 63. A drive larger than 8.4 Gbyte cannot therefore be identified as such by the standard INT 13h BIOS functions, even with translation.

This is where the *Enhanced BIOS* comes in. As is the case with so much in this field, lax use of terminology leads to so much possible confusion. The terms "enhancements" and "extensions" have been used by various sources to apply to those modifications that were made to the traditional (sometimes now called the *legacy*) INT 13h BIOS functions. These are the code modifications that enable CHS translation to take place, by, for example, using the bit shifting or assisted LBA methods that we discussed earlier. Unfortunately, the same terminology tends to be applied by the same sources to something that is quite different: the *INT 13h Extensions*.

The legacy INT 13h functions range from 00h to 1Ah; the extensions specify completely new INT 13h functions which range in value from 41h to 48h. That is not all that is different. The register conventions have been changed to permit the passing of data structures and all addressing information is now passed via such structures rather than having to be limited by the size of some register. The size of the field in the data structure used for the starting LBA address is four bytes, enabling disks as large as 2^{64} sectors to be connected. This, of course, far exceeds the capacity of the IDE/ATA interface itself, which can only deal, as we have seen in Table 5.11, with 2^{28} sectors. Nevertheless, this capability moves the barrier from 8.4 Gbyte to 127.5 Gbyte.

The INT 13h extensions Function 48h, "Get Drive Parameters", obtains its information about the drive from words 60 and 61 in the data structure that the IDE/ATA "Identify Device" command returns. This double word value holds the drive's maximum LBA address, and thus its full capacity can be recognized.

The extended BIOS still has the legacy INT 13h functions, so, for disks smaller than 8.4 Gbyte, it can operate as we have described earlier. For disks greater than 8.4 Gbyte, however, the operating system and the using software must be able to make use of the INT 13h BIOS Extensions and address the disk in LBA mode.

The *Microsoft/IBM INT 13h Extensions* document describes the original *de facto* standard, and a superset of this is the *BIOS Enhanced Disk Drive Specification* (Phoenix, 1995, 1998). Most BIOS manufacturers use this *Phoenix Enhanced BIOS* specification, though a competing and incompatible version, the *Western Digital Enhanced IDE Implementation Guide,* was also published. Disks formatted using BIOS extensions based on the Western Digital specification may be unreadable on other BIOSes, the majority of which use the Phoenix specification. We have mentioned this Phoenix specification before in footnotes when we discussed the background to the legacy problem and the CHS translation options.

From all that has been said before, another obvious possibility for overcoming the 8.4 Gbyte problem is a dynamic drive overlay (DDO) such as EZ-Drive or Disk Manager which simulates these INT 13h BIOS extensions; but note that we must still have an operating system and software that is able to make use of them and can address the disk in LBA mode.

Summary of BIOS Interface Issues

Figure 5.19 shows a summary of the major interfacing issues that arise between the BIOS and IDE/ATA drives.

Communication between the applications software and the BIOS is by means of the legacy INT 13h BIOS interface. This expects CHS addressing (sometimes known as Logical CHS) and has cylinder, head and sector per track maximum sizes of 1024, 256 and 63 respectively. This gives us the 8.4 Gbyte limit as well as the 1024 cylinder problem. If we are to exceed the 8.4 Gbyte limit, the applications software must use the INT 13h extensions (functions in the range 41h to 48h) and LBA.

With an old BIOS no CHS translation is carried out and LBA is not possible. We therefore have the 1024 cylinder problem and the 528 Mbyte limit, unless we use a dynamic drive overlay. The 528 Mbyte limit stems from having to use the minimum set of the two interface geometries: Logical CHS being 1024, 256 and 63 and Physical CHS being 65536, 16, 255 giving a minimum set of 1024, 16, 63 from which the 528

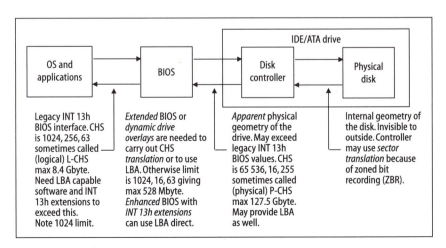

Fig. 5.19 Summary of BIOS interface issues.

Mbyte value results. With a more recent translating or extended BIOS the limitations of Logical CHS and Physical CHS geometries taken together no longer need apply since the BIOS can trade excessive cylinder size for spare head capacity[62]. If the drive supports LBA, similar translations can be performed by the BIOS between the legacy Logical CHS interface and LBA. A very modern BIOS will provide the INT 13h extensions and these entail the direct use of LBA. The BIOS will pass LBA addresses direct to the drive, provided that the drive is also able to use LBA. If the drive is not LBA capable, the BIOS will have to translate the LBA addresses into Physical CHS addresses before passing them to the drive.

Communication between the drive and the BIOS is across the IDE/ATA interface. This may use CHS addressing (sometimes known as Physical CHS) and has cylinder, head and sector per track maximum sizes of 65536, 16 and 255 respectively. This gives a theoretical maximum of 127.5 Gbyte. LBA may be used directly if the drive supports this.

Finally, for completeness, we have shown the internal interface between the controller and the disk itself. This may perform sector translation, particularly where zoned bit recording is in use. The Physical CHS addresses specified at the IDE/ATA interface are not, in such cases, an accurate representation of the physical structures inside the drive.

Summary of BIOS Translation Options

Figure 5.20 shows a summary of the translation options that may be carried out by the three different classes[63] of BIOS. The old BIOS class can only provide a straight through capability of Logical CHS to Physical CHS. No translation or LBA is possible.

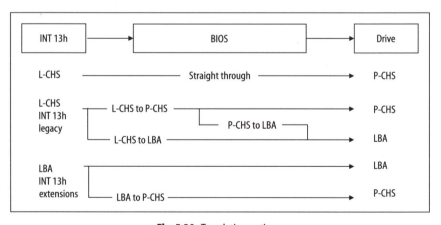

Fig. 5.20 Translation options.

---

62 This form of translation is often marked as *Large* in CMOS setup. Note that the geometry entered in setup should be the Physical CHS and not the Logical CHS. If we set *Auto-detect* the Physical CHS geometry is obtained by the BIOS querying the controller and using the returned results for its translation algorithm.

63 For a more detailed treatment of BIOS types see Landis (1995a).

The translating or extended BIOS class can perform translations from Logical CHS to Physical CHS, from Physical CHS to LBA and from Logical CHS to LBA. The enhanced BIOS or INT 13h extensions BIOS class can perform LBA direct and translation from LBA to Physical CHS. Each higher level class can, in addition, perform all the functions of the classes below it.

From a forensic computing viewpoint, we need to recall that there are a variety of possible translation algorithms and not all BIOS implementations are the same. We also need to be aware that there are at least two different and incompatible implementations of the INT 13h extensions: that of Phoenix (1995, 1998) and most other BIOS manufacturers, and that of Western Digital (1997a, undated b). The problem for the forensic computing analyst arises when there is a need to host a hard disk in a system other than the original machine. We need to be very sure that the Physical CHS or LBA addresses calculated by our host BIOS are exactly those that would have been calculated by the original BIOS given the same Logical CHS addresses, and vice versa.

We should also be aware that some protected mode operating systems that do not use INT 13h directly have their own drivers and these will have to make assumptions about the translation that has been used in formatting and writing to the disk. Using such software when a drive has been rehosted needs to be done with much caution.

The POST/Boot Sequence

Before we start this section we need to remind ourselves of addressing in real mode and the layout of the PC memory and its use. We will then look in turn at the *start of boot* sequence, the *Power On Self Test* (POST) processes, the BIOS, the CMOS and the bootstrap loader.

Addressing in Real Mode

Internally, the Intel 8086 and 8088 microprocessor chips on which the PC was first based have 16 bit registers and hence the maximum number that they can contain is $2^{16} - 1$ which is 65535 in decimal or FFFFh in hexadecimal. If a single register were to be used for memory addressing, the maximum size of memory that could be accessed would thus be 64 kbyte. However, the Intel 8086 and 8088 chips actually have 20 address lines in their external address bus and so are capable of accessing addresses up to $2^{20} - 1$, which is 1 048 575 in decimal or FFFFFh in hexadecimal. This permits the maximum size of memory to be 1 Mbyte.

In order to provide the external 20 bit address, two 16 bit registers are used together, as shown in Fig. 5.21. One 16 bit register is known as the *segment register* and the other as the *offset register*. The segment register value is multiplied by 16 (the equivalent of a shift left by 4 binary places) before being added to the offset register value to give a 20 bit external address value as shown.

In the example we see a segment register holding the value 2308h being shifted left by 4 places and then being added to an offset register holding the value 4B75h. The result forms the external 20 bit address of 27BF5h. Also shown in the figure is the

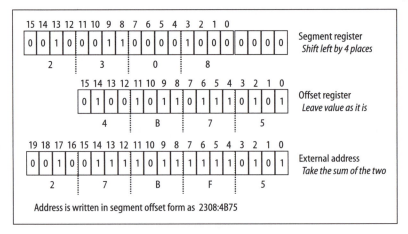

Fig. 5.21 Addressing in real mode.

standard way in which the segment and offset addresses are written. In this case we see 2308:4B75 as the segment:offset values, with no "h" being necessary since hexadecimal is always implied. This form of segment:offset addressing means that any given external address may be specified in a variety of ways. For example, the external address 130 decimal or 82 hexadecimal could be expressed as any of the following:

$$0000{:}0082 = 0 + 130$$
$$0001{:}0072 = 16 + 114$$
$$0002{:}0062 = 32 + 98$$
$$\dots$$
$$0008{:}0002 = 128 + 2$$

In practice, PC programmers tend to use blocks of code and data which reside within 64 kbyte memory segments[64]. The Intel 8086 and 8088 microprocessor chips have both data segment (DS) and code segment (CS) registers, among a number of others. It is common practice when programming to set the DS and CS registers to the start of the main data segment and the start of the main code segment memory addresses respectively. That way, any references to code or data in the current code or data segments may be made by means of 16 bit offset values, sometimes called *near pointers*. Only when it is required to refer to code or data in some other segment is it necessary to specify both the 16 bit segment and the 16 bit offset values of the address giving rise to what is sometimes known as a *far pointer*. What then has to happen is that the appropriate segment register, either DS or CS, depending upon whether we are dealing with data or code, has to be loaded with the 16 bit far pointer segment value before the 16 bit far pointer offset value can be used and the external address

---

64 The *memory model* determines the number of code and data segments that are made available to the program. The *small* model has one 64 kbyte data segment and one 64 kbyte code segment. The *large* model has multiple 64 kbyte data segments and multiple 64 kbyte code segments. A number of other such models are possible.

calculated. We can now see that the 4 byte entries in the interrupt vector table are in effect far pointers which allow any place in the 1 Mbyte memory to be accessed.

Memory Layout

The original Intel 8086 and 8088 microprocessors had only the one mode of operation, and within this was implemented the segment:offset addressing architecture that we have discussed above. It is this architecture that is used by MS-DOS, dating from the days of the original PC. In order to maintain backward compatibility with the MS-DOS operating system, all subsequent Intel microprocessor chips in the PC range have included an operating mode that provides this segment:offset addressing mechanism. It is known as *real mode*, and within it we can only address up to 1 Mbyte of memory because of the internal segment:offset design and the 20 bit external address lines of the original chips. The Intel 80286 and i386SX microprocessors have in fact 24 bit external address lines and can thus address up to $2^{24} - 1 = 16\ 777\ 215$ or 16 Mbyte of memory and the Intel i386DX, i486 and early Pentium microprocessors have 32 bit external address lines and can thus address up to $2^{32} - 1 = 4\ 294\ 967\ 295$ or 4 Gbyte of memory. These greatly enhanced capabilities only work however when the micro-processor is switched to a different operating mode, called *protected mode*[65], within which a quite different form of addressing architecture is employed. The memory above the 1 Mbyte real mode limit is known as *extended memory*.

In order to discuss the various memory issues, an expanded version of Fig. 5.12 is shown in Fig. 5.22. Here we see the 1 Mbyte memory area that is addressable in real mode. In fact it extends above the 1 Mbyte point because of a design fault that was made into a feature. The segment:offset addressing scheme clearly permits at the top of the memory the following segment:offset values[66]:

FFFF:000F = FFFFFh = 1 048 575 = 1 Mbyte – 1

FFFF:0010 = 100000h = 1 048 576 = 1 Mbyte exactly

FFFF:0011 = 100001h = 1 048 577 = 1 Mbyte + 1

...

FFFF:FFFF = 10FFEFh = 1 114 095 which is all but 16 bytes
of the next 64 kbyte block above.

In the original PC there were only 20 address lines (A0 to A19), so programs which tried to address 100000h or above using the permitted segment:offset values of FFFF:0010 up to FFFF:FFFF caused a *wraparound* such that the leading 1 bit (address line A20) was ignored and the external memory addresses of 0 up to FFEFh were accessed instead. This design fault was turned into a useful feature when the Intel 386 microprocessor came along and memory above 1 Mbyte could be addressed in protected mode. In this case, address lines A20 and above are implemented of course

---

65 There is a third mode known as *virtual 8086* mode which we will not consider any further here.

66 Note that FFFF:000F is the same external address as F000:FFFF.

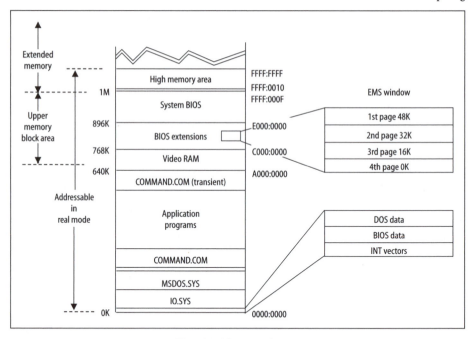

Fig. 5.22 PC memory layout.

for protected mode addressing and it was decided to utilize address line A20 in real mode as well. A switch was provided to activate address line A20 and with that active, instead of wraparound occurring, all but 16 bytes of the 64 kbyte segment above 1 Mbyte became addressable in real mode. This became known as the *high memory area*. The A20 switch has to be controlled carefully because some early versions of MS-DOS rely on the wraparound feature being present. Control of the switch is invested in the software driver HIMEM.SYS, which not only gives real mode access to the high memory area but also enables access to the rest of the extended memory[67]. It does this by switching the processor into protected mode in order to access data in extended memory and then back again into real mode in order to permit MS-DOS to function properly. It often does this in conjunction with another software driver, EMM386.SYS. This driver takes the extended memory provided by HIMEM.SYS and uses it to emulate *expanded memory* or to provide *Upper Memory Blocks* (UMBs) or both[68].

Expanded memory was a concept jointly developed by Lotus, Intel and Microsoft to provide access on the original PC to a much larger memory area than was possible using the 20 bit external address lines directly. The concept (see Fig. 5.22) entails allocating a spare 64 kbyte slot in the upper memory area where the adaptor card and BIOS extension ROMs are usually fitted. This slot is then viewed as an EMS window

---

67 See the XMS 3.0 specification available from http://www.skylab.org/~sabre/os/S4MemManagement/ as XMS30.TXT.

68 See the Lotus Intel Microsoft (LIM 4) Expanded Memory System (EMS) Specification available from http://www.skylab.org/~sabre/os/S4MemManagement/ as LIMEMS41.TXT.

which contains four 16 kbyte pages. The pages can be physically mapped onto four 16 kbyte areas of memory on a card populated with up to 8 Mbyte of memory. The four pages can each be switched to access *any* 16 kbyte memory area on the card, and thus programs can have real mode access to a maximum of 8 Mbyte of memory, albeit only 64 kbyte at a time.

As mentioned above, the driver EMM386.SYS provides an emulation of the EMS card facility. Very few systems these days have separate EMS memory cards. Instead, EMM386.SYS takes the high memory made available by HIMEM.SYS and uses that as though it was being accessed from an EMS memory card. This therefore gives us one means of providing real mode access to extended memory blocks. There are a number of other proprietary *memory managers* that operate in a similar fashion.

The expanded memory provided by EMM386.SYS is used in a number of ways to reduce the loading of the very limited 640 kbyte region. Software drivers may be loaded in emulated expanded memory by means of the DEVICEHIGH command in CONFIG.SYS and terminate and stay resident programs may similarly be loaded in emulated expanded memory by means of the LOADHIGH command in AUTOEXEC.BAT. In addition, BIOS code can be copied into emulated expanded memory and the addressing and interrupt vectors adjusted accordingly. The advantage of this is that execution of code in, for example, 64 bit extended memory DRAM tends to be faster than execution of the same code in 8 bit BIOS ROM[69]. Extended memory used in this way is often called *Shadow RAM*. Finally, using HIMEM.SYS, parts of MS-DOS can be loaded directly into the high memory area by means of the DOS=HIGH command.

The Start of the Bootstrap Sequence

Figure 5.23 shows the start of the bootstrap sequence in three separate sections. The BIOS code begins in ROM at F000:FFF0, which is the same external address as FFFF:0000, just 16 bytes from the top of the 1 Mbyte real mode memory. This is shown in the upper section of Fig. 5.23.

The microprocessor, immediately after switch on, is set by hardware to start its execution of code from this location. It is the commencement of the *cold boot*. The instruction sequence EA 5B E0 00 F0 decodes as a far jump (EA) to a full segment:offset address which follows in the next four bytes. However, we need to recall that Intel implements little endian storage, which means that the two bytes 5B E0 must be switched to become the 16 bit value E05B and the two bytes 00 F0 become F000. In addition we need to note that the offset address is the first pair and the segment address is the second pair. Hence the jump is to F000:E05B. The remaining 10 bytes to the top of memory hold data concerning the date of the BIOS and the model of PC for which it is designed.

The middle section of Fig. 5.23 shows the code at F000:E05B, the location to which the first section causes the microprocessor to jump. The code starts B bytes into the F000:E050 line with the sequence E9 12 70. This decodes as a near *relative* jump, meaning that the segment address value is the current segment and the offset address value is taken to be relative to the current address value. We have to

---

69 See page 12 of *SE440BX Motherboard Product Guide* (Intel, 1998a).

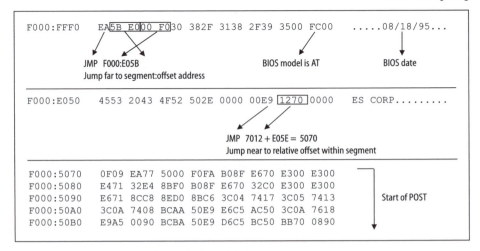

Fig. 5.23 Start of the bootstrap sequence.

note first the little endian reversal of the two address bytes to become 7012 and then
that the address of the *next* instruction is E05E, which is the relative value that has to
be added to the 7012. This gives E05E + 7012 = 5070 using 16 bit arithmetic. The
result therefore is an instruction to jump to the current segment (F000) with offset
address 5070.

The bottom section of Fig. 5.23 shows some of the code that starts at this address. It
is in fact the start of the Power on Self Test, or POST, sequence and we will be looking
at some of the processes carried out by this code in the next section.

Before we leave Fig. 5.23, however, it is useful to note that in some systems the EA
5B bytes at the beginning of the cold boot sequence are replaced by code bytes CD
19 after the cold boot has completed. These translate to INT 19h which is the *warm
boot* BIOS interrupt which gets activated by the CTRL-ALT-DEL keyboard sequence
on most systems. In case you might be wondering how code in ROM gets changed,
the answer is of course, that it does not. This change can only be made if the BIOS
code has been placed in shadow RAM, in which case it is the shadow RAM version
that gets changed and not the ROM itself.

Typical Actions by POST

The POST sequence software, held in the ROM BIOS, initializes as necessary and
then carries out diagnostic tests on each of the various hardware components of the
system. Before entering each step in the sequence, the BIOS writes a one byte identifying code, usually to I/O port 80h, which signals a successful completion of the
previous step. This code is commonly referred to as a *POST code*.

By means of a special *POST code reader* the last valid code sent to the port can be
observed. Such a reader may simply consist of an ISA plug-in card with a seven-
segment display to show the POST code value. In the event of a hardware failure,
often signalled by some kind of system lockup, the value on this display can give a
good indication of the device that has failed by taking note of the last action that was

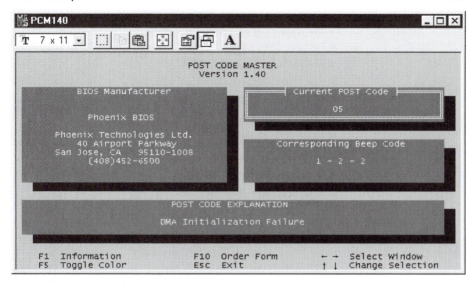

Fig. 5.24 POST code monitor and database.

successful. BIOS and motherboard specifications often include a table of port 80h POST codes[70] and specialist software can be obtained that operates in conjunction with a POST reader to identify POST code values for a range of current BIOSes. An example screenshot from a typical program[71] of this type is shown in Fig. 5.24.

The reason for needing POST codes is not difficult to see. Because much of the POST diagnostic testing is taking place before the display system has been activated, error messages cannot be written to the screen as they would be when the display becomes active. It is for this reason also that the system speaker is used to generate so-called *beep codes*. As well as writing a POST code to port 80h, the BIOS may, when there is an error, send a specific sequence of beeps to the system speaker. Some beep codes are simply a number of same length beeps, some are a combination of low and high tones, some are a series of long and short beeps and some are a series of beeps and pauses. These latter are usually shown as 1-2-2-3, which is read as: 1 beep, pause, 2 beeps, pause, 2 beeps, pause, 3 beeps. The meanings of each of these beep sequences should be listed[72] in BIOS and motherboard specifications together with any BIOS text error messages which can be written after the display becomes active.

One point of significance for the forensic computing analyst is that a successful completion of all the POST diagnostic tests normally results in a single short beep being sent to the speaker just prior to the loading of the operating system. Making a note, on hearing this short beep, can provide some useful formal assurance that the computer concerned was operating correctly at the time that it was being used, in that it had signalled a successful passing of all of its POST diagnostic tests.

---

70 The codes seem to be unique to the particular BIOS. See, for example, Appendix 3 and Intel (1998a, p. 75).

71 See for example, *Post Code Master Version 1.40* (MicroSystems, undated).

72 See Appendix 4 and Intel (1998b, p. 57).

Table 5.13 Typical actions by POST – part I.

- Perform function check of CPU
- Test BIOS ROM checksum
- Test CMOS RAM checksum
- Test/initialize DMA controller
- Test/initialize keyboard controller
- Check first 64 kbyte RAM
- Test/initialize interrupt controller
- Test/initialize cache controller
- Test/initialize video controller

First, the POST tests individual functions of the processor, its registers and some instructions (see Table 5.13). If the processor passes these tests, a checksum is then computed for each of the ROMs that form the BIOS and these computed values are compared with those stored within the ROMs to give some assurance that the BIOS code has not become corrupted. A similar check is made of the CMOS RAM which we will consider further in a moment. Each chip on the main board is then tested and initialized as necessary. These include the DMA controller, the keyboard controller, the first 64 kbyte of RAM, the interrupt controller, the cache controller and the video controller. Of course, once the video controller is tested and initialized, any POST error messages can now be sent to the display screen.

After the main board has been tested, the POST tests the other peripherals such as the serial and parallel interfaces and the remaining RAM above 64 kbyte (see Table 5.14). It then tests and initializes the floppy disk and hard drive controllers before setting up the BIOS variables. The BIOS data area, as we have already seen in Fig. 5.22, is located at the very beginning of the real mode memory. It is 256 bytes long starting at address 0040:000 and it is sometimes called the *BIOS variable range* or the *BIOS variable segment*[73]. The values in this segment can be examined and interpreted using specialist software such as BIOSR.COM (Postuma, 1995).

Table 5.14 Typical actions by POST – part II.

- Test/initialize serial and parallel interfaces
- Check RAM above 64 kbyte
- Test/initialize floppy disk and hard drive controllers
- Set up BIOS variables
- Set up the interrupt vector table
- Search for BIOS extensions
- System and video BIOS may be transferred to shadow RAM
- Initiate bootstrap loader

---

73 See, for example, Tischer and Jennrich (1996, pp. 67 *et seq.*).

Table 5.15 CMOS RAM.

- Complementary Metal Oxide Semiconductor
  - 64 bytes of battery-backed RAM
  - Contains BIOS user-adjustable configuration details
  - Replaces multitude of DIP switches
- SETUP
  - Used to alter the CMOS settings
  - Entered during boot via F1 key, for example
- Typical settings
  - Date and time
  - Hard drive types and geometry
  - Memory configuration
  - Power management
  - Password protection

The CMOS RAM

The POST routines obtain some of the information required to establish the BIOS variables from the CMOS RAM (see Table 5.15).

The original PC-AT had 64 bytes of CMOS battery-backed RAM that was part of the Motorola MC 146818 real-time clock chip. More recent systems[74] contain 256 bytes of CMOS battery-backed RAM in the real-time clock chip which is all reserved for use by the BIOS. The CMOS RAM is not included in the real mode memory address space but is accessed via the port addresses[75], 70h and 71h, of the real-time clock. As we saw earlier, disk drive parameters as well as many other motherboard configuration details are held in the CMOS RAM which replaced the multitude of on-board DIP (Dual Inline Package) switches which were to be found on the old PC-XT.

Because of the importance of this configuration information and, in particular, because the hard disk may not boot if the disk geometry parameters in the CMOS RAM become corrupted[76], it is a good idea to save the details on to a separate floppy disk. A good example of software specially written for the purpose of saving and restoring the CMOS RAM details is the program CMOSRAM2 . EXE (Mosteller, 1995).

To allow the user to alter the CMOS settings, the BIOS gives access to a program called SETUP during the boot sequence. SETUP is normally entered by pressing a special key combination such as DEL or ESC or CTRL-ESC or CRTL-ALT-ESC or F1 or F2, to name but a few examples, just after the POST diagnostic sequence has completed. On the other hand, some BIOSes permit SETUP to be entered at any time by pressing, for example, CTRL-ALT-ESC.

Typically the CMOS RAM will contain information such as the date and time settings, the hard drive types and disk geometry parameters, the memory configuration including any EMS and shadow memory, any power management or password

---

74 See, for example, Intel (1998a, p. 18).

75 70h is used to specify the CMOS address with an OUT instruction and 71h is used to read or write data to that address using an IN or OUT instruction respectively.

76 Which, of course, will inevitably happen when the backup battery dies.

protection settings, as well as the checksum, referred to above, which is used by the POST routines to confirm that none of this data has become corrupted.

Continuing with POST

After setting up the BIOS variables, the interrupt vector table is built (see Table 5.14). We discussed interrupts earlier and saw that they force the processor temporarily to halt the program currently being executed, saving enough information to permit a subsequent return, and then to execute some interrupt handler program associated with the interrupt number. We also saw that an interrupt may be caused either by an external hardware event or by an internal software code.

In fact, all calls to the BIOS and the MSDOS functions are made via internal software code interrupts. The Intel 8088 microprocessor design has some 256 interrupt vectors in its interrupt vector table and each entry in the table, as we have seen, consists of 4 bytes: the 16 bit offset address and the 16 bit segment address of the start of the program code for that particular interrupt. The table is located from address 0000:0000 to address 0000:03FF and it is this table that is built at this time.

Because the vector table is held in RAM and is rebuilt each time we go through the POST/boot sequence, interrupt vectors can easily be overwritten if new facilities need to be added. This is typically what happens at POST/boot time when extension cards have been added which themselves contain either replacement or updated BIOS functions in their own on-board ROM chips.

Part of the POST/boot sequence includes the search for BIOS extensions, as shown in the flowchart of Fig. 5.25, which is the next step in the process. These, you will recall, are in the memory area C000:0000 to F400:0000, so the search is carried out across this area by looking for the two identifier bytes 55AAh which always start a BIOS extension[77]. If a BIOS extension is found, the initialization function for that extension is called at this time. This will often add or alter a vector in the interrupt vector table, thus enabling subsequent execution of code in this BIOS extension in preference to the code of the standard BIOS function.

Once the search for BIOS extensions is complete, the POST/boot sequence may then transfer BIOS program code into shadow RAM to improve performance before, finally, initiating the *bootstrap loader.*

Initiating the Bootstrap Loader

All bootable floppies have a *boot sector* placed by high-level formatting at the standard fixed position of cylinder 0, head 0, sector 1, on the floppy disk. Similarly, all hard disks have a *master boot record* placed at the same position of cylinder 0, head 0, sector 1 on the hard disk. In this way, both DOS and the BIOS can access floppy and hard disk bootstrap information without knowing which form of data carrier is being used. At the end of POST, the BIOS code reads the sector at cylinder 0, head 0,

---

77 Following the two byte 55AAh identifier is a 1 byte size of ROM field in units of 512 bytes and after this is a two byte relative address field of the start of the initialization function.

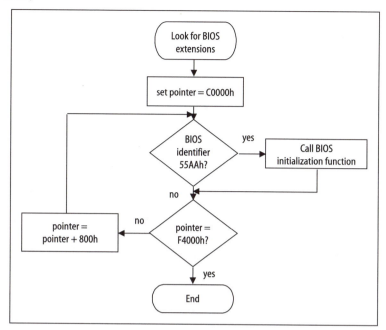

Table 5.25 Search for BIOS extensions.

sector 1 by means of INT 19h[78]. It tries first the floppy drive, and, if a floppy disk is present it reads from that. If a floppy disk is not present, it tries the hard disk, and reads from that[79]. In either case, it loads the 512 byte sector from the disk into memory starting at address 0000:7C00. Once the sector has been written into memory, the BIOS branches to the first byte at offset 00h of the sector in memory and starts to execute the values it finds there as program code.

If the sector has been loaded from a floppy disk, these first few bytes will cause a jump to the start address of the bootstrap loader, the code for which is held within the sector that has just been loaded. As the bootstrap loader code for an MS-DOS system executes, it checks to see whether the hidden system files IO.SYS and MSDOS.SYS[80] are present on the disk. If the loader program finds them, they too are loaded into main memory to build the MS-DOS operating system and the bootstrap loading process continues. If these files are not found, we then get the familiar "Non-System disk or disk error ..." message.

If, on the other hand, the boot is taking place from a hard disk rather than a floppy disk, the first few bytes at the beginning of the sector will cause a jump to the start address of the *partition analysis program*, the code for which will be contained within the sector that has just been loaded. This program investigates the partition

---

78 It is INT 19h that is invoked when we depress the CTRL-ALT-DEL keys for a warm boot.

79 Though note that the order in which drives are booted can often be changed in SETUP.

80 IBMBIOS.SYS and IBMDOS.SYS in the case of PC-DOS.

table, also contained within the sector that has just been loaded, and determines which (if any) is the current *active* (or *bootable*) *partition* on the hard disk. Having determined the active partition, it then reads the first sector of that partition, loading the 512 bytes of the sector into memory again starting at address 0000:7C00, and overwriting what is already there. From here, it continues as for the floppy disk case, jumping to the first byte at offset 00h of the sector in memory and starting to execute the values it finds there as program code. This will be the partition boot sector. In many ways, the hard disk partition appears to the system just like a large floppy disk. We will look at this process in some more detail when we have looked at the master boot record and the partition tables.

The Master Boot Record and Partitions

Figure 5.26 shows a hexadecimal listing of part of the master boot record (MBR) from a typical hard disk. As we have seen, the MBR is held at cylinder 0, head 0, sector 1 on the hard disk and it is, like nearly all sectors on modern hard disks, 512 (or 200h) bytes long.

In the listing we have shown two parts of the sector: the first part is from addresses 00h to 2fh and the second part is from addresses 160h to 1ffh, which is the end of the sector. As we outlined above, the POST/boot sequence causes this sector to be loaded into memory at address 0000:7C00 onwards and it then causes a jump to the first address at offset 00h executing what it finds there as code. In fact, for the example in Fig. 5.26, all the bytes up to 1bdh form the partition analysis program, which is different from the standard FDISK version because an EZ-Drive DDO has been installed on this disk. We can infer that this is the case by looking at the text bytes that start at 19ch and read: "(C)1993-95 Micro House Int'l". The standard FDISK version of the partition analysis program extends only from 00h to d9h with zeros from that point on to 1bdh. For an excellent detailed exposition of the standard partition analysis program see Landis (1997a).

Examination of the analysis program shows that it simply searches the four entries in the partition table for an active partition. If an active partition is found, it

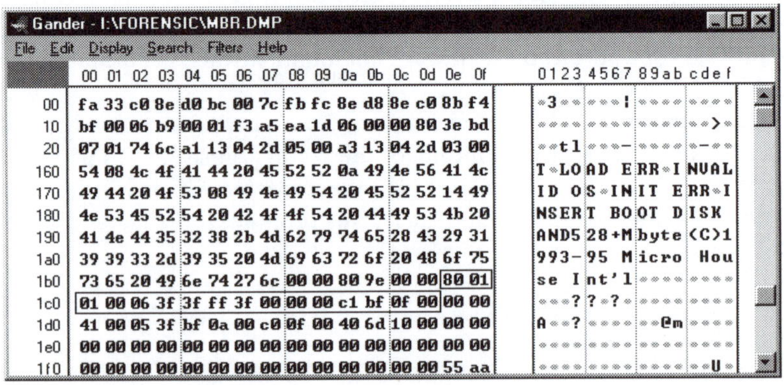

Fig. 5.26 Part of the master boot record.

continues to look at the remaining entries to make sure that there is only the one active entry otherwise it displays the message "Invalid Partition Table". If there is only the one active entry, it uses an INT 13h call to fetch the boot sector that is specified by the CHS address of that entry, and it overwrites the memory area from 0000:7C00 with this new sector. It then jumps to the first address at offset 00h of the sector keeping a pointer to the active partition table entry.

The partition table always starts at offset address 1beh in the master boot record sector. There can only be four entries in the master boot record partition table and each entry is 16 bytes long. The first entry of our example master boot record is shown outlined in Fig. 5.26. The four entries take us to offset address 1fdh in the sector and the final two bytes of the partition table are always of value 55h and aah, as shown.

Table 5.16 shows the use of each of the bytes in the partition table entry. The first byte is the *boot flag* which indicates whether or not the partition is active, the value being either 80h for active or 00h for not. It is useful to note that it is this boot flag value which is used to identify the device in the INT 13h call to fetch the boot sector of the active partition. Because the active flag is always 80h, this is one of the reasons why normally only the first hard disk, that is the device with the identifier 80h, can be used as the boot drive.

The next three bytes, starting from offset 01h, hold the CHS start address of the partition, that is, where the boot sector is. All eight bits of the first byte, offset 01h, are used to represent the heads value, giving a maximum of 255. The two most significant bits of the second byte, offset 02h, together with the 8 bits of the third byte, offset 03h, form the 10 bit value for cylinders, giving a maximum of 1023. Finally, the remaining 6 bits of the second byte, offset 02h, form the sectors value with a maximum of 63. What this tells us is very important. We have come up against the 528 Mbyte barrier again. If the drive is larger than 528 Mbyte, then this CHS address must be a *translated* address, that is, what we called an L-CHS rather than a P-CHS. It also means that our boot sector for the active partition may not reside beyond cylinder 1023.

The next byte, at 04h, indicates the type of partition. Although only five types are shown in Table 5.16, there are in fact many more than this, with a possible maximum

Table 5.16 Partition table entry.

Offset	Meaning	Notes
00	1 byte boot flag	80h = active (bootable) 00h = inactive (not bootable)
01–03	3 bytes start of partition	h7–h0 | c9 c8 s5–s0 | c7–c0 *max: c 1023, h 255, s 63*
04	1 byte partition type	0 = not used, 1 = DOS 12 bit FAT, 4 = DOS 16 bit FAT, 5 = Extended DOS, 6 = DOS > 32 Mbyte and many more
05–07	3 byte end of partition	h7–h0 | c9 c8 s5–s0 | c7–c0 *max: c 1023, h 255, s 63*
08–0b	4 bytes LBA address of start sector relative to start of disk (little endian)	
0c–0f	4 bytes number of sectors in the partition (little endian)	

of 256. Because of the importance of these types to the forensic computing analyst in helping to identify the use to which the partition is being put, a detailed list of all those currently known is given in Appendix 5.

At offset 05h, another three bytes are used to specify the CHS address of the last sector of the partition, in exactly the same format as that used for the start address. Naturally, the same comments apply about this having to be a translated CHS address if the disk size is greater than 528 Mbyte.

At offset 08h, four bytes are used to represent the start sector in LBA address form, that is, as a single number relative to the start of the disk, with the first sector on the disk being LBA 0. One word of caution might be appropriate here. In calculating this value it is essential to remember that it is held in little endian format. Finally, the last four bytes, commencing at offset 0ch, represent the number of sectors in the partition, again held in little endian format.

This analysis allows us now to determine the meaning of all the entries in the partition table in Fig. 5.26. At 1beh the value 80h identifies this as the active partition. The following three bytes, at 1bfh to 1c1h, describe the starting CHS address of this active partition as cylinders 0, heads 1, sectors 1, in the following way:

Address	Value	Interpretation				Result
1bfh	01h	= 00000001	= heads	= 1	H	
1c0h	01h	= 000001	= sectors	= 1	S	
		00	= cylinders			
1c1h	00h	= 00000000	= cylinders	= 0	C	

At 1c2h we note that the partition type is 06h, which is a DOS partition greater than 32 Mbyte, sometimes known as *BIGDOS*. Then the three bytes at 1c3h to 1c5h describe the CHS address of the end of the partition as cylinders 255, heads 63 and sectors 63 in the following way:

Address	Value	Interpretation				Result
1c3h	3fh	= 00111111	= heads	= 63	H	
1c4h	3fh	= 111111	= sectors	= 63	S	
		00	= cylinders			
1c5h	ffh	= 11111111	= cylinders	= 255	C	

Starting at 1c6h we have the four bytes of the LBA address as 3f 00 00 00. Recalling that this number is held in little endian format, we reorder these to be 00 00 00 3f and calculate the number as 3fh = LBA sector 63. Similarly, at 1cah we have the four bytes of the partition size as c1 bf 0f 00, and again reordering these gives us 00 0f bf c1 which is fbfc1h = 1 032 129 sectors. With a sector size of 512 bytes this results in a partition size of 1 032 129 × 512/(1024 × 1024) = 504 Mbyte.

Figure 5.27 shows the Norton Disk Editor[81] "partition table view" of the same partition table. It is particularly important to note that Norton Disk Editor uses *Side* for *Head* and lists the table in *Side Cylinder Sector* order and not in the CHS order

```
Physical Sector: Cyl 0, Side 0, Sector 1

+------+----+--------------------+--------------------+----------+-----------+
|      |    | Starting Location  |  Ending Location   | Relative | Number of |
|System|Boot|Side Cylinder Sector|Side Cylinder Sector| Sectors  | Sectors   |
+------+----+--------------------+--------------------+----------+-----------+
|BIGDOS| Yes|   1      0       1  | 63    255      63  |       63 |   1032129 |
|EXTEND| No |   0    256       1  | 63    522      63  |  1032192 |   1076544 |
|unused| No |   0      0       0  |  0      0       0  |        0 |         0 |
|unused| No |   0      0       0  |  0      0       0  |        0 |         0 |
+------+----+--------------------+--------------------+----------+-----------+
```

Fig. 5.27 Partition table entries – Norton Disk Editor partition table view.

that we (in common with most other writers) have been using throughout! Since Norton Disk Editor is an important tool, that will be used quite frequently, this is a major source of potential confusion. It is now left as an exercise to the reader (see exercises at the end of the chapter) to confirm from Fig. 5.26 the details for the second (EXTEND) entry in the partition table.

Unwritten Rules for Partition Tables

As we described in the section on formatting, the partition table is constructed by the program FDISK (or some similar utility) at the time the high-level formatting process is carried out. There do not seem to be any formal written rules laid down about how partition tables should work, although most versions of FDISK appear to conform with the set of unwritten rules[82] that are shown in Table 5.17.

Table 5.17 Unwritten rules for partition tables.

- In the master boot record there can only be up to four *primary* partition entries *or* up to three *primary* partition entries and up to one *extended* partition entry.
- In an extended partition there can be up to one *secondary* partition entry and up to one *extended* partition entry.
- Only primary partitions can be marked as "active" (that is, bootable) and only one of them can be marked as such at any one time.
- It is usual for a partition table to start at head 0, sector 1 of a cylinder and the boot record to start at head 1, sector 1 of a cylinder.
- The slots in the partition table can be used in any order and an unused slot can occur in the middle of the table.
- Some operating systems may indicate that a partition spans or starts beyond cylinder 1024 by setting the starting and ending CHS values all to ffh.

---

81 See Norton Utilities, Disk Editor, Symantec (1999).

82 See *How it Works – Partition Tables* (Landis, 1997b).

As we have seen, up to four 16 byte partition entries can be held in the master boot record partition table from 1beh to 1fdh. Each of these four entries may refer to a *primary* partition, that is, a partition that can contain a bootstrap loader in the first sector[83] together with associated operating system code elsewhere in the partition. There will normally be a file system, appropriate to the particular operating system, also set up in the partition. Any primary partition entry can be flagged as "active" or "bootable", but only one such partition entry can be flagged at any one time. When one primary partition is flagged as active, file systems in other primary partitions are not generally accessible; thus the file system in a primary partition is accessed, for all practical purposes, only by the operating system that is booted from that partition. As we have seen, the partition analysis program in the master boot record looks for this one "active" or "bootable" partition entry and from this partition it loads the bootstrap loader which in turn loads the operating system code from that partition into the main memory. In this way, up to four[84] different operating systems may reside on the same hard disk, in different partitions, with only one of them being active at any one time. Special software[85] may be used to select from a menu of different operating systems that may be loaded at boot time, and this is usually achieved simply by installing a modified partition analysis program in the master boot record.

Extended Partitions

To overcome the limitation of having only four partitions on the disk, one of the entries in the master boot record partition table can be set instead to be an *extended* partition entry by means of the partition type values 05h or 0fh (see Appendix 5). This *first extended partition*, which takes up a primary partition slot, is essentially no more than a *container* for one or more enclosed *logical* or *secondary* partitions. The first sector of the first extended partition holds another partition table, with the rest of that sector usually set to zeros. This extended partition table (see Fig. 5.28) starts at

	00	01	02	03	04	05	06	07	08	09	0a	0b	0c	0d	0e	0f	0 1 2 3 4 5 6 7 8 9 a b c d e f
1a0	00	00	00	00	00	00	00	00	00	00	00	00	00	00	00	00	
1b0	00	00	00	00	00	00	00	00	00	00	00	00	00	00	00	01	
1c0	41	00	06	3f	7f	7c	3f	00	00	00	81	b0	07	00	00	00	A ··? ·!?· ···· ····
1d0	41	7d	05	3f	7f	f9	c0	b0	07	00	c0	b0	07	00	00	00	A}·? ···· ···· ····
1e0	00	00	00	00	00	00	00	00	00	00	00	00	00	00	00	00	···· ···· ···· ····
1f0	00	00	00	00	00	00	00	00	00	00	00	00	00	00	55	aa	···· ···· ···· ·U·

Fig. 5.28 Extended partition table.

---

83 This is the *boot sector*, sometimes also called the *boot record*.

84 However, some operating systems can be booted from an extended partition so it is possible to have more than four.

85 See, for example, *BootMagic* (PowerQuest, 1998).

the same offset address within the sector as the master boot record partition table, that is, at 1beh, and although it is four 16 byte partition entries in length, terminated as before by 55h aah, it is only permitted to hold a maximum of *two* partition entries.

The first of these entries is likely to specify a *logical* partition, sometimes referred to as a *secondary* partition, and this partition may contain a file system and, exceptionally, an operating system. If an operating system is to be used, it must be one that is capable of being booted from a logical partition (as opposed to a primary partition). Operating systems with this feature include: Windows NT, OS/2 and Linux. The second entry in the extended partition table may specify another extended partition which itself starts with an extended partition table.

Terminology is likely to get in the way again here. These inner secondary extended partitions are rather different from the outer primary extended partition, although the same partition type code is used throughout and they are all referred to simply as extended partitions. The outer or first extended partition is a container for all the logical partitions; the inner secondary extended partitions each contain just a single logical partition. This is shown diagrammatically in Fig. 5.29.

Here we see a master boot record (marked mbr) at CHS 0,0,1 with two entries in the partition table. The first entry is a primary partition starting at CHS 0,1,1 and ending at CHS 255,63,63. This would be the active partition and would contain the operating system. It would be allocated the drive letter "C:" by MS-DOS. The second entry is the first extended partition starting at CHS 256,0,1 and ending at CHS 522,63,63. This partition is never allocated a drive letter and, as can be seen from the diagram, it simply acts as a container for the three logical partitions. In the first sector (CHS 256,0,1) of the first extended partition we find the extended partition table (marked ept1) and this contains two entries. The first is a logical partition

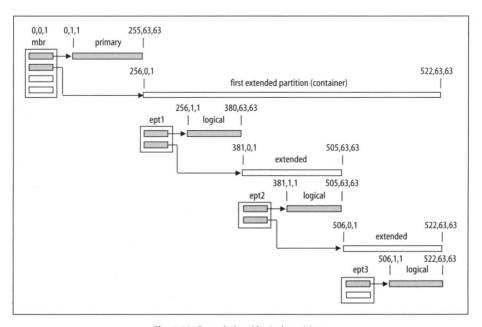

Fig. 5.29 Extended and logical partitions.

starting at CHS 256,1,1 and ending at CHS 380,63,63. If there were no other drives with a primary partition in the system, this logical partition would be allocated the logical drive letter "D:" by MS-DOS[86]. The second entry in the extended partition table at CHS 256,0,1 is a secondary extended partition. This starts at CHS 381,0,1 and ends at CHS 505,63,63. We can see from the diagram, that, unlike the first extended partition, which contains all the logical partitions, this secondary extended partition contains only one logical partition. At the beginning of the partition (CHS 381,0,1), we find another extended partition table, marked ept2 in the diagram, again with two entries. The first entry is a logical partition starting at CHS 381,1,1 and ending at CHS 505,63,63. If there were no other drives with a primary partition in the system, this logical partition would be allocated the logical drive letter "E:" by MS-DOS. The second entry in the extended partition table, ept2, at CHS 381,0,1 is another secondary extended partition. This starts at CHS 506,0,1 and ends at CHS 522,63,63. At the beginning of this partition (CHS 506,0,1), we find another extended partition table, marked ept3, this time with only one entry. This entry is a logical partition starting at CHS 506,1,1 and ending at CHS 522,63,63. If there were no other drives with a primary partition in the system, this logical partition would be allocated the logical drive letter "F:" by MS-DOS.

This explanation of how extended partitions are constructed does not entirely agree with some of the current literature on the subject. It is, however, an accurate representation of what has been found in a series of experiments carried out by the authors. For more details of these experiments, see Appendix 6.

Hidden Partitions

It is possible, using specialist software, to mark a partition as "hidden" such that the operating system will no longer access it. PartitionMagic (PowerQuest, 1996) uses a partition type of 16h to hide a primary DOS partition originally of type 06h. The benefit of doing this, apart from the obvious use to hide information, becomes clear when there are two or more hard drives in a system, each of which have extended partitions. We earlier described the way in which DOS assigns drive letters, first to all primary partitions across all drives in drive number order, and then to all extended partitions, again in drive number order. As a result, the drive letter assignment to the drive shown in Fig. 5.29 is "C:" to the primary partition at CHS 0,1,1; "D:" to the extended partition at CHS 256,1,1; "E:" to the extended partition at CHS 381,1,1; and "F:" to the extended partition at CHS 506,1,1.

Now consider the situation where there is a second drive in the system with, for example, a primary partition starting at CHS 10,1,1 and an extended partition starting at CHS 300,1,1. The drive letter assignment to this configuration would be "C:" to the primary partition at CHS 0,1,1 of the first drive, followed by "D:" to the primary partition at CHS 10,1,1 of the second drive, then "E:" to the extended partition at CHS 256,1,1 of the first drive, "F:" to the extended partition at CHS

---

86 MS-DOS allocates drive letters at boot time alphabetically from C, first to all accessible primary partitions across all drives and then to all logical partitions.

381,1,1 of the first drive; "G:" to the extended partition at CHS 506,1,1 of the first drive, and finally, "H:" to the extended partition at CHS 300,1,1 of the second drive.

What is evident from this is that the drive letter assignment to the extended partitions of the first drive will change if the second drive is removed. For the forensic computing analyst, in particular, who will probably wish to mount hard drives in removable trays, this can be a significant disadvantage. One way round this problem is to partition the second drive with a very small primary DOS partition[87] and then mark it as hidden. In this way, the primary partition of the second drive no longer gets assigned a drive letter, "D:", which is at the heart of the problem. The analyst may therefore come across hidden partitions which have been set up essentially for this purpose.

More Places to Hide

As indicated in Figure 5.29, it is normal practice for partition tables (mbr or ept) to start at head 0, sector 1 of a cylinder and the first sector of the partition proper, that is the boot record, to start at head 1, sector 1 of a cylinder. The consequence of this practice is that there will invariably be a number of unused sectors at the beginning of each partition, between the partition table sector and the boot record sector. For example, in Fig. 5.29 it can be seen that sectors CHS 0,0,2 to CHS 0,0,63, sectors CHS 256,0,2 to CHS 256,0,63, sectors CHS 381,0,2 to CHS 381,0,63 and sectors CHS 506,0,2 to CHS 506,0,63 are all unused. Clearly, information could be safely hidden in these sectors without any risk of it being detected by normal use of the file systems. As we described earlier (see section on CHS Translation Options), some of these sectors are precisely where software such as EZ-Drive places its Dynamic Drive Overlays (DDOs). They are also very good places where viruses might hide.

In addition, we may note that only the master boot record (mbr) normally contains a partition analysis program. The extended partition tables (ept1, ept2 and ept3) just contain the one or two entries of the extended partition table starting at 1beh and leaving most of the sector unused. Again, this is a good place to hide things.

The Boot Sector

We should now return to the boot sector (sometimes also referred to as a *boot record*), which we considered briefly in a previous section. We may recall that floppy disks have a boot sector placed at cylinder 0, head 0, sector 1 of the disk by the high-level formatting process. Similarly, a boot sector or boot record is placed in the first sector of a primary or a logical partition on a hard disk when that partition is formatted. As mentioned earlier, this means that each formatted hard disk partition looks to the system in many ways just like a large floppy disk.

Figure 5.30 shows a hexadecimal listing of the first few bytes of the actual boot sector at cylinder 0, head 1, sector 1 of the primary partition that is referred to in Figs. 5.27 and 5.29. It is shown in Fig. 5.27 as the entry marked "BIGDOS", meaning that it is an MS-DOS file partition that is greater than 32 Mbyte in size. Most of the boot

---

87 All drives must have at least one primary partition.

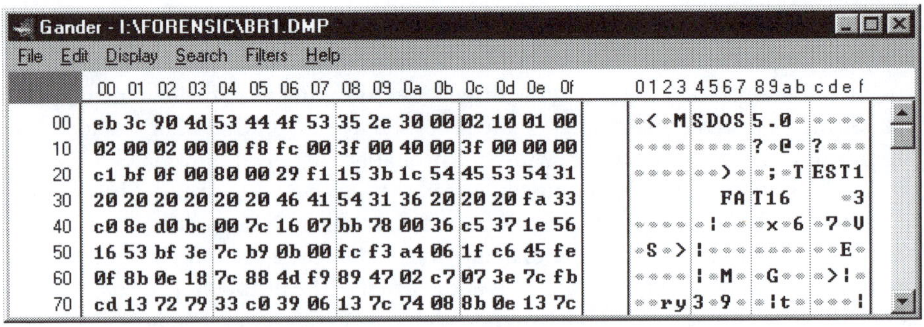

```
Gander - I:\FORENSIC\BR1.DMP                                        _ □ ×
File  Edit  Display  Search  Filters  Help

        00 01 02 03 04 05 06 07 08 09 0a 0b 0c 0d 0e 0f   0123 4567 89ab cdef

  00   eb 3c 90 4d 53 44 4f 53 35 2e 30 00 02 10 01 00   «<«M SDOS 5.0« ««««
  10   02 00 02 00 00 f8 fc 00 3f 00 40 00 3f 00 00 00   «««« «««« ?«@« ?«««
  20   c1 bf 0f 00 80 00 29 f1 15 3b 1c 54 45 53 54 31   «««« ««)« «;«T EST1
  30   20 20 20 20 20 20 46 41 54 31 36 20 20 20 fa 33        FA T16  «3
  40   c0 8e d0 bc 00 7c 16 07 bb 78 00 36 c5 37 1e 56   «««« «|«« «x«6 «7«V
  50   16 53 bf 3e 7c b9 0b 00 fc f3 a4 06 1f c6 45 fe   «S«> |««« «««« ««E«
  60   0f 8b 0e 18 7c 88 4d f9 89 47 02 c7 07 3e 7c fb   «««« |«M« «G«« «>|«
  70   cd 13 72 79 33 c0 39 06 13 7c 74 08 8b 0e 13 7c   ««ry 3«9« «|t« ««««
```

Fig. 5.30 Hexadecimal view of part of the boot sector or boot record.

sector contains the bootstrap loader program code that we referred to above, but, in addition, there is a block of data called the *BIOS parameter block* (BPB) that contains detailed information about the particular floppy disk or hard disk partition on which this boot sector resides. It should be noted, in passing, that although each operating system will follow the same rules for creating the master boot record and the partition tables, they can do whatever they like within the partition and they will almost certainly have their own boot sector format.

Recalling that this MS-DOS boot sector will have been loaded into memory starting from address $0000:7C00$, the first bytes to be executed as program code will be:

```
0000:7C00  EB3C   JMP to 7C02 + 3C
0000:7C02  90     NOP
0000:7C03  4D     BIOS parameter block
...
0000:7C3E  FA     Start of loader program
```

which represents a relative jump around the BIOS parameter block to the start of the loader program at $0000:7C3E$. The loader program then gets a copy of the disk parameter table, modifies it using information from the BIOS parameter block and then sets an interrupt vector to point to the altered disk parameter table. It then computes the sector address of the root directory, and reads the first sector into memory. It confirms that the first two entries in the root directory are the hidden system files IO.SYS and MSDOS.SYS, and if this is the case, it then reads the first three sectors of IO.SYS into memory. If this is not the case, it causes the message "Non-System disk or disk error ..." to be displayed. Finally, once the three sectors of IO.SYS have been successfully loaded into memory, the bootstrap loader transfers control to the beginning of the IO.SYS program which then proceeds to build the rest of the operating system. For an excellent detailed analysis of the floppy disk boot sector code see Landis (1995b).

The BIOS parameter block starts at $0000:7C03$ (offset 03h in the boot record) and continues to $0000:7C3D$ (offset 3dh in the boot record) inclusive. The details of all the information held in this parameter block are shown in Table 5.18. Listed here are the offset addresses in hexadecimal form from the boot record of Fig. 5.30 together with the use to which each field is put, the values in hexadecimal

Table 5.18 BIOS parameter block.

Offset	Use	Hex values	Meaning
03–0a	OEM name and version	4d 53 44 4f 53 35 2e 30	MSDOS5.0
0b–0c	Bytes per sector	00 02	512
0d	Sectors per cluster	10	16
0e–0f	Reserved sectors	01 00	1
10	Number of FATs	02	2
11–12	Root directory entries	00 02	512
13–14	Total sectors (unused)	00 00	0
15	Media descriptor byte	f8	f8h
16–17	Sectors per FAT	fc 00	252
18–19	Sectors per track	3f 00	63
1a–1b	Number of heads	40 00	64
1c–1f	Hidden sectors	3f 00 00 00	63
20–23	Total sectors	c1 bf 0f 00	1032129
24	Physical drive number	80	128
25	Reserved	00	0
26	Extended boot signature	29	29h
27–2a	Volume serial number	f1 15 3b 1c	1c3b15f1h
2b–35	Volume label	54 45 53 54 31 20 20 20 20 20 20	TEST1
36–3d	File system ID	46 41 54 31 36 20 20 20	FAT16

obtained from Fig. 5.30 and the interpretation that is to be placed on each field. Note, once again, that all the decimal numbers are converted using little endian format.

Although it is important to be aware of the low-level details, we do not need to do all this interpretation ourselves. Figure 5.31 shows the Norton Disk Editor Boot Record view of the same boot sector listed in Fig. 5.30. From this we can obtain many of the details about the hard disk partition. The first point of interest to note is the Norton Disk Editor reference in the heading to "Sector 0". This is because Norton Disk Editor is being used in "logical" mode, that is, a mode in which the sectors are counted from zero from the beginning of the logical partition. This is in contrast with "physical" mode, where sectors are counted from the very beginning of the hard disk itself. The corresponding physical mode heading produced by Norton Disk Editor for this boot record is "Physical Sector: Cyl 0, Side 1, Sector 1".

The first item of Fig. 5.31 identifies the operating system for which this partition was formatted and we note that this partition has the standard 512 bytes per sector. We also see that there are 16 sectors to the *cluster*, and this is a term which we will be discussing in a later section. The "Reserved sectors at beginning" entry refers to the number of sectors reserved for the boot record. In all the MS-DOS systems so far seen this has always been a single sector, as it is in the case of Windows 95 FAT16.

```
Sector 0
                                    OEM ID: MSDOS5.0
                           Bytes per sector: 512
                         Sectors per cluster: 16
                 Reserved sectors at beginning: 1
                                 FAT Copies: 2
                      Root directory entries: 512
                        Total sectors on disk: (Unused)
                     Media descriptor byte: F8 Hex
                            Sectors per FAT: 252
                          Sectors per track: 63
                                      Sides: 64
                       Special hidden sectors: 63
                  Big total number of sectors: 1032129
                     Physical drive number: 128
             Extended Boot Record Signature: 29 Hex
                        Volume Serial Number: 1C3B15F1 Hex
                             Volume Label: TEST1
                          File System ID: FAT16
```

Fig. 5.31 The boot sector – Norton Disk Editor boot record view.

However, for Windows 95 FAT32 and Windows 98 FAT32, more than one[88] sector is allocated for the boot record.

Two independent copies of the *File Allocation Table* (FAT) are kept because this is the key means by which resources are allocated to files and any damage to the FAT can cause serious loss of data. Keeping two copies helps reduce the risk of data loss. Again, we will discuss the FAT in more detail in a later section. The *root directory* is of fixed size in FAT16 systems and the "Root directory entries" figure defines how many directory entries can be held in this partition. Here we see a figure of 512, and since each entry is 32 bytes long, this indicates that the root directory is 512 × 32 = 16 384 bytes or 32 sectors in size. In passing, it is worth noting that this next field "Total sectors on disk" was one of the reasons for the infamous 32 Mbyte maximum partition size that existed for MS-DOS versions before 4.0. Only two bytes are available for this value (see offsets 13–14h in Table 5.18), which give us 65 536 as the maximum number of sectors and result in a maximum partition size of 65 536 × 512 = 32 Mbyte. This was overcome in MS-DOS version 4 and above by using an alternative field of 4 bytes ("Big total number of sectors") at offsets 20–23h in the boot sector. The "Media descriptor byte" identifies the kind of medium that is in use; here we see f8h, which signals that this is a hard disk as opposed to some specific floppy disk. A variety of media types are defined for the various floppy disks, but only one value, f8h, is used for all hard disks. Details of the specific hard disk can, of course, be obtained from the CMOS RAM. The size of each FAT is given as 252 sectors and then there are figures for sectors per track (63) and number of heads (64) both entirely as expected. The "Special hidden sectors" entry refers to the number of sectors on the disk before the start of the first partition, and this is the "Relative Sectors" number we noted before against the BIGDOS entry in the partition table in Fig. 5.27.

---

88 In the Windows 98 FAT32 system currently used by the author, this figure is 32.

Similarly, we saw the "Big total number of sectors" figure of 1032129 as the "Number of Sectors" value for the same BIGDOS entry in the partition table in Fig. 5.27. The "Physical drive number" is 128 or 80h indicating that this is drive 0 and the next three entries are just signatures and labels. Finally, the "File System ID" signals that this is formatted as a DOS FAT16 partition.

The MS-DOS operating system uses *logical sector numbers* (LSNs) which start from 0 at the very beginning of the partition. Given the details from the boot record, and knowing that MS-DOS uses a fixed structure of boot sector, FAT 1, FAT 2, root directory and files area, we can now draw up the layout of this logical partition as seen by MS-DOS. The first sector (LSN 0), contains the boot record, and then there are 252 sectors for the first FAT (LSN 1 to LSN 252), followed by a further 252 sectors for the second FAT (LSN 253 to LSN 504). After this comes the root directory with 32 sectors (LSN 505 to LSN 536) and finally the start of the files area proper at LSN 537, which would appear to continue to LSN 1 032 128 (that is, the "Big total number of sectors" less 1, since LSN counting starts at 0). However, the files area only actually extends to LSN 1,032,120, and this is because of the cluster size which we will be looking at in the next section. The details of the partition are shown in Fig. 5.32.

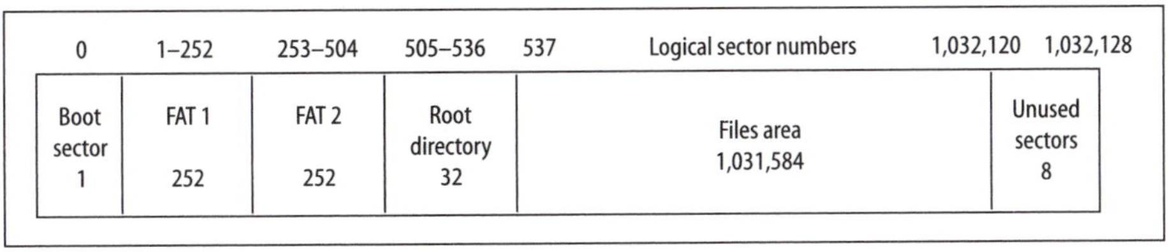

0	1–252	253–504	505–536	537	Logical sector numbers	1,032,120	1,032,128
Boot sector	FAT 1	FAT 2	Root directory		Files area		Unused sectors
1	252	252	32		1,031,584		8

Fig. 5.32 Layout of the partition.

FATs, Directories and File Systems

From the viewpoint of MS-DOS, each hard disk partition (or floppy disk) provides us with a set of logical sectors, each of 512 bytes in size, which are sequentially numbered from 0 to the end of the partition or floppy disk. However, we need more than just a sequence of sectors to make an effective file management system. We need to have structures in place that permit the sectors to be viewed as a set of files. There are two fundamental requirements here: one is for a means by which a file can be named and its characteristics can be recorded, and the other is for a mechanism by which files, which use more than just a single sector, can have their sector numbers recorded in an appropriate order. A number of strategies are possible to meet these two requirements and different operating systems typically use different approaches, with the result that they are rarely compatible with one another. MS-DOS meets the first requirement by means of the root directory[89] and the second requirement by means of the File Allocation Table or FAT. Before looking at the specific details of our example partition, we will consider the principles as outlined in Fig. 5.33.

---

89 There was only one directory for MS-DOS version 1. Since version 2 subdirectories are also permitted, as we will see later.

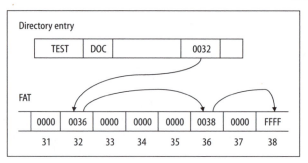

Fig. 5.33 Principles of the MS-DOS file system.

FATs and Clusters

Here we see a much simplified directory entry for a file called TEST.DOC. The original MS-DOS file naming scheme allows for 8 upper-case[90] characters in the filename and 3 upper-case characters in the file extension. By convention, the filename is shown separated from the file extension by a period, hence the reference: TEST.DOC. The directory entry has been simplified by removing references to various file characteristics such as the file attributes, the time and date created and the file size, for example, and we will be coming back to all this in a moment. What is shown in the entry is a numeric pointer to a logical *cluster* or *allocation unit*. For the time being we will make the assumption[91] that the cluster is equivalent to a sector. The pointer here shows that the first part of the file TEST.DOC is contained in logical cluster 0032.

The lower part of the diagram shows some of the entries in the File Allocation Table or FAT. At entry 32 we find a pointer to logical cluster 0036. This indicates that the second part of the file TEST.DOC is contained in logical cluster 0036. At entry 36 we find a pointer to logical cluster 0038. This indicates that the third part of the file TEST.DOC is contained in logical cluster 0038. Finally, at entry 38 we find the value FFFF, which signals the end of the cluster sequence. What the combination of the directory entry and the FAT has told us is that the file TEST.DOC is contained in the cluster sequence 0032–0036–0038. This system permits files to be spread over any number of clusters, which need not be either sequential or contiguous. Clearly, there are improvements in access time to be obtained if the clusters of a file are sequential and contiguous, since disk head movement is then minimized. After a period of use, the file system is likely to become fragmented with portions of files spread all over the partition. For this reason, *defrag* programs are often used to reassign, as far as possible, sequential and contiguous cluster sequences to all files in order to improve the file access efficiency.

Referring back to Fig. 5.32, we may note that the first logical sector number available to the files area is LSN 537. Continuing, for the moment, with our

90 Together with numerals and a limited set of other symbols.

91 Which is correct for floppy disks.

assumption that clusters are equivalent to sectors, this would then form logical cluster 2. You may wonder why clusters should start at 2 and not 0. Cluster 0 in the FAT would have to have a reference to 000 and as this is used in the FAT to indicate a free cluster it cannot be allocated. In addition, a special signature is used to identify the start of the FAT, and this utilizes the first two cluster positions in the FAT. This signature is always `Fx FF FF FF` for 16 bit FATs and `Fx FF FF` for 12 bit FATs, where `Fx` is the value of the media descriptor byte (for hard disks this is `F8`). The first available cluster, therefore, is always 2.

We have now made several references variously to FAT16, FAT32, 16 bit FATs and 12 bit FATs and it is perhaps useful at this stage to consider what these mean. They all simply refer to the number of bits used in the FAT to describe one entry. So, a 12 bit FAT (FAT12 or more often just FAT) uses 12 bits (1.5 bytes) per FAT entry, a 16 bit FAT (FAT16) uses 16 bits (2 bytes) per FAT entry and a 32 bit FAT (FAT32) uses 32 bits (4 bytes) per FAT entry. The possible values that may be given to each entry in the FAT are listed in Table 5.19. In addition to what has been described before, we see that FF0–FF6h values (and the equivalent FFF0–FFF6h values for the 16 bit FAT) are reserved, FF7h (and FFF7h) permits a cluster to be marked as bad, and FF8–FFFh (and FFF8–FFFFh) are all valid indicators of the last cluster in a file. In passing, we may note that clusters marked in the FAT as bad are another possible place in which to hide information.

The original MS-DOS FAT used 12 bits per entry, and the consequence of this is that only 2^{12} (that is, 4096) allocation units or clusters can be addressed. In fact, the number is less than this since 000h and 001h are not used and FF0h to FFFh are reserved or used for other purposes, leaving 002h to FEFh (2 to 4079) as the range of possible clusters. If we are to use one sector per cluster, as we have assumed above, the maximum number of sectors that we can address is 4078, and this at 512 bytes per sector gives us $4078 \times 512 = 2\ 087\ 936$ bytes, which is slightly less than 2 Mbyte. This would mean that the largest disk we can deal with is only 2 Mbyte in size. This is quite satisfactory for conventional floppy disks and is precisely what is used by MS-DOS for the standard floppy. For larger disks, however, we need to use more than one sector per cluster. For disks up to 16 Mbyte, MS-DOS uses eight sectors per cluster with a 12 bit FAT (making the cluster size $8 \times 512 = 4$ kbyte) and it uses a 16 bit FAT for disks of 16 Mbyte and above in accordance with Table 5.20.

The significance of the cluster size is, of course, that this is the smallest unit of disk memory that can be allocated at a time. Even if we have a file of only one or two bytes, we are forced to allocate a minimum of 32 kbyte to that file if the disk is larger than

Table 5.19 FAT cluster values.

FAT12 value	FAT16 value	Meaning
000h	0000h	Available for allocation
001h	0001h	Never used
FF0–FF6h	FFF0–FFF6h	Reserved
FF7h	FFF7h	Bad cluster
FF8–FFFh	FFF8–FFFFh	Last cluster in file
xxxh	xxxxh	Next cluster in file

Table 5.20 MS-DOS hard disk cluster sizes.

Logical drive size	FAT type	Sectors per cluster	Cluster size
0–15 Mbyte	12 bit	8	4 kbyte
16–127 Mbyte	16 bit	4	2 kbyte
128–255 Mbyte	16 bit	8	4 kbyte
256–511 Mbyte	16 bit	16	8 kbyte
512–1023 Mbyte	16 bit	32	16 kbyte
1024–2047 Mbyte	16 bit	64	32 kbyte

1024 Mbyte. There are, therefore, real advantages in partitioning a large disk into a number of smaller logical drives in order to reduce the cluster size in each of the partitions and hence the amount of wasted space. This wasted space between the end of the file and the rest of the cluster is known as *slack space*. The cluster size and the FAT type are decided by the FORMAT program when high-level formatting is carried out on the partition and the rules applied are those that are implied by Table 5.20.

You may have noted that the maximum sectors per cluster value in Table 5.20 does not exceed 64, resulting in a maximum cluster size of 32 kbyte. The argument for this is understood to be that some 16 bit programs make the assumption that the number of bytes per cluster (which must be a power of two) will fit into a 16 bit word and, of course, the value 65 536 (which is the next bytes per cluster power of two greater than 32 768) is just too large by 1. The consequence of this is that no normal FAT16 partition may exceed 32 768 (the maximum cluster size that will fit into a 16 bit word) times 65 536 (the maximum number of clusters[92] available with a 16 bit FAT) = 2 Gbyte. This is where the MS-DOS 2 Gbyte maximum partition limit comes from. Although it is possible, using Windows NT utilities, to produce FAT16 partitions which have 128 sectors per cluster (64 kbyte) and are 4 Gbyte in size, such partitions are not recommended by Microsoft[93] for use with MS-DOS or Windows 9x.

Returning for a moment to Fig. 5.32, we can now also see why the files area does not extend to the very end of the partition. The total number of sectors available for the files area is 1 032 128 – 536 = 1 031 592. Dividing this by the cluster size, 16, we obtain 64 474 clusters, with a remainder of 8 sectors. This means that the last 8 sectors in the partition cannot be addressed by the file system, which extends only to LSN 64 474 × 16 + 536 = 1 032 120. Here is yet another good place to hide information.

With Windows 95 OEM Service Release 2 (OSR2) and Windows 98, Microsoft[94] introduced an updated version of the FAT system called FAT32. This uses four bytes per FAT entry (32 bits, hence FAT32) and can address 2^{32} = 4 294 967 296 clusters. Given that the maximum possible number of sectors is also 2^{32} = 4 294 967 296 (see "Total sectors" offset 20–23 in Table 5.18), and we can now address them all at one

---

92 The actual number is slightly less than this since we must subtract 0000, 0001 and FFF0 to FFFF from the range.

93 See *Problems Accessing FAT16 Drives Larger than 2GB* (Microsoft Corporation, 1999a).

94 See *Description of FAT32 File System* (Microsoft Corporation, 1998b).

sector per cluster, we could have disks as large as $4\,294\,967\,296 \times 512 =$ $2\,199\,023\,255\,552$ bytes = 2 Tbyte. In practice, one sector per cluster is not used, largely because the size[95] of the FAT itself becomes far too unwieldy and only 28 bits of the 32 are used for the cluster number. A cluster size of 8 sectors per cluster (4 kbyte) is used for partitions up to 8 Gbyte, 16 sectors per cluster (8 kbyte) for partitions up to 16 Gbyte, 32 sectors per cluster (16 kbyte) for partitions up to 32 Gbyte, and 64 sectors per cluster (32 kbyte) for partitions above 32 Gbyte. The other major difference with FAT32 is that the root directory is no longer of fixed size and is held in a cluster chain just like other files.

Figure 5.34 shows, in Norton Disk Editor FAT view, a small part of the first FAT for the same example partition that we referred to in Figs. 5.30, 5.31 and 5.32 and Table 5.18. From this we can readily see that one file probably starts at cluster 2, continues with clusters 3, 4 and 5, and ends with cluster 6. It is a safe bet that the next file starts with cluster 7 and continues with 8, 9 and 10 and ends with cluster 11. However, to confirm all this, we really need to examine the root directory, and it is this that we will look at next.

```
Sector 1
Clusters 2 - 255
                      3         4         5         6    <EOF>        8
       9       10       11    <EOF>       13        14       15       16
      17       18    <EOF>        0        0         0        0        0
       0        0        0    <EOF>    <EOF>     <EOF>    <EOF>        0
       0        0        0        0        0         0        0        0
       0        0        0        0        0         0        0        0
       0        0        0        0        0         0        0        0
       0        0        0        0        0         0        0        0
```

Fig. 5.34 The 1st FAT – Norton Disk Editor FAT view.

The Root Directory

As described earlier, MS-DOS directory entries are each 32 bytes in length. The first 8 bytes of the entry (see Table 5.21) are the eight characters of the filename, padded out, if necessary, with spaces (20h) to the end of the field. The first byte of the filename has a special significance depending upon its value. If it is 00h, it indicates that the entry has not been used before and we have reached the last entry in the directory list. If it is e5h, which corresponds to the character "σ", then the directory entry has been deleted. We will look at file and subdirectory deletion in a later section. If it is the value 05h, then this indicates that the first filename character should be "σ", which cannot, of course be stored as such without signalling a deleted entry! Finally, if it is the value 2eh, which corresponds to the character ".", this

---

[95] At 1 sector per cluster with 4 bytes per entry for the FAT, a 2 Gbyte partition would require $4 \times 2\,147\,483\,648/512 = 16\,777\,216$ bytes = 16 Mbyte of space for each of the two FATs, making a total requirement of 32 Mbyte.

Table 5.21 32 byte directory entry.

Offset	Meaning
00–07h	Filename 8 bytes padded with spaces
08–0ah	File extension 3 bytes padded with spaces
0bh	File attributes 1 byte
0c–15h	Reserved (MS-DOS 1.0–6.22) 10 bytes
16–17h	Time of last change 2 bytes
18–19h	Date of last change 2 bytes
1a–1bh	First cluster 2 bytes
1c–1fh	File size 4 bytes

signifies that this entry refers to a directory and we will say more about that in a moment.

The next three bytes are the three characters of the file extension, again padded out as necessary with spaces (20h) to the end of the field. It should be noted that the period that separates the filename from the file extension in all MS-DOS 8.3 references is not actually held in the directory entry.

The next byte in the sequence is the file attributes byte (see Fig. 5.35). This indicates whether the file is write protected, hidden, a system file or changed since it was last backed up by an archive program. In addition, the entry may, instead of referring to a file, be a volume label or a subdirectory. If the volume label bit is set (only one entry in the root directory may have this bit set), the filename and file extension fields are taken together without an intervening period as the 11 byte volume name for the partition. If the subdirectory bit is set, the "first cluster" field points to a subdirectory rather than to a file, though in many ways the subdirectory can be considered as a special case of a file.

The next 10 bytes in the directory entry are reserved in MS-DOS 1.0 to 6.22. In passing, we should note that seven of these bytes are used in MS-DOS 7 and Windows 95 for additional date and time information and two of them are used in FAT32 systems to specify the additional two bytes (making four in all) that are required for the "first cluster" value (see later section). Following the reserved bytes are two bytes (in little endian order) used to specify the time of creation or last change made to the file and then a further two bytes (also in little endian order) to specify the date of

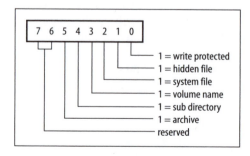

Fig. 5.35 File attributes byte.

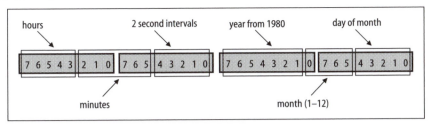

Fig. 5.36 Time and date field bytes.

creation or last change made to the file. These four bytes have a very specific structure, as shown in Fig. 5.36. Looking at them in sequence, the first five bits specify the hours, the next six bits specify the minutes and the last five bits specify the number of two second intervals. To obtain the actual seconds we need to multiply the value from this field by 2. For the date fields, the first seven bits specify the number of years since 1980, the next four bits specify the month number, 1 to 12, and the last five bits specify the day of the month, 1 to 31.

The next field in Table 5.21 identifies the starting cluster for the file or subdirectory to which this entry refers. For FAT16 we simply need two bytes as given here, but for FAT32, as mentioned above, two more bytes are needed and these are taken from the reserved field. Note that these numbers are all little endian and that, for FAT32, the "first cluster" field contains the least significant values. The final field in Table 5.21 is the file length in bytes, and this is held little endian in the last four bytes of the entry.

Figure 5.37 shows the root directory details in hexadecimal of the example partition. Taking the first entry we see that at offsets 00–07h is the filename "IO" padded out with spaces and at offsets 08–0ah is the file extension "SYS". At offset 0bh is the file attributes byte of value 27h, and this represents a write protected, hidden, system file with the archive bit set. Offsets 0c–15h are not used and are set to 00h. At offsets 16–17h is the time of the last update as 3280h (little endian, of course). In binary this is 0011 0010 1000 0000, and when divided up as in Fig. 5.36 this is

```
Gander - I:\FORENSIC\ROOT.DMP
File  Edit  Display  Search  Filters  Help

      00 01 02 03 04 05 06 07 08 09 0a 0b 0c 0d 0e 0f      0 1 2 3 4 5 6 7 8 9 a b c d e f

  00  49 4f 20 20 20 20 20 20 53 59 53 27 00 00 00 00      IO        SYS '  « » « «
  10  00 00 00 00 00 00 80 32 3e 1b 02 00 76 9e 00 00      » » « » » » 2 > » » » u » » »
  20  4d 53 44 4f 53 20 20 20 53 59 53 27 00 00 00 00      MSDO S    SYS '  » » » «
  30  00 00 00 00 00 00 80 32 3e 1b 07 00 fa 94 00 00      » » » » » » 2 > » » » » » » »
  40  43 4f 4d 4d 41 4e 44 20 43 4f 4d 20 00 00 00 00      COMM AND  COM   » » » »
  50  00 00 00 00 00 00 80 32 3e 1b 0c 00 5b d5 00 00      » » » » » » 2 > » » » [ » » »
  60  e5 42 4c 53 50 41 43 45 42 49 4e 20 00 00 00 00      » BLS PACE BIN   » » » »
  70  00 00 00 00 00 00 80 32 3e 1b 13 00 f6 fa 00 00      » » » » » » 2 > » » » » » » »
  80  54 45 53 54 31 20 20 20 20 20 20 28 00 00 00 00      TEST 1       (  » » » »
  90  00 00 00 00 00 00 4c 74 0a 27 00 00 00 00 00 00      » » » » » » Lt » ' » » » » »
  a0  53 55 42 31 20 20 20 20 20 20 20 10 00 00 00 00      SUB1         »  » » » »
  b0  00 00 0f 27 00 00 20 50 0f 27 1b 00 00 00 00 00      » » » '    P » ' » » » » »
  c0  52 45 43 59 43 4c 45 44 20 20 20 16 00 a1 e8 52      RECY CLED    »  » » » R
  d0  0f 27 0f 27 00 00 e9 52 0f 27 1d 00 00 00 00 00      » ' » ' » » R » ' » » » » »
  e0  00 00 00 00 00 00 00 00 00 00 00 00 00 00 00 00      » » » » » » » » » » » » » »
  f0  00 00 00 00 00 00 00 00 00 00 00 00 00 00 00 00      » » » » » » » » » » » » » »
```

Fig. 5.37 Hexadecimal view of the root directory.

equivalent to 00110 hours, 010100 minutes, and 00000 × 2 seconds giving us 06:20:00. Similarly the date of the last update is at offsets 18–19h and is 1b3eh in little endian. In binary this is 0001 1101 0011 1110, and when divided up as in Fig. 5.36, this is equivalent to 0001110 years from 1980, 1001 number of month, and 11110 day of month giving us 1993/9/30. At offsets 1a–1bh is the first cluster number in little endian, that is 0002 and finally, at offsets 1c–1fh, is the file size in little endian, that is 00009e76h, which is equivalent to 40 566 in decimal.

Deleted Files

Immediately below the three files, IO.SYS, MSDOS.SYS and COMMAND.COM specified in this root directory, there is a deleted file which used to be DBLSPACE.BIN starting at offset 60h. The first character of the name has been overwritten with the deleted marker e5h. When files are deleted in the MS-DOS file system, the directory entry for the file is not removed, it is simply marked as deleted in this way. If we look at the first cluster field for the file at offsets 7a–7bh we find that the value 0013 (decimal 19) is still present, as is the original file size at offsets 7c–7fh of 0000faf6h (decimal 64 246). If we look, however, at the FAT table of Fig. 5.34, we see that clusters 19 to 26 are all set to 0, although clusters 27 to 30 are in use, all marked with <EOF>. This suggests that the DBLSPACE.BIN file originally used clusters 19 to 26, but these were returned to the available pool once the file had been deleted. What is important from a forensic viewpoint, however, is that on deletion of a file, MS-DOS does not delete the information contained in the clusters; it merely marks them as available for reallocation. It is therefore quite possible to restore a file that has been deleted provided the clusters of the file have not been reused. The deleted directory entry will often contain details of the first cluster and the file length, as is the case here, and this can greatly assist the process. Programs such as UNDELETE.EXE and UNERASE.EXE attempt to automate the recovery of deleted files, but an analyst using Norton Disk Editor, for example, is likely to be much more effective in difficult cases.

The degree of success obtained in undeleting a file is obviously related to the likelihood of the original file clusters being reallocated by MS-DOS. In early versions of MS-DOS (1.0 and 2.0), a search for the next free cluster to be allocated was always made from the beginning of the FAT, but in later versions a more complicated algorithm is used, and an unused cluster near the other clusters of the file being extended is sought.

Volume Label and Subdirectory Entries

The next entry beneath the deleted file entry is a volume label, TEST1, and beneath that are two subdirectory entries, SUB1 and RECYCLED. Examination of the volume label shows that the volume name extends over the 11 bytes of offsets 80–8ah and is padded out with spaces. The file attributes byte at 8bh is of value 28h and this signifies that the volume name and the archive bits are set. The time field, at offsets 96–97h, is 744ch, and this gives 0111 0100 0100 1100, which divides up as 01110 hours, 100010 minutes and 01100 × 2 seconds, and results in 14:34:24. The date field, at

```
Sector 505
Name      .Ext ID      Size     Date      Time   Cluster   76 A R S H D V
------------------------------------------------------------------------------
IO         SYS  File    40566  30/ 9/93   6:20am        2      A R S H - -
MSDOS      SYS  File    38138  30/ 9/93   6:20am        7      A R S H - -
COMMAND    COM  File    54619  30/ 9/93   6:20am       12      A - - - - -
ŎBLSPACE   BIN  File    64246  30/ 9/93   6:20am       19      A - - - - -
TEST1           Vol         0  10/ 8/99  14:34pm        0      A - - - - V
SUB1            Dir         0  15/ 8/99  10:01am       27      - - - - D -
RECYCLED        Dir         0  15/ 8/99  10:23am       29      - - S H D -
```

Fig. 5.38 Norton Disk Editor directory view of the root directory.

offsets 98–99h, is 270ah, and this gives 0010 0111 0000 1010, which divides up as 0010011 years from 1980, 1000 number of month, and 01010 day of month, and results in 1999/8/10. The first cluster field at offsets 9a–9bh and the file size field at offsets 9c–9fh are both seen to be zero.

For the subdirectory SUB1 a similar analysis could be performed, and here we would find that the directory bit is set in the file attributes byte at offset abh (value is 10h) and that the first cluster is at 001bh (offsets ba–bbh), which is decimal 27.

Although it is important to be able to analyze the details in this way, Norton Disk Editor provides a directory view which can be used to show most of this information for us. Such a view of the example directory is given in Fig. 5.38.

From our previous analysis, all the entries in the table of Fig. 5.38 should be self-evident. The start sector of the root directory is 505, which conforms with our analysis of Fig. 5.32. The only unexplained item is the heading 76, which simply refers to the two reserved bits in the attribute byte. In passing, we might also note that the RECYCLED subdirectory has been added automatically to our partition by Windows 98. It is a system, hidden, directory and it is noteworthy because it breaks our forensic rules of not changing the evidence during examination. Using Windows 95 or 98 to examine a disk will result in changes such as this being made.

Subdirectories

As mentioned above, a subdirectory can be considered to be a special case of a file. It is, in fact, a file that contains directory entries in just the same format as the root directory. The contents of a subdirectory may be file entries or further subdirectory entries but, unlike the root directory, because subdirectories are specified as a cluster chain they are not constrained to being of fixed length.

Figure 5.39 shows a hexadecimal view of the subdirectory SUB1. In common with all subdirectories, the first two entries are pre-defined. The first, as can be seen from offsets 00–0ah is called " . " and stands for this directory itself. Its attribute byte at offset 0bh has just the directory bit set (10h) and the first cluster value at offsets 1a–1bh is 001bh or decimal 27, which from Fig. 5.38 we can see is the first cluster of this subdirectory SUB1. The second entry at offsets 20–2ah is similarly called " . . ", and this stands for the parent directory of this directory. The parent, in this case, is the root directory and the first cluster for that is shown at offsets 3a–3bh as 0000. Apart from these two entries, all the other entries in the subdirectory will either be filename entries or subdirectory entries in the form that we have seen before, with

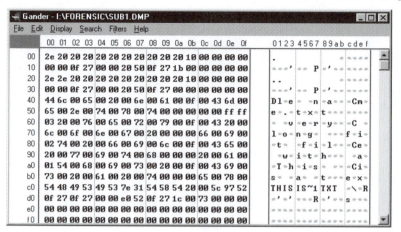

Fig. 5.39 Hexadecimal view of a subdirectory.

one exception, that of the *long filename* (LFN), which we could also find in the root directory.

Long Filenames

Figure 5.40 shows the Norton Disk Editor directory view of the subdirectory, SUB1, that we were examining in hexadecimal form in Fig. 5.39. This shows clearly the two entries for "." and ".." and confirms the details that we established above. It also shows four entries marked "LFN" and a normal file entry named THISIS~1.TXT.

With Windows 95 and 98, Microsoft removed the 8.3 limitation to file and directory names and introduced the long filename, which can be up 255 characters in length. Both upper- and lower-case letters are permitted and the range of other characters has also been increased. However, in order to maintain compatibility with MS-DOS and to continue to operate within the existing file system, the long filename is spread over a number of standard 32 byte directory entries and it is always matched with a *short filename* (SFN) alias which conforms to the old 8.3 naming conventions. Windows automatically generates the SFN alias from the long filename. In our example case, the long filename is This is a text file with a very long file name.txt and the SFN generated by Windows is THISIS~1.TXT. Although the actual generation algorithm is quite complicated in detail, most of the

```
Cluster 27, Sector 937
Name       .Ext ID      Size      Date      Time     Cluster   76 A R S H D V
----------------------------------------------------------------------------
  .              Dir        0   15/ 8/99   10:01am      27      - - - - D -
  ..             Dir        0   15/ 8/99   10:01am       0      - - - - D -
le name.txt      LFN                                     0      - R S H - V
 very long fi    LFN                                     0      - R S H - V
t file with a    LFN                                     0      - R S H - V
This is a tex    LFN                                     0      - R S H - V
THISIS~1 TXT     File      115   15/ 8/99   10:23am      28      A - - - - -
```

Fig. 5.40 Norton Disk Editor directory view of the subdirectory SUB1.

principles are clear from this example. Lower case is translated to upper case, spaces are removed and the first six characters of the resulting LFN are then used followed by a "~" and a digit to make the SFN up to 8 characters. If there is a file extension specified, the first three characters of this are used. The reason for the "~" and the digit at the end is to permit Windows to differentiate from, say, another long filename such as This is a shorter file name.txt, which would then receive an SFN of THISIS~2.TXT[96].

One consequence of this approach that is important for a forensic analyst to be aware of, is that SFNs of copied files, which are generated by Windows at the time of the copy, may be different in different directories. This is because the value of the last digit in the SFN will depend on whether there are one or more files with similar starting LFNs in the directory to which the copy is being made. Although the LFN of the copied file will always be the same as the original, the SFN may not.

Returning to our subdirectory entry for THISIS~1.TXT in Fig. 5.40, we see that this is in exactly the same format as that for the other files we have seen in Fig. 5.38. What we do need to look at a little more closely are the four LFN entries which specify the long filename. We can see that as many 32 byte directory entries as are necessary are used to record the LFN. Each entry can hold a maximum of 13 characters of the long filename since each of the characters is recorded in *Unicode*[97] and requires two bytes to represent it. We can relate the four entries of the example back to the hexadecimal view of Fig. 5.39 by noting that they start at offsets 40h, 60h, 80h and a0h respectively. The first byte in each entry is the sequence number; that is, it specifies the order in which the entries are to be taken to restore the text of the long filename. We can see clearly what that order should be in the example LFN by inspection of Fig. 5.40, and if we examine offsets a0h, 80h, 60h and 40h in that order we see the values 01h, 02h, 03h and 44h in the relevant first bytes. The last byte in this sequence of four has bit 6 set as well as the value 04h (thus giving 44h) to indicate that it is the last entry of the long file name. Bits 7 and 5 of this byte are unused.

Table 5.22 shows the details of the LFN directory entry. Offset 0bh, the file attributes byte, is always set to 0fh. This gives file attributes (see Fig. 5.35) of read-only, hidden, system and volume, as we see in Fig. 5.40. After some testing, it was found that directory entries with these attributes were mostly ignored by existing software, so such LFN entries could generally be used with legacy systems. At offset 0dh is the checksum byte, which is the checksum of certain fields in the associated SFN directory entry and is used by Windows to detect orphaned or corrupt LFN entries.

Additional Times and Dates

Finally, as we mentioned above, it should be noted that the 10 reserved bytes in the normal file directory entry are used in MS-DOS 7, Windows 95 and Windows 98

---

96 If we were to have more than nine files of This is ..., the tenth would become THISI~10.TXT, and so on.

97 This is a complex subject. The code has been designed to meet the computer needs of the vast variety of human languages and not just those of English. For more details see the Unicode home page at http://www.unicode.org/.

Table 5.22 LFN directory entry.

Offset	Meaning
00h	Sequence number 1 byte
01–0ah	First five characters of LFN in Unicode 10 bytes
0bh	File attributes 1 byte (always 0fh)
0ch	Type indicator 1 byte
0dh	Checksum 1 byte
0e–19h	Next six characters of LFN in Unicode 12 bytes
1a–1bh	First cluster 2 bytes (always 0000h)
1c–1fh	Next two characters of LFN in Unicode 4 bytes

systems for additional dates and times. The details of these are shown in Table 5.23. Using the same format as that shown in Fig. 5.36, the file creation time is held in little endian form in offsets 0e–0fh, the file creation date is similarly held in offsets 10–11h and the last access date is held in offsets 12–13h. At offsets 14–15h are the high two bytes of the 4 byte start cluster for FAT32 systems. The difference between these various times and dates is as follows: the original time and date stamp of the file is that as given at offsets 16–19h; the creation time and date on the MS-DOS 7 or Windows system is that as given at 0e–11h, and the last access date, read or write, made to the file is that as given at offsets 12–13h.

If we examine the "THISIS~1.TXT" entry in the subdirectory in Fig. 5.39 we find that the reserved ten bytes are in use, unlike many of the entries in the root directory of Fig. 5.37, which have their corresponding ten bytes set to 0. The reason for this difference has nothing whatsoever to do with root or subdirectories, but is solely because the LFN entries and the associated SFN alias in the subdirectory were generated using Windows 98, which has this additional time and date capability, whereas some entries in the root directory were generated by MS-DOS 6.20, which does not.

Hiding and Recovering Information

In this section we first briefly review where information might be hidden on a disk and then we consider the possibility of recovering information that has not

Table 5.23 Additional time and date fields.

Offset	Meaning
0ch	Reserved 1 byte
0dh	10 millisecond units past creation time 1 byte
0e–0fh	File creation time 2 bytes
10–11h	File creation date 2 bytes
12–13h	Last access date 2 bytes
14–15h	High word of start cluster (FAT32) 2 bytes

necessarily been deliberately hidden. A variety of opportunities exist for hiding information on hard disks, as listed below:

- With older controllers, sectors or tracks might be marked as bad within the controller when in fact they are perfectly good and are being used to hide information. This technique requires a high level of technical expertise (see Bad Sector Mapping and A Possible Place to Hide).

- Some partitions may be deliberately marked as hidden using, for example, PartitionMagic (see Hidden Partitions).

- The accessible partitions may not use the whole of the disk. This may be accidental or deliberate. The partition table may have been modified using, for example, a disk editor, so that one or more of the working partitions are no longer recorded. These conditions can be tested for by comparing the physical disk size with the sum of all the indicated partition sizes.

- The translated disk geometry may not permit access to the entire physical disk. We saw this with Fig. 5.8, where a physical geometry of 4095 cylinders and 16 heads translates to only 1023 cylinders and 64 heads. This is because 4095 is not exactly divisible by 4 and it results in a loss of $(4095 - 1023 \times 4) \times 16 \times 63 = 3024$ sectors. With a different BIOS, these sectors might have been accessible.

- Logical partitions may not fill the whole of the first extended partition (see Extended Partitions).

- Unassigned sectors following the partition tables and between partitions may have been used to hide information. Even the extended partition table sectors themselves should be examined, since only the last 66 bytes of the sector are used by the system for the partition table (see More Places to Hide).

- The usable files area may not extend to the end of the defined partition because of the cluster size (see Fig. 5.32). Any last few sectors should be checked.

- Clusters may have been marked in the FAT as bad and then used to hide information (see FATs and Clusters).

Opportunities exist for the recovery of information that has not been deliberately hidden but has perhaps been deleted or has been saved unwittingly in various buffers or temporary files:

- It may be possible to restore some or all of any deleted files, where clusters have not yet been reused, by following the cluster chains in the FAT (see Deleted Files).

- Where a file does not use all of the last (or only) cluster assigned to it, there may be information from previous files still accessible beyond the end of the sector in which the current file ends and up to the end of the cluster. This is known as *cluster slack space*.

- Where the last part of a file does not completely fill the standard sector buffer, there may be information from a previous file beyond the end of the file and up to the end of the sector buffer. This is known as *buffer slack space*.

- Clusters currently unallocated may contain information from previous files.

- System files, such as the Windows swap file, may contain printer and other temporary file buffers that are no longer directly accessible.

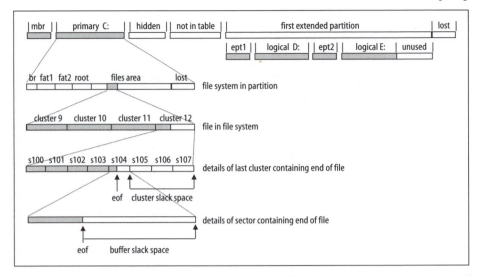

Fig. 5.41 Summary of disk and file issues.

Figure 5.41 shows a summary of many of these issues in diagrammatic form. The first line in the diagram shows a map of the physical disk. As expected, this starts with a master boot record (mbr) and continues with a primary partition which has been allocated the drive letter C: This is followed by a hidden partition which would appear in the partition table with the partition type byte set to hidden. Next is a partition marked "not in table". This represents a partition that has been used but whose entry has been edited out of the partition table. Then comes the first extended partition container in the form that we have seen before. This takes up the rest of the disk except for the part marked "lost". This represents those sectors that cannot be accessed because of the translated disk geometry. Between each partition and the partition tables we see unused space, and this occurs because partition tables always start at head 0 sector 1 and boot records start at head 1 sector 1.

Within the first extended partition container we see an extended partition table followed by a logical partition that has been allocated the drive letter D: and this is followed by another extended partition table and another logical partition that has been allocated the drive letter E:. We also see beyond this last partition that there is unused space within the first extended partition container. In addition, we may note that once again between each logical partition and the extended partition tables there is unused space for precisely the same reasons as before.

The diagram also shows, for the primary C: partition, an exploded view of the file system in the partition, and we note the possibility of lost sectors at the end of the files area because of the need to divide sectors exactly by the sectors per cluster value (always a power of two). We have shown, in addition, an exploded view of a typical file which uses the four clusters 9 to 12 for its data. We note that the end of the file (eof) occurs part way through cluster 12 and on examining an exploded view of this cluster we see that it is made up of the eight sectors 100 to 107. Again we note that the end of file occurs in sector 104, which means that sectors 105, 106 and 107 are not used at all by this file. These three sectors are known as *cluster slack space*. Further, an exploded view of sector 104, which contains the end of file, shows that only part of the sector buffer is taken up with file data. From the end of the file to the end of the sector will be information that was in the buffer before this file update was written. This information is known as *buffer slack space*.

RAID

Before leaving this chapter we should just mention Redundant Arrays of Inexpensive Disks or RAID. The concept came from the University of California at Berkeley in the mid-1980s and the original paper[98] on the subject was published at SIGMOD in 1988. Today, the word "inexpensive" that was used by the original designers is more often replaced by the word "independent".

A RAID system is a set of independent disks which appear to the operating system as a single drive. The paper defines five levels of RAID, numbered 1 to 5, which adopt various strategies to utilize the independent disks in different ways to improve the overall reliability and performance of the RAID system. RAID improves reliability by distributing data over multiple drives and calculating and storing parity information about it. This redundancy permits data to be restored if a drive fails. RAID improves performance by distributing the disk read processes over several disks so that transfers can be taking place in parallel.

RAID Level 0

Strictly speaking RAID Level 0 is not a RAID system at all and it was not described in the original paper. It is, however, referred to as such and it has therefore been included in this discussion. RAID Level 0 uses what is known as *sector striping* to increase performance. This means that sectors or blocks are written in turn to different drives. So, for example, given three drives, sector 1 of a file would be written to drive 1, sector 2 to drive 2, sector 3 to drive 3 and then sector 4 to drive 1 again, and so forth. The file would be *striped* across the three drives. Such striping does not need to be at the sector or block level, it can be at the byte or even the bit level. RAID Level 0 does not provide any redundancy or improved reliability, but it can be used to improve overall performance.

RAID Level 1

RAID Level 1 uses *mirroring* or *duplexing* to improve data reliability. Mirroring simply means that each drive has a duplicate, and when data is written to one drive it is simultaneously mirrored or duplicated on the second. If one drive fails, the other can be used to restore the data. Clearly the process of having to write to both drives increases the performance overheads.

---

98 *A Case for Redundant Arrays of Inexpensive Disks (RAID)* (Patterson *et al.*, 1988).

RAID Level 2

This system distributes data across multiple drives at the bit level, using Hamming code error detection and correction. A system with four data drives, for example, would also require three parity drives for the error detecting and correcting codes. Because it operates at the bit level, every disk access occurs in parallel, making the transfer of large amounts of contiguous data particular efficient, and the degree of redundancy is the highest of any of the RAID levels.

RAID Levels 3 and 4

RAID Level 3 combines striping at the byte level with a single drive assigned for parity. So, typically, there might be four data drives and one parity drive in such a system. Byte 1 of a transfer would then be written to drive 1, byte 2 to drive 2, byte 3 to drive 3 and byte 4 to drive 4, then a parity value byte for those 4 bytes would be calculated and written to the parity drive; after that, byte 5 would be written to drive 1 again, and so forth.

RAID level 4 is very similar. This system combines striping at the sector or block level with a single drive assigned for parity. So, with four data drives and one parity drive, sector 1 is written to drive 1, sector 2 to drive 2, sector 3 to drive 3 and sector 4 to drive 4, then a parity sector is calculated and written to the parity drive; following that, sector 5 is written to drive 1 again, and the process continues as before.

RAID Level 5 and Other RAID Levels

This approach combines sector or block striping with distributed parity. In this system there is no dedicated parity disk; parity sectors or blocks are written to the next available disk in sequence. So, given, for example, five disks as before, sector 1 is written to disk 1, sector 2 to disk 2, sector 3 to disk 3, sector 4 to disk 4 and sector 5 to disk 5; then the parity sector is calculated and written to disk 1, and then sector 6 is written to disk 2 and so forth. The parity sectors are therefore distributed across all the disks.

Formally, only RAID Levels 1 to 5 have been defined, but references to RAID 0, RAID 0/1, RAID 6, RAID 7 and RAID 10 are in common usage and these are effectively accepted extensions to the original specification. For a comprehensive and clear treatment of RAID see Appendix C to Zacker (1995).

Exercises

5.1   By comparing Fig. 5.42 with Fig. 5.6, show that this RLL encoded signal represents the character "Y" and sketch the equivalent MFM encoded signal.

5.2   Figure 5.43 shows part of the listing from the Find-ATA program for a Quantum Pioneer hard disk. Using Fig. 5.8 as an example, calculate, assuming 512 bytes per sector, the capacities in bytes for the columns marked

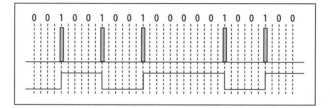

Fig. 5.42 RLL encoded signal.

```
Drive: QUANTUM Pioneer SG 1.0A      Port: Primary (01F0h)
            Hardware    DOS          Current  Max ECC: 4 bytes

Cylinders: 2097         524          2097
    Heads: 16           64           16
  Sectors: 63           63           63
 Capacity: □,□□□,□□□,□□□ □,□□□,□□□,□□□ □,□□□,□□□,□□□

      LBA Mode:    Yes      □□□□□□□
```

Fig. 5.43 Part of the Find-ATA analysis of a Quantum Pioneer.

"Hardware", "DOS" and "Current" and also the number of sectors in LBA mode. In addition, determine the number of sectors that are inaccessible on this disk as a result of the translation shown.

5.3 Determine all the details of the second partition in the partition table of the master boot record shown in Fig. 5.26, starting from address 1ceh, and confirm that these are correctly given by the Norton Disk Editor view in Fig. 5.27.

5.4 Analyze the directory record for the entry "SUB1" at offset a0h in Fig. 5.37 and show that it conforms with the detail give by the Norton Disk Editor directory view in Fig. 5.38.

5.5 Analyze the subdirectory record for the entry "THISIS~1.TXT" at offset c0h in Fig. 5.39 and determine the values of the additional time and date fields.

References

ANSI (1996) *ANSI X3.279-1996 - AT Attachment Interface with Extensions (ATA-2)*, American National Standards Institute, 11 West 42nd Street, New York, NY 10036.

Clarke, A. R. M. and Powys-Lybbe, D. (1986) *The Amstrad CP/M Plus*, MML Systems Ltd, London.

Duncan, R. (1988) *Advanced MSDOS Programming*, Microsoft Press, Redmond, WA.

Finch, S. G. (ed.) (1995) Information technology - AT Attachment Interface with Extensions (ATA-2), *Working Draft, Proposed American National Standard, X3T10 948D, Revision 3*, 17 January. URL: http://fission.dt.wdc.com/.

IBM (1995) *No-ID sector format*, Dr Steven R Hetzler, IBM Research Division, Almaden Research Center, San Jose, CA. URL: http://www.storage.ibm.com/oem/tech/noid.htm.

IBM (1998) *IBM Deskstar 25GP and Deskstar 22GXP Hard Disk Drives*, IBM Storage Systems Division, 5600 Cottle Road, San Jose, CA 95193. URL: http://www.ibm.com/harddrive/.

IBM (1999) *Disk Manager (version 9.47)*, 25 March, IBM Storage Systems Division, 5600 Cottle Road, San Jose, CA 95193. URL: http://www.storage.ibm.com/techsup/hddtech/welcome.htm.

Intel (1998a) *SE440BX Motherboard Technical Product Specification*, March, Intel Corporation, PO Box 5937, Denver, CO 80217-9808.

Intel (1998b) *SE440BX Motherboard Product Guide*, Intel Corporation, PO Box 5937, Denver, CO 80217-9808.

Landis, H. (1995a) *How It Works – BIOS Types, CHS Translation, LBA and Other Good Stuff, Version 4a*, URL: http://web.idirect.com/~frank/docs/chs.txt.

Landis, H. (1995b) *How It Works – DOS Floppy Disk Boot Sector, Version 1a*, hiw@sugs.talisman.com.

Landis, H. (1997a) *How It Works – Master Boot Record, Version 1b*, hiw@sugs.talisman.com.

Landis, H. (1997b) *How It Works – Partition Tables, Version 1e*, hiw@sugs.talisman.com.

Majors, N. (1995) *Technicians' Guide to PC Hard Disk Subsystems*, Data Recovery Labs. URL: http://www.wi.leidenuniv.nl/ata/hdtech.html.

Maxtor (1996) *Maxtor's CrystalMax 1080 Model Number 84320A8, Rev A 3/18/96*. T. Gilmer, IDE.EXE Compressed File of all IDE Drive Specs. URL: http://www.maxtor.com/products/products.html.

Messmer, H.-P. (1997) *The Indispensable PC Hardware Book*, Addison-Wesley, Reading, MA.

Micro Firmware (1998) *Issues with Hard Drives over 4GB*, Micro Firmware Tech Support, 330 W Gray Street, Norman, Oklahoma. URL: http://www.firmware.com/support/.

Microsoft Corporation (1999a) *Problems Accessing FAT16 Drives Larger Than 2 GB*, Article ID: Q127851, 15 January, http://support.microsoft.com/support/kb/articles/Q127/8/51.asp.

Microsoft Corporation (1999b) *Description of FAT32 File System*, Article ID: Q154997, 8 August, http://support.microsoft.com/support/kb/articles/Q154/9/97.asp.

MicroSystems, *POST CODE MASTER Version 1.40*, MicroSystems Development, Inc. 4100 Moorpark Ave. Suite #104, San Jose, CA 95117.

Mosteller, T. (1995) CMOSRAM2.EXE, Tellerware, 1872 Rampart Lane, Lansdale, PA 19446-5051.

Patterson, D. A., Gibson, G. A. and Katz, R. H. (1988) A case for redundant arrays of inexpensive disks (RAID), *SIGMOD Conference 1988*, pp. 109–116.

Phoenix (1995) *BIOS Enhanced Disk Drive Specification Version 1.1*, 9 May 1995, Phoenix Technologies Ltd, 2575 McCabe Way, Irvine, CA 92714. URL: http://www.phoenix.com/.

Phoenix (1998) *BIOS Enhanced Disk Drive Specification, Version 3.0*, 12 March, Phoenix Technologies Ltd, 2575 McCabe Way, Irvine, CA 92714. URL: http://www.phoenix.com/.

Postuma, P. (1995) *BIOS Reporter, version 1.1*, ppostuma@nbnet.nb.ca, 16 Fullyer Drive, Quispamsis, NB, Canada E2G 1Y7.

PowerQuest (1996) *PartitionMagic 3.0 User Guide*, PowerQuest Corporation, 1083 N State Street, Orem, UT. URL: http://www.powerquest.com/.

PowerQuest (1998) *BootMagic User Guide*, PowerQuest Corporation, PO Box 1911, Orem, UT 84059-1911.

Quantum (1996), *Quantum Fireball™ 1.0/1.2/1.7/2.1/2.5/3.2/3.8 GB AT Product Manual*, Chapter 5, Table 5.1, Quantum Corporation, October.

Seagate (1991a) *Specifications for ST-506*, URL: http://www.seagate.com/cgi-bin/view.cgi?/mfm/st506.txt.

Seagate (1991b) *Specifications for ST-412*, URL: http://www.seagate.com/cgi-bin/view.cgi?/mfm/st412.txt.

Seagate (1994) *FIND-ATA.EXE v1.0, An ATA Interface Identify Drive Utility*, Seagate Technology, Inc., B-5 Technical Support, 920 Disc Drive, Scotts Valley, CA 95066. URL: http://www.seagate.com/support/disc/faq/faq96029.shtml.

Seagate (1995a) *SGATFMT4.EXE v4.0, Seagate Format Drive Utility*, Seagate Technology, Inc. URL: http://www.seagate.com/support/disc/faq/faq96029.shtml.

Seagate (1995b) *NFDisc v1.20, Partition Record display and maintenance*, Seagate Technology, Inc. URL: http://www.seagate.com/support/disc/faq/faq96029.shtml.

Seagate (1997a) *Cheetah 4.5- to 9.1-Gbyte capacity disc drives.* URL: http://www.seagate.com/, publication number 1480-002.

Seagate (1997b) *Low level Formatting an ATA (IDE) Hard Drive*, Seagate Technology, Inc., B-5 Technical Support, 920 Disc Drive, Scotts Valley, CA 95066. URL: http://www.seagate.com/support/disc/faq/faq96029.shtml.

Seagate (1997c) *Seagate Fast ATA/Fast ATA-2 Fact Sheet*, Seagate Technology, Corporate Communications. URL: http://www.seagate.com/.

Seagate (1998) *FAQ Disk Manager Basics, BIOS Limitations*, Seagate Technology, Inc. URL: http://www.seagate.com/support/disc/faq/bioslmt.shtml.

Symantec (1999) *Norton Utilities Version 4, User's Guide, Norton Disk Editor*, Symantec Corporation, Peter Norton Group, 10201 Torre Avenue, Cupertino, CA 95014.

Tischer, M. and Jennrich, B. (1996) *PC Intern, The Encyclopedia of System Programming*, Abacus, Data Becker Edition.

Western Digital (1997a) *Enhanced IDE Interface*, Western Digital Corporation, 8105 Irvine Center Drive, Irvine, CA 92618. URL: http://www.wdc.com/.

Western Digital (1997b) *Drive Parameters*, 25 March, Western Digital Corporation, 8105 Irvine Center Drive, Irvine, CA 92618. URL: http://www.wdc.com/.

Western Digital (1998a) *Large Disk Integration*, 7 October, Western Digital Corporation, 8105 Irvine Center Drive, Irvine, CA 92618. URL: http://www.wdc.com/.

Western Digital (1998b) *8.4 GB Capacity Barrier*, Western Digital Corporation, 8105 Irvine Center Drive, Irvine, CA 92618. URL: http://www.wdc.com/.

Western Digital (1999) *EZ-Drive FAQ Sheet*, 9 March, Western Digital Corporation, 8105 Irvine Center Drive, Irvine, CA 92618. URL: http://www.wdc.com/.

Western Digital (undated a) *User's Guide WD1003V-MM1 Winchester Disk Controller (also MM2, SR1 and SR2).* URL: http://www.wdc.com/.

Western Digital (undated b) *Enhanced IDE Implementation Guide, Version 5*, Western Digital Corporation, 8105 Irvine Center Drive, Irvine, CA 92618. URL: http://www.wdc.com/.

Zacker, C. (1995) *Upgrading and Repairing Networks*, Que, San Francisco, CA.

6.   The Treatment of PCs

Introduction

Up to this point, we have concentrated on the technical issues: on how computers work and their construction; on how information is stored; and, in particular, on how and where information can be hidden or inadvertently left on hard disk drives. This technical understanding gives us both the knowledge and the confidence that will enable us to find information of evidential value from a PC. However, unless we carry out the investigative processes in ways which guarantee the integrity of that evidence, it is unlikely to be admissible in court. We thus now need to concern ourselves with perhaps the most important part of all: the processes that we need to carry out and the practices that we need to observe in order to extract information from PCs and present it as admissible evidence in court. In this chapter we are going to consider the treatment of PCs and will be looking at the topics listed below:

- A guide to good practice
- The principles of computer-based evidence
- Search and seizure
- Intelligence, preparation and briefing
- At the search scene
- The operating dilemma
- Shutdown, seizure and transportation
- Computer examinations
- Physical disks and logical drives
- Interpreting partition tables
- Imaging and copying

In the next chapter, we will be looking at the rather different processes involved in the treatment of electronic organizers.

We first look at the principles of computer-based evidence as recommended in the ACPO *Good Practice Guide*. Then we look at the problems of mounting a search and seizure operation and the issues that might occur on-site when seizing computers from a suspect's premises. Guidelines are given for each of the major activities, including the shutdown, seizure and transportation of the equipment. The next section considers the receipt of the equipment into the analyst's laboratory and the process of examination and the production of evidence. An example of a specific disk with a number of partitions set up on it is then described in detail, and full guidance is given on interpreting the host of figures that result. Finally, the issues of imaging and copying are outlined and compared.

▪ ▪

The ACPO *Good Practice Guide*

The Association of Chief Police Officers (ACPO) Crime Committee have produced a *Good Practice Guide for Computer Based Evidence*, the most recent version of which is version 2, dated 23 June 1999 (ACPO, 1999). The document is written as a guide to good practice when dealing with computers and other electronic devices in the possession of a suspect. It is intended for use by officers attending a search and seizure operation, by investigating officers, by computer evidence recovery personnel and by external consulting witnesses. The *Good Practice Guide* is fully supported by the authors of this book.

The Principles of Computer-Based Evidence

Four principles have been established and these, together with a brief explanation from the *Good Practice Guide*, are reproduced here, with the kind permission of ACPO:

- *Principle 1*
  No action taken by Police or their agents should change data held on a computer or other media which may subsequently be relied upon in Court.
- *Principle 2*
  In exceptional circumstances where a person finds it necessary to access original data held on a target computer that person must be competent to do so and to give evidence explaining the relevance and the implications of their actions.
- *Principle 3*
  An audit trail or other record of all processes applied to computer-based evidence should be created and preserved. An independent third party should be able to examine those processes and achieve the same result.
- *Principle 4*
  The Officer in charge of the case is responsible for ensuring that the law and these principles are adhered to. This applies to the possession of, and access to, information contained in a computer. They must be satisfied that anyone accessing the computer, or any use of a copying device, complies with these laws and principles.

Explanation of the Principles

Data held on a computer is no different from information or text contained on a document. For this reason evidence that is based on a computer or on computer media is subject to the same rules and laws that apply to documentary evidence.

The Doctrine of Documentary evidence may be explained as: "*The onus is on the prosecution to show to the Court that the evidence produced is no more and no less now than when it was first taken into the possession of police*".

Operating systems and other programs frequently alter and add to the contents of the computer's storage space. This happens automatically without the user necessarily being aware that the data has been changed. In order to comply with the principles of computer-based evidence, a copy should be made of the entire target device. Partial or selective file copying should not be readily considered as an alternative. The copy or copies should be made onto media that should be retained for examination and subsequent Court use.

In a minority of cases it may not be possible to obtain an image using a recognized imaging device. In these circumstances it may become necessary for the original machine to be accessed to recover the evidence. With this in mind it is essential that any such access is made by a witness who is competent to give evidence to a Court of Law. It is essential to objectively show to a Court that the continuity and integrity of the evidence has been preserved. It is necessary to demonstrate to the Court how evidence has been recovered, showing each process through which the evidence was obtained. Evidence should be preserved to an extent that a third party is able to repeat the same process and arrive at the same result as that presented to a Court.

Search and Seizure

Forensic Computing bears a certain similarity to that ancient recipe for jugged hare, the initial line of which optimistically states "First go forth and capture a suitable hare". This chapter, which is primarily aimed at law enforcement personnel, outlines the procedures to be followed for a search and seizure operation where one of the key aims is to take possession of, or image, one or more suspect computers.

The primary objective for an operation of this kind is to secure all evidence in such a manner that its integrity cannot later be challenged and that it is obtained under circumstances which ensure its admissibility in Court.

Pre-Search Intelligence

While it is accepted that there will be occasions when an urgent and immediate search operation is thrust upon the team, most search and seizure tasks should be thoroughly well pre-planned. It is during this stage that as much intelligence as possible is gathered about the premises, the occupants, the users and the computer systems that are located inside. It is vital that the number of computers, their types, operating systems and connections are all known before entry. This will then permit the search team to be prepared with the right equipment and the right expertise, including if necessary any outside experts, and will enable them to deal with the systems correctly and efficiently once entry has been effected.

Some key decisions will have to be made prior to entry. If the premises contain a large network it may well be that it is only possible to target certain specific machines and image those within the time allowed. Such machines will need to be identified prior to the search, if at all possible. If seizure of machines is the objective then justification must exist not only for the seizure itself but also for the effect on the suspects once seizure has taken place. It will be rare for a business to continue to operate effectively after its computers have been removed, and there are likely to be adverse effects as a result of any on-site imaging or copying.

Intelligence about the actual systems installed in the target premises may indicate the need for an independent expert to be engaged to give advice at the scene. If known individual targets have been identified consideration could be given to using expertise within the company to assist with advice and information on their systems. Such persons should only be used if it is clear that they have no possible involvement in the matter under investigation. These people are not bound to help and some may even be obstructive because of the disturbance to their workplace.

Contingency planning is also important where information and intelligence is sketchy, incomplete or inadequate. Search team leaders should be in a position to obtain further assistance immediately, in terms of expertise or additional personnel, should they come across unexpected systems at the scene.

The timing of the operation, if possible, should be set outside the normal operating hours of the suspect systems. If an office environment is the target, going in with the cleaner at 7 a.m. is a good idea, since then the premises and the machines can be safely secured before the daily business gets under way.

Pre-Search Preparation

The team allocated to the task of seizing the machines should ensure that they have the following items, in addition to the normal search and seizure equipment:

- *An adequate toolkit*
  This should contain an array of flat and crosshead screwdrivers, a small pair of pliers, wire cutters for cutting cable ties, and a clean 1/2 inch paintbrush for cleaning away dust and dirt.

- *A search kit*
  This should comprise an array of plastic, paper and padded bags, adhesive and tie-on labels, tape and elastic bands for securing leads, plastic crates and flat pack boxes for removal of items, and blankets or foam sheets for padding during carriage. Each item, or package of items, should be sealed on seizure, particularly individual computer units containing data storage items. Coloured pens and labels can be used to identify all connections. Plastic bags should not be used for individual packaging of single electronic components as they may create a static charge which could damage the component.

- *Search forms and sketch plan sheets*
  A sketch plan identifying the locations of items seized should always be made, and a master property form with associated numbering should be used to list and identify items against the labels placed on them. All seal numbers must also be listed.

- *Still and video cameras*
  Screenshots of operating machines are useful to prove correct shutdown procedures, and *in situ* pictures are a boon to proving later the proximity of items to

suspects and the general layout of the premises. Video is good for recording the removal of complicated connections, although labels should still be used as well.

- *Disk boxes*
  These are for the removal of floppy disks found on the premises. It is essential to ensure that all floppy disks can be identified as to their exact location at seizure.
- *Mobile telephone*
  This is useful to obtain further assistance or advice while on-site. It should not be used near computer equipment.
- *Blank floppy disks*
  A number of clean, blank, floppy disks should be prepared beforehand and thoroughly erased to ensure that no previous data is present. These may be used to save files, prior to switching off, on computers found running.
- *A torch*
  Very useful for searching those little unlit places where connecting leads tend to be tucked away.

The Search Briefing

An operational order for any pre-planned search should be prepared allocating tasks and giving details of the aims and objectives of the search. If computers are involved the person in overall charge must be aware of the ACPO *Good Practice Guide* (ACPO, 1999). All officers who may be involved in the operation should attend the briefing. One possible exception to this may be the computer forensic analysts if it is felt that they should retain a degree of independence from the case itself. Not only should the briefing contain the intelligence information and the logistics of the search but it must also include a briefing to all officers on the likely presence of computers and the methods of seizure, the staff available to do this, and how they may be contacted. Distinct warnings should be given to discourage enthusiastic and untrained amateurs from tampering with the equipment. Such tampering could lead to contamination of any evidence found and its exclusion from subsequent Court proceedings. Use of samples or some visual representations of the equipment likely to be found will assist in its identification by untrained personnel.

The briefing must include the provisions of any warrant or similar order under which the search and seizure are authorized. It is particularly important that any conditions attached are strictly adhered to (see practical notes in later section).

At the Search Scene

The first priority at the search scene is to gain total control both of the premises and of the occupants. Identification of the numbers and locations of computers present will then permit control to be taken of the computers themselves and their environment. Suspects should be kept clear of all machines and any connections to them, including power, network and telephone. The method and order of seizure can then be assessed and the imaging and copying workload identified if required.

It is not possible in these pages to cover all possible permutations of computers, networks and connections. The advice that follows may need to be modified to allow for the particular configuration faced by the search team. In general terms, where a major network is involved, planning should be done well prior to the search. It is likely that on-site imaging will offer the only reasonable solution to such configurations. For small networks and standalone machines, subject to the issues of disruption to the business already mentioned, seizure is probably the more convenient option, allowing machines to be imaged later and in more controlled circumstances.

To ensure the integrity of any item seized, particularly those items which contain data, security seals should be used on all property containers and the serial numbers entered onto the search log.

The Operating Dilemma

On all occasions where search teams find machines that are switched on and operating they face a dilemma. By allowing the equipment to complete its current task they may gain, or they may lose, evidence. A value judgement has therefore to be undertaken.

As an example, consider a modem or network connection which is operating and is clearly transferring data. It may be that the system is receiving a vital email which contains damning evidence against the suspect. On the other hand it could be receiving a similar email which completely exonerates the suspect from any wrong doing. Added to these possibilities, the file being received might be routine and of no evidential value but is overwriting some other important evidence on the hard disk. The question is whether to interrupt this transaction or not. Will evidence thereby be gained or lost? That is the dilemma.

The search team need to make a decision immediately and it should be based on their knowledge of the enquiry and the likelihood of relevant evidence being gained or lost, regardless of whether it benefits the prosecution or the defence. To assist in their decision, they will need to examine the contents of and active computer screens to try to determine what is happening. Needless to say, whatever decision is taken, the circumstances must be recorded in detail.

Machines Which Are Switched Off

The following is a list of actions which should be taken in order when dealing with machines which are already switched off when their seizure takes place:

- One of the most important of all is to start logging all your actions.
- Disconnect any external data communication lines ensuring that such disconnection will not impinge upon the activities of other members of the search team. This will isolate the machine from any external electronic access and help prevent the loss or overwriting of data. If possible, physically trace where the connection goes and note the details. (See also *The Operating Dilemma* section above.)
- Be satisfied that the computer is actually switched off. Check that it is not in sleep mode or using a blank screen saver. LED indicators on the case of the machine or the monitor may indicate that power is applied. DO NOT SWITCH ON. Be warned that some laptops will power up when the lid is raised.

- Photograph or video the connections *in situ*. Label all cables and sockets so that the machine can be reconstructed exactly at a later time. Remove the cables.

- Remove, package and seal all items noting individual identification, serial numbers and the like. Sealing an item in front of a suspect is always a good idea. Record all seal and label numbers in the search log.

- Check the area for Post-it® notes, diaries, notepads and the like which may have passwords recorded on them. Consider asking the user if passwords are required for the machine or any of the applications and what they are. Note any replies in the log.

- Consider the seizure of printers and paper samples, if relevant. Some printouts can be associated with a particular printer using forensic techniques. Take advice before the search on this matter.

- If equipment is to be examined physically for fingerprints, ensure that aluminium powder is not used, as it is a conductor of electricity and can damage the equipment. Any such examination should take place after imaging with the machine, including the power supply unit, thoroughly cleaned internally and externally afterwards. It should then be tested by a competent engineer before it is reused or returned.

Machines Which Are Switched On

The following is a list of actions which should be taken in order when dealing with machines which are already switched on, or suspected to be so, when their seizure takes place:

- As before, one of the most important of all is to start logging all your actions. In particular, note all keystrokes made at the keyboards and all responses that appear on the displays. The use of photographs or video is a distinct advantage in these circumstances.

- Disconnect any external data communication lines ensuring that such disconnection will not impinge upon the activities of other members of the search team. This will isolate the machine from any external electronic access and help prevent the loss or overwriting of data. If possible, physically trace where the connection goes and note the details. (See also *The Operating Dilemma* section above.)

- Check the monitor to confirm that it is actually switched on and powered.

- If the screen is blank, note that it may be running a blank screen saver.

- If the DOS prompt, or what appears to be a DOS prompt, is visible, check for the mode of operation. Use the EXIT command to determine whether this is Windows' full-screen DOS mode. Record the screen state.

- If programs are running note and record screen states and save any open files to floppy disk. *Do not* instigate a write to the hard disk. Shut down all open applications when data is saved. Switch power off when the machine has been cleared.

- Proceed as from the fourth item in the section *Machines Which Are Switched Off* above.

Shutdown Procedures for Servers

Because servers may be so critical to a business, special procedures need to be observed here.

- As before, one of the most important of all is to start logging all your actions. In particular, note all keystrokes made at the keyboards and all responses that appear on the displays. The use of photographs or video is a distinct advantage in these circumstances.
- Ensure that the expertise is available for the particular operating system of the server. Note that nearly all server operating systems (Unix, Linux, Windows NT etc.) require to write system information back to the disk before power is turned off. Failure to permit this may result in corrupted disks which could inhibit not only the extraction of evidence but also the restoration of the system for subsequent use by the business.
- Follow exactly the correct operating system procedure for shutting down the server, then proceed as from the fourth item in the section *Machines Which Are Switched Off* above.

Seizure – What Should Be Taken

When a system is seized and dismantled, it is essential that it be capable of identical reconstruction. The following items should be taken:

- The main system unit.
- The keyboard and mouse.
- Any external expansion units or cards.
- All connecting leads.
- Any dongles. These are software security devices, often with connectors that are plugged into the parallel port.
- Power supply units, particularly for laptops.

In addition, the following peripheral items may be taken, if deemed relevant:

- External backup devices, such as Jaz, Zip and tape drives.
- Printers. It may be possible to associate output documents with particular printers.
- Modems. Some of these can contain a memory of telephone numbers.
- Scanners.
- Digital cameras.
- PCMCIA cards and leads.

All electronic media found should be taken for examination. In this case, the exhibit bags should be labelled rather than the items themselves. Typical items are:

- Any hard disks not fitted within machines
- All floppy disks.

- Any CD-ROM and CD-RW discs.
- Backup tapes and cartridges of whatever format.
- Video tapes, if a video backup system is fitted.

Other items that may be considered for seizure are as follows:

- Personal organizers, palmtops, PIMs and PDAs. Remember to consider battery replacement if these are retained in storage.
- Mobile telephones. Most of these have a memory of numbers and other data.
- Landline telephones. Some of these have a memory of numbers.
- Answering machines. Some of these have memory.
- Fax machines. Some of these have memory, some retain a duplicate record.
- Dictating machines and tapes.
- Multi-purpose units. That is, combinations of some of the above.

Transport and Storage of IT Equipment

It is important to remember that most IT equipment is susceptible to magnetic fields and therefore removal and storage methods should be such as to avoid exposure to them. There are also considerations with regard to static electrical charges on components which have been separately packaged as well as the effect of condensation on items packaged in plastic bags. Hard disks in particular can be damaged by dropping or other impact. Useful tips for storage as well as removal are as follows:

- Keep all items away from magnetic sources, such as loudspeakers, radios, electrical motors and the like.
- Store at room temperature, not in a damp cellar or garage. Avoid damp and protect from dust.
- Take care when stacking to ensure that fragile items are protected from damage.
- Avoid physical shocks.
- Generally the use of tough, breathable, paper bags and sacks or aerated plastic bags is the preferred option for most items.

Particular care should be taken with the following items:

- The main system unit. This should be handled with care and kept upright in a secure place when transporting so that it cannot fall over or be subject to shocks.
- Monitors. These are best transported screen down on the back seat of a car and secured by an elasticated strap or something similar.
- Hard disks. For individual components and circuit boards use anti-static bags, tough paper bags or wrap in paper and use aerated plastic bags.
- Electronic media such as floppy disks, tape cartridges and so forth. These must not be folded, bent or stored under heavy objects. Do not label the item itself; label the bag in which it is stored.
- Personal organizers, palmtops, PIMs and PDAs. Protect any exposed keyboard from inadvertent pressure. The use of a stiff cardboard sheet around the item can

prevent this. Place the organizer in a sealed envelope or something similar to prevent operation through a sealed evidence bag. Consider the need to change batteries regularly.

Practical Notes

Evidence produced from a suspect's computer tends often to be quite damning, and thus it becomes the major target for the defence during the usual round of applications to get evidence excluded. The evidence itself cannot usually be argued with; it is either present on the computer or it is not. The continuity of the evidence, however, must be demonstrable and its integrity unblemished. The use of security seals and a record of their breaking and replacement goes a long way to avoiding allegations of the planting of evidence on machines or into images before examination.

At the time of writing there continues to be inconsistency with regard to the interpretation of some legislation. In particular, where warrants are being executed, it is being argued that the seizure of a computer system was unlawful because the whole of the content of that machine could not be shown as being evidentially *relevant*. It is the term relevant which is the crux of this argument. Under a Police and Criminal Evidence Act warrant the material searched for must be relevant evidence, together with other considerations. Thus, it is argued, the police are only empowered to remove those files which directly contain evidence of the offence being investigated. If this argument is upheld, and the precedent set, the implications for searches are immense. It suggests that all data must be searched at the scene and its relevance established before it can be removed, presumably only as copies of the relevant files rather than the whole machine, disk or image. It is not possible to predict the outcome of this and other arguments, so it is advisable that practitioners keep up to date with current decisions and changes in legislation in order to avoid breaching the "current" interpretation. This area is relatively new. The law should settle down eventually once arguments like the above have been tested and resolved.

Another point on warrants arose in the case of R v Du'Kett and others. Lengthy applications were made to exclude all the evidence found on Du'Kett's machines. Du'Kett was the main defendant in a network of software pirates and Cambridgeshire police executed a warrant at his home and seized a number of machines and huge amounts of software. The machines were examined and provided the majority of the evidence and intelligence identifying the other members of the network. It was clear that if the evidence from the first machines examined could be excluded, all evidence following the information found would also have to be excluded. The defence decided to attack the issue, legality and execution of the warrant.

The first target was the formal information document. Having obtained a copy of the police copy of this document they made enquiries of the magistrates clerk. It was erroneously assumed that the copy they obtained was a copy of the information after the warrant had been issued. It was alleged that the application for the warrant was illegal because the information had not been signed by a magistrate. The original could not be found among the Court archives, but eventually the defence accepted that their application was based upon a false assumption and withdrew. The second line of attack followed the ruling of R v Reading Justices [and others] where it was shown that although a warrant was issued to a constable it was effectively executed by others. The constable was simply present while the search was carried out. In the Du'Kett case it was alleged that the search was orchestrated by a member of FAST, who was present, and that the police officers were simply assisting him. Therefore the execution was unlawful. This application was also withdrawn after argument.

The lessons to be learned from the above are:

- Keep a copy of the original information and mark it as such.
- Provided that the Court agrees, obtain a copy of the information after it has been marked up as the warrant is granted.
- Ensure that any parties, other than those to which the warrant is granted (usually the police), are actually named on the warrant and the reason why they are present is given. This would apply to any external assistants or experts.
- Keep a copy of the warrant itself.
- Keep a copy of the briefing document. This should include the role and reason for the presence of any individual who is named on the warrant. Ensure that during execution the persons to whom the warrant is issued are demonstrably in charge of the search with others purely assisting or advising. The roles must be clear.

Computer Examination – Initial Steps

Having dealt with the seizure of machines in the previous section, this section deals with the reception of the machine at the place of examination, up to the point at which data, which may be of evidential value, is actually examined and analyzed.

In our trek from the search and seizure of the machines through the process of their examination to the production of evidential material at Court, it is apparent that we must bear a number of important matters in mind. Of these, the ACPO principles, outlined above, give us the good practice that we must apply to the process of examination. This results in the following:

- The integrity of the original data must be preserved; therefore we will have to use non-intrusive examination techniques (Principle 1).
- If the original data has to be examined, for whatever reason, the analyst must be competent to do so and to give evidence explaining their actions. Trained and qualified staff must be used (Principle 2).
- An audit trail is required and an independent party must be able to reproduce the same actions and get the same result. We must therefore keep a full log of all actions (Principle 3).

The prime objective of the analyst is to recover and secure, from whatever medium is examined, a true copy of the data stored on that medium. This should be done, wherever possible, without any alteration to the original data as a whole. The process for the recovery of evidence is a forensic exercise; thus only forensically sound hardware, software and procedures should be used.

Full records of all actions taken must be kept. It is common that the brief given to the analyst is not as full as it could be, or the suspect may change his or her explanation at a later stage. Even the recording of a minor matter may play a pivotal part in proving or disproving a claim made by one side or the other. Although not generally aimed at persons who will give expert evidence, this book promotes the principle that a forensic computer analyst will give unbiased evidence or, where required by the Court, expert evidence based upon the facts, and will stand apart from any loyalty to the prosecution or the defence, regardless of who may be the employer.

Reception of Machines and Media

All items should be received in sealed bags. Continuity from person to person should be recorded by the exchange of signatures and a formal identification of the item, particularly the seal number. Local procedures will need to be followed with regard to the detail of the actual records kept, but the log of events of the item for examination should be started at this point and signed appropriately by the person delivering it.

From this stage the security of the item, and any information held upon it, is the responsibility of the person receiving it. Precautions should be taken to ensure that there is no accidental or deliberate tampering, and work on and storage of these items should be in a secure environment.

Electrical Safety

A brief word on electrical safety is appropriate here. Most organizations employ a Safety at Work Officer, and there may be organizational guidelines in addition to the mandatory regulations. If the analyst is not fully conversant with these, reference should be made to the Safety at Work Officer. It should be noted that different officers actually interpret the regulations in differing ways. Further advice is also available from Local Authority Health and Safety Officers. The analyst might consider obtaining certification in Portable Appliance Testing (IEE, undated) and obtaining a copy of the Electricity at Work Regulations 1989 (HMSO, 1989; HSE Books, 1998; IEE, 1994).

Static Electricity

Many of the components within a computer are susceptible to damage by the discharge of static electricity, particularly the integrated circuits or chips. The analyst should take steps to discharge any body-held static charge prior to any physical examination of a machine simply by touching a known earth connection. In addition the use of anti-static straps and non-conducting tools will help to minimize the risk of static discharge damage.

External Physical Examination

First record the date and time of the breaking of the seal and then physically examine the item. If there is external damage which may have an effect upon the normal operation of the machine the only real alternative is to remove the medium from the machine and deal with this separately, on a host machine.

The external examination should also include recording details of the machine itself, such as make, model serial number and any identifying marks, scratches, stickers and the like.

Internal Physical Examination

Before embarking on an internal examination, it is important to bear in mind that the objective is to ensure that the machine is safe for imaging. Any deconstruction or detailed examination of parts should be left until the analyst is satisfied that a good image or images have been obtained. If a component is on the verge of breaking down it is more likely to do so if it is disturbed.

Once the external case has been removed it is a good idea to step back, place hands in pockets and carry out a purely visual inspection first. The majority of PC cases are designed so that most components and contents can be seen without removal of internal items. At this point it should be obvious to the practised eye if there is anything in the case which should not be there. It has been known for drug dealers to record transactions on their computer and place their stock inside the actual machine.

If there is anything in the case which warrants removal as an exhibit it is always better to get a specialist to remove it or at the very least to seek advice from one. If removal has to be done by the analyst then the use of protective rubber gloves is recommended and immediate bagging and sealing of the exhibit should be carried out. Photographs or video which record the item *in situ* and its subsequent removal can be beneficial.

When the visual inspection and record is complete, and subject to the rider at the beginning of this section, a closer inspection can take place, recording the expansion cards and internal devices present. Records should include the details of all hard disks fitted and their specifications, with particular regard to the disk drive parameters, where these are given on the disk. Any unconnected disks are best removed and dealt with on a host machine. Where any internal serial numbers are stated these should be recorded.

Proper recording of the internals of a particular machine can be of importance in demonstrating that the machine was capable of some particular operation, such as, for example, being able to play sound files or to connect to the Internet.

When satisfied that the machine is safe to operate and the details have been recorded the analyst may then move to the next step, that of booting the machine in preparation for imaging or copying.

Imaging and Copying

Physical Disks and Logical Drives

Before discussing imaging and copying it is important that the reader understands fully the implications of the earlier chapter on Disk Geometry, in particular the

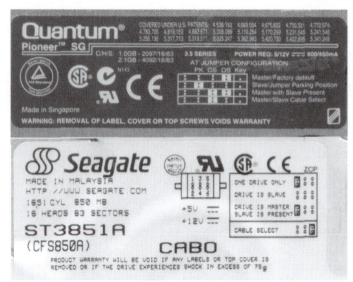

Fig. 6.1 Quantum and Seagate disk labels.

principles of CHS addressing. We must be able to identify the areas on the disk which may hold data to be copied or imaged. The "shape" and size of all hard disks are dictated by the physical characteristics of the disk itself as specified by the manufacturer. This invariably takes the form of a CHS statement on the case of the disk and within its own electronics to enable automatic detection by the computer on which it is to be used. Figure 6.1 Shows two examples of labels affixed to hard disks.

The CHS figures shown are the physical parameters of the disk. It is these figures which will be recognized by the machine and recorded internally in the BIOS variables, depending upon whether any translation is required or not. Physical disks are usually referred to by number. For example, when moving between physical and logical views of a disk in Norton Disk Editor, drives are referred to as Hard Disk 1, Hard Disk 2 etc., in physical view, and Disk A, Disk C, Disk D etc, in logical view.

The difference between the physical disk and the logical drive is a most important concept. The physical disk can be held in your hand; a logical drive is a different animal altogether and is created by partitioning.

Partitioning is covered in detail in Chapter 5. In short, a physical disk can be partitioned into one or more logical drives. Partitioning, using MS-DOS FDISK or a similar utility, permits users to choose the size of logical drive or drives which they wish to create on the physical hard disk. It is possible to partition a disk with areas that do not fall within partitions, so these areas would be unavailable to users. Alternatively, using readily available software, one can move part of the physical disk in and out of a partition at will and thus 'hide' the data contained therein. It thus follows that the forensic computer analyst must be aware of this and other possible scenarios and ensure that all the data on a disk is obtained and available for examination and analysis. Some imaging systems permit users to choose the type of image to be taken. Choices involving physical disks and logical drives are available. Users must be fully aware of the meanings of these terms and the implications of each type of image in terms of the data actually captured.

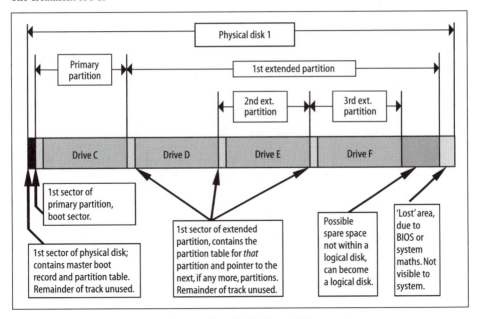

Fig. 6.2 Example partitioned disk.

In order to identify the areas of data which may be obtained by an image we will consider the example of a partitioned MS-DOS disk, as illustrated in Fig. 6.2.

The diagram is a schematic of what a partitioned DOS disk actually "looks" like. The physical disk extends from the very first sector at CHS 0,0,1 to the end of the disk, as reported by the BIOS (see the next section *Interpreting Partition Tables* for an explanation of this). The first logical drive always begins at CHS 0,1,1.

A physical image of this drive should capture all data within the area defined as "Physical Disk", including areas not within a logical drive. The image will thus contain all data from all areas of the disk which are capable of having data stored within them, whether defined for use or not. A logical image of a drive will contain only the data within the area of the defined drive. For example, a logical image of the primary partition in Fig. 6.2 will only contain the data from the area shown as that allocated to Drive C.

Interpreting Partition Tables

This topic is best illustrated by working through an example. Figure 6.3 is a schematic of a typical hard disk drive, a Seagate ST3851A with a CHS marking on the case of cylinders 1651, heads 16, and sectors 63. It has been partitioned using MS-DOS 6.22 `FDISK` to four partitions of 200 Mbyte, 250 Mbyte, 200 Mbyte and 160 Mbyte. The four partition tables are as shown, using slightly revised Norton Disk Editor partition table views. We need to remember that cylinders count from 0, heads from 0 and sectors from 1 in CHS addressing and that Norton Disk Editor uses a different sequence in its tables of Side, Cylinder and Sector. We have reordered them in Fig. 6.3 to the more traditional CHS form in an attempt to avoid more confusion than is necessary.

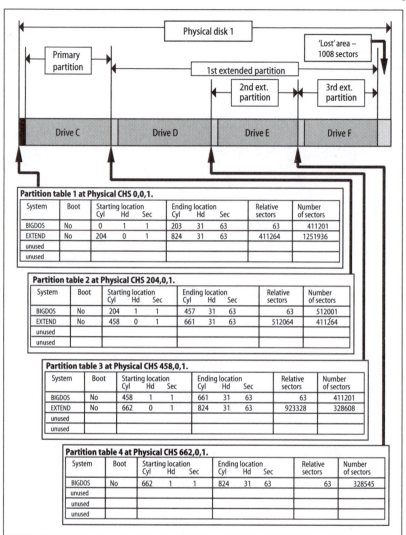

Fig. 6.3 Interpreting partition tables.

We also need to recall that "Relative Sectors" (see Chapter 5) is the logical block addressing (LBA) sector number from the beginning of the physical disk. For the primary partition, this starts immediately after the Master Boot Record track[1]; all tracks of course being 63 sectors in length. Note that the number is LBA 63 and not LBA 64 because LBA sector counting starts from 0. We should note also that the first extended partition (the container marked EXTEND in partition table 1) by default extends to the end of that part of the physical disk that is accessible to the BIOS. We will consider this issue further in a moment. The second and subsequent extended

---

1 A *track*, you will recall, being one head position of a cylinder.

partitions (marked EXTEND in partition tables 2 and 3) are nested within the first extended partition and their "Relative Sectors" declarations each refer to their LBA starting sector relative to the beginning of the first extended partition. However, the three logical partitions (marked BIGDOS in partition tables 2, 3 and 4) have "Relative Sectors" declarations which refer to their starting sector *relative to the beginning of their respective extended partitions* and not to the beginning of the first extended partition. This can be a source of some considerable confusion. In each case, the logical partition starts immediately after the extended partition table track and is at LBA 63 relative to the start of the respective extended partition. Finally we should note that the CHS addresses of the various boundaries are always at cylinder perimeters.

In order to fully understand and analyze the partition tables we must first know what the physical CHS parameters are. They have already been given as CHS 1651, 16, 63, on the disk label but we must also know what the BIOS "sees" when it detects the disk. The test machine that was used to create these tables has an auto-detecting BIOS, and the disk was actually detected as CHS 825, 32, 63. Using the BIOS detect disk utility gives us three choices, as shown in Table 6.1.

Table 6.1 BIOS disk detect options.

Choice	Size (Mbyte)	Cylinders	Heads	Sectors	Type
1	851	825	32	63	LBA
2	852	1651	16	63	NORMAL
3	851	825	32	63	LARGE

Choice 1 is recommended, but it is important to note that the disk size changes between the choices. We know that the manufacturer's parameters are given by choice 2, which results in a total disk size of $1651 \times 16 \times 63 = 1\,664\,208$ sectors. On the other hand, the default values obtained from auto-detection are $825 \times 32 \times 63 = 1\,663\,200$ sectors. We see, therefore, that there are 1008 sectors, representing some 500 kbyte, which are not addressed by the BIOS. This is the so-called 'Lost' area referred to in Fig. 6.3. The differences, as we have seen before, are due to the need for translation of the disk parameters (see Chapter 5). Any physical image that is using the auto-detected parameters will not see the 'Lost' area. However, imaging a disk in its home machine will usually ensure that the correct[2] parameters are loaded by the BIOS. When hosting a drive elsewhere it is very important to check, if possible, the BIOS and CMOS settings of the home machine to ensure that the correct parameters are used.

Now we know that the disk, as seen by the BIOS, is of a total length of 1 663 200 sectors we can look at the partition tables to check exactly what areas are occupied by logical disks and what areas, if any, fall outside the partitions.

---

2 By *correct* here we mean those parameters which were set when the disk was written to by the user.

| **Explanation and notes** | **Areas accounted for** |

Partition Table 1, at LBA 0, CHS 0, 0, 1

1. This starts with the master boot record and partition table 1 in the first sector. The remainder (62 sectors) of the track is not used.

> LBA 0 to 62
> CHS 0, 0, 1 to 0, 0, 63

2. Drive C is defined as starting at LBA 63 and is of 411201 sectors in size.

> LBA 63 to 411263
> CHS 0, 1, 1 to 203, 31, 63

3. The first extended partition is defined as starting at LBA 411264 and is of 1251936 sectors in size. It thus stretches to end at sector LBA 1663199. Recognizing that LBA counting starts at 0, we note that this therefore uses 1663200 sectors, which is the size that was auto-detected. We therefore now know that the whole physical disk is within partitions. We do not, however, yet know to what extent the logical drives occupy this area. The first logical drive occupying all or part of this extended partition will be declared in a partition table in the first sector of the extended partition, at LBA 411264, CHS 204, 0, 1.

> LBA 411264 to 1663199
> CHS 204, 0, 1 to 824, 31, 63

Partition Table 2, at LBA 411264, CHS 204, 0, 1

1. This starts with partition table 2 in the first sector. The remainder (62 sectors) of the track is not used.

> LBA 411264 to 411326
> CHS 204, 0, 1 to 204, 0, 63

2. Drive D is defined as starting at sector 63 relative to the start of the partition, hence it starts at 411264 + 63 = LBA 411327. It is of 512001 sectors in size.

> LBA 411327 to 923327
> CHS 204, 1, 1 to 457, 31, 63

3. A second extended partition is defined as starting at sector 512064 relative to the start of the extended partition, hence it starts at 411264 + 512064 = LBA 923328. It is of 411264 sectors in size. The second logical drive occupying all or part of this extended partition will be declared in a partition table in the first sector of this extended partition, at LBA 923328, CHS 458, 0, 1.

> LBA 923328 to 1334591
> CHS 458, 0, 1 to 661, 31, 63

Partition Table 3, at LBA 923328, CHS 458, 0, 1

1. This starts with partition table 3 in the first sector. The remainder (62 sectors) of the track is not used.

> LBA 923328 to 923390
> CHS 458, 0, 1 to 458, 0, 63

2. Drive E is defined as starting at sector 63 relative to the start of the partition, hence it starts at 923328 + 63 = LBA 923391. It is of 411201 sectors in size.

LBA 923391 to 1334591
CHS 458, 1, 1 to 661, 31, 63

3. A third extended partition is defined as starting at sector 923328 relative to the start of the extended partition, hence it starts at 411264 + 923328 = LBA 1334592. It is of 328608 sectors in size. The third logical drive occupying all or part of this extended partition will be declared in a partition table in the first sector of this extended partition, at LBA 1334592, CHS 662, 0, 1.

LBA 1334592 to 1663199
CHS 662, 0, 1 to 824, 31, 63

Partition Table 4, at LBA 1334592, CHS 662, 0, 1

1. This starts with partition table 4 in the first sector. The remainder (62 sectors) of the track is not used.

LBA 1334592 to 1334654
CHS 662, 0, 1 to 662, 0, 63

2. Drive F is defined as starting at sector 63 relative to the start of the partition, hence it starts at 1334592 + 63 = LBA 1334655. It is of 328545 sectors in size.

LBA 1334655 to 1663199
CHS 662, 1, 1 to 824, 31, 63

We have now accounted for all 1663200 sectors (LBA 0 to LBA 1663199) and all 825 cylinders (from zero), 32 heads (from 0) and 63 sectors (from 1). The whole of this disk is addressed within partitions apart from the master boot record and the partition table tracks. Note also the 1008 lost sectors which have not been addressed by this BIOS. Do note, and be very wary of, the complex counting conventions that have to be used.

An Explanation of Imaging

Now that we fully understand the "shape" and size of the suspect disk we can consider what an image of it actually is. The principle of imaging itself is to obtain all the data present on the disk, whether it be "live" data or data in an unused area, in such a way that it can be examined as if the original disk itself was being examined. To obtain an image it is normal to use specialist software which reads the suspect disk from its very beginning to its very end, and creates an image file that contains all the data read in the same order. The image file, depending upon format and hardware used, can then be laid down on a disk of similar or larger capacity. Data appearing in a particular sector of the suspect disk will then appear in the same sector on the target disk.

To give an analogy, taking an image of a disk is similar to taking a copy of a video tape by connecting two tape machines together, recording on one and playing back on the other, and running both tapes from beginning to end. The copy tape (the target) will contain not only the film that was perhaps taped last night but also the adverts before it and, at the end, all the odds and ends of previous recordings, just as on the original tape.

Generally, it is believed that an image of a hard disk drive when it is laid down on another drive is a true "mirror" image of the original. This is very definitely *not* the case. Where this belief came from is not clear. Possibly it was from one of the manufacturers of imaging hardware and software, where a salesperson's over-simplified explanation of what the product actually did became the standing view. It is understandable that such a simplified picture was, and to some extent still is, used to enable non-technical staff to visualize the concepts.

The actual situation is very different. As a result of improved electronics and modern advanced methods of manufacture, defects within the hard disk itself are not seen by the normal user. Although there are minor defects on a vast proportion of new disks, these defects do not detract from the actual storage area of the disk itself. A number of differing methods are used (as we discussed in Chapter 5) to avoid the defective areas by moving the data to another place on the disk. The map of the disk, within its own electronics, takes these areas into account when accessing the disk and returning the data required. All of this takes place within the disk itself and is totally invisible elsewhere. It therefore follows that although images may be a complete bit-by-bit copy of the electronic patterns on the original disk, it is not necessarily the case[3] that the data is in exactly the same place on the surface of one of the platters on the image copy as it is on the original disk. It is therefore not a mirror image. It should be emphasized that these storage changes from original to image copy are invisible outside of the disk itself, and so have no bearing on the imaging process or on any other operation involving the disk, including forensic exami-nation. However, from the point of view of giving evidence, it is essential that the analyst understands the true nature of the situation, and is thus able to deal with the most searching of technical questions.

There is one further point about knowing the physical size of the suspect disk, and that is knowing the extent of it when the image is laid down on another disk. If the examination software uses a physical address it will, of course, search the whole of the target disk when executed. Such a search will include the area of any larger disk between the end of the image and the end of the disk. Being able to identify the last sector of the image, and thus being able to curtail searching at that point, may save the analyst a lot of search time.

Copying

In some cases it is necessary to copy files from a suspect or target disk to another storage medium. Use of the MS-DOS COPY command or drag and drop in Windows[4] is an acceptable practice as the utilities are tried and tested. For floppy disks DISKCOPY is perfectly adequate. It is strongly recommended that any floppy disks or hard drives that are used for temporary storage are completely erased before use in order to avoid any possible claims of contamination.

---

3   Indeed, it is very unlikely.

4   Though note the problems with copying LFNs in Windows, see Chapter 5.

A Brief Comparison of Imaging and Copying

In the early days of forensic computing, before imaging was widely available, most recovered evidence was in the form of copied files or raw sectors. When imaging became the norm, the use of copying decreased. However, copying does have some advantages over imaging, and, in this final section we will make a brief comparison of the two.

Imaging	Copying
Images usually need re-loading before viewing can take place.	Copies can be viewed immediately.
Imaging can be a lengthy process.	Copying can be used when convenient or expedient, or, to recover evidence from "unusual" machines or those which are unsuitable for imaging.
Special equipment is required. Solutions are offered which use software alone or specialist hardware and software.	No special equipment or software requirements.
Can be expensive both in terms of equipment and some media.	Carries no additional costs.
Training in the specific solution is required often at a considerable cost.	Little training required.
Captures and preserves all data on a disk, including deleted files, swap files, slack space, FAT unallocated space and FAT unaddressed space.	Applies to files only.
Reconstructed disk can be "run". Acknowledged as the better solution, preserving date and time stamps and enhancing continuity and integrity of any evidence found.	

References

ACPO (1999) *Good Practice Guide for Computer Based Evidence, Version 2*, Association of Chief Police Officers of England, Wales and Northern Ireland, ACPO Crime Committee, 23 June.

IEE (undated) *City & Guilds Portable Appliance Testing Course.* See http://www.iee.org.uk/Profdev/Courses/cg_pat.htm.

HMSO (1989) *The Electricity at Work Regulations 1989, Statutory Instrument 1989 635*, HMSO, London.

HSE Books (1998) *Memorandum of Guidance on the Electricity at Work Regulations 1989, HSR 25*, HMSO, London.

IEE (1994) *The IEE Code of Practice for In-Service Inspection and Testing of Electrical Equipment*, IEE, London.

7. *The Treatment of Electronic Organizers*

Introduction

In this chapter, our main concern is with the extraction of admissible evidence from electronic organizers, although other specialist electronic devices may be treated in a similar way. The topics that we will cover are:

- Principles of operation
- Batteries and memories
- Password protection
- Switching on the organizer
- Application of the ACPO guideline principles
- Seizure of organizers
- Examination and what may be possible
- Dealing with the password
- Open heart surgery

We begin by outlining the principles associated with electronic organizers and identifying their major characteristics. We then go on to consider the application of the ACPO *Good Practice Guide* principles and to recommend some guidelines for seizure of organizers. Finally, we discuss the examination of organizers and look particularly at how admissible evidence might be obtained from protected areas.

Electronic Organizers

Electronic organizers range from very small, very cheap devices that can hold no more than a few tens or so of telephone entries up to large, relatively expensive units that are as powerful as desktop PCs and that can hold vast numbers of text, sound, graphics and other types of computer files. Examples of some typical organizers can be seen in Fig. 7.1.

Some of the larger organizers are now using the Windows CE operating system (see Fig. 7.2) which then makes them fully compatible with Windows based PCs. Such systems often have Windows CE versions of the Microsoft Office suite pre-loaded,

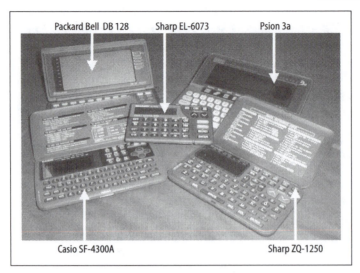

Fig. 7.1 Some typical organizers.

Fig. 7.2 A Windows CE organizer – the HP 320 LX.

with a view to providing a user with mobile use of the Office programs together with facilities for automatic updating and synchronization with their desktop PC system. Despite this move, there is still an immense variety in the types of electronic organizer that are available, and this variety appears currently to be increasing rather than moving, as did the development of the PC, to a standard product. A current database, which is known to be incomplete, records over 70 different manufacturers of electronic organizers with more than 450 different models between them, and most of these models are quite different in operation from one another.

Principles of Operation

Electronic organizers may be called Digital Diaries, Palmtops, Memo Masters, Databank Calculators and so forth. Although each may perform differently from one another in detail, all organizers follow a similar basic design. They contain a small microcomputer with a miniature keyboard and a liquid crystal display together with memory chips in which all the information is stored. In short, they are no different, in principle, from the black box model of an information processing system that we met at Fig. 3.20. The amount of memory available for storage is often indicated in the name of the organizer, for example: 2KB, 15KB, 32KB and so forth. KB, as you might expect, stands for kbyte and 1KB represents approximately enough storage room for a thousand or so characters of text information. The memory is usually kept active by batteries and if these fail, all information contained in the organizer is likely to be lost[1]. Often there are two sets of batteries: a main set which is designed to run the display, keyboard and microcomputer when the organizer is switched on; and a backup battery which maintains information in the memory if and when the main batteries become discharged. These two sets of batteries are shown in Fig. 7.3 together with the microcomputer, which, in this case uses *chip on board* (COB) technology (see later section) and the memory chip which here uses a standard *dual in line* (DIL) package. This particular memory chip is volatile static random access memory (SRAM), hence the need for battery backup, and it can store 128 kbyte of information.

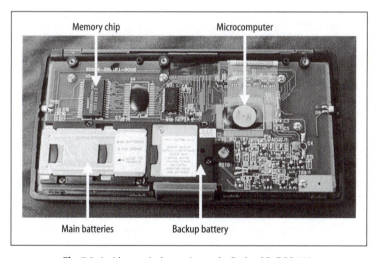

Fig. 7.3 Inside a typical organizer – the Packard Bell DB 128.

---

1   In some very recent organizers, use has been noted of serial EEPROM memory. This does not require any kind of battery support to maintain its information content and it is claimed to have a data retention that is better than 200 years! See Microchip (1997).

Two Important Points about Batteries

Most current organizers use SRAM for their internal memory and thus require some form of electrical power to be present at all times if they are to retain the information that they hold. This leads to two important points for an analyst to be aware of:

- Just because the display is not working when the organizer is switched on does not mean that all the information is necessarily lost. It may be that the main set of batteries have failed and hence the display cannot operate, but that a backup battery is still active. In this case, on replacing the main batteries, we should still be able to recover all the information that is held.

- Removal of all the batteries will normally guarantee a loss of all the information in the memory. We have used the word "normally" here because some systems retain a small charge which will often keep the memory active for several minutes even with all the batteries removed. However, switching the organizer on when all the batteries are removed will usually dissipate this charge very quickly and cause all the information to be lost. It is thus particularly important not to return the organizer to a suspect until forensic analysis has been completed. It is the work of a moment to remove the batteries and thus possibly destroy incriminating evidence[2].

Memory Extensions

Many of the larger organizers have means by which the internal memory capacity can be extended through the use of add on devices which are also often used for backing up information. These may be called by proprietary names such as "IC Cards", "Solid State Disks" or "Memory Disks" and they may be fitted into plug in slots on the organizer which are specially designed for this purpose. They may either contain free random access memory (RAM) which extends the organizer's capacity, or read-only memory (ROM) programs which extend the organizer's functionality. They may be very large in capacity, capable of holding, for example, as much as 10 million characters of text information (10 Mbyte), and are often significantly larger than the internal memory of the organizer itself. The RAM devices may contain either standard SRAM memory chips, similar to those in the organizer, with their own integral lithium battery on the device, or a form of *Flash EPROM* memory chips that do not require backup batteries. The ROM devices may be one-time-programmable ROM or masked ROM; see SIBO Software Development Kit (Psion, 1992).

Figure 7.4 shows a typical solid state disk (SSD), manufactured by Psion PLC, resting on top of the rear casing of a Psion 3a organizer. Clearly visible in the figure are the main and backup batteries as well as the two SSD drive slots, both of which have their doors slightly open. The SSD may be pushed into either slot to give access, in this case, to a further 128 kbyte of Flash EPROM.

In memory terms, the Psion Series 3 range tends to be on the medium to large size compared with other organizers. The one shown in Fig. 7.4 has 2 Mbyte of internal

---

2   An organizer was received for analysis on one occasion where the batteries were neatly sealed in a separate evidence bag so as not to allow any possible leakage to damage the organizer.

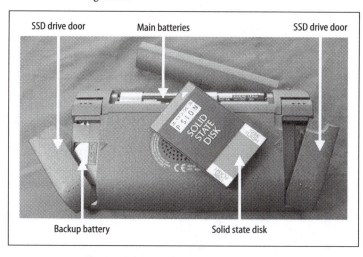

Fig. 7.4 Solid state disks (SSDs) – the Psion 3a.

memory and can thus hold close to 2 million characters of information. Although it uses a different operating system from MS-DOS it can be fairly described as a pocket-sized PC.

Figure 7.5 shows a Sharp IQ 8000 organizer on top of which has been placed a Sharp IC card. The organizer is a 64 kbyte model and the IC card may be pushed into a slot that is at the rear of the top casing. The IC card may have a list of commands printed on one side that provides a customized touch pad for the functions of the card. The standard touch pad is visible in Fig. 7.5 on the top right-hand side of the organizer. The IC card in this example is a combination card with 64 kbyte of EPROM and 32 kbyte of battery-backed SRAM.

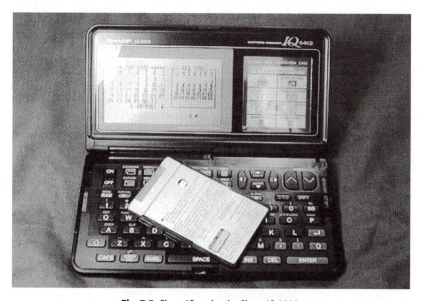

Fig. 7.5 Sharp IC card – the Sharp IQ 8000.

Significance of Memory Type

In the context of organizers, we have now referred to several different kinds of memory and it is important to understand the significance of each type from a forensic computing viewpoint.

With static RAM (SRAM), the kind of RAM that is to be found in the main memory of most organizers, we must maintain some form of electrical power connected if we are to retain its contents. However, we also have the ability to read from and write to such memory anywhere at will. We can reuse it over and over again for different purposes. We might, through the operating system of the organizer, write a telephone number into one part of the memory and, at some later time, when we no longer require that number, overwrite that part of the memory with details of a memo to do something. SRAM is very flexible and reusable, but it is volatile. If all electrical power is lost, so is all the information contained.

With the older form of EPROM (erasable programmable read-only memory), such as that referred to in the IC card shown in Fig. 7.5, the memory can be written to (programmed) once using a relatively high voltage[3] and thereafter only be read from. However, it will retain the programmed information for a very considerable time without the need for any form of batteries. This class of memory used to be known as WORM (write once read many) memory and the word "erasable" in the name refers to the ability to bulk erase the whole of the memory by subjecting the chip to ultra-violet light. Doing this then allows the EPROM to be reprogrammed with a different set of information. The quartz window which is used to subject the chip to ultraviolet radiation when erasing can just be seen as a small circle on the casing of the IC card in Fig. 7.5. The programming and erasing of this kind of EPROM requires specialist equipment and the analyst is unlikely to come across many such EPROMs that have been programmed by a user.

However, a more recent form of EPROM, called Flash EPROM, no longer requires the use of specialist equipment to program or erase it. Although still a WORM memory, such devices can appear to the user as though they are SRAM. It is this form of memory which is used by Psion in its Flash SSDs. They are often used for backup purposes and for databases and Psion has written file management software which exploits the non-volatility of EPROM, without exposing the user to the problems of WORM. The file management software achieves this by having a *validity* bit associated with each record stored. When the record is first written, the validity bit is not programmed and the record is seen by the file management system to be valid for all subsequent reads. When a change to that record is required, however, a completely new copy of the revised record is written and the validity bit of the now outdated record is programmed to make it invalid. In this way, the SSD appears through the file management system to be just like SRAM; changes can be made to records as required. However, it is important to recognize that the same memory locations are not being reused; instead they are being marked invalid and new memory locations are being used for each change. Two important consequences of this approach result:

---

3   12.5 V compared with 5 V in the example given. This is normally done using a special
    EPROM programmer.

- The SSD fills up as records are changed and the actual used space becomes larger than the apparent used space. Eventually, when the SSD is full, consideration has to be given to erasing it. With this form of EPROM[4], erasure of the whole memory is done electrically by applying a high voltage as for writing. In the Psion file management system, this process is known as formatting.

- Every change made to the file system is still recorded in the SSD although not accessible through the Psion file management system. Specialist forensic software can be used to access all these changes, which may have considerable evidential value.

More recent developments in flash technology have led to EPROM chips that can be erased a byte or a block at a time[5] rather than having to erase the entire chip, and we see such technology in applications such as flash memory for the BIOS of a PC, where infrequent updates can be easily made. Perhaps most important of all, however, has been the development of the so-called *CompactFlash* (CF) device[6]. This consists of flash EPROM memory chips controlled by a complete ATA (IDE) compatible disk controller on the card so that the entire unit appears to be a tiny (at least in form factor) solid state IDE disk. At the time of writing (August 1999) production capacities are being quoted at up to 192 Mbyte, with 256 Mbyte units expected to ship in the first quarter of 2000. A full and detailed specification[7] for such devices has been produced and they are in common use in applications such as digital cameras, mobile phones and electronic organizers. Psion uses CompactFlash memory, which it calls *Memory Disk*, in the Psion Series 5 range of organizers. However, it should be noted that the memory disk as a system operates just like non-volatile SRAM, so there is no opportunity to access all previous records as there is with SSDs.

Perhaps the most important point to come out of this section is a note for arresting officers and search and seizure teams:

- An insignificant little IC card, or an SSD or a CF memory disk may contain several hundred times the amount of information that is held within the organizer itself.

It should also be noted that some IC cards, SSDs and CF memory disks may contain programs rather than provide additional memory. They will normally be marked as such, often with some form of commercial label. They are frequently used for games, spreadsheets, databases (for example, wine, food, route finding and so forth), finance packages, dictionaries and the like.

Password Protection

Most electronic organizers have one or more password-based security features that are intended to protect against unauthorized access to the data held within them.

---

4   Sometimes referred to as EEPROM, electrically erasable programmable read-only memory.

5   See *Boot Block Flash Memory Technology* (Micron, 1999a).

6   See *CompactFlash* (Micron, 1999b).

7   See *CF+ and CompactFlash Specification* (CompactFlash Association, 1999).

These security features may protect at the level of the *system*, the *file*, the *compartment* or the *record*. From a forensic computing viewpoint, where passwords are not known, it is necessary to defeat such security features if all the evidence is to be accessed. Different approaches may need to be employed against the four different categories of security feature.

At the *system* level, a password may be required before any significant system function can be carried out. This may prevent the operation of an external communications link or deny access to information about the amount of memory in use as well as preventing any access to the user data held within the organizer.

At the *file* level, a password may be used to generate a key which is then used to apply an encryption algorithm to the file. Usually, a separate one-way hash of the password is also added to the encrypted file. Subsequent decryption occurs only when the correct password is offered and this is signified when the hash generated using the offered password matches the hash held within the file. The decryption key is then generated using the offered password and this is applied to decrypt the file.

At the *compartment* level, two separate areas exist, at least conceptually, and both may hold a number of different record categories: such as telephone, memo and schedule, for example. One area is unprotected and is accessible by default and the other is protected by a password. Offering the correct password causes the organizer to switch access from the records in the unprotected area to the records in the protected area.

Finally, at the *record* level, any individual record, be it telephone, memo or schedule, may be "marked" as "secret". In the default situation, only those records that are not marked as secret are accessible. Offering the correct password causes the organizer to make accessible *all* records, both secret and non-secret.

Switching On the Organizer

The significance of switching on the organizer varies across the entire range. It is important to appreciate that pressing the ON button will always change the internal memory state of the organizer and hence the evidence in some respect or another. The value of each keystroke made on the keyboard is stored in the keyboard buffer of the internal memory, so the act of pressing the ON button itself changes that memory buffer. Although this change is unlikely, in itself, to affect any user data held, what happens thereafter depends on the operating system of the organizer and what other keystrokes are made. If it is a Windows CE operating system, changes to a number of files can take place as the operating system becomes active, in a manner very similar to that of a Windows-based system starting up on a PC. Some other operating systems, which maintain date and time stamping of files, will also change file attributes when those files are opened and closed, again resulting in some aspect of the evidence being changed.

Application of the ACPO *Good Practice Guide* Principles

With a PC, the essential concern, as we saw in Chapter 6, is not to change the evidence on the hard disk and to produce an image which represents its state exactly as it was when seized. With an organizer, there is no hard disk and the concern has to be to change the evidence in the main memory as little as possible and then only in the certain knowledge of what is happening internally. The possibility of producing an image of the memory rarely exists.

This results in one major difference between the treatment of PCs and the treatment of organizers. To access the organizer it will almost certainly have to be switched on, *which effectively means that Principle 1*[8] *cannot be complied with*. It is therefore essential to ensure that Principle 2[9] is complied with because we can rarely image the memory and we thus have to work on the original evidence. This means that the competence of the analyst and Principle 3[10], the generation of a detailed audit trail, are even more important.

Guidelines for Seizure

On seizure the organizer should not be switched on. It should be placed in some form of sealed envelope before being put into a sealed evidence bag. This procedure prevents the organizer from being opened and accessed while still sealed in the evidence bag, a situation that can easily arise with some organizers.

Figure 7.6 is an example of how not to do it. This organizer could easily be opened and operated while still sealed in the bag. There can thus be no real guarantee about the continuity of this evidence.

If switched on when found, consideration should be given to switching the organizer off using the off switch in order to preserve battery life. A note of the time and date of this process should be made and the organizer should then be packaged and sealed as stated above.

A search should also be conducted for associated devices such as IC cards, solid state disks and memory disks as well as for any means of connecting the organizer to a PC.

The organizer should never be returned to the accused at the scene or prior to the evidence recovery procedures being completed. Depressing the RESET button or the removal of all the batteries can result in the complete loss of all information held in the organizer.

A competent person should examine the organizer at an early stage, and should replace the batteries as necessary to prevent any loss of evidence. This process should be repeated at regular intervals of a month or so to preserve the evidence until the case is complete. A competent person who understands the specific implications of the particular model should access the organizer. As recommended in the

---

8 No action taken by Police or their agents should change data held on a computer or other media which may subsequently be relied upon in Court.

9 In exceptional circumstances where a person finds it necessary to access original data held on a target computer that person must be competent to do so and to give evidence explaining the relevance and the implications of their actions.

10 An audit trail or other record of all processes applied to computer-based evidence should be created and preserved. An independent third party should be able to examine those processes and achieve the same result.

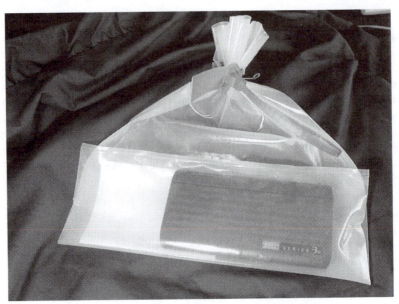

Fig. 7.6 How not to seal an organizer in an evidence bag.

Explanation of the Principles (see Chapter 6) it is essential that a witness who is competent to give evidence to a Court of Law makes this access.

It is of paramount importance that anyone handling electronic organizers prior to their examination, treats them in such a manner that will give the best opportunity for any recovered data to be admissible in evidence in any later proceedings.

Examination of Organizers and What May Be Possible

Provided that either the main or backup batteries are still operational, and the organizer is not faulty, it should be possible to obtain details of all the unprotected information, through the display screen, by normal use of the organizer. This is the recommended approach, since it may be easily audited and repeated by others. This approach also applies to unprotected information in IC cards, SSDs and memory disks. It requires that the examiner be thoroughly familiar with the particular organizer, is aware of any alterations to the memory that are unavoidable and is careful to ensure that no inadvertent changes are made. It is vital that a log of all the keystrokes together with any resulting displays is maintained.

It may be possible to obtain details of protected information in the organizer. To achieve this, either the passwords will have to be obtained, or the security features of the particular organizer will have to be defeated. There are a number of possible approaches to this problem and these are considered in outline in a later section. Having obtained access to any protected area, the recommended approach is again to access details through the display screen by normal use of the organizer.

Where password-protected information is stored in an encrypted form and the password cannot be obtained, it may be possible to break the encryption by exploiting known weaknesses in the encryption algorithm.

In most organizers, information is stored in the memory in a very structured way. In particular, it is normally held in the form of a record and the first part of the record may contain information about how long it is, what type of information it contains, whether or not it is password-protected, and so forth. There may in addition be a marker which indicates that a record has been deleted. When a user deletes information from the organizer, the information itself is rarely removed. Rather, the marker associated with the record is simply set to indicate that the information is now deleted. This is very similar in concept to the deletion of files in the MS-DOS directory system. It does mean, however, that if we are able to access the memory of the organizer directly, we may be able to restore some of the deleted information. A similar problem to that of undeleting MS-DOS files arises here also. The memory space taken up by deleted records will be reused by the organizer when new information is entered and deleted information will eventually be overwritten. This technique also applies to flash SSDs, as we mentioned earlier, and here we can possibly restore deleted files as well as deleted records.

A Set of Protocols

Because of the wide variety of different organizer models that are current, no attempt has been made here to outline the specific procedure that should be adopted to process any particular organizer. The required procedures vary greatly from model to model and manufacturer to manufacturer not only with regard to the keystrokes that need to be entered and the displays that result, but also in the measures that may be needed to defeat any security features and to access any password-protected areas.

Building on the experience of a large number of past cases, a database has been constructed and a set of protocols for dealing with specific models of organizer has been established. These protocols utilize the best practice so far found for each model and are revised and updated in the light of further experience with that model. A generic example of a protocol, in outline, is as follows:

- Open a new log and note the date and time. Commence a detailed physical external examination of the organizer. Log any noticeable damage and any markings. Open doors to any IC card, SSD drive, memory disk, modem or other PCMCIA type slots. Note the details, including serial numbers and locations, of any IC cards, SSDs, memory disks, modems or other PCMCIA type devices that are found installed. Note the serial number of the organizer, its type and size of RAM. Label the organizer with a signed and dated case identification.

- If appropriate, connect a mains adaptor. Switch on. Log the display details and, in particular, the displayed date and time. Also log the current date and time of this action. Check for any low battery states and replace batteries, as necessary, in accordance with the manufacturer's instructions. Log all keystrokes made throughout. Note whether a system password has been set.

- If a system password is set, then first try any passwords that have been given by the case officer. Log all attempts made and note all results. If this is not successful, then use appropriate measures to attempt to defeat security features.
- When the system password has been dealt with, log all screen details. With the larger organizers, determine whether the screen is displaying from within an open file. *Do not close any files at this stage.*
- If appropriate, access the system directory and log all file and directory details and in particular all file date and time stamps.
- Note all files that are open together with their displayed details. Try to save copies of open files to a clean pre-prepared IC card, SSD or memory disk. Close all open files and log that this has been done. Re-examine the directory structure and note all changes to date, time and size stamps for the closed files.
- Where a personal computer (PC) link to the organizer is available, run diagnostics on the PC and produce a printed copy of the results. If the PC is working correctly, connect to the organizer using the appropriate PC link system. Transfer copies of all files in the organizer to the PC.
- Transfer copies of all files from the PC to a similar test organizer.
- Commence a detailed examination of each file in the test organizer and in the PC and log all details found. This is done to preserve as far as possible the integrity of the evidence organizer and prevent inadvertent keystrokes during this phase of the examination from altering the evidence.
- Repeat the entire examination using the evidence organizer and compare the results with those logged previously.
- Carry out a diagnostic test on the evidence organizer to establish that it is working correctly. If it is not, try to establish the nature of the failure and make an assessment of what effect, if any, this might have on the information that has been obtained.

Dealing with the Password

There are a number of approaches that can be used to attempt to deal with an unknown password. It is better, however, from an evidential point of view if the actual password itself can be determined, rather than have to subvert it, because then access to the protected information can be demonstrated to the Court.

The first approach we have called *second guessing*. It is surprising how often someone who has set a password uses that same password elsewhere in their organizer. As a matter of routine we will examine all the diary entries looking for the pet name of a partner, say, which might turn out to be the key to the protected area. It is useful to have some knowledge of the domestic affairs of the suspect. As well as pet names, we find that nicknames, car numbers, telephone numbers, initials of children in age order and so forth are often used. Many people cannot be bothered with more than one password and they may use the same one for other systems as well. It is therefore worth inquiring whether there are any other organizers involved, as well as PCs and Internet accounts.

With some organizers, so-called *back doors* have been established. These are undocumented key sequences that have been made available by the manufacturer to aid diagnostic testing and maintenance of the organizer. In some cases they reboot the organizer into a service mode. Where we have found these, we have sometimes been able to use the manufacturer's diagnostic mode to examine the internal memory, find the password set by the user and then type in that password to unlock the protected area. This must be done with great care. Selecting the wrong diagnostic (and it is not evident what is what) can cause the organizer to run a destructive memory test, causing a total loss of all information.

Many organizers have a copy or *backup mode* whereby some or all of the information held in one organizer can be copied to a second identical or very similar model. The manufacturer normally supplies a suitable connector for this purpose. For those organizers that offer a complete backup, it is sometimes the case that the password will also have been passed between the two organizers during the data transfer. By accessing, electronically, the connector between the two organizers and monitoring the signals using a PC, it is possible to reconstruct an image of all the characters that have been passed, including the password. If we back up the evidence machine to a test machine in this way, we can then simply scan the reconstructed image within the PC to find the password sequence and then enter that into the evidence machine. In some cases, where the password is not held in the main organizer memory but instead in the on-chip memory of the microcomputer, we do not obtain the password information. However, the image should contain all the protected as well as the unprotected records, so access to all the evidence is still possible.

Where the organizer has a serial port or a PC link, it is possible that it may respond to what we have called a *magic bullet*. For what we again believe are test and diagnostic purposes, an undocumented character sequence transmitted into the serial port may cause the organizer to enter a service mode or even, in some cases, to send an entire image of its memory back across the link. The image may or may not contain the details of the password, depending upon whether it is held in main memory or in the on-chip memory of the microcomputer. Again, the image should contain all the protected as well as the unprotected records.

Open Heart Surgery

Finally, if all the foregoing methods fail, we are left only with *open heart surgery*. In this we try to open up the organizer while it is still fully operational and intervene directly in its internal workings. We have in the past used two different forms of intervention.

- In the first, we established from a very detailed analysis of a test organizer precisely where in the memory of that organizer a flag indicating that the password was set was actually located. Having found the exact place, we connected a specially made piece of electronic hardware to the memory chip which physically changed the password marker in the memory chip from on to off. When the organizer was switched back on, it decided that no password had been set.

● The second approach we have used much more frequently. This entails transferring an image of the entire memory of the organizer directly into a PC.

Figure 7.7 demonstrates neatly one of the difficulties with this technique. The figure shows the internal workings of a particular organizer with three battery holders on the left of the diagram. Two of these are for the main batteries and one is for the backup battery and as soon as dismantling of the organizer starts, the batteries all fall out. For the sake of clarity, we have not shown it in the figure, but it is essential to connect alternative power supplies to the organizer if the information in the memory is to be retained. This is usually done by soldering external power connections directly on to the printed circuit board as the dismantling process proceeds. As an alternative, we have used electronically controlled machine tools to cut, very accurately, a hole in the rear casing so that we could access the memory chip without disturbing the spring-loaded battery carriers.

As can be seen from Fig. 7.7, the memory chip is in a standard DIL package, although the microcomputer is implemented using chip on board (COB) technology. It is thus possible to connect to the memory chip using a spring-loaded SOIC connector, and this is shown in Fig. 7.8.

In the figure we can see how the SOIC connector sits cleanly over the memory chip and makes contact with each of its legs. The connections, brought out at the top of the clip, are then taken via ribbon cable to a specially designed interface board, which in turn is connected to a PC. Specially written programs in the PC are then used to drive the interface board and through it the organizer memory, causing it to read out all the information the chip contains to the PC. What we have done, in effect, is to make the organizer memory an extension of the PC and then simply copied an image of the organizer memory directly to the hard disk of the PC. As in the case of the backup and magic bullet images, analysis of this image may result in the password being obtained. In any event, both protected and unprotected records are usually stored in the same memory, so access to all the evidence should now be possible.

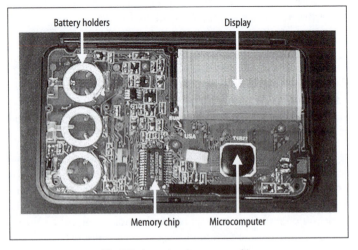

Fig. 7.7 Accessing the memory chip.

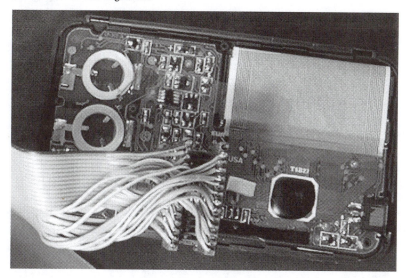

Fig. 7.8 Connecting to the memory chip.

Problems arise with organizers that use chip on board technology throughout to implement both the microcomputer and the memory, as we see in the example of Fig. 7.9. Making contact with this memory chip is much more difficult. It is not in a standard DIL package where the significance of each of the connections is known nor are there any legs on a package to give easy access to those connections.

The only realistic approach is to try to use a jig as shown in Fig. 7.10. The organizer has been locked into place with a specially drilled sheet of plastic above it and spring-loaded pins have been pushed through the plastic to make contact with specific plated through holes on the printed circuit board. Pins have been positioned to make contact with all the data and address bus lines and these in turn have been connected via ribbon cable to the PC interface.

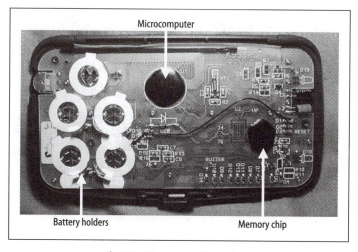

Fig. 7.9 Chip on board technology.

Fig. 7.10 Using a jig.

However, this approach is only effective where the microcomputer and the memory are in separate chips since it is only then that the address and data buses need to be implemented as connections on the printed circuit board. Where the memory is on the same chip as the microcomputer, as is the case in Fig. 7.11, there is no longer any point in trying to access connections on the printed circuit board since the required buses are all internal to the chip.

This kind of technology is currently posing a problem for the forensic computing analyst, though a number of possible approaches are being followed up. One such, for example, involves the removal of the resin from the surface of the chip and then

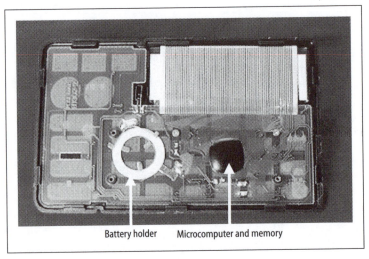

Battery holder   Microcomputer and memory

Fig. 7.11 Microcomputer and memory on same chip.

examining the chip under a powerful microscope with a view to trying to make contact with the internal buses by means of optical fibres. A second approach examines the radiated waveforms from the microcomputer under various conditions of operation. Yet a third approach looks at the performance of the chips when operating with very high or very low power supply values.

A Final Word about Electronic Organizers

The electronic organizer can hold vast amounts of information which may have considerable significance from an evidential point of view. To maintain the integrity of this potential evidence, it is essential that the organizer is only accessed by a competent person as explained in Principle 2 of the ACPO Guidelines. The recommendation, following seizure of an electronic organizer, is therefore not to tamper with it in any way but to place it immediately into a sealed envelope and then into a sealed evidence bag, so that it can be examined by a competent person. However, occasions may arise, where the demands of the case require immediate access to the information that may be held in a seized electronic organizer. This has to be an operational decision, where the risk of possible contamination of the evidence is weighed against the importance of immediate intelligence. In order to preserve the evidence, as far as possible, a formal approach should be adopted, with all actions taken and the reasons for them being logged, including all the keystrokes made and the displays obtained.

References

ACPO (1999) *Good Practice Guide for Computer Based Evidence V2.00*, The Association of Chief Police Officers (ACPO) Computer Crime Group.

CompactFlash Association (1999) *CF+ and CompactFlash Specification Revision 1.4*, 7/99, CompactFlash Association, P.O. Box 51537, Palo Alto, CA 94303. URL: http://www.compactflash.org/.

Microchip (1997) *24LC01B/02B Modules, Document DS21222A*, 8/97, Microchip Technology Incorporated, 2355 West Chandler Blvd., Chandler, AZ 85224-6199. URL: http://www.microchip.com/.

Micron (1999a) *Boot Block Flash Memory, TN-28-01, FT01.p65 – Rev. 2/99*, Micron Technology Inc., 8000 S. Federal Way, PO Box 6, Boise, ID 83707-0006. URL: http://www.micron.com/.

Micron (1999b) *CompactFlash, FC02.p65 – Rev. 2/99*, Micron Technology Inc., 8000 S. Federal Way, PO Box 6, Boise, ID 83707-0006. URL: http://www.micron.com/.

Psion (1992) *'C' Software Development Kit*, Volume II, PLIB Reference, 10 June, Psion PLC.

8. *Looking Ahead (Just a Little Bit)*

Introduction

We have attempted, in this book, to offer a basic foundation for the professional practice of forensic computing. Our aim has been to put in place sufficient theory and good practice as to enable professionals to continue their development from a sound and confident starting point. To do this effectively, we have had to limit the scope of what we have talked about and there is therefore much that we have not been able to cover in the time and space available.

We started with the concepts of information and information storage and we continued with the fundamental principles that underlie all digital computers. From here on, however, we have tended to concentrate on the personal computer (PC) and, in particular, on the PC running either MS-DOS or one of the Microsoft Windows operating systems. That is not to say that there are no other architectures or operating systems that need to be considered; just that the PC with Microsoft software is the configuration that the practising forensic computing analyst is most likely to come across today. Cases involving the Apple Macintosh are occasionally met with, as are cases involving PCs which use other operating systems, such as Linux. Although we can expect the incidence of cases such as these to increase slightly, a considerable increase of PC cases is very likely to result from the myriad of retailers who are now targeting the rapidly expanding domestic computer market in this country. All seem to be offering ever higher and higher performance PCs, invariably bundled with Microsoft Windows software. It is this trend, we would claim, that justifies the approach we have taken in the book to concentrate upon the PC as the example.

However, the other systems, although quite different in detail, do not in any way detract from the principles that we have established for the PC, so the theoretical and procedural grounding of the earlier chapters is still applicable.

What this chapter is about, however, are issues that may change the ways in which we currently deal with PCs (and other electronic devices) because of overriding technical or legal problems. The "looking ahead" is very deliberately "just a little bit" because the state and application of this technology beyond a few months or so is notoriously difficult to predict. Well known authoritative statements from the past explaining for example, that computers may weigh no more than 1.5 tons[1], that there

---

1 "Computers in the future may weigh no more than 1.5 tons"; *Popular Mechanics*, forecasting the relentless march of science, 1949.

is a world market for maybe five[2], and that there is no reason any one would want a computer in their home[3], only serve to illustrate this point.

■ ■

Bigger and Bigger Disks

At the time of writing, an advertisement[4] in a national newspaper offers a 600 MHz PC with 128 Mbyte of RAM and a 27 Gbyte hard disk for just over £1500. This quite typical pricing puts high-performance PCs within the financial reach of many ordinary people and ensures that their use is going to become even more widespread. However, it is the size of the hard disk that poses the greatest potential problem for the forensic computing analyst.

Although we were aware of many apocryphal stories about the quantity of paper such disk sizes can represent, we felt, for this book, that we should provide an authenticated version. We started with a 500 sheet pack of 80 g A4 paper and found this to be 2.25 inches thick. A typical page, with 1 inch margins all round, was filled with 12 point characters and this was found to contain 3,600 of them. We are thus able to determine that 2.25 inches of paper, or 500 sheets, represents $500 \times 3600 = 1\ 800\ 000$ characters, or, in computing terms, 1 800 000 bytes. From this, we can establish that 1,000,000 bytes represents 2.25/1.8 = 1.25 inches.

Therefore, 27 Gbyte, which equals $27 \times 1024 \times 1024 \times 1024$ bytes or 28 991 029 248 bytes represents 28 991.029 248 × 1.25 inches, which is 36 238.79 inches or 36 238.79/ 12 feet which is equal to 3020 feet (920 metres).

To put this height into context, Nelson's Column, in Trafalgar Square, London, is a mere 170 feet high and equates only to 1.5 Gbyte. However, Big Ben at 320 feet equates to about 2.8 Gbyte and the Eiffel Tower at 1050 feet equates to about 9.4 Gbyte (see Fig. 8.1). There are no buildings or monuments that are as high as the equivalent of 27 Gbyte! A good rule of thumb to remember is that 1 Gbyte represents a column of A4 paper sheets about 110 feet high.

We have already reached the situation where it is quite impractical to consider printing out all of the information that might be contained in commonly used hard disks of today. Quite apart from the physical problems of producing and handling stacks of paper that could be up to several thousands of feet in height, we need also to note the time that will be required to search through such massive quantities of information, even with the aid of automated tools. Hard disk capacities, even for entry level domestic systems, have now passed all practical limits for indiscriminate printing and they show every prospect of continuing to increase in size in the future. We need to look at how we can sensibly handle this particular problem.

---

2   "I think there is a world market for maybe five computers"; Thomas Watson, chairman of IBM, 1943.

3   "There is no reason anyone would want a computer in their home"; Ken Olson, president, chairman and founder of Digital Equipment Corp., 1977.

4   Time Computers Ltd, *The Express*, Tuesday 4 January 2000, p. 49.

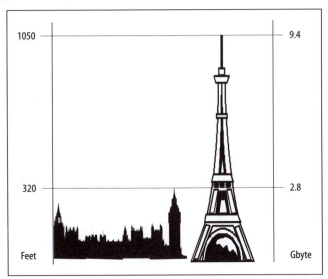

Fig. 8.1 Heights in Gbyte.

Unfortunately, we have no easy answers. The days when the case officer could say "…just print out all that's on the disk and I will decide what is relevant" have long gone. The forensic computing analyst is going to have to work closely with the case officer and search the disk (or preferably an image of the disk – but see later) specifically for items of relevance. That requires specialist tools as well as specialist knowledge, and few such tools currently exist. Many analysts write their own tools, and these are increasingly being shared within the community. However, this too poses a problem, which the community has yet to address. Should not all such tools be accredited by some recognized body so that the integrity of evidence obtained using them can be explained in Court?

To Image or not to Image?

There are other legal traps here for the unwary. Simply looking on the hard disk for information that may support a prosecution by the case officer is seen by some as unacceptable. There may reside on the hard disk evidence that demonstrates the innocence of the accused and the view is that this too should be retrieved. Where the size of the hard disk is small enough, or the quantity of information held is very limited, printouts of all the evidence can be produced, with copies going to both the prosecution and the defence. Here the problem does not arise, as both parties have access to everything. Some now argue that, in the case of much larger disks, containing much greater quantities of information, it is sufficient for both parties to receive a certified image[5] of the disk and for each then to access from their image whatever they require. However, this too may not be possible or practical in the

5   Again, the imaging software should be accredited.

future. The standard CD-ROM, which has been the most frequently used medium for certified images in the past, can only store some 650 Mbyte and so, for a 27 Gbyte hard disk, we require some 40 CD-ROMs for each image. Although DVDs may provide a more practical alternative in time, DVD writers are still too expensive for most authorities to purchase. More significant, however, is the view held by some authorities that imaging is no longer the appropriate approach.

This view is held not just because of the practical problems of imaging very large disks but also because of the legal and ethical issues of seizing such vast quantities of information, much of which is unlikely to be relevant to the case. This issue is particularly pertinent where *legal privilege* is involved and where it is essential that only relevant evidence is accessed. At the time of writing, these matters have not yet been tested in Court, but the expectation is that they soon will be and we then may need to rethink the whole policy of imaging.

What might replace it is difficult to see. Imaging has a number of very real advantages. By taking identical and unmodifiable certified images of the disk at the time of seizure and passing a copy to prosecution and a copy to defence we can be certain of the integrity of the evidence, given that the imaging tool is accredited. Analysts can examine the image without fear of corrupting the evidence and can also, if required, generate additional hard disk versions from their image for examining files and executing software packages on a test machine. Perhaps equally important, where a business is involved, the PC with its hard disk can be returned to the user so that work may continue as soon as the imaging is complete. If a non-imaging approach were to be adopted, the PC could not be returned to the user until *analysis* was complete, which, for a large hard disk, might take many days.

Perhaps the most effective solution, particularly where legal privilege is involved, is for a Court to authorize and oversee the imaging of the hard disk, so that the evidence is captured and retained with a high degree of integrity, and then for the Court to decide what parts of the image are to be made available to the various parties.

Networked Systems Add to the Problems

A 27 Gbyte hard disk on a standalone computer may seem problematic enough, but this can be magnified many times over where a network of computers is involved. Here we may have very many hard disk servers, each of which is far larger than the standalone disk, and each of which is accessible from any point in the network. To confound the problem, some or all of these servers may be in the jurisdictions of other nations, geographically separate from the systems that are being seized and subject to quite different legal systems.

In such cases, imaging of anything other than the local disks is unlikely to be feasible, and making accesses beyond the local system may not even be legal. Current thinking tends to favour the seeking of guidance from the local systems administration, where they are not involved in the case, and selectively accessing only material which is relevant to the case, thereby occasioning minimum disruption to the network and the business. Where this cannot be done, then disconnecting the external network, closing the local systems down and imaging the hard disks that are accessible seems to be the only fallback position.

Encryption

The final issue we consider in this brief look ahead is the problem of encryption. Although the capability has been around for a long time, it is only relatively recently that cases have started to appear where strong encryption has been used. There is now an increasing range of user-friendly programs available that enable strong encryption to be applied with little knowledge or effort by the user.

We will mention first weak encryption. For some time, many well-known word processor, spreadsheet and other similar application programs have incorporated built-in encryption by means of password protection. When a file is password-protected it is saved on hard disk in an encrypted form. Frequently, these programs have used encryption algorithms that are unpublished and weak; that is, they contain flaws that permit cryptanalysts to perform decryption without knowledge of the password. The protection offered by such algorithms, such as it is, often relies upon the fact that the algorithm is unknown, though this can always be established by reverse engineering the code. A number of companies sell software products which can be used to break such weak algorithms and decrypt the file or, alternatively, retrieve the original password from the file.

In the case of strong encryption, the algorithm is published and is well known and does not rely upon any obfuscation for protection. Indeed, the view of the crypto-graphic community is that publication of the algorithm permits peer review to take place and allows any possible weaknesses to be thoroughly examined. Algorithms that have continued to remain unbroken in such a spotlight can therefore justifiably claim the title "strong".

Despite concerns by some nations about the misuse of such cryptography, software products incorporating strong encryption are now widely available throughout the world. Forensic computing analysts are likely to encounter the effects of such software in three main areas: email transactions, encrypted files on a hard disk and encrypted partitions on a hard disk. In what follows we mention a variety of specific software products. In doing so, we are not in any way endorsing a particular product; rather simply using it as an exemplar with which we are familiar for the particular kind of functionality that it exhibits.

Encryption of Email

Perhaps the best known of the email encryption systems is Pretty Good Privacy or PGP (Garfinkel, 1995). Figure 8.2 shows a block diagram view of a PGP email message being passed from Ted (on the left-hand side of the figure) to Alice (on the right-hand side of the figure). PGP is not a cryptographic algorithm; rather it is a system for managing cryptographic keys and messages.

PGP uses two forms of encryption: private key (also known as symmetric) encryption and public key (also known as asymmetric) encryption. With private key

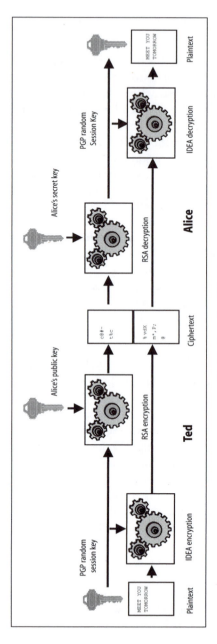

Fig. 8.2 Pretty Good Privacy.

encryption, the same secret key is used both to encrypt plain text to ciphertext and to decrypt ciphertext to plain text. The problem here is: how do you safely distribute your secret key to your distant correspondent so that they can decrypt your messages? With public key encryption, different (but mathematically related) keys are used to encrypt plain text to ciphertext (the public key) and to decrypt ciphertext to plain text (the secret key). Key distribution is solved here by a user generating a public/secret key pair and then distributing openly the public key to everyone with whom they wish to communicate. Only the corresponding secret key will decrypt messages encrypted with that public key and that secret key is kept secure by the user. The problem here is that the mathematical computations involved in public key encryption and decryption are as much as 1000 times slower than the equivalent encryption and decryption computations for private key encryption. Long messages would therefore take an unacceptable period of time to encrypt and decrypt using public key cryptography.

PGP overcomes both problems by using the two methods together. In Fig. 8.2 we note, on the left-hand side, that Ted wishes to send the message "MEET YOU TOMORROW" to Alice. We first assume that Alice has used her PGP to generate a public/secret key pair, and has distributed her public key to, among others, Ted. She will, of course, have retained her secret key privately to herself. In order to send Ted's message, Ted's PGP system now automatically generates a random "session key" of 128 bits and then uses (for example) the IDEA[6] private key encryption algorithm with this session key to encrypt the message "MEET YOU TOMORROW" to ciphertext. In parallel, PGP also takes the random session key and encrypts that using (for example) the RSA[7] public key encryption system and Alice's public key to produce a ciphertext version of the session key. The two pieces of ciphertext, one representing the private key encryption of the message "MEET YOU TOMORROW" and the other representing the public key encryption of the random session key, are now merged and transmitted out onto the open network.

On receipt by Alice, her PGP system demerges the two parts and uses her secret key together with the RSA public key decryption algorithm to convert the ciphertext of the session key back to the original plain text. The PGP system then uses this decrypted session key together with the IDEA private key decryption algorithm to convert the ciphertext of the message back to the original plain text as shown.

From the viewpoint of the practical forensic computing analyst, there is not a great deal that can be done about breaking the encryption of either of these algorithms. However, assuming access to Alice's computer, the most profitable approach would be to try to establish the password that protects Alice's *secret key ring*: the place where PGP keeps her secret keys. Given that, PGP could then be used to decrypt all messages sent to Alice that use her public key. Although such passwords are well protected by PGP, many people use a Windows "front end" that is designed to hide the complexity of using DOS-based PGP from the user.

---

6 International Data Encryption Algorithm. For details see *Applied Cryptography* (Schneier, 1996, pp. 319–325).

7 Named after its three inventors: Ron Rivest, Adi Shamir and Leonard Adelman. For details see *Applied Cryptography* (Schneier, 1996, pp. 466–474).

Sometimes the security of such programs falls well short of that of the PGP program itself, and it may be possible to find the secret key ring password, which has at some stage had to pass through the Windows front end. The password may have been saved in the Windows Registry, or in an .ini file, or in a Windows temporary file or perhaps even in the Windows swap file. It is certainly worth searching these areas for possible passwords or pass phrases.

Hiding Folders and Encrypting Files

There is now a wide variety of user-friendly programs which users might employ to make access by others to their files more difficult. Some allow individual files or complete folders of files to be hidden on the hard disk, while others encrypt files and folders. The first of these is exemplified by Magic Folders[8], a program which makes selected folders on the hard disk and all the files within those folders invisible to all applications. Folders and files cannot be deleted, viewed, modified or executed and to all intents and purposes they do not exist. Through the use of a password, however, normal and complete access can be restored. From a forensic computing viewpoint, however, there should be no real problem with accessing the hidden files or folders. The file data remains on the hard disk in its original form; only the operating system (and thus all applications that use the operating system for file access) are convinced that the files do not exist. Programs that access the disk directly and, in particular, disk editing tools, will readily find the hidden files.

Presumably for this reason, the same company produces an enhanced product called Encrypted Magic Folders, which, in addition to the hiding of files and folders, also encrypts and decrypts the files as they are accessed. This means that the files always remain on the hard disk in an encrypted form. This is quite different from other systems, whereby a file is either all completely in an encrypted form or all completely in a plain text form. PC-Magic has developed its own encryption algorithms which operate at the byte level and ensure that only the sequence of bytes that have currently been requested by the access are decrypted and passed to the file system. Since these are not published algorithms, it is not known how difficult or otherwise it may be to break this encryption. However, attempting to obtain the password is still probably the most effective policy.

An alternative approach is exemplified by programs such as Cryptext[9] and Data Fortress[10]. In the case of Cryptext, a strong cryptographic algorithm, RC4[11], is used to encrypt a specified file and overwrite the plain text version on the hard disk. Again, a password is used to control access to the process and a hashed version of this password is stored with the file using the SHA-1[12] algorithm. Decryption occurs when the correct password is given and the encrypted version is then converted to

---

8 See PC-Magic Software at http://www.pc-magic.com/.

9 See Cryptext at http://www.tip.net.au/~njpayne/.

10 See Data Fortress at http://montgomery.hypermart.net/DataFortress/.

11 "RC" apparently refers to "Ron's Code" or "Rivest Cipher" after the designer Ron Rivest. For details see *Applied Cryptography* (Schneier, 1996, pp. 318 and 397).

plain text and this plain text is used to overwrite the encrypted version on the hard disk. These facilities are made readily accessible to the user by means of a right mouse button click on a file that displays a menu providing "encrypt" and "decrypt" options. The Data Fortress program uses a similar technique. In this case the strong encryption is provided by the Blowfish[13] algorithm. Again, the most effective policy is probably to attempt to obtain the password. However, where plain text is overwritten by ciphertext, the work of Peter Gutmann (1996) may be of interest. In his paper he describes how it may be possible to access information from a hard disk after it has been overwritten with new information. This would be of particular value where a plain text version of a file is overwritten with the encrypted version.

Hard Disk Encryption on the Fly

The final technique that we will mention here concerns encrypting a hard disk or a hard disk partition "on the fly". This technique works by producing an encrypted container file which, using special software, can be then be mounted to appear to the operating system as a virtual drive with its own drive letter. The drive is made accessible by means of a password and then all accesses typically pass through some form of cryptographic driver. That is, plain text is converted to encrypted form on being written to the disk and encrypted text is converted to plain text on being read from the disk. In the case of the BestCrypt[14] product this driver uses the IDEA algorithm, which has been mentioned earlier. E4M[15] is a similar "on the fly" encryption product which supports a range of different algorithms, such as IDEA, Blowfish, DES[16] and triple-DES, CAST[17] and MDC[18].

A Final Word

The technology in this field is advancing at an unprecedented rate and we can only anticipate that the task of the forensic computing analyst is going to become ever more challenging. We believe that a good grasp of the theoretical and practical principles along the lines that we have presented in this book is an essential

---

12 Secure Hash Algorithm. For details see *Applied Cryptography* (Schneier, 1996, pp. 442–445).

13 This algorithm has been designed by the author of Applied Cryptography and is in the public domain. For details see *Applied Cryptography* (Schneier, 1996, pp. 336–339).

14 See Jetico, Inc. at http://www.jetico.sci.fi/home.htm.

15 15. See *Encryption for the Masses* at http://www.e4m.net/main.html.

16 Data Encryption Standard. For details see *Applied Cryptography* (Schneier, 1996, pp. 265–301).

17 The authors, Carlisle Adams and Stafford Tavares, claim that CAST refers to their design approach, but note their initials. For details see *Applied Cryptography* (Schneier, 1996, pp. 334–335).

18 Message Digest Cipher. For details see *Applied Cryptography* (Schneier, 1996, p. 353).

prerequisite for the professional analyst. However, we also believe that what we have talked about here is only the very beginning, and that there is so much more to do. We hope that our readers find, as we do, that they are entering one of the most stimulating, exciting and rewarding disciplines that there is today, and we look forward to our community working together to solve many of these difficult problems that are about to descend upon us.

References

Garfinkel, S. (1995) *PGP – Pretty Good Privacy*, O'Reilly & Associates Inc., San Francisco.

Gutmann, P. (1996) Secure deletion of data from magnetic and solid-state memory, *Sixth USENIX Security Symposium Proceedings*, San Jose, CA, 22–25 July. See also `http://www.cs.aukland.ac.nz/~pgut001/secure_del.htm`.

Schneier, B. (1996) *Applied Cryptography, Protocols, Algorithms and Source Code in C*, John Wiley & Sons, New York.

Bibliography

ACPO (1999) *Good Practice Guide for Computer Based Evidence, Version 2*, Association of Chief Police Officers of England, Wales and Northern Ireland, ACPO Crime Committee, 23 June 1999.

Adams, C. K. (1981) *Master Handbook of Microprocessor Chips*, Tab Books Inc., New York.

Aikenhead, M. (1995) Legal knowledge based systems: some observations for the future, *Web Journal of Current Legal Issues*, [1995] 2 Web JCLI, 19 May. URL: http://www.newcastle.ac.uk/~nlawwww/articles2/aiken2.html.

Akdeniz, Y. (1996) Section 3 of the Computer Misuse Act 1990: an antidote for computer viruses!, *Web Journal of Current Legal Issues*, [1996] 3 Web JCLI, 24 May. URL: http://www.newcastle.ac.uk/~nlawwww/1996/issue3/akdeniz3.htm.

Akdeniz, Y. (1997) UK Government policy on encryption, *Web Journal of Current Legal Issues*, [1997] 1 Web JCLI, 28 February. URL: http://www.newcastle.ac.uk/~nlawwww/1997/issue1/akdeniz1.htm.

Anderson, M. R. (1996), Erased files often aren't, *Government Technology Magazine*, November. URL: http://www.govtech.net/1997/gt/jan/jan-justice&technology2/jan-justice&technology2.shtm.

ANSI (1996) *ANSI X3.279-1996 – AT Attachment Interface with Extensions (ATA-2)*, ANSI, 11 West 42nd Street, New York, NY 10036. URL: http://fission.dt.wdc.com./pub/standards/x3t13/t13.htm.

Apple Computer Inc. (1999) *More About IEEE 1394 and FireWire*. URL: http://developer.apple.com/hardware/FireWire/More_about_Firewire.htm.

Atzberger, P. and Zolli, A. (1996) Portable Network Graphics, *Trincoll Journal*. URL: http://www.trincoll.edu/~tj/tj10.31.96/articles/tech.html.

Barrett, N. (1997) *Digital Crime – Policing the Cybernation*, Kogan Page, London.

Binary Research (1997) Ghost URL: http://www.ghostsoft.com/.

Blackstock, S. (undated) *LZW and GIF explained*. URL: http://excel.riga.lv/encyclopedia/gif.html.

Borland (1994) *Borland C++ User's Guide, Version 4.5*, Borland International, Inc., 100 Borland Way, PO Box 660001, Scotts Valley, CA 95067-0001.

Born, G. (1997) *The File Formats Handbook*, International Thompson Publishing, London.

Bowker, A. L. and Drinkard, L. N. (1996) Downloading: using computer software as an investigative tool, *Law Enforcement Bulletin*, Federal Bureau of Investigation, June. URL: http://www.fbi.gov/leb/june961.txt.

Brown, S. (1998) *Hard Disk Partitioning, Why and How (for MS-DOS/Windows PCs)*, 18 November. URL: http://www.concentric.net/~Brownsta/hd-partn.htm.

Chandler, D. (1994) *Semiotics for Beginners*, UWA. URL: http://www.aber.ac.uk/~dgc/semold.html.

Choo, A. L.-T. and Mellors, M. (1995) Undercover police operations and what the suspect said (or didn't say), *Web Journal of Current Legal Issues*, [1995] 2 Web JCLI, 19 May. URL: http://www.newcastle.ac.uk/~nlawwww/articles2/choo2.html.

Clarke, A. R. M. and Powys-Lybbe, D. (1986) *The Amstrad CP/M Plus*, MML Systems Ltd, London.

Clede, B. (1993) Investigating computer crime is every department's concern, *Law and Order*, July. URL: http://ourworld.compuserve.com/homepages/BillC/compcrim.htm.

CompactFlash Association (1999) *CF+ and CompactFlash Specification Revision 1.4*, 7/99, CompactFlash Association, P.O. Box 51537, Palo Alto, CA 94303. URL: `http://www.compactflash.org/`.

Computers & Law (1996) Discovery of computer data, *Computers & Law*, Spring. URL: `http://wings.buffalo.edu/law/Complaw/CompLawPapers/printup.htm`.

Corel (1997) *WordPerfect Document File Format*, Corel WordPerfect Suite 8 Software Development Kit in `Corel/SDKs/Suite8/DOCS/B_1DOCIN.HTM`.

Committee of Ministers (1995) *Concerning Problems of Criminal Procedure Law Connected with Information Technology*, Recommendation No. R (95) 13 of the Committee of Ministers to Member States, Council of Europe, 11 September. URL: `http://www.privacy.org/pi/intl_orgs/coe/info_tech_1995.html`.

Compaq (1997a) *Power-on Self-Test (POST)*, 17 March. URL: `http://172.18.229.243/support/techzone/solutions/post.html`.

Compaq (1997b) *Power-on Self-Test Messages*, 17 March. URL: `http://172.18.229.243/support/techzone/solutions/8361.html`.

Cramer, J. (1997) Legal Research on the Internet, *Computers & Law*, 28 April. URL: `http://wings.buffalo.edu/Complaw/CompLawPapers/cramer.htm`.

Darwin, I. F. (1992) *file(0) synopsis*, URL: `http://www.neosoft.com/neosoft/man/file.1.htm`.

Dees, T. M. (1994) Dealing with Computer Evidence, Originally published in *Law Enforcement Technology* magazine, August. URL: `http://www.rrinvestigations.com/articles/computerevidence.htm`.

Department of Justice (1994) *Federal Guidelines for Searching and Seizing Computers*, US Department of Justice, Criminal Division, Office of Professional Development and Training, July. URL: `http://evidence.finder.com/FTP/dojgui.html`.

Digital Research Inc. (1987) *Operator's and Programmer's Guide for the Amstrad CPC6128 and PCW8256*, William Heinemann Ltd, London.

Dockery, M. (1995) *Digital Discovery and Recovery: A New Kind of Evidence Gathering*, Dockery Associates. URL: `http://www.pimall.com/nais/n.digit.discer.html`.

Downing, R. (1995) Magill and the Software Directive: are they interoperable?, *Web Journal of Current Legal Issues*, [1995] 4 Web JCLI, 28 September. URL: `http://www.newcastle.ac.uk/~nlawwww/articles4/downing4.html`.

Duncan, R. (1988) *Advanced MS-DOS Programming*, Microsoft Press, Redmond, WA.

Elonex (1995) *Elonex MT-500/I System Board Configuration Guide*, August, Elonex plc, 2 Apsley Way, London NW2 7LF.

Elonex (1997) *MS-5156 User's Manual, Rev 1.21*, September, Elonex plc, 2 Apsley Way, London NW2 7LF.

EPIC (1994) EPIC Analysis of New Justice Department Guidelines on Searching and Seizing Computers, The Electronic Privacy Information Center, *Criminal Law Reporter*, Vol. 56, No. 12 (21 December). URL: `http://cpsr.org/cpsr/privacy/epic/guidelines_analysis.txt`.

Falbo, F. R. (1997) *The Ref – Hardware Specs at Your Fingertips*, 1 September. URL: `http://theref.c3d.rl.af.mil/theref.html`.

Feldman, M. (ed.) *Graphics File Formats*, URL: `http://excel.riga.lv/encylopedia/bmp.html`.

Finch, S. G. (ed.) (1995) *Information technology – AT Attachment Interface with Extensions (ATA-2)*, Working Draft, Proposed American National Standard, X3T10 948D, Revision 3, 17 January. URL: `http://fission.dt.wdc.com/`.

Freer, J. (1987) *Systems Design with Advanced Microprocessors*, Pitman, London.

Garfinkel, S. (1995) *PGP – Pretty Good Privacy*, O'Reilly & Associates Inc., San Francisco.

Gilbert, H. (1996) *Surviving the Next Operating System*. URL: `http://pclt.cis.yale.edu/pclt/opsys/default.htm`.

Gutmann, P. (1996) Secure deletion of data from magnetic and solid-state memory, *Sixth USENIX Security Symposium Proceedings*, San Jose, CA, 22–25 July. See also http://www.cs.aukland.ac.nz/~pgut001/secure_del.htm.

Hamilton, E. (1992) *JPEG File Interchange Fomat Version 1.02*, C-Cube Microsystems, 1778 McCarthy Blvd, Milpitas, CA 95035.

Hinckley, K. (1995) *The GIF format as intellectual property*. URL: http://www.utopia.com/.

HMSO (1989) *The Electricity at Work Regulations 1989*, Statutory Instrument 1989 635, HMSO, London.

Hoey, A. (1996) Analysis of The Police and Criminal Evidence Act, s.69 – Computer Generated Evidence, *Web Journal of Current Legal Issues*, [1996] 1 Web JCLI, 25 January. URL: http://www.newcastle.ac.uk/~nlawwww/1996/issue1/hoey1.html.

Hoffman, G. (1995) *Computer Crime – Legal Enforcement in the age of the Internet*, URL: http://www.privnet.com/~hoffmang/jomc191/paper.html.

HSE Books (1998) *Memorandum of Guidance on the Electricity at Work Regulations 1989*, HSR 25, HMSO, London.

IBM (undated) *Understanding EDO (Hyper Page Mode)*, IBM Applications Note, International Business Machines Corp. URL: http://www.chips.ibm.com/.

IBM (1995) *No-ID sector format*, Dr Steven R. Hetzler, IBM Research Division, Almaden Research Center, San Jose, CA. URL: http://www.storage.ibm.com/oem/tech/noid.htm.

IBM (1996a) Synchronous DRAMs: The DRAM of the Future, *IBM MicroNews*, First Quarter, 4–6.

IBM (1996b) *Understanding DRAM Operation*, IBM Applications Note, 12/96, International Business Machines Corp. URL: http://www.chips.ibm.com/.

IBM (1996c) *Understanding VRAM and SGRAM Operation*, IBM Applications Note, 12/96, International Business Machines Corp. URL: http://www.chips.ibm.com/.

IBM (1997) *Understanding Static RAM Operation*, IBM Applications Note, 03/97, International Business Machines Corp. URL: http://www.chips.ibm.com/.

IBM (1998a) *Getting beyond the ATA 8.4 GB limit*, Dr Steven R. Hetzler, IBM Storage Systems Division, 5600 Cottle Road, San Jose, CA 95193. URL: http://www.storage.ibm.com/hardsoft/diskdrdl/library/8.4gb.htm.

IBM (1998b) *IBM Deskstar 25GP and Deskstar 22GXP Hard Disk Drives*, IBM Storage Systems Division, 5600 Cottle Road, San Jose, CA 95193. URL: http://www.ibm.com/harddrive/.

IBM (1999) *Disk Manager (version 9.47)*, 25 March, IBM Storage Systems Division, 5600 Cottle Road, San Jose, CA 95193. URL: http://www.storage.ibm.com/techsup/hddtech/welcome.htm

IEE (undated) *City & Guilds Portable Appliance Testing Course*. See http://www.iee.org.uk/Profdev/Courses/cg_pat.htm.

IEE (1994) *The IEE Code of Practice for In-Service Inspection and Testing of Electrical Equipment*, IEE, London.

Intel (1979) *The 8086 Family User's Manual*, October, Intel Corporation.

Intel (1998a) *SE440BX Motherboard Technical Product Specification*, March, Intel Corporation, PO Box 5937, Denver, CO 80217-9808.

Intel (1998b) *SE440BX Motherboard Technical Product Guide*, February, Intel Corporation, PO Box 5937, Denver, CO 80217-9808.

Kahn, J. R. (1989) *Implications of Computer Technology and Use for the Law of Evidence*. URL: http://www.accesscom.com/~jkahn/computer_evidence.html.

Kegel, D. (1997) *Dan Kegel's Fast Hard Drives Page*, 19 April. URL: http://www.kegel.com/drives/.

Khambata, A. J. (1982) *Microprocessors/Microcomputers Architecture, Software, and Systems*, John Wiley & Sons, New York.

Kozierok, C. M. (1998) *The PC Guide, Site Version: 1.80*, 16 December. URL: http://www.PCGuide.com/.

Landis, H. (1995a) *ATA/ATA-1/ATA-2/IDE/EIDE/etc FAQ Part 1 of ? -- The Basics, Version 0b, 7 February.* URL: `http://web.idirect.com/~frank/docs/ata.txt`.

Landis, H. (1995b) *How It Works – CHS Translation, Plus BIOS Types, LBA and Other Good Stuff, Version 4a.* URL: `http://web.idirect.com/~frank/docs/chs.txt`.

Landis, H. (1995c) *How It Works – DOS Floppy Disk Boot Sector, Version 1a.* URL: `http://web.idirect.com/~frank/docs/dbr.txt`.

Landis, H. (1995d) *How It Works – OS2 Boot Sector, Version 1a.* URL: `http://web.idirect.com/~frank/docs/os2br.txt`.

Landis, H. (1997) *How It Works – Master Boot Record, Version 1b.* hiw@sugs.talisman.com.

Landis, H. (1998a) *ATA News,* February. hiw@sugs.talisman.com.

Landis, H. (1998b) *Facts and Fiction (FnF),* February. hiw@sugs.talisman.com.

Landis, H. (1998c) *How it Works – Partition Tables, Version 1e and Version 1h.* hiw@sugs.talisman.com.

Landis, H. (1999a) *ATADRVR ATA/ATAPI Low Level Driver, User's Guide, Version 13H.* atadrvr@sugs.talisman.com.

Landis, H. (1999b) *Using DMA with ATA or ATAPI.* atadrvr@sugs.talisman.com.

Landis, H. (1999c) *Using PIO with ATA or ATAPI.* atadrvr@sugs.talisman.com.

Lash, A. (1995) Time to call in the cybertroops, *Open Computing,* July. URL: `http://www.wcmh.com/oc/features/previous/9507insb.html#cybertroops`.

Liebenau, J. and Backhouse, J. (1990) *Understanding Information: An Introduction,* Macmillan Press, Basingstoke.

Lim, W. and Valentino, R. (1996) *comp.sys.ibm.pc.hardware, Frequently Asked Questions (Draft),* 30 August. URL: `http://www.circa.ufl.edu/comp.net/help/faqs/pc.txt`.

Lord, D. (1991) Gander for Windows. URL: `http://www.gsw.com/welcome/2112.htm`.

Majors, N. (1996) *Technicians' Guide to PC Hard Disk Subsystems,* Data Recovery Labs, 26 February. URL: `http://www.datarec.com/tech1.html`.

Maxtor (1996) *Maxtor's CrystalMax 1080 Model Number 84320A8, Rev A 3/18/96 T.* URL: `http://www.maxtor.com/products/products.html`.

McCarvel, R. T. (1996) *Taking the Fourth Amendment to Bits: The Department of Justice Guidelines for Computer Searches and Seizures,* 17 October. URL: `http://www.seanet.com/~rod/comp_4a.html`.

McLean, P. T. (ed.) (1995) *Information technology – AT Attachment-3 Interface(ATA-3), Working Draft, X3T10 2008D, Revision 5,* 6 October. URL: `http://fission.dt.wdc.com/`.

Messmer, H.-P. (1997) *The Indispensable PC Hardware Book,* 3rd edn, Addison-Wesley, Reading, MA.

Microchip (1997) *24LC01B/02B Modules, Document DS21222A, 8/97,* Microchip Technology Incorporated, 2355 West Chandler Blvd., Chandler, AZ 85224-6199. URL: `http://www.microchip.com/`.

Micro Firmware (1998a) *Issues with Hard Drives over 4GB,* Micro Firmware Tech Support, 330 W Gray Street, Norman, OK. URL: `http://www.firmware.com/support/`.

Micro Firmware (1998b) *Notes on Installing Hard Drives Larger Than 2 Gigabytes,* Micro Firmware Tech Support, 330 W Gray Street, Norman, OK. URL: `http://www.firmware.com/support/`.

Micro Firmware (1998c) *Problems with New Partition Types Used by WIN95 FDISK,* Micro Firmware Tech Support, 330 W Gray Street, Norman, OK. URL: `http://www.firmware.com/support/`.

Micro Firmware (1998d) *Some Technical Info on Hard Drives,* Micro Firmware Tech Support, 330 W Gray Street, Norman, OK. URL: `http://www.firmware.com/support/bios/hdtecg.htm`.

Micron (1999a) *Boot Block Flash Memory, TN-28-01,FT01. p65 – Rev. 2/99,* Micron Technology Inc., 8000 S. Federal Way, PO Box 6, Boise, ID 83707-0006. URL: `http://www.micron.com/`.

Micron (1999b) *CompactFlash, FC02. p65 – Rev. 2/99,* Micron Technology Inc., 8000 S. Federal Way, PO Box 6, Boise, ID 83707-0006. URL: `http://www.micron.com/`.

Microsoft Corporation (1999a) *Description of FAT32 File System,* Article ID: Q154997, 8 August. URL: `http://support.microsoft.com/support/kb/articles/Q154/9/97.asp`.

Microsoft Corporation (1999b) *Problems Accessing FAT16 Drives Larger Than 2 GB,* Article ID: Q127851, 15 January. URL: `http://support.microsoft.com/support/kb/articles/Q127/8/51.asp`.

MicroSystems (undated) *POST CODE MASTER Version 1.40,* MicroSystems Development, Inc., 4100 Moorpark Ave. Suite #104, San Jose, CA 95117.

Moher, R. K. (1996) Computer Crime: Tips on Securing and Recovering Electronic Data, *New York Law Journal,* 17 December. URL: `http://www.ljextra.com/securitynet/articles/121796s2.html`.

Mosteller, T. (1995) *CMOSRAM2.EXE,* Tellerware, 1872 Rampart Lane, Lansdale, PA 19446-5051.

Mueller, S. (1998) *Upgrading and Repairing PCs,* 8th edn, Macmillan Computer Publishing, Basingstoke.

Murray, J. D. and vanRyper, W. (1996). *Encyclopedia of Graphics File Formats.* O'Reilly & Associates, San Francisco.

National Committee on Information Technology Standards (NCITS) (1998) *Technical Committee T13 AT Attachment,* URL: `http://www.ncits.org/`.

National Computer Security Center (undated) *A Guide to Understanding Data Remanence in Automated Information Systems,* National Computer Security Center, NCSC-TG-025, Library No. 5-236,082, Version-2. URL: `http://bilbo.isu.edu/security/isl/drinais.html`.

Norton, P. (1988a) *The Norton Disk Companion,* Peter Norton Computing Inc.

Norton, P. (1988b) *The Norton Trouble Shooting Guide for Disks,* Peter Norton Computing Inc.

Norton, P. and Goodman, J. (1997) *Peter Norton's Inside the PC,* 7th edn, SAMS Publishing, New York.

Ogren, J. (undated) *ST506/412 Connector.* URL: `http://ftp.sunet.se/co_ST506.html`.

Patterson, D. A., Gibson, G. A. and Katz, R. H. (1988) A Case for Redundant Arrays of Inexpensive Disks (RAID), *SIGMOD Conference 1988,* pp. 109–116.

Phoenix (1998) *BIOS Enhanced Disk Drive Specification, Version 3.0,* 12 March, Phoenix Technologies Ltd, 2575 McCabe Way, Irvine, CA 92714. URL: `http://www.phoenix.com/`.

PKWARE Inc. (undated) *Application Notes for PKZIP.* URL: `ftp://ftp.pkware.com/appnote.zip`.

Pollitt, M. M. (undated a) *A Five-Step Approach to Forensic Examinations,* Special Agent, Federal Bureau of Investigation, Baltimore, MD.

Pollitt, M. M. (undated b) *Computer Forensics: an approach to evidence in cyberspace,* Special Agent, Federal Bureau of Investigation, Baltimore, MD.

Pollitt, M. M. (1995a) Forensic use of a peer to peer network, *Second International Conference on Computer Evidence,* Baltimore, MD, 10–15 April.

Pollitt, M. M. (1995b) Principles, practices, and procedures: an approach to standards in computer forensics, *Second International Conference on Computer Evidence,* Baltimore, MD, 10–15 April.

Postuma, P. (1995) *BIOS Reporter, version 1.1,* `ppostuma@nbnet.nb.ca`; 16 Fullyer Drive, Quispamsis, NB, Canada E2G 1Y7.

PowerQuest (1996) *PartitionMagic 3.0 User Guide,* PowerQuest Corporation, 1083 N State Street, Orem, UT. URL: `http://www.powerquest.com/`.

PowerQuest (1997) *Primary, Extended, Logical, Free Space! What Do I Need!,* PowerQuest Corporation, 1083 N State Street, Orem, UT. URL: `http://support.powerquest.com/logical.htm`.

PowerQuest (1998) *BootMagic User Guide,* PowerQuest Corporation, PO Box 1911, Orem, UT 84059-1911.

Psion (1992) *'C' Software Development Kit, Volume II, PLIB Reference,* 10 June, Psion PLC.

Quantum (1996) *Quantum Fireball TM 1.0/1.2/1.7/2.1/2.5/3.2/3.8 GB AT Product Manual,* Chapter 5, Table 5.1, Quantum Corporation, October. URL: http://www.quantum.com/.

Quantum (1997a) *An Immediate Solution to Breaking the 528 MB DOS Barrier,* Quantum Corporation. URL: http://www.karmaint.com.tr/qntm_528mb1.html.

Quantum (1997b) *Ultra AT – A Quantum White Paper,* Quantum Corporation. URL: http://www.quantum.com/.

Quantum (1999) *Breaking the 2.1 Gigabyte Barrier,* Quantum Corporation. URL: http://www.quantum.com/.

Quinlan, D. (1996) *magic-numbers: file(1) specification.* URL: http://earthspace.net/~esr/magic-numbers/mail-archive/0016.htm.

Raymond, E. S. (1996) *rfc-draft.* URL: http://sagan.earthspace.net/~esr/magic-numbers/rfc-draft/.

Raymond, E. S. (1997) *The Magic Numbers Group Home Page.* URL: http://sagan.earthspace.net/~esr/magic-numbers/mail-archive/0014.htm.

Risley, D. (1997) *PC Mechanic, Hard Drives.* URL: http://pcmech.pair.com/hdindex.htm/.

Rodrigue, J.-P. (undated) *What is BIOS? (Mini FAQ).* URL: http://www.sysopt.com/bios/biosdef.htm.

Rodrigue, J.-P. and Croucher, P. (1997) *The BIOS Survival Guide,* URL: http://www.lemig.umontreal.ca/bios/bios_sg.htm.

Rosch, W. L. (1997) *Hardware Bible,* Electronic Edition, 18 April. URL: http://www.eet.alfredtech.edu/courses/Elet5224/ebook/newtoc.htm.

Rosenblatt, K. S. (1996) How to investigate computer intrusion: a checklist, *Government Technology,* October. URL: http://www.govtech.net:80thePoint/1996/gt/oct/oct1996-management/oct1996-management.htm.

Schneier, B. (1996) *Applied Cryptography, Protocols, Algorithms and Source Code in C,* John Wiley & Sons, New York.

Schwartz, M. (1997a) *Elser Word convertress.* URL: http://wwwbs.cs.tu-berlin.de/~schwartz/pmh/elser/elser.html.

Schwartz, M. (1997b) *LAOLA file system.* URL: http://wwwbs.cs.tu-berlin.de/~schwartz/pmh/guide.html.

Seagate (1991a) *Specifications for ST-412.* URL: http://www.seagate.com/cgi-bin/view.cgi?/mfm/st412.txt.

Seagate (1991b) *Specifications for ST-506.* URL: http://www.seagate.com/cgi-bin/view.cgi?/mfm/st506.txt.

Seagate (1994) *FIND-ATA.EXE v1.0, An ATA Interface Identify Drive Utility,* Seagate Technology, Inc., B-5 Technical Support, 920 Disc Drive, Scotts Valley, CA 95066. URL: http://www.seagate.com/support/disc/faq/faq96029.shtml.

Seagate (1995a) *NFDisc v1.20, Partition Record display and maintenance,* Seagate Technology Inc. URL: http://www.seagate.com/support/disc/faq/faq96029.shtml.

Seagate (1995b) *SGATFMT4.EXE v4.0, Seagate Format Drive Utility.* URL: http://www.seagate.com/support/disc/faq/faq96029.shtml.

Seagate (1996) *FindSector v1.0, Sector level display and maintenance.* URL: http://www.seagate.com/support/disc/faq/faq96029.shtml.

Seagate (1997a) *Cheetah 4.5- to 9.1-Gbyte capacity disc drives.* URL: http://www.seagate.com/.

Seagate (1997b) *Low Level Formatting an ATA (IDE) Hard Drive,* Seagate Technology, Inc., B-5 Technical Support, 920 Disc Drive, Scotts Valley, CA 95066. URL: http://www.seagate.com/support/disc/faq/faq96029.shtml.

Seagate (1997c) *Seagate Fast ATA/Fast ATA-2 Fact Sheet,* Seagate Technology, Corporate Communications. URL: http://www.seagate.com/support/disc/faq/fastfs.shtml.

Seagate (1998a) *DiscWizard.* URL: http://www.seagate.com/disc/discwizard/discwizshtml.

Seagate (1998b) *FAQ Disk Manager Basics, BIOS Limitations*, Seagate Technology. URL: http://www.seagate.com/support/disc/faq/bioslmt.shtml.

Seagate (1998c) *Ultra ATA Advanced ATA Storage Interface*. URL: http://www.seagate.com/support/disc/papers/ultra_ata.shtml.

Silverglate, H. A. and Viles, T. C. (1991) Constitutional, legal, and ethical considerations for dealing with electronic files in the age of cyberspace, *Federal Enforcement Conference*, Washington, DC, 16–17 May. URL: http://www.eff.org/pub/Global/USA/Legal/search_and_seizure.speech.

Smith, R. E. (1997) *Internet Cryptography*, Addison-Wesley, Reading, MA.

Solutions by Design (1997) *Hard Disk Sub-Systems*, Solutions by Design (Australia) Pty Ltd, 22 August. URL: http://www.solbydes.com.au/sbd/hdtech1.htm.

Sommer, P. (1995) *Forensic Computing CSRC Research Project*. URL: http://csrc.lse.ac.uk/csrc/forncomp.htm.

Steunebrink (1997) *The BIOS IDE Harddisk Limitations*. URL: http://www.inter.nl.net/hcc/J.Steunebrink/bioslim.htm.

Stevens, C. E. (1995) *BIOS Enhanced Disk Drive Specification Version 1.1*, Phoenix Technologies Ltd, 9 May. URL: http://www.ptltd.com/desktop/edd2c.pdf.

Stevens, C. E. and Broyles, P. J. (1997) *ATAPI Removable Media Device BIOS Specification Version 1.0*, Compaq Computer Corporation and Phoenix Technologies Ltd, 30 January. URL: http://www.ptltd.com/desktop/armdbs10.pdf.

Stone, R. (1995) Exclusion of Evidence under Section 78 of the Police and Criminal Evidence Act: Practice and Principles, *Web Journal of Current Legal Issues*, [1995] 3 Web JCLI, 18 July. URL: http://www.newcastle.ac.uk/~nlawwww/articles3/stone3.html.

Susskind, R. (1996) *The Future of Law: Facing the Challenges of Information Technology*, Oxford University Press, Oxford. Review article by Charlesworth, A. (1997) *Web Journal of Current Legal Issues*, [1997] 3 Web JCLI, 30 June. URL: http://www.newcastle.ac.uk/~nlawwww/1997/issue3/charles3.htm.

Symantec (1995) *Norton Utilities for Windows 95 User's Guide*, Symantec Corporation, 1995, Peter Norton Group, 10201 Torre Avenue, Cupertino, CA 95014.

Symantec (1999) *Norton Utilities Version 4, User's Guide, Norton Disk Editor*, Symantec Corporation, Peter Norton Group, 10201 Torre Avenue, Cupertino, CA 95014.

Tauritz, D. R. (1995) *EIDE/MIO Mini FAQ v0.2*, 15 January. URL: http://www.wi.leidenuniv.nl/ata/minifaq.html.

Tischer, M. and Jennrich, B. (1996) *PC Intern, The Encyclopedia of System Programming*, Abacus, Data Becker Edition.

Townsend, S. and Hale, B. (1996) *Post Memory Manager Specification Version 1.0*, Phoenix Technologies Ltd and Intel Corporation, 20 September. URL: http://www.ptltd.com/desktop/pmm10.pdf.

UN (1994) *International review of criminal policy – United Nations Manual on the prevention and control of computer-related crime*, URL: http://www.ifs.univie.ac.at/~pr2gq1/rev4344.html.

Unisys (undated) *License Information on GIF and Other LZW-based Technologies*. URL: http://corp2.unisys.com/LeadStory/lzwfaq.html.

USB (1998) *Universal Serial Bus Specification, Revision 1.1*, 23 September, Compaq Computer Corporation, Intel Corporation, Microsoft Corporation, NEC Corporation. URL: http://www.us.org/developers/data/usb11.pdf.

van Staten, E. (1997) *Harddrive Related Terms and Tricks*, 04/16/1997. URL: http://www.computercraft.com/docs/evsterms.htm.

von Neumann, J. (1945) *First Draft of a Report on the EDVAC*, 30 June, Contract No W-670-ORD-492, Moore School of Electrical Engineering, University of Pennsylvania, Philadelphia.

Wehman, J. and Haan, P. (1998) *The Enhanced IDE/Fast-ATA/ATA-2 FAQ, V1.92*, 23/1/1998. URL: http://www.wi.leidenuniv.nl/ata/.

Weitz, H. (1997) Trial Practice In The Computer Age: Use of Computer-Generated Evidence, *Web Law Review*, Winter. URL: http://www.eaglelink.com/law-review/3w97.html.

Western Digital (undated a) *Enhanced IDE Implementation Guide, Version 5*, Western Digital Corporation, 8105 Irvine Center Drive, Irvine, CA 92618. URL: http://www.wdc.com/.

Western Digital (undated b) *User's Guide WD1003V-MM1 Winchester Disk Controller (also MM2, SR1 and SR2)*, Western Digital Corporation, 8105 Irvine Center Drive, Irvine, CA 92618. URL: http://www.wdc.com/.

Western Digital (1997a) *Drive Parameters*, 25 March, Western Digital Corporation, 8105 Irvine Center Drive, Irvine, CA 92618. URL: http://www.wdc.com/.

Western Digital (1997b) *Enhanced IDE Interface*, Western Digital Corporation, 8105 Irvine Center Drive, Irvine, CA 92618, URL: http://www.wdc.com/.

Western Digital (1998a) *8.4 GB Capacity Barrier*, Western Digital Corporation, 8105 Irvine Center Drive, Irvine, CA 92618. URL: http://www.wdc.com/.

Western Digital (1998b) *Large Disk Integration*, 10/07/1998, Western Digital Corporation, 8105 Irvine Center Drive, Irvine, CA 92618. URL: http://www.wdc.com/.

Western Digital (1999) *EZ-Drive FAQ Sheet*, 9 March, 8105 Irvine Center Drive, Irvine, CA 92618. URL: http://www.wdc.com/.

Williams, R. (1996) *Data Powers of Ten*, URL: http://www.cacr.caltech.edu/~roy/dataquan/.

Zacker, C. (1995) *Upgrading and Repairing Networks*, Appendix C, RAID, Que, San Francisco. URL: http://www.mcp.com/que/.

Zander, M. (1985) *The Police & Criminal Evidence Act 1984*, Sweet & Maxwell, London.

Ziv, J. and Lempel, A. (1977) A universal algorithm for sequential data compression, *IEEE Transactions on Information Theory*, Vol 23, No 3, pp. 337–343.

Appendix 1. *Common Character Codes*

American Standard Code for Information Interchange (ASCII)

This is by far the most common of the character codes. It was originally defined as a 7 bit code (hexadecimal 00 to 7F) and includes a number of control characters (00h to 1Fh) that were used with teleprinter and communications terminals. It is listed below in decimal, hexadecimal and octal.

Dec	Hex	Oct	Char	Dec	Hex	Oct	Char	Dec	Hex	Oct	Char	Dec	Hex	Oct	Char
0	00	000	NUL	32	20	040	SP	64	40	100	@	96	60	140	`
1	01	001	SOH	33	21	041	!	65	41	101	A	97	61	141	a
2	02	002	STX	34	22	042	"	66	42	102	B	98	62	142	b
3	03	003	ETX	35	23	043	#	67	43	103	C	99	63	143	c
4	04	004	EOT	36	24	044	$	68	44	104	D	100	64	144	d
5	05	005	ENQ	37	25	045	%	69	45	105	E	101	65	145	e
6	06	006	ACK	38	26	046	&	70	46	106	F	102	66	146	f
7	07	007	BEL	39	27	047	'	71	47	107	G	103	67	147	g
8	08	010	BS	40	28	050	(	72	48	110	H	104	68	150	h
9	09	011	TAB	41	29	051	)	73	49	111	I	105	69	151	i
10	0A	012	LF	42	2A	052	*	74	4A	112	J	106	6A	152	j
11	0B	013	VT	43	2B	053	+	75	4B	113	K	107	6B	153	k
12	0C	014	FF	44	2C	054	,	76	4C	114	L	108	6C	154	l
13	0D	015	CR	45	2D	055	−	77	4D	115	M	109	6D	155	m
14	0E	016	SO	46	2E	056	.	78	4E	116	N	110	6E	156	n
15	0F	017	SI	47	2F	057	/	79	4F	117	O	111	6F	157	o
16	10	020	DLE	48	30	060	0	80	50	120	P	112	70	160	p
17	11	021	DC1	49	31	061	1	81	51	121	Q	113	71	161	q
18	12	022	DC2	50	32	062	2	82	52	122	R	114	72	162	r
19	13	023	DC3	51	33	063	3	83	53	123	S	115	73	163	s
20	14	024	DC4	52	34	064	4	84	54	124	T	116	74	164	t
21	15	025	NAK	53	35	065	5	85	55	125	U	117	75	165	u
22	16	026	SYN	54	36	066	6	86	56	126	V	118	76	166	v
23	17	027	ETB	55	37	067	7	87	57	127	W	119	77	167	w
24	18	030	CAN	56	38	070	8	88	58	130	X	120	78	170	x
25	19	031	EM	57	39	071	9	89	59	131	Y	121	79	171	y
26	1A	032	SUB	58	3A	072	:	90	5A	132	Z	122	7A	172	z
27	1B	033	ESC	59	3B	073	;	91	5B	133	[	123	7B	173	{
28	1C	034	FS	60	3C	074	<	92	5C	134	\	124	7C	174	|
29	1D	035	GS	61	3D	075	=	93	5D	135	]	125	7D	175	}
30	1E	036	RS	62	3E	076	>	94	5E	136	^	126	7E	176	~
31	1F	037	US	63	3F	077	?	95	5F	137	_	127	7F	177	DEL

Windows ANSI Character Set

A number of different extensions have been made to the original ASCII character set to utilize the codes from 80h to FFh. One that is often met with is the Windows ANSI character set. The range from 00h to 7Fh is as for the ASCII character set. The extended portion of the set is shown below with blanks for codes that do not display.

Dec	Hex	Oct	Char	Dec	Hex	Oct	Char	Dec	Hex	Oct	Char	Dec	Hex	Oct	Char
128	80	200		160	A0	240		192	C0	300	À	224	E0	340	à
129	81	201		161	A1	241	¡	193	C1	301	Á	225	E1	341	á
130	82	202	‚	162	A2	242	¢	194	C2	302	Â	226	E2	342	â
131	83	203	ƒ	163	A3	243	£	195	C3	303	Ã	227	E3	343	ã
132	84	204	„	164	A4	244	¤	196	C4	304	Ä	228	E4	344	ä
133	85	205	…	165	A5	245	¥	197	C5	305	Å	229	E5	345	å
134	86	206	†	166	A6	246	¦	198	C6	306	Æ	230	E6	346	æ
135	87	207	‡	167	A7	247	§	199	C7	307	Ç	231	E7	347	ç
136	88	210	ˆ	168	A8	250	¨	200	C8	310	È	232	E8	350	è
137	89	211	‰	169	A9	251	©	201	C9	311	É	233	E9	351	é
138	8A	212	Š	170	AA	252	ª	202	CA	312	Ê	234	EA	352	ê
139	8B	213	‹	171	AB	253	«	203	CB	313	Ë	235	EB	353	ë
140	8C	214	Œ	172	AC	254	¬	204	CC	314	Ì	236	EC	354	ì
141	8D	215		173	AD	255		205	CD	315	Í	237	ED	355	í
142	8E	216		174	AE	256	®	206	CE	316	Î	238	EE	356	î
143	8F	217		175	AF	257	¯	207	CF	317	Ï	239	EF	357	ï
144	90	220		176	B0	260	°	208	D0	320	Ð	240	F0	360	ð
145	91	221	'	177	B1	261	±	209	D1	321	Ñ	241	F1	361	ñ
146	92	222	'	178	B2	262	²	210	D2	322	Ò	242	F2	362	ò
147	93	223	"	179	B3	263	³	211	D3	323	Ó	243	F3	363	ó
148	94	224	"	180	B4	264	´	212	D4	324	Ô	244	F4	364	ô
149	95	225	•	181	B5	265	µ	213	D5	325	Õ	245	F5	365	õ
150	96	226	–	182	B6	266	¶	214	D6	326	Ö	246	F6	366	ö
151	97	227	—	183	B7	267	·	215	D7	327	×	247	F7	367	÷
152	98	230	˜	184	B8	270	¸	216	D8	330	Ø	248	F8	370	ø
153	99	231	™	185	B9	271	¹	217	D9	331	Ù	249	F9	371	ù
154	9A	232	š	186	BA	272	º	218	DA	332	Ú	250	FA	372	ú
155	9B	233	›	187	BB	273	»	219	DB	333	Û	251	FB	373	û
156	9C	234	œ	188	BC	274	¼	220	DC	334	Ü	252	FC	374	ü
157	9D	235		189	BD	275	½	221	DD	335	Ý	253	FD	375	ý
158	9E	236		190	BE	276	¾	222	DE	336	Þ	254	FE	376	þ
159	9F	237	Ÿ	191	BF	277	¿	223	DF	337	β	255	FF	377	ÿ

IBM Extended ASCII Character Set

Another extension that is often met with is the IBM Extended ASCII Character set. This extended set includes the familiar line drawing characters and is shown below.

Dec	Hex	Oct	Char	Dec	Hex	Oct	Char	Dec	Hex	Oct	Char	Dec	Hex	Oct	Char
128	80	200	Ç	160	A0	240	á	192	C0	300	└	224	E0	340	α
129	81	201	ü	161	A1	241	í	193	C1	301	┴	225	E1	341	β
130	82	202	é	162	A2	242	ó	194	C2	302	┬	226	E2	342	Γ
131	83	203	â	163	A3	243	ú	195	C3	303	├	227	E3	343	π
132	84	204	ä	164	A4	244	ñ	196	C4	304	─	228	E4	344	Σ
133	85	205	à	165	A5	245	Ñ	197	C5	305	┼	229	E5	345	σ
134	86	206	å	166	A6	246	ª	198	C6	306	╞	230	E6	346	µ
135	87	207	ç	167	A7	247	º	199	C7	307	╟	231	E7	347	τ
136	88	210	ê	168	A8	250	¿	200	C8	310	╚	232	E8	350	Φ
137	89	211	ë	169	A9	251	⌐	201	C9	311	╔	233	E9	351	Θ
138	8A	212	è	170	AA	252	¬	202	CA	312	╩	234	EA	352	Ω
139	8B	213	ï	171	AB	253	½	203	CB	313	╦	235	EB	353	δ
140	8C	214	î	172	AC	254	¼	204	CC	314	╠	236	EC	354	∞
141	8D	215	ì	173	AD	255	¡	205	CD	315	═	237	ED	355	φ
142	8E	216	Ä	174	AE	256	«	206	CE	316	╬	238	EE	356	ε
143	8F	217	Å	175	AF	257	»	207	CF	317	╧	239	EF	357	∩
144	90	220	É	176	B0	260	░	208	D0	320	╨	240	F0	360	≡
145	91	221	æ	177	B1	261	▒	209	D1	321	╤	241	F1	361	±
146	92	222	Æ	178	B2	262	▓	210	D2	322	╥	242	F2	362	≥
147	93	223	ô	179	B3	263	│	211	D3	323	╙	243	F3	363	≤
148	94	224	ö	180	B4	264	┤	212	D4	324	╘	244	F4	364	⌠
149	95	225	ò	181	B5	265	╡	213	D5	325	╒	245	F5	365	⌡
150	96	226	û	182	B6	266	╢	214	D6	326	╓	246	F6	366	÷
151	97	227	ù	183	B7	267	╖	215	D7	327	╫	247	F7	367	≈
152	98	230	ÿ	184	B8	270	╕	216	D8	330	╪	248	F8	370	°
153	99	231	Ö	185	B9	271	╣	217	D9	331	┘	249	F9	371	•
154	9A	232	Ü	186	BA	272	║	218	DA	332	┌	250	FA	372	·
155	9B	233	¢	187	BB	273	╗	219	DB	333	█	251	FB	373	√
156	9C	234	£	188	BC	274	╝	220	DC	334	▄	252	FC	374	ⁿ
157	9D	235	¥	189	BD	275	╜	221	DD	335	▌	253	FD	375	²
158	9E	236	₧	190	BE	276	╛	222	DE	336	▐	254	FE	376	■
159	9F	237	ƒ	191	BF	277	┐	223	DF	337	▀	255	FF	377	□

In addition to the codes from 80h to FFh, the IBM Extended Character set, also defines printable codes for the control characters from 00h to 1Fh. These are shown in this next table:

Dec	Hex	Oct	Char	Dec	Hex	Oct	Char	Dec	Hex	Oct	Char	Dec	Hex	Oct	Char
0	00	000		1	01	001	☺	2	02	002	☻	3	03	003	♥
4	04	004	♦	5	05	005	♣	6	06	006	♠	7	07	007	●
8	08	010	◘	9	09	011	○	10	0A	012	◙	11	0B	013	♂
12	0C	014	♀	13	0D	015	♪	14	0E	016	♫	15	0F	017	☼
16	10	020	►	17	11	021	◄	18	12	022	↕	19	13	023	‼
20	14	024	¶	21	15	025	§	22	16	026	▬	23	17	027	↨
24	18	030	↑	25	19	031	↓	26	1A	032	→	27	1B	033	←
28	1C	034	∟	29	1D	035	↔	30	1E	036	▲	31	1F	037	▼

Appendix 2. Some Common File Format Signatures

Hex signature	File type	Description
xx[1] xx xx xx af 11	FLI	Graphics – Autodesk Animator
xx xx xx xx af 12	FLC	Graphics – Autodesk 3D Studio
xx xx 2d 6c 68 35 2d - l h 5 -	LZH	Archive – LHA archive file
00 00 00 02	MAC	Graphics – MAC Picture format
00 00 01 00	ICO	Graphics – Windows icon format
00 00 02 00 04 04	WKS	Spreadsheet – Lotus 1-2-3
00 00 02 00 05 04	WRK	Spreadsheet – Symphony
00 00 02 00 06 04	WK1	Spreadsheet – Lotus 1-2-3
00 00 02 00 06 04	WR1	Spreadsheet – Symphony
00 00 1a 00 00 10	WK3	Spreadsheet – Lotus 1-2-3
00 00 1a 00 02 10	WK4	Spreadsheet – Lotus 1-2-3
00 01 00 08	IMG	Graphics – GEM Image format
01 00 00 00	PIC	Spreadsheet graph – Lotus 1-2-3
02	DBF	Database – dBASE II
03	DBF	Database – dBASE III
03	DBF	Database – dBASE 1V
03	DBF	Database – FoxPro
09 00 04 00 07 00 01 00		Spreadsheet – Excel BIFF2[2]
09 02 06 00 00 00 01 00		Spreadsheet – Excel BIFF3
09 04 06 00 00 04 00 01	XLW	Spreadsheet – Excel BIFF4
0a	PCX	Graphics – ZSOFT Paintbrush
2e 73 6e 64 . s n d		Sound – NeXT/Sun audio format
31 be 00 00 00 ab	DOC	Word processor – MS Word 4
31 be 00 00 00 ab	WRI	Word processor – MS Write
32 be 00 00 00 ab	WRI	Word processor – MS Write
34 12	PIC	Graphics – PC Paint
38 42 50 53 8 B P S	PSD	Graphics – Adobe Photoshop
3a de 68 b1	DCX	Graphics – CAS fax format
41 48 A H	PAL, PIC	Graphics – Dr Halo format
42 4d B M	BMP	Graphics – Windows bitmap
43 54 4d 46 C T M F	CMF	Sound – Creative music format
43 72 65 61 74 69 76 65 C r e a t i v e 20 56 6f 69 63 65 20 46 V o i c e F	VOC	Sound – Creative voice format

Hex signature	File type	Description
69 6c 65 1a i l e		
44 61 6e 4d D a n M	MSP	Graphics – Windows Paint
45 59 45 53 E Y E S	CE1, CE2	Graphics – ComputerEyes format
46 4f 52 4d F O R M	LBM	Graphics – Interchange file format
47 49 46 38 37 61 G I F 8 7 a	GIF	Graphics – graphics interchange format
47 49 46 38 39 61 G I F 8 9 a	GIF	Graphics – graphics interchange format
49 42 4b 1a I B K	IBK	Sound – Soundblaster instrument bank
49 49 I I	TIF	Graphics – tag image file format Intel (little endian)
49 4d 44 43 I M D C	IC1, IC2, IC3	Graphics – Atari Imagic film format
4c 69 6e 53 L i n S	MSP	Graphics – Windows 3.x Paint
4d 47 43 M G C	CRD	Database – Windows 3.x Cardfile
4d 4d M M	TIF	Graphics – tag image file format Motorola (big endian)
4d 54 68 64 M T h d	MID	Sound – standard MIDI format
4d 5a M Z	EXE, DLL, DVR COM, SYS	Executable files
50 4b P K	ZIP	Archive – Pkzip archive file
50 4d 43 43 P M C C	GRP	General – Windows group file
50 c3 P	CLP	Graphics – Windows 3.x clipboard
52 49 46 46 xx xx xx xx R I F F 41 56 49 20 A V I	AVI	Graphics – Resource interchange file format (RIFF) wrapping Audio/video interleavedfile
52 49 46 46 xx xx xx xx R I F F 52 4d 49 44 R M I D	RMI	Sound – Resource interchange file format (RIFF) wrapping Windows MIDI file
52 49 46 46 xx xx xx xx R I F F 57 41 56 45 W A V E	WAV	Sound – Resource interchange file format (RIFF) wrapping Windows WAVE file
53 42 49 1a S B I	SBI	Sound – Soundblaster instrument format
56 44 56 49 V D V I	AVS	Graphics – Intel digital video interface
59 a6 6a 95	RAS	Graphics – SUN raster format
5a 4f 4f 20 Z O O	ZOO	Archive – Zoo archive file
6d 6f 6f 76 m o o v	QTM	Graphics – Apple quick time format

Hex signature	File type	Description
7b	DBF	Database – dBASE 1V
7b 5c 72 74 66 31 { \ r t f 1	RTF	Word processor – rich text format
83	DBF	Database – dBASE III
83	DBF	Database – dBASE 1V
83	DBF	Database – FoxPro
8b	DBF	Database – FoxPro
9b a5	DOC	Word processor – Winword 1.0
b5 a2 b0 b3 b3 b0 a2 b5	CAL	Calendar – Windows 3.x calendar
ba be eb ea	ANI	Graphics – NEOchrome animation
d0 cf 11 e0 a1 b1 1a e1		Wrapper file used for variety of Microsoft applications
d7 cd c6 9a	WMF	Graphics – Windows metafile format
db a5	DOC	Word processor – Winword 2.0
f5	DBF	Database – FoxPro
fe db	SEQ	Graphics – Cyber paint
fe dc	SEQ	Graphics – Cyber paint
ff 57 50 43 -1 W P C	WPD	Word processor – WordPerfect
ff 57 50 43 -1 W P C	WPG	Graphics – WordPerfect Graphic
ff d8	JPG	Graphics – JPEG/JFIF format
ff ff	GEM	Graphics – GEM Metafile format
ff ff ff ff	SYS	Executable system file

1. "xx" is used to indicate "don't care". In other words, we have for this case four leading bytes whose values can be anything (don't care) followed by af 11.
2. Excel binary interchange format.

Appendix 3. A Typical[1] Set of POST Codes

Hex code	Description of POST operation
02h	Verify real mode
03h	Disable non-maskable interrupt (NMI)
04h	Get processor type
06h	Initialize system hardware
08h	Initialize chipset with initial POST values
09h	Set IN POST flag
0Ah	Initialize CPU registers
0Bh	Enable CPU cache
0Ch	Initialize caches to initial POST values
0Eh	Initialize I/O component
0Fh	Initialize the local bus IDE
10h	Initialize power management
11h	Load alternate registers with initial POST values
12h	Restore CPU control word during warm boot
13h	Initialize PCI bus mastering devices
14h	Initialize keyboard controller
16h	BIOS ROM checksum
17h	Initialize cache betore memory autosize
18h	8254 timer initialization
1Ah	8237 DMA controller initialization
1Ch	Reset programmable interrupt controller
20h	Test DRAM refresh
22h	Test keyboard controller
24h	Set ES segment register to 4 GB
26h	Enable A20 line
28h	Autosize DRAM
29h	Initialize POST memory manager
2Ah	Clear 512 KB base RAM
2Ch	RAM failure on address line xxxx
2Eh	RAM failure on data bits xxxx of low byte of memory bus
2Fh	Enable cache before system BIOS shadow
30h	RAM failure on data bits xxxx of high byte of memory bus
32h	Test CPU bus-clock frequency
33h	Initialize POST dispatch manager
34h	Test CMOS RAM
35h	Initialize alternate chipset registers
36h	Warm start shut down
37h	Reinitialize the chipset (motherboard only)
38h	Shadow system BIOS ROM
39h	Reinitialize the cache (motherboard only)
3Ah	Autosize cache

Hex code	Description of POST operation
3Ch	Configure advanced chipset registers
3Dh	Load alternate registers with CMOS values
40h	Set Initial CPU speed
42h	Initialize interrupt vectors
44h	Initialize BIOS interrupts
45h	POST device initialization
46h	Check ROM copyright notice
47h	Initialize manager for PCI option ROMs
48h	Check video configuration against CMOS RAM data
49h	Initialize PCI bus and devices
4Ah	Initialize all video adapters in system
4Bh	Display QuietBoot screen
4Ch	Shadow video BIOS ROM
4Eh	Display BIOS copyright notice
50h	Display CPU type and speed
51h	Initialize EISA motherboard
52h	Test keyboard
54h	Set key click if enabled
56h	Enable keyboard
58h	Test for unexpected interrupts
59h	Initialize POST display service
5Ah	Display prompt "Press F2 to enter SETUP"
5Bh	Disable CPU cache
5Ch	Test RAM between 512 and 640 KB
60h	Test extended memory
62h	Test extended memory address lines
64h	Jump to UserPatchl
66h	Configure advanced cache registers
67h	Initialize multiprocessor APIC
68h	Enable external and processor caches
69h	Setup System Management Mode (SMM) area
6Ah	Display external L2 cache size
6Ch	Display shadow-area message
6Eh	Display possible high address for UMB recovery
70h	Display error messages
72h	Check for configuration errors
74h	Test real-time clock
76h	Check for keyboard errors
7Ah	Test for key lock on
7Ch	Set up hardware interrupt vectors
7Eh	Initialize coprocessor if present
80h	Disable onboard Super I/O ports and IRQs
8lh	Late POST device initialization
82h	Detect and install external RS232 ports
83h	Configure non-MCD IDE controllers
84h	Detect and install external parallel ports
85h	initialize PC-compatibie PnP ISA devices
86h	Re-initialize onboard I/O ports
87h	Configure motherboard configurable devices
88h	Initialize BIOS Data Area
89h	Enable Non-Maskable Interrupts (NMls)
8Ah	Initialize extended BIOS data area
8Bh	Test and initialize PS/2 mouse
8Ch	Initialize diskette controller
8Fh	Determine number of ATA drives

Hex code	Description of POST operation
90h	Initialize hard-disk controllers
9lh	Initialize local-bus hard-disk controllers
92h	Jump to UserPatch2
93h	Build MPTABLE for multiprocessor boards
94h	Disable A20 address line (ReI. 5.1 and earlier)
95h	install CD-ROM for boot
96h	Clear huge ES segment register
97h	Fix up multiprocessor table
98h	Search for option ROMs
99h	Check for SMART Drive
9Ah	Shadow option ROMs
9Ch	Set up power management
9Eh	Enable hardware interrupts
9Fh	Determine number of ATA and SCSI drives
A0h	Set time of day
A2h	Check key lock
A4h	Initialize typematic rate
A8h	Erase F2 prompt
AAh	Scan for F2 key stroke
ACh	Enter SETUP
AEh	Clear IN POST flag
B0h	Check for errors
B2h	POST done - prepare to boot operating system
B4h	One short beep before boot
B5h	Terminate QuietBoot
B6h	Check password (optional)
B8h	Clear global descriptor table
B9h	Clean up all graphics
BAh	Initialize DMI parameters
BBh	Initialize PnP Option ROMs
BCh	Clear parity checkers
BDh	Display MultiBoot menu
BEh	Clear screen (optional)
BFh	Check virus and backup reminders
C0h	Try to boot with INT 19h
Clh	Initialize POST Error Manager (PEM)
C2h	Initialize error logging
C3h	Initialize error display function
C4h	Initialize system error handler

1. These codes are taken from the SE440BX Motherboard Technical Product Specification, by permission of Intel Corporation.

Appendix 4. *Typical BIOS Beep Codes and Error Messages*

Intel[1] SE440BX Motherboard

Beep code	POST code	Explanation
1-2-2-3	16h	BIOS ROM checksum
1-3-1-1	20h	Test DRAM refresh
1-3-1-3	22h	Test Keyboard Controller
1-3-3-1	28h	Autosize DRAM
1-3-3-2	29h	Initialize POST Memory Manager
1-3-3-3	2Ah	Clear 512 KB base RAM
1-3-4-1	2Ch	RAM failure on address line xxxx
1-3-4-3	2Eh	RAM failure on data bits xxxx of low byte of memory bus
1-4-1-1	30h	RAM failure on data bits xxxx of high byte of memory bus
2-1-2-2	45h	POST device initialization
2-1-2-3	46h	Check ROM copyright notice
2-2-3-1	58h	Test for unexpected interrupts
2-2-4-1	5Ch	Test RAM between 512 and 640 KB
1-2	98h	Search for option ROMs. One long, two short beeps on checksum failure

One long beep followed by several short beeps indicates a video problem. One short beep indicates that POST completed normally.

Error message	Explanation
Diskette drive A error	Drive A is present but fails the POST diskette tests. Check that the drive is defined with the proper diskette type in Setup and that the diskette drive is installed correctly.
Extended RAM Failed at offset :nnnn	Extended memory not working or not configured properly at offset nnnn.
Failing Bits: nnnn	The hexadecimal number nnnn is a map of the bits at the RAM address (System, Extended, or Shadow memory) that failed the memory test. Each 1 in the map indicates a failed bit.
Fixed Disk 0 Failure or Fixed Disk 1 Failure or Fixed Disk Controller Failure	Fixed disk is not working or not configured properly. Check to see if fixed disk installed properly. Run Setup to be sure the fixed-disk type is correctly identified.

Error message	Explanation
Incorrect Drive A type – run SETUP	Type of diskette drive for drive A not correctly identified in Setup.
Invalid NVRAM media type	Problem with NVRAM (CMOS) access.
Keyboard controller error	The keyboard controller failed test. Try replacing the keyboard.
Keyboard error	Keyboard not working.
Keyboard error nn	BIOS discovered a stuck key and displayed the scan code nn for the stuck key.
Keyboard locked – Unlock key switch	Unlock the system to proceed.
Monitor type does not match CMOS – Run SETUP	Monitor type not correctly identified in Setup.
Operating system not found	Operating system cannot be located on either drive A or drive C. Enter Setup and see if fixed disk and drive A are properly identified.
Parity Check 1	Parity error found in the system bus. BIOS attempts to locate the address and display it on the screen. If it cannot locate the address, it displays ????.
Parity Check 2	Parity error found in the I/O bus. BIOS attempts to locate the address and display it on the screen. If it cannot locate the address, it displays ????.
Press <F1> to resume, <F2> to Setup	Displayed after any recoverable error message. Press <F1> to start the boot process or <F2> to enter Setup and change any settings.
Real-time clock error	Real-time clock fails BIOS test. May require motherboard repair.
Shadow RAM Failed at offset: nnnn	Shadow RAM failed at offset nnnn of the 64 KB block at which the error was detected.
System battery is dead – Replace and run SETUP	The CMOS clock battery indicator shows the battery is dead. Replace the battery and run Setup to reconfigure the system.
System cache error – Cache disabled	RAM cache failed the BIOS test. BIOS disabled the cache.
System CMOS checksum bad – run SETUP	System CMOS RAM has been corrupted or modified incorrectly, perhaps by an application program that changes data stored in CMOS. Run Setup and reconfigure the system either by getting the default values and/or making your own selections.
System RAM Failed at offset: nnnn	System RAM failed at offset nnnn of the 64 KB block at which the error was detected.
System timer error	The timer test failed. Requires repair of system motherboard.

Elonex² MT-500/I System Board

Beeps	Error message	Description
1 beep	Refresh Failure.	The memory refresh circuitry on the motherboard is faulty.
2 beeps	Parity Error.	Parity error in the first 64KB of memory.
3 beeps	Base 64KB Memory Failure.	Memory failure in the first 64KB of memory.
4 beeps	Timer Not operational.	Memory failure in the first 64KB of memory, or Timer 1 on the motherboard is not functioning.
5 beeps	Processor Error.	The CPU on the board generated an error.
6 beeps	8042 Gate A20 Failure.	The keyboard controller may be bad. The BIOS cannot switch to protected mode.
7 beeps	Processor Exception Interrupt Error.	The CPU generated an exception interrupt
8 beeps	Display Memory Read/Write Error.	The system video adapter is either missing or its memory is faulty. This is not a fatal error.
9 beeps	ROM Checksum Error.	The ROM checksum value does not match the value encoded in the BIOS.
10 beeps	CMOS Shutdown Register Read/Write Error.	The shutdown register for CMOS RAM failed.
11 beeps	Cache Error/External Cache Bad.	The external cache is faulty.

Error message	Explanation
8042 Gate – A20 Error	Gate A20 on the keyboard controller (8042) is not working.
Address Line Short!	Error in the address decoding circuitry on the motherboard.
Cache Memory Bad, Do Not Enable Cache!	Cache memory is defective.
CH-2 Timer Error	Most systems include two timers. There is an error in timer 2.
CMOS Battery State Low	CMOS RAM is powered by a battery. The battery power is low.
CMOS Checksum Failure	After CMOS RAM values are saved, a checksum value is generated for error checking. The previous value is different from the current value. Run Setup.
CMOS System Options Not Set	The values stored in CMOS RAM are either corrupt or nonexistent. Run Setup.
CMOS Display Type Mismatch	The video type in CMOS RAM does not match the one detected by the BIOS. Run Setup.
CMOS Memory Size Mismatch	The amount of memory on the motherboard is different than the amount in CMOS RAM. Run Setup.
CMOS Time and Date Not Set	Run Setup to set the date and time in CMOS RAM.
Diskette Boot Failure	The boot disk in floppy drive A: is corrupt. It cannot be used to boot the system. Use another boot disk and follow the screen instructions.

Error message	Explanation
Display Switch Not Proper	Some systems require that a video switch on the motherboard be set to either colour or monochrome. Turn the system off, set the switch, then power on.
DMA Error	Error in the DMA (Direct Memory Access) controller.
DMA #1 Error	Error in the master DMA channel.
DMA #2 Error	Error in the slave DMA channel.
FDD Controller Failure	The BIOS cannot communicate with the floppy disk drive controller.
HDD Controller Failure	The BIOS cannot communicate with the hard disk drive controller.
INTR #1 Error	Interrupt channel 1 failed POST.
INTR #2 Error	Interrupt channel 2 failed POST.
Invalid Boot Diskette	The BIOS can read in floppy drive A: but cannot boot the system.
Keyboard is locked... Unlock It	The keyboard lock on the system is engaged. The system must be unlocked to continue.
Keyboard Error	There is a timing problem with the keyboard.
KB/Interface Error	There is an error in the keyboard connector.
Off Board Parity Error	Parity error in memory installed in an expansion slot. The format is: OFF BOARD PARITY ERROR ADDR (HEX) = (XXXX). XXXX is the hex address where the error occurred.
On Board Parity Error	Parity error in motherboard memory. The format is: ON BOARD PARITY ERROR ADDR (HEX) = (XXXX). XXXX is the hex address where the error occurred.
Parity Error ????	Parity error in system memory at an unknown address.

1. These beep codes and error messages are taken from the SE440BX Motherboard Product Guide, by permission of Intel Corporation.
2. These beep codes and error messages are taken from the MT-500/I Series Configuration Guide, by kind permission of Elonex plc.

Appendix 5. *Disk Partition Types*

Type	Use
00	Unused partition
01	DOS, Primary Partition (12-bit FAT, <16MB)
02	XENIX root
03	XENIX user
04	DOS, Primary Partition (16-bit FAT, >=16MB and <32MB)
05	DOS, Extended Partition using standard INT 13
06	DOS, Primary Partition (16-bit FAT, >32MB) using standard INT 13
07	OS/2 HPFS, Windows NT NTFS, QNX, or Adv UNIX
08	OS/2, DELL, Commodore DOS, AIX – boot or file system
09	AIX – boot or file system, Coherent swap
0A	OS/2 Boot Manager, OPUS, Coherent swap
0B	FAT 32 partition
0C	FAT 32 partition LBA using INT 13 extensions
0D	Possibly a type 07 LBA
0E	FAT 16 partition LBA using INT 13 extensions – otherwise same as 06
0F	Extended partition LBA using INT 13 Extensions – otherwise same as 05
10	OPUS
11	OS/2 Boot Manager: Inactive type 01
12	Compaq diagnostics partition
13	–
14	OS/2 Boot Manager: Inactive type 0, Novell DOS 7.0 FDISK
15	–
16	OS/2 Boot Manager: Inactive type 06, used by PartitionMagic to hide a partition
17	OS/2 Boot Manager: Inactive type 07
18	AST Windows swap file, Compaq System Diagnostics
19	–
to	–
20	–
21	Reserved
22	–
23	Reserved
24	NEC version of MS-DOS
25	–
26	Reserved
27	–
to	–
30	–
31	Reserved
32	–
33	Reserved
34	Reserved

Type	Use
35	–
36	Reserved
37	–
to	–
3B	–
3C	PowerQuest PartitionMagic recovery partition
3D	–
to	–
3F	–
40	VENIX 80286
41	Personal RISC Boot, PowerPC boot
42	Secure File System (Peter Gutmann)
43	–
to	–
4E	–
4F	Oberon boot and data
50	OnTrack Disk Manager read-only DOS partition
51	OnTrack Disk Manager read/write DOS partition, Novell
52	CP/M, Microport System V/386
53	OnTrack Disk Manager write-only partition
54	OnTrack Disk Manager non-DOS partition (DDO)
55	Micro House EZ-Drive non-DOS partition
56	Golden Bow VFeature partition
57	–
to	–
60	–
61	Storage Dimensions SpeedStor partition
62	–
63	UNIX System V/386, Mach, MtXinu BSD 4.3 on Mach, GNU HURD
64	Speedstor, Novell
65	Novell 286 Netware
66	Novell 386 Netware
67	Novell
68	Novell
69	Novell
6A	–
to	–
6F	–
70	DiskSecure Multi-Boot
71	Reserved
72	–
73	Reserved
74	Reserved
75	PC/IX IBM
76	Reserved
77	–
to	–
7F	–
80	Minix (ver. 1.4a and earlier)
81	Minix (ver. 1.4b and later), Mitac Advanced Disk Manager, Linux
82	Prime, Linux swap, Solaris UNIX
83	Linux ext2fs
84	OS/2 hiding a type 04
85	–
86	Reserved

Type	Use
87	HPFS FT mirrored partition
88	–
to	–
92	–
93	Amoeba file system
94	Amoeba bad block table
95	–
to	–
98	–
99	Mylex EISA SCSI
9A	–
to	–
A0	–
A1	Reserved
A2	–
A3	Reserved
A4	Reserved
A5	FreeBSD/386
A6	Reserved
A7	–
A8	–
A9	NetBSD
AA	–
to	–
B0	–
B1	Reserved
B2	–
B3	Reserved
B4	Reserved
B5	–
B6	Reserved
B7	BSDI file system or secondary swap
B8	BSDI swap or secondary file system
B9	–
to	–
BD	–
BE	Solaris boot partition
BF	–
C0	–
C1	DR-DOS LOGIN.EXE-secured 12-bit FAT
C2	–
C3	–
C4	DR-DOS LOGIN.EXE-secured 16-bit FAT
C5	–
C6	DR-DOS LOGIN.EXE-secured Huge
C7	HPFS FT disabled mirrored partition, Cyrnix Boot
C8	–
to	–
D7	–
D8	CP/M 86
D9	–
DA	–
DB	Concurrent DOS, CP/M and CTOS
DC	–
to	–

Type	Use
E0	–
E1	SpeedStor 12-bit FAT extended partition
E2	–
E3	Storage Dimensions, DOS read-only
E4	SpeedStor 16-bit FAT extended partition
E5	Reserved
E6	Reserved
E7	–
to	–
F0	–
F1	Storage Dimensions
F2	DOS 3.3+ second partition, some OEM customized DOS
F3	Reserved
F4	SpeedStor, large partitions, Storage Dimensions
F5	–
F6	Reserved
F7	–
to	–
FD	–
FE	Lan Step, SpeedStor partitions over 1024 cyl, IBM PS/2 IML
FF	UNIX Bad Block Tables

This information has been obtained from the following sources:

Landis, H. (1998) *How It Works – Partition Tables, Version 1h*, 12 December. hiw@sugs.talisman.com.

Seagate (1995) *NFDisc v1.20, Partition Record display and maintenance.* URL: http://www.seagate.com/support/disc/faq/faq96029.shtml.

van Staten, E. (1997) *Harddrive Related Terms and Tricks*, 04/16/1997. URL: http://www.computercraft.com/docs/evsterms.htm.

Wirzenius, L. (1997) *Partition Types (from Linux FDISK)*, 4 May. URL: http://linux.ichannel.gr/LDP/LDP/sag/node38.html.

Appendix 6.   *Extended Partitions*

Introduction

Because there appeared to be some doubt in the current literature about the detailed structure of extended partitions, comparative experiments were carried out to determine the actual structures that result when FDISK and PartitionMagic are used successively to partition the same hard disk. The disk used was a Quantum Pioneer SG 1.0A, which had a manufacturer's label marked "C/H/S 1.0GB 2097/16/63". This indicates a maximum possible capacity of:

$$2097 \times 16 \times 63 = 2\,113\,776 \text{ sectors}$$
$$2\,113\,776 \times 512 = 1\,082\,253\,312 \text{ bytes}$$
$$1\,082\,253\,312 / (1024 \times 1024) = 1032.12 \text{ Mbyte}$$

The disk was partitioned, on each occasion, with a primary DOS partition of 504.0 Mbyte and an extended DOS partition of the remaining space, which was reported as 525.7 Mbyte. The extended partition was then further partitioned into three logical partitions of 246.1 Mbyte, 246.1 Mbyte and 33.4 Mbyte respectively. It is this disk which was used as the example for Fig. 5.29, repeated here as Fig. A6.1 for convenience.

The partitioning process was carried out using, in the first instance, PQMAGICT.EXE (PartitionMagic by Powerquest Version 3.03.256) and then, after deleting all partitions, using FDISK.EXE (MS-DOS Version 6). The results obtained from both partitioning processes were found to be identical in terms of the partition tables that were produced. Norton Disk Editor was used to analyze these partition tables and both hexadecimal and partition table views were obtained.

It may be noted that this hard disk has not been partitioned right to the very end of all the available physical sectors, although the maximum number of sectors that were accessible to the partitioning programs was used. The last partitioned CHS address is seen to be 522,63,63, which gives the number of available sectors as $523 \times 64 \times 63 = 2,108,736$[1]. This may be confirmed from the master boot record partition table, shown in Fig. A6.2, where the number of sectors on the disk can be calculated as 63 + 1 032 129 (BIGDOS) + 1 076 544 (EXTEND) = 2 108 736. This compares with the 2 113 776 sectors calculated from the physical number of cylinders, heads and

---

1   Recall that cylinders and heads in CHS addresses are counted from 0 and not 1.

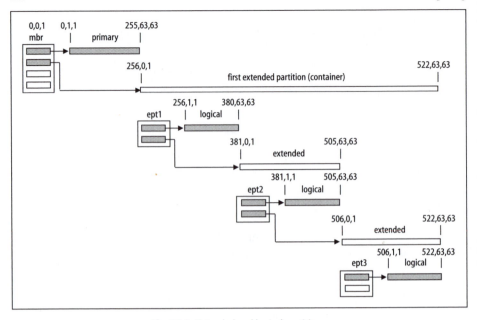

Fig. A6.1 Extended and logical partitions.

```
                              Disk Editor
                      Norton Utilities for Windows 95
                          August  3, 1999 4:57pm

                            * * * * * * * * * * * * * * *
                              Partition Table
                            * * * * * * * * * * * * * * *


Physical Sector: Cyl 0, Side 0, Sector 1
+------+----+-------------------+-------------------+----------+----------+
|      |    | Starting Location | Ending Location   | Relative | Number of|
|System|Boot|Side Cylinder Sector|Side Cylinder Sector| Sectors | Sectors  |
+------+----+-------------------+-------------------+----------+----------+
|BIGDOS| Yes|  1      0     1   | 63    255    63   |      63  | 1032129  |
|EXTEND| No |  0    256     1   | 63    522    63   | 1032192  | 1076544  |
|unused| No |  0      0     0   |  0      0     0   |       0  |       0  |
|unused| No |  0      0     0   |  0      0     0   |       0  |       0  |
+------+----+-------------------+-------------------+----------+----------+
```

Fig. A6.2 Partition table for master boot record.

sectors given on the manufacturer's label. This difference occurs because the translating algorithm which swaps cylinders for heads, in this case dividing cylinders by 4
and multiplying heads by 4, causes the last few cylinders to be inaccessible because
the total number of cylinders is not exactly divisible by 4.

Results

Both PartitionMagic and FDISK gave exactly the same results, and these are shown, in both hexadecimal and Norton Disk Editor Partition Table views, in Figs. A6.3–A6.9.

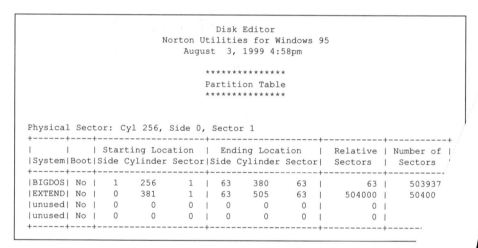

Fig. A6.3 Partition table for master boot record – hexadecimal.

```
                            Disk Editor
                   Norton Utilities for Windows 95
                      August  3, 1999 4:58pm

                        ****************
                        Partition Table
                        ****************


Physical Sector: Cyl 256, Side 0, Sector 1
+------+----+-------------------+-------------------+-----------+-----------+
|      |    | Starting Location | Ending Location   | Relative  | Number of |
|System|Boot|Side Cylinder Sector|Side Cylinder Sector| Sectors  |  Sectors  |
+------+----+-------------------+-------------------+-----------+-----------+
|BIGDOS| No |  1     256      1 |  63     380     63 |        63 |    503937 |
|EXTEND| No |  0     381      1 |  63     505     63 |    504000 |     50400 |
|unused| No |  0       0      0 |   0       0      0 |         0 |           |
|unused| No |  0       0      0 |   0       0      0 |         0 |           |
+------+----+-------------------+-------------------+-----------+-------.
```

Fig. A6.4 Partition table for the first extended partition.

Fig. A6.5 Partition table for the first extended partition – he'

```
                              Disk Editor
                    Norton Utilities for Windows 95
                        August  3, 1999 4:58pm

                         ****************
                          Partition Table
                         ****************


Physical Sector: Cyl 381, Side 0, Sector 1
+------+----+--------------------+--------------------+----------+----------+
|      |    | Starting Location  | Ending Location    | Relative | Number of|
|System|Boot|Side Cylinder Sector|Side Cylinder Sector|  Sectors |  Sectors |
+------+----+--------------------+--------------------+----------+----------+
|BIGDOS| No |   1    381      1  | 63    505      63  |       63 |   503937 |
|EXTEND| No |   0    506      1  | 63    522      63  |  1008000 |    68544 |
|unused| No |   0      0      0  |  0      0       0  |        0 |        0 |
|unused| No |   0      0      0  |  0      0       0  |        0 |        0 |
+------+----+--------------------+--------------------+----------+----------+
```

Fig. A6.6 Partition table for the second extended partition.

Fig. A6.7 Partition table for the second extended partition – hexadecimal.

```
                              Disk Editor
                    Norton Utilities for Windows 95
                        August  3, 1999 4:58pm

                         ****************
                          Partition Table
                         ****************


Physical Sector: Cyl 506, Side 0, Sector 1
+------+----+--------------------+--------------------+----------+----------+
|      |    | Starting Location  | Ending Location    | Relative | Number of|
|System|Boot|Side Cylinder Sector|Side Cylinder Sector|  Sectors |  Sectors |
+------+----+--------------------+--------------------+----------+----------+
|BIGDOS| No |   1    506      1  | 63    522      63  |       63 |    68481 |
|unused| No |   0      0      0  |  0      0       0  |        0 |        0 |
|unused| No |   0      0      0  |  0      0       0  |        0 |        0 |
|unused| No |   0      0      0  |  0      0       0  |        0 |        0 |
+------+----+--------------------+--------------------+----------+----------+
```

Fig. A6.8 Partition table for the third extended partition.

```
Gander - I:\FORENSIC\EPT3.DMP                                    _ □ ✕
File  Edit  Display  Search  Filters  Help

       00 01 02 03 04 05 06 07 08 09 0a 0b 0c 0d 0e 0f    0123 4567 89ab cdef

 1b0   00 00 00 00 00 00 00 00 00 00 00 00 00 00 00 01    ⊹⊹⊹⊹ ⊹⊹⊹⊹ ⊹⊹⊹⊹ ⊹⊹⊹⊹    ▲
 1c0   41 fa 06 3f bf 0a 3f 00 00 00 81 0b 01 00 00 00    A⊹⊹? ⊹⊹?⊹ ⊹⊹⊹⊹ ⊹⊹⊹⊹
 1d0   00 00 00 00 00 00 00 00 00 00 00 00 00 00 00 00    ⊹⊹⊹⊹ ⊹⊹⊹⊹ ⊹⊹⊹⊹ ⊹⊹⊹⊹
 1e0   00 00 00 00 00 00 00 00 00 00 00 00 00 00 00 00    ⊹⊹⊹⊹ ⊹⊹⊹⊹ ⊹⊹⊹⊹ ⊹⊹⊹⊹
 1f0   00 00 00 00 00 00 00 00 00 00 00 00 00 00 55 aa    ⊹⊹⊹⊹ ⊹⊹⊹⊹ ⊹⊹⊹⊹ ⊹⊹U⊹    ▼
```

Fig. A6.9 Partition table for the third extended partition – hexadecimal.

Appendix 7. *Registers and Order Code for the Intel 8086*

Intel 8086 Registers

The Intel 8086 has 8 general-purpose registers which are 16 bits (two bytes or one word) in size. They are known as: AX, BX, CX, DX, SI, DI, BP and SP (stack pointer). The first four, AX, BX, CX and DX may also be addressed as 8 general purpose 8 bit (one byte) registers AH, AL, BH, BL, CH, CL, DH and DL. There are also 4 segment registers which are 16 bits (two bytes or one word) in size. These are known as: CS (code segment), DS (data segment), ES (extra segment) and SS (stack segment).

Intel 8086 Hexadecimal Order Code

Hex	Instruction	Description
00	ADD	Add byte register into byte
01	ADD	Add word register into word
02	ADD	Add byte into byte register
03	ADD	Add word into word register
04	ADD	Add immediate byte into AL
05	ADD	Add immediate word into AX
06	PUSH ES	Push ES onto stack
07	POP ES	Pop ES from stack
08	OR	Logical-OR byte register into byte
09	OR	Logical-OR word register into word
0A	OR	Logical-OR byte into byte register
0B	OR	Logical-OR word into word register
0C	OR	Logical-OR immediate byte into AL
0D	OR	Logical-OR immediate word into AX
0E	PUSH CS	Push CS onto stack
0F		
10	ADC	Add with carry byte register into byte
11	ADC	Add with carry word register into word
12	ADC	Add with carry byte into byte register
13	ADC	Add with carry word into word register
14	ADC	Add with carry immediate byte into AL
15	ADC	Add with carry immediate word into AX
16	PUSH SS	Push SS onto stack

Hex	Instruction	Description
17	POP SS	Pop SS from stack
18	SBB	Subtract with borrow
19	SBB	Subtract with borrow word register from word
1A	SBB	Subtract with borrow byte from byte register
1B	SBB	Subtract with borrow word from word register
1C	SBB	Subtract with borrow immediate byte from AL
1D	SBB	Subtract with borrow immediate word from AX
1E	PUSH DS	Push DS onto stack
1F	POP DS	Pop DS from stack
20	AND	Logical-AND byte register into byte
21	AND	Logical-AND word register into word
22	AND	Logical-AND byte into byte register
23	AND	Logical-AND word into word register
24	AND	Logical-AND immediate byte into AL
25	AND	Logical-AND immediate word into AX
26		
27	DAA	Decimal adjust AL after addition
28	SUB	Subtract byte register from byte
29	SUB	Subtract word register from word
2A	SUB	Subtract byte from byte register
2B	SUB	Subtract word from word register
2C	SUB	Subtract immediate byte from AL
2D	SUB	Subtract immediate word from AX
2E		
2F	DAS	Decimal adjust AL after subtraction
30	XOR	Exclusive-OR byte register into byte
31	XOR	Exclusive-OR word register into word
32	XOR	Exclusive-OR byte into byte register
33	XOR	Exclusive-OR word into word register
34	XOR	Exclusive-OR immediate byte into AL
35	XOR	Exclusive-OR immediate word into AX
36		
37	AAA	ASCII adjust AL after addition
38	CMP	Subtract byte register from byte for compare
39	CMP	Subtract word register from word for compare
3A	CMP	Subtract byte from byte register for compare
3B	CMP	Subtract word from word register for compare
3C	CMP	Subtract immediate byte from AL for compare
3D	CMP	Subtract immediate word from AX for compare
3E		
3F	AAS	ASCII adjust AL after subtraction
40	INC	Increment word register 0 by 1
41	INC	Increment word register 1 by 1
42	INC	Increment word register 2 by 1
43	INC	Increment word register 3 by 1
44	INC	Increment word register 4 by 1
45	INC	Increment word register 5 by 1
46	INC	Increment word register 6 by 1
47	INC	Increment word register 7 by 1
48	DEC	Decrement word register 0 by 1
49	DEC	Decrement word register 1 by 1
4A	DEC	Decrement word register 2 by 1
4B	DEC	Decrement word register 3 by 1
4C	DEC	Decrement word register 4 by 1
4D	DEC	Decrement word register 5 by 1

Hex	Instruction	Description
4E	DEC	Decrement word register 6 by 1
4F	DEC	Decrement word register 7 by 1
50	PUSH	Push word register 0 onto stack
51	PUSH	Push word register 1 onto stack
52	PUSH	Push word register 2 onto stack
53	PUSH	Push word register 3 onto stack
54	PUSH	Push word register 4 onto stack
55	PUSH	Push word register 5 onto stack
56	PUSH	Push word register 6 onto stack
57	PUSH	Push word register 7 onto stack
58	POP	Pop word register 0 from stack
59	POP	Pop word register 1 from stack
5A	POP	Pop word register 2 from stack
5B	POP	Pop word register 3 from stack
5C	POP	Pop word register 4 from stack
5D	POP	Pop word register 5 from stack
5E	POP	Pop word register 6 from stack
5F	POP	Pop word register 7 from stack
60		
61		
62		
63		
64		
65		
66		
67		
68		
69		
6A		
6B		
6C		
6D		
6E		
6F		
70	JO	Jump short if overflow
71	JNO	Jump short if not overflow
72	JB	Jump short if below
	JC	Jump short if carry
	JNAE	Jump short if not above or equal
73	JAE	Jump short if above or equal
	JNB	Jump short if not below
	JNC	Jump short if not carry
74	JE	Jump short if equal
	JZ	Jump short if zero
75	JNE	Jump short if not equal
	JNZ	Jump short if not zero
76	JBE	Jump short if below or equal
	JNA	Jump short if not above
77	JA	Jump short if above
	JNBE	Jump short if not below or equal
78	JS	Jump short if sign
79	JNS	Jump short if not sign
7A	JP	Jump short if parity
	JPE	Jump short if parity even
7B	JPO	Jump short if parity odd

Hex	Instruction	Description
	JNP	Jump short if not parity
7C	JL	Jump short if less
	JNGE	Jump short if not greater or equal
7D	JGE	Jump short if greater or equal
	JNL	Jump short if not less
7E	JLE	Jump short if less or equal
	JNG	Jump short if not greater
7F	JG	Jump short if greater
	JNLE	Jump short if not less or equal
80 /0	ADD	Add immediate byte into byte
80 /1	OR	Logical-OR immediate byte into byte
80 /2	ADC	Add with carry immediate byte into byte
80 /3	SBB	Subtract with borrow immediate byte from byte
80 /4	AND	Logical-AND immediate byte into byte
80 /5	SUB	Subtract immediate byte from byte
80 /6	XOR	Exclusive-OR immediate byte into byte
80 /7	CMP	Subtract immediate byte from byte for compare
81 /0	ADD	Add immediate word into word
81 /1	OR	Logical-OR immediate word into word
81 /2	ADC	Add with carry immediate word into word
81 /3	SBB	Subtract with borrow immediate word from word
81 /4	AND	Logical-AND immediate word into word
81 /5	SUB	Subtract immediate word from word
81 /6	XOR	Exclusive-OR immediate word into word
81 /7	CMP	Subtract immediate word from word for compare
82		
83 /0	ADD	Add immediate byte into word
83 /1	OR	Logical-OR immediate byte into word
83 /2	ADC	Add with carry immediate byte into word
83 /3	SBB	Subtract with borrow immediate byte from word
83 /4	AND	Logical-AND immediate byte into word
83 /5	SUB	Subtract immediate byte from word
83 /6	XOR	Exclusive-OR immediate byte into word
83 /7	CMP	Subtract immediate byte from word for compare
84	TEST	AND byte register with byte for flags
85	TEST	AND word register with word for flags
86	XCHG	Exchange byte register with byte
87	XCHG	Exchange word register with word
88	MOV	Move byte register into byte
89	MOV	Move word register into word
8A	MOV	Move byte into byte register
8B	MOV	Move word into word register
8C /0	MOV	Move ES into word
8C /1	MOV	Move CS into word
8C /2	MOV	Move SS into word
8C /3	MOV	Move DS into word
8D	LEA	Calculate offset and place in word register
8E /0	MOV	Move memory word into ES
	MOV	Move word register into ES
8E /2	MOV	Move memory word into SS
	MOV	Move word register into SS
8E /3	MOV	Move memory word into DS
	MOV	Move word register into DS
8F	POP	Pop memory word from stack
90	NOP	No Operation

Hex	Instruction	Description
91		
92		
93		
94		
95		
96		
97		
98	CBW	Convert byte into word
99	CWD	Convert word to doubleword
9A	CALL	Call far segment, immediate 4-byte address
9B	WAIT	Wait until BUSY inactive
9C	PUSHF	Push flags onto stack
9D	POPF	Pop flags from stack
9E	SAHF	Store AH into flags
9F	LAHF	Load AH with flags
A0	MOV	Move byte, offset immediate word, into AL
A1	MOV	Move word, offset immediate word, into AX
A2	MOV	Move AL into byte, offset immediate word
A3	MOV	Move AX into word, offset immediate word
A4	MOVS	Move byte [SI] to ES:[DI]
	MOVSB	Move byte DS:[SI] to ES:[DI]
A5	MOVS	Move word [SI] to ES:[DI]
	MOVSW	Move word DS:[SI] to ES:[DI]
A6	CMPS	Compare bytes ES:[DI] from [SI]
	CMPSB	Compare bytes ES:[DI] from DS:[SI]
A7	CMPS	Compare words ES:[DI] from [SI]
	CMPSW	Compare words ES:[DI] from DS:[SI]
A8	TEST	AND immediate byte into AL for flags
A9	TEST	AND immediate word into AX for flags
AA	STOS	Store AL to byte [DI], advance DI
	STOSB	Store AL to byte ES:[DI], advance DI
AB	STOS	Store AX to word [DI], advance DI
	STOSW	Store AX to word ES:[DI], advance DI
AC	LODS	Load byte [SI] into AL, advance SI
	LODSB	Load byte [SI] into AL, advance SI
AD	LODS	Load word [SI] into AX, advance SI
	LODSW	Load word [SI] into AX, advance SI
AE	SCAS	Compare bytes AL - ES:[DI], advance DI
	SCASB	Compare bytes AX - ES:[DI], advance DI
AF	SCAS	Compare words AL - ES:[DI], advance DI
	SCASW	Compare words AX - ES:[DI], advance DI
B0	MOV	Move immediate byte into byte register 0
B1	MOV	Move immediate byte into byte register 1
B2	MOV	Move immediate byte into byte register 2
B3	MOV	Move immediate byte into byte register 3
B4	MOV	Move immediate byte into byte register 4
B5	MOV	Move immediate byte into byte register 5
B6	MOV	Move immediate byte into byte register 6
B7	MOV	Move immediate byte into byte register 7
B8	MOV	Move immediate word into word register 0
B9	MOV	Move immediate word into word register 1
BA	MOV	Move immediate word into word register 2
BB	MOV	Move immediate word into word register 3
BC	MOV	Move immediate word into word register 4
BD	MOV	Move immediate word into word register 5

Hex	Instruction	Description
BE	MOV	Move immediate word into word register 6
BF	MOV	Move immediate word into word register 7
C0		
C1		
C2	RET	Return near
C3		
C3	RET	Return near
C4	LES	Load doubleword into ES and word register
C5	LDS	Load doubleword into DS and word register
C6	MOV	Move immediate byte into byte
C7	MOV	Move immediate word into word
C8		
C9		
CA	RETF	Return far
CB	RETF	Return far
CC	INT 3	Interrupt 3
CD	INT	Interrupt number immediate byte
CE	INTO	Interrupt 4 if overflow is set
CF	IRET	Interrupt return
D0 /0	ROL	Rotate 8-bit byte left once
D0 /1	ROR	Rotate 8-bit byte right once
D0 /2	RCL	Rotate 9-bit quantity left once
D0 /3	RCR	Rotate 9-bit quantity right once
D0 /4	SAL	Multiply byte by 2, once
	SHL	Multiply byte by 2, once
D0 /5	SHR	Unsigned divide byte by 2, once
D0 /7	SAR	Signed divide byte by 2, once
D1 /0	ROL	Rotate 16-bit word left once
D1 /1	ROR	Rotate 16-bit word right once
D1 /2	RCL	Rotate 17-bit quantity left once
D1 /3	RCR	Rotate 17-bit quantity right once
D1 /4	SAL	Multiply word by 2, once
	SHL	Multiply word by 2, once
D1 /5	SHR	Unsigned divide word by 2, once
D1 /7	SAR	Signed divide word by 2, once
D2 /0	ROL	Rotate 8-bit byte left CL times
D2 /1	ROR	Rotate 8-bit byte right CL times
D2 /2	RCL	Rotate 9-bit quantity left CL times
D2 /3	RCR	Rotate 9-bit quantity right CL times
D2 /4	SAL	Multiply byte by 2, CL times
	SHL	Multiply byte by 2, CL times
D2 /5	SHR	Unsigned divide byte by 2, CL times
D2 /7	SAR	Signed divide byte by 2, CL times
D3 /0	ROL	Rotate 16-bit word left CL times
D3 /1	ROR	Rotate 16-bit word right CL times
D3 /2	RCL	Rotate 17-bit quantity left CL times
D3 /3	RCR	Rotate 17-bit quantity right CL times
D3 /4	SAL	Multiply word by 2, CL times
	SHL	Multiply word by 2, CL times
D3 /5	SHR	Unsigned divide word by 2, CL times
D3 /7	SAR	Signed divide word by 2, CL times
D4	AAM	ASCII adjust after multiply
D5	AAD	ASCII adjust before division
D6		
D7	XLAT	Set AL to memory byte [BX + unsigned AL]

Hex	Instruction	Description
D7	XLATB	Set AL to memory byte DS:[BX + unsigned AL]
D8		
D9		
DA		
DB		
DC		
DD		
DE		
DF		
E0		
E0	LOOPNE	jump short if CX/=0 and not equal
	LOOPNZ	jump short if CX/=0 and ZF=0
E1	LOOPE	jump short if CX/=0 and equal
	LOOPZ	jump short if CX/=0 and zero
E2	LOOP	jump short if CX/=0
E3	JCXZ	Jump short if CX register is zero
E4	IN	Input byte from immediate port into AL
E5	IN	Input word from immediate port into AX
E6	OUT	Output byte AL to immediate port
E7	OUT	Output word AX to immediate port
E8	CALL	Call near
E9	JMP	Jump near
EA	JMP	Jump far
EB	JMP	Jump short
EC	IN	Input byte from port DX into AL
ED	IN	Input word from port DX into AX
EE	OUT	Output byte AL to port number DX
EF	OUT	Output word AX to port number DX
F0	LOCK	Assert BUSLOCK signal
F1		
F2	REPNE	Repeat following CX times or until ZF=1
	REPNZ	Repeat following CX times or until ZF=1
F3	REP	Repeat following CX times
	REPE	Repeat following CX times or until ZF=0
	REPZ	Repeat following CX times or until ZF=0
F4	HLT	Halt
F5	CMC	Complement carry flag
F6 /0	TEST	AND immediate byte with byte for flags
F6 /2	NOT	Reverse each bit of byte
F6 /3	NEG	Two's complement negate byte
F6 /4	MUL	Unsigned multiply (AX = AL * byte)
F6 /5	IMUL	Signed multiply (AX = AL * byte)
F6 /6	DIV	Unsigned divide AX by byte
F6 /7	IDIV	Signed divide AX by byte
F7 /0	TEST	AND immediate word with word for flags
F7 /2	NOT	Reverse each bit of word
F7 /3	NEG	Two's complement negate word
F7 /4	MUL	Unsigned multiply (DXAX = AX * word)
F7 /5	IMUL	Signed multiply (DXAX = AX * word)
F7 /6	DIV	Unsigned divide DXAX by word
F7 /7	IDIV	Signed divide DXAX by word
F8	CLC	Clear carry flag
F9	STC	Set carry flag
FA	CLI	Clear interrupt enable flag
FB	STI	Set interrupt enable flag

Hex	Instruction	Description
FC	CLD	Clear direction flag
FD	STD	Set direction flag
FE /0	INC	Increment byte by 1
FE /1	DEC	Decrement byte by 1
FF /0	INC	Increment word by 1
FF /1	DEC	Decrement word by 1
FF /2	CALL	Call near, offset absolute at word
FF /3	CALL	Call far segment, address at doubleword
FF /4	JMP	Jump near to word (absolute offset)
FF /5	JMP	Jump far
FF /6	PUSH	Set [SP-2] to memory word

Answers to Exercises

Chapter 2

2.1 (a) (1) 01010111 01110110
  (2) 30295
  (3) 22390
  (4) +87 and +118
  (5) 87.4609375
  (6) 5776
  (7) 5776
  (8) W v

(b) (1) 10000000 01111111
  (2) 32640
  (3) 32895
  (4) −128 and +127
  (5) 128.49609375
  (6) 807?
  (7) 807F
  (8) ? ?

(c) (1) 01000110 01011001
  (2) 22854
  (3) 18009
  (4) +70 and +89
  (5) 70.34765625
  (6) 4659
  (7) 4659
  (8) F Y

(d) (1) 0000101 10001000
  (2) 34821
  (3) 1416
  (4) +5 and −120
  (5) 5.53125
  (6) 0588
  (7) 0588
  (8) ? ?

(e) (1) 00110111 10011001
  (2) 39223
  (3) 14233

       (4) +55 and –103
       (5) 55.59765625
       (6) 3799
       (7) 3799
       (8) 7 ?
  (f) (1) 01110010 00111111
       (2) 16242
       (3) 29247
       (4) +114 and +63
       (5) 114.24609375
       (6) 723?
       (7) 723F
       (8) r ?
  (g) (1) 10010001 01000010
       (2) 17041
       (3) 37186
       (4) –111 and +66
       (5) 145.2578125
       (6) 9142
       (7) 9142
       (8) ? B
  (h) (1) 01010101 01100001
       (2) 24917
       (3) 21857
       (4) +85 and +97
       (5) 85.37890625
       (6) 5561
       (7) 5561
       (8) U a

2.2 (a) 01000011 01111111
     (b) 00011000 10101011
     (c) 01000010 01111010
     (d) 00011001 00000100
     (e) 01001010 00001100
     (f) 11011111 11001000
     (g) 11111100 11000100
     (h) 01100111 11000000

2.3 (a) 01000001 01000000 00000000 00000000
     (b) 01000001 10000000 00000000 00000000
     (c) 01000010 11111110 00000000 00000000
     (d) 11000010 11111110 00000000 00000000

2.4 (a) +24.75
     (b) –24.75
     (c) +1986.0
     (d) –5025.0

2.5   (a) This is confirmed as a graphics file of GIF format by the file signature "GIF89a" at address 00H to 05H.

(b) The image width is at address 06H of value 80 02 which in little endian becomes 0280H and is equal to 640 in decimal. Similarly, the image height is at address 08H of value e0 01 which in little endian becomes 01e0H and is equal to 480 in decimal.

(c) This is a colour image. The global colour table starts at address 0dH and although the first triple is 00 00 00, the second is 80 00 00 which, because all values are not the same, is not a grey-scale value.

Chapter 3

3.1   Table 3A.1 is the finger check table for Question 1. The counter register starts at 31 referring to the instruction "load 07" and the execution of this results in the gp register being set to 03H. Meanwhile, the counter register has been stepped to 33. The next instruction, at 33, is "add 07" and the result of this execution is that 03H is added to 03H in the gp register giving 06H. Again, the counter register has been stepped, now to 35, and so the instruction "add 07" is executed, resulting once again in 03H being added to the gp register now to give 09H. Again, the counter register has been stepped, now to 37, and so the instruction "store 08" is executed. This results in the value in the gp register, 09H, being put into memory address 8. The counter register is now at 39, where we leave the example. The overall effect of this sequence is to multiply the value in address 07 by 3 (using successive addition) and to place the result in address 08.

Table 3A.1 Finger check of Exercise 3.1.

Counter register	Doing		Using code	gp	Address	
	Code	Action			07	08
31	01	load	07	03	03	01
33	04	add	07	06	03	01
35	04	add	07	09	03	01
37	02	store	08	09	03	09
29						

3.2 Below is listed the complete finger check table for this code and data sequence:

Counter register	Doing		Using code	gp	Address					
	Code	Action			05	06	07	08	09	0a
31	01	load	05	04	04	00	01	01	00	01
33	02	store	06	04	04	04	01	01	00	01
35	01	load	07	01	04	04	01	01	00	01
37	04	add	08	02	04	04	01	01	00	01
39	02	store	09	02	04	04	01	01	02	01
3b	01	load	08	01	04	04	01	01	02	01
3d	02	store	07	01	04	04	01	01	02	01
3f	01	load	09	02	04	04	01	01	02	01
41	02	store	08	02	04	04	01	02	02	01
43	01	load	06	04	04	04	01	02	02	01
45	05	subtract	0a	03	04	04	01	02	02	01
47	02	store	06	03	04	03	01	02	02	01
49	08	jbnz	16	03	04	03	01	02	02	01
4b−16=35	01	load	07	01	04	03	01	02	02	01
37	04	add	08	03	04	03	01	02	02	01
39	02	store	09	03	04	03	01	02	03	01
3b	01	load	08	02	04	03	01	02	03	01
3d	02	store	07	02	04	03	02	02	03	01
3f	01	load	09	03	04	03	02	02	03	01
41	02	store	08	03	04	03	02	03	03	01
43	01	load	06	03	04	03	02	03	03	01
45	05	subtract	0a	02	04	03	02	03	03	01
47	02	store	06	02	04	02	02	03	03	01
49	08	jbnz	16	02	04	02	02	03	03	01
4b−16=35	01	load	07	02	04	02	02	03	03	01
37	04	add	08	05	04	02	02	03	03	01
39	02	store	09	05	04	02	02	03	05	01
3b	01	load	08	03	04	02	02	03	05	01
3d	02	store	07	03	04	02	03	03	05	01
3f	01	load	09	05	04	02	03	03	05	01
41	02	store	08	05	04	02	03	05	05	01
43	01	load	06	02	04	02	03	05	05	01
45	05	subtract	0a	01	04	02	03	05	05	01
47	02	store	06	01	04	01	03	05	05	01
49	08	jbnz	16	01	04	01	03	05	05	01
4b−16=35	01	load	07	03	04	01	03	05	05	01
37	04	add	08	08	04	01	03	05	05	01
39	02	store	09	08	04	01	03	05	08	01
3b	01	load	08	05	04	01	03	05	08	01
3d	02	store	07	05	04	01	05	05	08	01
3f	01	load	09	08	04	01	05	05	08	01
41	02	store	08	08	04	01	05	08	08	01
43	01	load	06	01	04	01	05	08	08	01
45	05	subtract	0a	00	04	01	05	08	08	01
47	02	store	06	00	04	00	05	08	08	01
49	08	jbnz	16	00	04	00	05	08	08	01
4b										

As can be seen, the final value of memory address 09 is 08. The sequence in memory address 09 is seen to be: 2, 3, 5, 8 ... which is the Fibonacci number sequence.

3.3 The program code and data segments for Exercise 3.3 are as shown in Fig. 3A.1.

program			data	
Memory address	Doing code	Using code	Memory address	Value
31	01	05	05	03
33	02	08	06	07
35	01	0a	07	00
37	02	07	08	00
39	01	07	09	01
3b	04	06	0a	00
3d	02	07		
3f	01	08		
41	05	09		
43	02	08		
45	08	0e		
47				

Fig. 3A.1 Program and data for Exercise 3.3.

For completeness, the finger check table for the above example is also shown as follows:

Counter register	Doing		Using code	gp	Address					
	Code	Action			05	06	07	08	09	0a
31	01	load	05	03	03	07	00	00	01	00
33	02	store	08	03	03	07	00	03	01	00
35	01	load	0a	00	03	07	00	03	01	00
37	02	store	07	00	03	07	00	03	01	00
39	01	load	07	00	03	07	00	03	01	00
3b	04	add	06	07	03	07	00	03	01	00
3d	02	store	07	07	03	07	07	03	01	00
3f	01	load	08	03	03	07	07	03	01	00
41	05	subtract	09	02	03	07	07	03	01	00
43	02	store	08	02	03	07	07	02	01	00
45	08	jbnz	0e	02	03	07	07	02	01	00
47−0e=39	01	load	07	07	03	07	07	02	01	00
3b	04	add	06	0e	03	07	07	02	01	00
3d	02	store	07	0e	03	07	0e	02	01	00
3f	01	load	08	02	03	07	0e	02	01	00
41	05	subtract	09	01	03	07	0e	02	01	00
43	02	store	08	01	03	07	0e	01	01	00
45	08	jbnz	0e	01	03	07	0e	01	01	00
47−0e=39	01	load	07	0e	03	07	0e	01	01	00
3b	04	add	06	15	03	07	0e	01	01	00
3d	02	store	07	15	03	07	15	01	01	00
3f	01	load	08	01	03	07	15	01	01	00

Counter register	Doing		Using code	gp	Address					
	Code	Action			05	06	07	08	09	0a
41	05	subtract	09	00	03	07	15	01	01	00
43	02	store	08	00	03	07	15	00	01	00
45	08	jbnz	0e	00	03	07	15	01	01	00
47										

As can be seen, the value in memory address 07 is 15H, which is 21 decimal, and this is the result of multiplying 7 by 3.

Chapter 5

5.1   From Fig. 5A.1 it can be seen that the RLL encoded signal forms the three RLL chunks 0010, 11, and 0010 resulting in the binary code 0 0101 1001 0. This is the hexadecimal value 59h with leading and trailing zeros, as was used in the example of Fig. 5.6. 59h is the ASCII code for the character "Y". Also shown in the diagram is the equivalent MFM encoding.

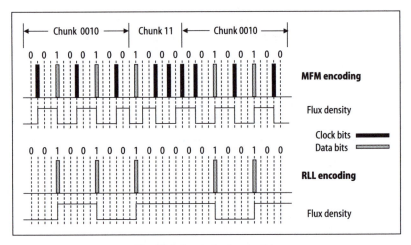

Fig. 5A.1 Results for Exercise 5.1.

5.2   The three byte capacities of Fig. 5A.2 are calculated as follows: for "Hardware" 2097 × 16 × 63 × 512 = 1 082 253 312; for "DOS" 524 × 64 × 63 × 512 = 1 081 737 216; and for "Current", the same as "Hardware". The LBA mode number of sectors is calculated from 2097 × 16 × 63 = 2 113 776. The translated number of sectors accessible is 524 × 64 × 63 = 2 112 768 resulting in a loss of 1008 sectors.

```
Drive: QUANTUM Pioneer SG 1.0A                    Port: Primary (01F0h)
  Serial #: 841714054902            CMOS Type: 47    Unit: 1 - Slave

              Hardware        DOS              Current       Max ECC: 4  bytes
Cylinders: 2097              524              2097
   Heads: 16                 64               16
 Sectors: 63                 63               63
Capacity: 1,082,253,312  1,081,737,216  1,082,253,312


                     Available  Information
R/W Multiple Mode:      Yes     8  sectors Max  Current: 8 sectors/block
         LBA Mode:      Yes     2113776
```

Fig. 5A.2 Results for Exercise 5.2.

5.3 The meaning of the second entry in the partition table at Fig. 5.26 is as follows. At 1ceh the value 00h identifies this as a non active partition. The following three bytes, at 1cfh to 1d1h, describe the starting CHS address of this active partition as cylinders 256, heads 0, sectors 1, in the following way:

Address	Value	Interpretation			Result	
1cfh	00h	= 00000000	= heads	= 0		H
1d0h	41h	= 000001	= sectors	= 1		S
		01	= cylinders			
1d1h	00h	= 00000000	= cylinders	= 256		C

At 1d2h we note that the partition type is 05h, which is an extended DOS partition. Then the three bytes at 1d3h to 1d5h describe the CHS address of the end of the partition as cylinders 522, heads 63 and sectors 63 in the following way:

Address	Value	Interpretation			Result	
1d3h	3fh	= 00111111	= heads	= 63		H
1d4h	bfh	= 111111	= sectors	= 63		S
		10	= cylinders			
1d5h	0ah	= 00001010	= cylinder	= 522		C

Starting at 1d6h we have the four bytes of the LBA address as 00 c0 0f 00. Recalling that this number is held in little endian format, we reorder these to be 00 0f c0 00 and calculate the number as fc000h = LBA 1 032 192. Similarly, at 1dah we have the four bytes of the partition size as 40 6d 10 00 and again, reordering these results in 00 10 6d 40 which is 106d40h = 1 076 544 sectors. With a sector size of 512 bytes this gives us 1 076 544 × 512/(1024 × 1024) = 525.65 Mbyte. These results are confirmed by the EXTEND entry in Fig. 5.27.

5.4 At offsets a0–a7h of Fig. 5.37 is the directory filename SUB1 padded out with spaces and at offsets a8–aah are a further three spaces for the directory extension. At offset abh is the file attributes byte of value 10h and this represents a subdirectory entry. Offsets ac–b1h are not used and are set to 00h. However, at offsets b2–b3h is the last access date of 270fh in little endian. In binary this is 0010 0111 0000 1111 and when divided up as in Fig. 5.36 this is equivalent to 0010011 years from 1980, 1000 number of month, and 01111 day of month, giving us 1999/8/15. At offsets b6–b7h is the time of the last update as 5020h. In binary this is 0101 0000 0010 0000 and when divided up as in figure 5.36, this is equivalent to 01010 hours, 000001 minutes, and 00000 × 2 seconds giving us 10:01:00. Similarly, the date of the last update is at offsets b8–b9h and is again 270fh in little endian, resulting in a date of 1999/8/15. At offsets 1ba–bbh is the first cluster number in little endian, that is 001b, which is 27 in decimal, and finally, at offsets bc–bfh is the file size of 0.

5.5   The additional time and date fields start at offset cch with the reserved byte 00h. At offset cdh is the 10 millisecond units past creation time of 5ch which is equivalent to decimal 92, giving 920 milliseconds. At offsets ce–cfh is the file creation time of 5297h in little endian. In binary this is 0101 0010 1001 0111 and when divided up as in Fig. 5.36 this is equivalent to 01010 hours, 010100 minutes, and 10111 × 2 seconds, giving us 10:20:46. Similarly the creation date is at offsets d0–d1h and is 270fh in little endian. In binary this is 0010 0111 0000 1111, and when divided up as in Fig. 5.36 this is equivalent to 0010011 years from 1980, 1000 number of month, and 01111 day of month, giving us 1999/8/ 15. The last access date is at offsets d2–d3h and is again 270fh, resulting in 1999/ 8/15. Finally, at offsets d4–d5h is the high word of the start cluster number for FAT32 systems that is 0000h here.

Glossary

2's complement

See two's complement.

A20

Address line 20. The segment-offset memory addressing architecture permits physical addresses up to 1 megabyte plus 64 kilobytes less 16 bytes. In the original 8088 processor, physical memory addresses could only extend to 1 byte below the 1 megabyte mark and any addresses above that value "wrapped around" to the beginning of memory again. Some early programs were written to take advantage of this feature. The 80286 and higher Intel processors, however, give access to physical addresses in real mode up to the limit of the segment-offset memory addressing architecture, and programs which expect wraparound are thus incompatible. To provide full compatibility with the 8088, circuitry is included in many systems which permits the twenty-first address line (A20) to be disabled, thus causing wraparound. *See also* HMA; Real mode.

ACPO

Association of Chief Police Officers.

Allocation unit

An MS-DOS file system memory unit consisting of a number of disk sectors. Also known as a cluster.

ANSI

American National Standards Institute.

ARLL

Advanced Run Length Limited. An encoding method used to store information magnetically on the surface of a disk.

ASCII

American Standard Code for Information Interchange. Character code in common use.

ASCIIZ

An ASCII string of characters which is terminated by an all zeros byte.

ATA

AT Attachment. ATA defines a standard specification for connecting hard disk drives to the PC. Further updates to the standard include ATA-2 and ATA-3.

ATAPI

ATA Packet Interface. A standard that permits CD-ROM and tape drives to be connected to the IDE (ATA) interface.

Back door

A feature left in a system for the convenience of designers and testers which may be used to defeat the security system.

BCD

Binary Coded Decimal. A format used for representing decimal numbers.

BCAI

Byte Count After Index. A code used in hard disks to identify the position in bytes on the disk relative to an index mark. *See* BFI.

Beep code

A specific set of beeps sent to the PC loudspeaker when a POST diagnostic fails.

BFI

Bytes From Index. A code used in hard disks to identify the position in bytes on the disk relative to an index mark. *See* BCAI.

Big endian

A method of forming a number from two bytes taken together. The higher valued bits are taken as being in the lower valued address.

BIOS

Basic Input–Output System. The name given to the system programs which provide basic input and output functions for the PC. Often held in ROM.

Bit

Binary digit. The elementary unit of information storage.

Boot

To "boot" is to execute the "bootstrap" code. The bootstrap is that sequence of code which is initiated at the instant of switching on the PC and which causes it to load its working programs. The word stems from the phrase: "to pull oneself up by one's bootstraps".

Boot sector

The first sector in a partition or on a floppy disk that contains the bootstrap loader code for the particular operating system. Also known as the boot record.

Bus

A set of parallel wires (or tracks on a printed circuit board) which connects one part of the PC to another.

Bus mastering

A mechanism whereby the memory and input–output devices, as well as the processor, can take control of the buses. *See also* DMA.

Byte

A group of 8 bits taken together. The fundamental unit of memory addressing.

Cache

Caching is a method of increasing performance by keeping frequently used data in more rapidly accessible and faster storage.

CCITT

International Telegraph and Telephone Consultative Committee.

CD-R

See CD-ROM

CD-ROM

Compact Disc Read-Only Memory. A means of storing up to 700 Mbyte of data on a disk which is very similar in appearance and method of working to an audio CD. Originally this was a read-only system (hence ROM), but there are now writable CDs (CD-R) and re-writable CDs (CD-RW).

CD-RW

See CD-ROM.

CF device

Compact Flash device. A proprietary name for a flash EPROM system.

Chipset

Often used to refer specifically to the set of controller chips on the motherboard of a PC.

CHS

Cylinder Head Sector. The basic form for addressing sectors on a disk. *See* LBA.

CISC

Complex Instruction Set Computer. Microprocessors which have a large and complex set of instruction codes. *See also* RISC.

Clean boot

A boot that carries out all the POST/boot activities from the very beginning of the sequence using a floppy disk that has been constructed to ensure that none of the hard disks are written to. *See also* boot.

Cluster

An MS-DOS file system allocation unit. It consists of a number of disk sectors.

CMOS

Complementary Metal-Oxide Semiconductor. A type of integrated circuit design known for its low power consumption.

CMOS RAM

A small amount of memory in the real-time clock chip that is preserved by the clock battery and is used for storing system configuration information.

COB

Chip On Board. A form of technology where the chip (or die) is connected directly to the printed circuit board without being packaged. A blob of resin is then placed over the die to protect it. Also known as Direct Chip Attach (DCA).

Cold boot

A boot that carries out all the POST/boot activities from the very beginning of the sequence. The system is starting from cold. *See also* boot.

CP/M

Control Program for Microcomputers. An operating system developed for the 8 bit Intel 8080 processor.

CRC

Cyclic Redundancy Check. A form of checksum used to detect certain kinds of error.

Cylinder

The narrow cylinder strip swept out at a particular head assembly position on all surfaces of all platters during one rotation of the disk. *See* track.

DAM

Data Address Mark. A low-level format marker on a disk surface.

Daughterboard

A subordinate printed circuit board that connects, often at right angles, to the motherboard in a PC. Sometimes known as a riser board.

DCA

Direct Chip Attach. A form of technology where the chip (or die) is connected directly to the printed circuit board without being packaged. A blob of resin is then placed over the die to protect it. Also known as Chip On Board (COB).

DDO

Dynamic Drive Overlay. Software that is resident on a hard disk and automatically loaded during the bootstrap sequence to provide CHS translation.

Defrag

Defragment. The process of reordering data on a disk in order to improve the efficiency of access.

DIL

Dual In-Line. A form of PC chip packaging and the socket for it.

DIMM

Dual In-line Memory Module. A small printed circuit board mounted with several memory chips which may be locked into a socket on the mother board of a PC. *See* SIMM.

DIP

Dual In-line Package. See DIL.

DMA

Direct Memory Access. A means by which input output devices and the internal memory unit can perform data transfer operations independently of the processor. The logic circuitry which provides this capability.

DOS

This strictly refers to any Disk Operating System, but it is often used as a synonym for MS-DOS.

DRAM

Dynamic Random Access Memory. A form of RAM that requires continuous refreshing, hence the word "dynamic". *See* SRAM.

DVD

Digital Versatile Disc or Digital Video Disc. A successor to the CD-ROM, and generally backwards compatible with it. This technology currently has a storage capacity of up to 17 Gbyte.

EBCDIC

Extended Binary Coded Decimal Interchange Code. A less commonly used character code from IBM.

ECC

Error-Correcting Code. A set of check bytes used to detect and correct certain kinds of errors.

ECHS

Extended CHS. The facility offered by a BIOS which incorporates CHS translation software.

EDO

Extended Data Out (sometimes called Hyper Page Mode). An architecture for DRAMs.

EEPROM

Electrically Erasable PROM. Read-only memory that can be repeatedly programmed, completely erased electrically and reprogrammed.

EIDE

Enhanced IDE. A standard originally used by Western Digital to refer to systems with ATA-2, ATAPI and dual IDE/ATA host adaptor facilities. Now in common use.

EISA

Extended Industry Standard Architecture. An improved version of the ISA standard PC bus architecture.

Enhanced BIOS

A BIOS that incorporates the INT 13h extensions.

EMM

Expanded Memory Manager. *See* Expanded memory.

EMS

Expanded Memory System. *See* Expanded memory.

EPROM

Erasable PROM. Read-only memory that can be repeatedly programmed, completely erased and reprogrammed.

ESDI

Enhanced Small Device Interface. A standard that was designed to improve on the ST412/506 interface. Now effectively obsolete.

Expanded Memory

A design developed by Lotus, Intel and Microsoft for accessing more than one megabyte of memory by bank-switching additional memory into the one megabyte real mode address space. LIM EMS stands for Lotus–Intel–Microsoft Expanded Memory System.

Expansion slots

The slots on a PC where expansion cards can be fitted to provide additional functionality.

Exponent

Part of a floating point number.

Extended Memory

Memory above the one megabyte address. Apart from the High Memory Area (*see* HMA), extended memory is only accessible when the processor is in protected mode.

FAT

File Allocation Table. A resource allocation mechanism used by the MS-DOS file system.

FCF

Forensic Computing Foundation Course. Postgraduate level course run by Cranfield University in conjunction with the UK Joint Agency Forensic Computer Group.

FCG

Forensic Computer Group. The UK Joint Agency Forensic Computer Group.

FDC

Floppy Disk Controller.

File signature

The characters at the beginning of a file which may be used to identify the type of file. Sometimes called the magic number.

Firewire

A new bus technology designed primarily for high-performance audio and multi-media applications.

Flash EPROM

EEPROM chips that permit erasure and reprogramming at the level of the block or the byte rather than having to erase the entire chip first.

Floating point

A binary representation of numbers held in scientific notation form.

FM

Frequency Modulation. An encoding method used to store information magnetically on the surface of a disk.

Form factor

The physical shape and size of a packaged chip or a disk.

FPM

Fast Page Mode. An architecture for DRAMs.

GIF

Graphic Interchange Format. A commonly used graphics file format.

Gigabyte

A unit of memory of value 2^{30} or 1 073 741 824 bytes.

GUI

Graphical User Interface. A user interface which provides graphic elements such as windows, icons, menus and pointers (WIMP) to control PC applications.

Head assembly

Mechanical assembly to which the heads of a hard disk unit are connected.

Hex

Abbreviation for numbers shown in the hexadecimal number system.

High-level format

The process of establishing a file system on a disk. *See* low level format.

HMA

High Memory Area. The area of memory (64 kilobytes less 16 bytes in size) that is immediately above the 1 megabyte address. *See also* A20.

HOL

High-Order Language. A high-level programming language.

HPM

Hyper Page Mode (sometimes called Extended Data Out). An architecture for DRAMs.

IAM

Index Address Mark. A low-level format marker on a disk surface.

IC Card

Proprietary name for an organizer memory card.

IDAM

ID Address Mark. A low-level format marker on a disk surface.

IDE

Integrated Drive Electronics, Intelligent Disk Electronics and similar interpretations. A hard drive interface standard. More usually now referred to as ATA.

IDE

Integrated Development Environment. A set of integrated programming tools for use by a programmer.

IEEE Format

Definition of standard floating point number formats.

INT

Software interrupt instruction code.

Interrupt vector

A four byte pointer to interrupt handling code.

I/O port address

The physical address (or range of addresses) that are assigned to a hardware device and which permit control instructions and data to be exchanged with that device.

IRQ

Interrupt request channel. The physical channel number assigned to a hardware device which permits interrupts to be passed from that device.

ISA

Industry Standard Architecture. A defined standard PC bus architecture which formalized and updated the PC-AT architecture.

ISO

International Organization for Standardization.

JFIF

JPEG File Interchange Format. A graphics file format.

JPEG

Joint Photographic Experts Group. A graphics standards committee.

Kilobyte

A unit of memory of value 2^{10} or 1024 bytes.

LBA

Logical Block Addressing. An alternative system for addressing sectors on a disk. *See* CHS.

L-CHS

Logical CHS address. *See* CHS.

LFN

Long File Name.

Little endian

A method of forming a number from two bytes taken together. The lower valued bits are taken as being in the lower valued address.

Local bus
Internal connection made between the processor bus and some expansion slots to improve graphics and disk performance. *See* VL-Bus.

Low-level format
The process of placing address and structure markers on a disk. See high-level format.

LSN
Logical Sector Number.

LZW
Lempel–Ziv–Welch. A file compression system named after its designers.

Magic number
A synonym for "file signature". The characters at the beginning of a file which may be used to identify the type of file.

Mantissa
Part of a floating point number.

Master boot record
The first sector on a hard disk containing the partition table and code which is used to analyse it.

MCA
Micro Channel Architecture. A proprietary IBM PC bus architecture.

Megabyte
A unit of memory of value 2^{20} or 1 048 576 bytes.

Memory disk
Proprietary name for an organizer memory card.

MFM
Modified Frequency Modulation. An encoding method used to store information magnetically on the surface of a disk.

MIPs
Millions of Instructions Per Second. Sometimes used as a measure of processor performance.

MMX
Multimedia extensions. An additional set of instructions designed for multimedia use and built into the later Intel Pentium processors.

Motherboard
The main printed circuit board of a PC to which all other elements are connected.

MS-DOS
The Microsoft Disk Operating System. The basic operating system found in most PCs.

MZR

Multiple Zone Recording. This is a system where different tracks on the surface of a disk have different numbers of sectors per track. *See also* ZBR; ZCAV.

Nibble

4 bits taken together. Half a byte.

Object code

The code executed by the target machine. Typically this will have been generated by a compiling system from source code written by a programmer.

Partition

A logical volume established on a hard disk.

PC

Personal Computer.

PC-AT

Personal Computer – Advanced Technology. The later architecture of the PC on which most modern PC systems are based.

P-CHS

Physical CHS address. *See* CHS.

PCI

Peripheral Component Interconnect. A new standard PC bus architecture designed by Intel for the Pentium range of processors.

PC-XT

Personal Computer – Extended Technology. The earlier architecture of the PC.

PGA

Pin Grid Array. A type of PC chip packaging and socket for it.

PGP

Pretty Good Privacy.

PIO

Programmed Input–Output. A means of data transfer that is carried out directly by the central processor. *See* DMA.

Platter

A disk coated with magnetic material which forms two surfaces of a hard disk unit.

PLCC

Plastic Leaded Chip Carrier. A form of PC chip packaging and the socket for it.

Plug and Play

Automatic detection and allocation of the resources (IRQ, I/O Address, DMA channel) that are required by a hardware device.

PNG

Portable Network Graphic. A relatively new graphics file format.

POST

Power-On Self Test. The sequence of tests that are executed when power is first switched on to the PC.

POST code

A specific code sent to an I/O port when a POST diagnostic fails.

PROM

Programmable ROM. Read-only memory that can be programmed after manufacture.

Protected Mode

One of the operating modes of the 80286 and higher Intel processors, in which a more complex addressing architecture than the segment offset system of real mode is used and the CPU enforces protection mechanisms designed to prevent one program from disrupting another. *See also* Real mode; Virtual-86 mode.

PS/2

A standard connector and socket used, typically, for the mouse and the keyboard.

RAID

Redundant Array of Inexpensive (or Independent) Disks.

RAM

Random Access Memory. The main (volatile) memory of the PC.

Real number

Synonym for floating point number.

Real mode

One of the operating modes of the 80286 and higher Intel processors, and the only operating mode of the 8088, 8086, 80186, and 80188 processors. In this mode, all addresses used by programs correspond directly to real physical addresses (thus the name Real *Address* Mode) and utilise the segment offset addressing architecture. See also Protected Mode and Virtual-86 Mode.

RISC

Reduced Instruction Set Computer. Microprocessors which have a small reduced set of instruction codes. *See also* CISC.

Riser board

A subordinate printed circuit board that connects, often at right angles, to the motherboard in a PC. Sometimes known as a daughterboard.

RLL

Run Length Limited. An encoding method used to store information magnetically on the surface of a disk.

ROM

Read-Only Memory. Non-volatile memory that cannot (normally) be changed. Used to contain, for example, the BIOS in a PC.

RSA

Rivest (Ron), Shamir (Adi), Adelman (Leonard). Inventors of the RSA security algorithm.

RTF

Rich Text Format. A word processor file format.

SCSI

Small Computer Systems Interface. A standard expansion bus typically used to connect a number of devices, such as hard disks, tape drives and CD-ROMs, to a computer.

SDRAM

Synchronous DRAM. DRAM operated synchronously with the processor clock.

Sector

For the purposes of addressing, a disk track is divided into a number of equal sized sectors. *See* Cylinder; Track.

SGRAM

Synchronous Graphics RAM. DRAM designed for graphics use with a high-speed serial port and operated synchronously with the processor clock.

SEC

Single Edge Connector. A form of PC chip packaging and the socket for it.

Shadow RAM

RAM used to hold copies of some or all of the BIOS code in order to achieve performance improvements.

SIMM

Single In-line Memory Module. A small printed circuit board mounted with several memory chips which may be locked into a socket on the motherboard of a PC. *See* DIMM.

Slack space

The space from the end of a file to the end of the last cluster containing the file.

Slot 1 or 2

The form factors of some recent Intel microprocessors.

SMART

Self Monitoring and Reporting Technology. A self monitoring and reporting system found on modern hard drives.

Socket 1 to 8

The form factors of many microprocessors since the 80486.

Source code

The original code written by the programmer. *See* Object code.

SRAM

Static Random Access Memory. A form of RAM that does not require refreshing, hence the word "static". *See* DRAM.

SSD

Solid State Disk. Proprietary name for an organizer memory card.

ST412/506

Early *de facto* standard for connecting hard disk drives to their controllers.

Terabyte

A unit of memory of value 2^{40} or 1 099 511 627 776 bytes

TIFF

Tagged Image File Format. A graphics file format.

TQPF

Thin Quad Flat Plastic. A form of PC chip packaging and the socket for it.

Track

The narrow circular strip swept out at a particular head assembly position on one surface of a platter during one rotation of the disk. *See* Cylinder.

Trash blocks

Unused areas within a document that may contain information unrelated to the document but of forensic significance.

Two's complement

A format used for representing binary numbers with negative values.

UDMA

Ultra-DMA. A relatively recent ATA standard that permits high-performance transfer rates and disk sizes that are greater than the 8.4 Gbyte limit. Also known as Ultra-ATA, Ultra33, Ultra66 etc.

UMB

Upper Memory Block.

Unicode

A two byte character code.

USB

Universal Serial Bus. A relatively new architecture that permits up to 127 peripheral devices to be daisy-chained on to a high-speed serial bus.

Ultra-ATA

See Ultra-DMA.

VDU

Visual Display Unit. The standard display unit of a PC.

VESA

Video Electronics Standards Association.

Virtual-86 mode

One of the operating modes of the 80386 and higher Intel processors in which user programs run as if the CPU were in real mode, while providing the protection and the address capabilities of protected mode to a supervisor program which oversees each of the 8086 virtual environments on which the user programs are running. *See also* Protected mode; Real mode.

VL-Bus
VESA Local Bus. An interim PC bus architecture designed by VESA for better graphics and disk performance. Used the local bus concept.

von Neumann, John
Famous mathematician credited (though some dispute this) with the invention of the stored program concept. A machine architecture which implements this concept.

VRAM
Video RAM. DRAM designed for graphics use with a high-speed serial port.

Warm boot
A boot that carries out the boot activities from part way though the sequence, often bypassing all of the POST. The system is starting from warm. *See also* Boot.

WIMP
Windows Icons Menus Pointers. A Graphical User Interface (GUI) which provides graphic elements such as windows, icons menus and pointers to control PC applications.

Winchester Drive
A term that originated from an early IBM drive that had 30 megabytes of removable media and 30 megabytes of fixed media. This gave rise to the name "30-30", which is the calibre of the famous rifle made by the Winchester gun factory. The term now refers to all PC hard drives.

Word
16 bits taken together. Two bytes. *See* and Big endian; Little endian.

WORM
Write Once Read Many times memory.

ZBR
Zoned Bit Recording. This is a system where different tracks on the surface of a disk have different numbers of sectors per track. *See also* MZR and ZCAV.

ZCAV
Zoned Constant Angular Velocity. This is a system where different tracks on the surface of a disk have different numbers of sectors per track. *See also* ZBR and MZR.

ZIF
Zero Insertion Force. Refers to a PC chip socket which has a locking and unlocking device and for which zero force is needed to insert or remove a chip.

Zip
A commonly used archive file format.

ZIP disk
A proprietary form of large (100–250 MByte) floppy-type disk.

Index